HOW UKRAINE BECAME A MARKET ECONOMY AND DEMOCRACY

Other Books by Anders Åslund

Private Enterprise in Eastern Europe, 1985

Gorbachev's Struggle for Economic Reform, 1989

Post-Communist Economic Revolutions: How Big a Bang? 1992

How Russia Became a Market Economy, 1995

Building Capitalism: The Transformation of the Former Soviet Bloc, 2002

How Capitalism Was Built: The Transformation of Central and Eastern Europe, Russia, and Central Asia, 2007

Russia's Capitalist Revolution: Why Market Reform Succeeded and Democracy Failed, 2007

HOW UKRAINE BECAME A MARKET ECONOMY AND DEMOCRACY

ANDERS ÅSLUND

PETERSON INSTITUTE FOR INTERNATIONAL ECONOMICS
WASHINGTON, DC
MARCH 2009

Anders Åslund has been deeply engaged in Ukraine and its economic reforms since 1985 and has published extensively. He boldly predicted the fall of the Soviet communist system in his *Gorbachev's Struggle for Economic Reform* (1989). He served as an economic adviser to the Ukrainian government from 1994 to 1997. He was one of the founders of the Kyiv School of Economics and remains its cochairman. In 2004 he cochaired a United Nations Blue Ribbon Commission for Ukraine, *Proposals for the President: A New Wave of Reform.*

He is the author of nine books, including *Russia's Capitalist Revolution: Why Market Reform Succeeded and Democracy Failed* (2007), which was named a Choice Outstanding Academic Title for 2008, and *How Capitalism Was Built: The Transformation of Central and Eastern Europe, Russia, and Central Asia* (2007), which the *Economist* magazine named one of the best books of the year in 2007. He coedited *Economic Reform in Ukraine: The Unfinished Agenda* (2000) and *Revolution in Orange* (2006).

Dr. Åslund joined the Peterson Institute for International Economics as senior fellow in 2006. He was the director of the Russian and Eurasian Program at the Carnegie Endowment for International Peace. He was founding director of the Stockholm Institute of Transition Economics and professor at the Stockholm School of Economics. He earned his doctorate from the University of Oxford.

PETER G. PETERSON INSTITUTE FOR INTERNATIONAL ECONOMICS
1750 Massachusetts Avenue, NW
Washington, DC 20036-1903
(202) 328-9000 FAX: (202) 659-3225
www.piie.com

C. Fred Bergsten, *Director*
Edward A. Tureen, *Director of Publications, Marketing, and Web Development*
Typesetting by Xcel Graphic Services
Printing by Edwards Brothers, Inc.
Cover photos: © Gleb Garanich/Reuters/Corbis; epa/Corbis; Sergey Dolzhenko/epa/Corbis

Map by Dave Merrill. Reprinted with permission of the publisher of *Revolution in Orange* edited by Anders Åslund (Washington, DC: Carnegie Endowment for International Peace, 2006, p. ix, www.carnegieendowment.org).

Printed in the United States of America
11 10 09 5 4 3 2 1

Library of Congress Cataloging-in-Publication Data

Åslund, Anders, 1952–
How Ukraine became a market economy and democracy / Anders Åslund.
p. cm.
1. Ukraine—Economic policy—1991–
2. Ukraine—Economic conditions—1991–
3. Democratization—Ukraine. I. Title.

HC340.19.A85 2009
330.9477—dc22

2008052694

For
Hans and Märit Rausing

Contents

Tables

Figures

Box

Preface

Ukraine was a fast-growing market economy until 2008, and it is a fragile democracy. Despite being one of the last postcommunist countries to opt for serious market economic reforms in the 1990s, it grew at an average of 7.5 percent a year from 2000 to 2007. By 2005, Freedom House ranked Ukraine as a free nation, the only country besides the Baltic states so labeled in the former Soviet Union.

In this book, Senior Fellow Anders Åslund probes how Ukraine transformed into a market economy and democracy and whether these achievements can hold in a challenging world, especially in the headwind of the current financial crisis. His comprehensive account of Ukraine's economic and political transformation covers the period from 1991, when Ukrainians overwhelmingly voted for their nation's independence, to 2008. It is the first book on the economic and political story of Ukraine covering this period in any language.

This volume completes Åslund's trilogy on postcommunist transformation, which he started when he arrived at the Institute in January 2006. The first book, *How Capitalism Was Built: The Transformation of Central and Eastern Europe, Russia, and Central Asia*, discusses postcommunist transition in 21 countries. The second, *Russia's Capitalist Revolution: Why Market Reform Succeeded and Democracy Failed*, considers key transition issues in Russia. This book focuses on the same topics in Ukraine.

During its first three years of independence, Ukraine focused on little but nation-building. As a consequence, political and economic reforms were ignored. The cost of delayed reforms proved considerable but the popular tolerance for this neglect was amazing. Ukrainians appear to have considered nation-building their all-dominant priority.

When Ukraine's market economic reforms did take place, they were fast and radical because only then could they succeed. The first round took place in the fall of 1994 and the second occurred in the first four months of 2000. Delayed reforms were to no advantage. On the contrary, the delay aggravated and prolonged the decline in GDP. To succeed, Ukrainian reforms had to be concentrated because only a combination of fear of crisis and determined policymaking could defeat the strong group that thrived on state subsidies and arbitrage between state-controlled and free prices. As in other postcommunist countries, the preconditions for market economic success included deregulation of prices and trade, privatization of most enterprises, and financial stabilization.

Ukraine became a real democracy with free and fair elections as well as free media after the Orange Revolution in November–December 2004. This democracy, however, is not very effective: Minimum legislation has been promulgated, corruption remains pervasive, and the state administration is malfunctioning. The crucial problem appears to be the constitutional order, which provides the president with flawed incentives. The president can exercise power only through his veto and by calling for new elections, which he is thus tempted to do all too often. A rational solution would be to move to a fully parliamentary system. The key question is whether Ukraine's democracy can survive such dysfunction, rendering constitutional amelioration of paramount importance.

Ukraine has gradually steered its foreign policy and trade toward the West, making clear its choice for Europe. A major breakthrough was its accession to the World Trade Organization in May 2008. The next big step is the negotiation of a European Association Agreement with the European Union, which will offer deep free trade and speed up Ukraine's integration into the European Union, although its prospect of eventual membership remains elusive. The United States should also offer a bilateral free trade agreement with Ukraine.

At the time of this writing, an unprecedented global financial crisis is testing Ukraine's economy. In particular, its large steel industry is facing a major structural predicament. The current crisis will undoubtedly bring about substantial changes in the economy as well as the economic system but also in the politics and the political system of Ukraine. At this juncture, it is important that the United States and the West engage with Ukraine to help it overcome these hurdles. Meanwhile, Ukraine is preparing for presidential elections in January 2010. We hope this book will help a broad audience understand Ukraine's current dilemma.

The Peter G. Peterson Institute for International Economics is a private, nonprofit institution for the study and discussion of international economic policy. Its purpose is to analyze important issues in that area and to develop and communicate practical new approaches for dealing with them. The Institute is completely nonpartisan.

The Institute is funded by a highly diversified group of philanthropic foundations, private corporations, and interested individuals. About 22 percent of the Institute's resources in our latest fiscal year were provided by contributors outside the United States, including about 9 percent from Japan. The Victor Pinchuk Foundation provides generous support for the Institute's Central and Eastern European program.

The Institute's Board of Directors bears overall responsibilities for the Institute and gives general guidance and approval to its research program, including the identification of topics that are likely to become important over the medium run (one to three years) and that should be addressed by the Institute. The director, working closely with the staff and outside Advisory Committee, is responsible for the development of particular projects and makes the final decision to publish an individual study.

The Institute hopes that its studies and other activities will contribute to building a stronger foundation for international economic policy around the world. We invite readers of these publications to let us know how they think we can best accomplish this objective.

C. Fred Bergsten
Director
January 2009

Acknowledgments

This book is a labor of love. I first visited Ukraine in 1985, and I was immediately taken by the country because of its dignity and friendliness. Since then, I have visited Ukraine ever so often, seeing how it has slowly transformed into a strong, self-confident nation. As this book reflects my work in Ukraine during two decades, I have many people to thank.

Tacitly hoping for reforms, I visited Ukraine about once a year, but reforms in Ukraine were late in coming. My wise benefactor was George Soros. From St. Antony's College in Oxford, I knew well a few friends of Ukraine, Nadia Diuk, John Hewko, and Emmanuel van der Mensbrughe. Around 1991, I met Bohdan Hawrylyshyn, Oleh Havrylyshyn, Myron Wasylyk, Peter Sochan, Natalie Jaresko, and Bohdan Krawchenko, who had enthusiastically returned to their native land, and I have greatly benefited from their wisdom. Roman Szporluk generously shared his historical insights.

In July 1994 Leonid Kuchma was unexpectedly elected president of Ukraine, and he was determined to revive the mismanaged economy. George Soros saw the opportunity, and I owe him a considerable debt for introducing me to President Kuchma and for providing financial support to our economic advisory group to the Ukrainian government. As director of Soros's Open Society Institute, John Fox eminently guided our work, and Bohdan Budzan was our local support. My friends Peter Boone and Simon Johnson came over immediately to assist in this endeavor, and so did my graduate students Eva Sundquist and Elisabeth Hopkins. Michael Zienchuk was already in place. Soon Professors Marek Dabrowski and Georges de Ménil joined us, and our group expanded to 27 at the most in 1997. I would particularly mention Hans-Gunnar Adén, Agha Ghazanfar,

Michael Blackman, Boris Najman, Marcin Luczynski, Oleksandr Rohozynskiy, Andrii Zhirny, and Oleksei Krivtsov. Svitlana Bocharova has continuously worked with me since 1995 and still does. I am immensely grateful to all of them.

We worked for a wonderful group of Ukrainian officials who reformed their land in the period 1994–97: President Leonid Kuchma, Minister of Economy Roman Shpek, Deputy Prime Minister for Economic Reform Viktor Pynzenyk, Chairman of the National Bank of Ukraine Viktor Yushchenko, Chairman of the State Property Fund Yuriy Yekhanurov, Deputy Prime Minister Ihor Mitiukov, Deputy Prime Minister Serhiy Tyhypko, and Minister of Justice Serhiy Holovatyi. We tried to assist them, and they were amazingly kind and grateful to us. We worked with several other officials, from whom I have learned a great deal: Volodymyr Lanovyi, Ihor Shumilo, Oleh Rybachuk, Andrii Goncharuk, Borys Tarasiuk, Anatoliy Halchynskiy, Serhiy Terekhin, Ivan Vasiunyk, Ihor Hryniov, Natalia Propokovich, Viktor Lysytskiy, Valeriy Lytvytskiy, Oleksandr Savchenko, and Tamara Solyanik. In 1996 I first had the pleasure of meeting Yuliya Tymoshenko, whose lucid analysis I have appreciated.

During this period, one journalist managed to attract attention to Ukraine, Chrystia Freeland of the *Financial Times*, whose company I thoroughly enjoyed.

In 1996, as a representative of George Soros, I participated in the founding of the Economics Education and Research Consortium, which later evolved into the Kyiv School of Economics. Its staff and current director Tom Coupé have assisted me in many ways. I have benefited from conversations with Robert Campbell, Fred Pryor, and Paul Gregory.

My old friend Carl Bildt has been persistently engaged in Ukraine. For many years, I have kept up with a group of Swedish businessmen in Ukraine, from which I wish to acknowledge Hans Rausing, Adolf Lundin, Bo Hjelt, Carl Sturén, Fredrik Svinhufvud, and Peter Elam Håkansson. I am enormously grateful for the hospitality and insights of Swedish Ambassadors Martin Hallquist, Åke Peterson, and John-Christer Åhlander, US Ambassadors Roman Popadiuk, William Miller, Steven Pifer, Carlos Pasqual, John Herbst, and William Taylor, and Raymond Asquith and Duncan Allan of the British Embassy. Of the World Bank representatives, I want to particularly praise Daniel Kaufmann and Luca Barbone, as well as Patrick Lenain from the IMF.

In Washington, I have enjoyed the many receptions and meetings at the Embassy of Ukraine with Ambassadors Yuriy Shcherbak, Anton Buteiko, Kostyatyn Gryshchenko, and Oleh Shamshur as well as Ukrainian diplomats Yuriy and Vira Yakusha, Oleksandr Potekhin, and Volodymyr Makukha.

In the early 2000s a new, colorful group of Ukrainian businessmen and politicians came to the fore. I had the pleasure of making their acquaintances, notably Victor Pinchuk, Rinat Akhmetov, Serhiy Taruta, Vitaliy

Haiduk, Inna Bohoslavskaya, Valeriy Khoroshkovskiy, Oleksandr Yaroslavskiy, Gennady Bogoliubov, Oleksandr Morozov, Mykola Azarov, Viktor Yanukovych, and Leonid Kozhara.

In 2004 UN Assistant Secretary General Kalman Mizsei asked me to co-chair with Oleksandr Paskhaver a Blue Ribbon Commission on proposals for a new wave of reform for Ukraine after the presidential elections, which I happily accepted. Our commission included my old friends, Marek Dabrowski, Georges de Ménil, and Oleksandr Rohozynskiy, as well as Iryna Akimova, Dan Bilak, Ihor Burakovskiy, Oleksandr Chalyi, Keith Crane, Adrian Karatnycky, Ihor Koliushko, Oleksandra Kuzhel, Dmytro Leonov, Vira Nanivska, Jerzy Osiatynski, and Ben Slay. We were ably assisted by Oleksandr Shevtsov and Tamara Zykova. Unfortunately, most of these reforms have not been implemented as yet, but they reflect a broad consensus about what needs to be done.

The Orange Revolution was an unforgettable experience. I followed it closely, and Michael McFaul and I edited a book on it. I learned a lot from him, Kalman Mizsei, Adrian Karatnycky, Nadia Diuk, Hryhoriy Nemyria, Olena Prytula, Taras Kuzio, Pavol Demes, and Oleksandr Sushko. In recent years, I have also greatly benefited from conversations with Thomas Eymond-Laritaz, Natalia Izosimova, Anna Derevyanko, and Jorge Zukoski.

During my 15 years in Washington, I have discussed Ukraine with many people. Among those not already mentioned, special thanks are due to Stanley Fischer and John Odling-Smee of the IMF, Lawrence Summers, David Lipton, Nancy Lee and Mark Medish of the US Treasury, James Wolfensohn and Johannes Linn at the World Bank, and Stephen Sestanovich and Eugene Fishel at the State Department. I have also greatly benefited from conversations with Zbigniew Brzezinski, Robert Zoellick, and James Harmon. I have been deeply involved in the community concerned with Ukraine here and would especially thank Bohdan Futey, Bruce Jackson, Morgan Williams, Nadia McConnell, George Chopiwsky, Orest Deychakivsky, and Stephen Larrabee.

Over the years, I have discussed Ukraine with many journalists and fondly remember conversations with Celestine Bohlen, Pilar Bonet, Judy Dempsey, Jackson Diehl, Inna Dubynsky, Fred Hiatt, Miroslava Gongadze, Adrian Karamzyn, Fred Kempe, Edward Lucas, Quentin Peel, Martin Walker, Ewa Wiekert, and Martin Wolf.

Although this book draws on previous writings, I wrote it as a whole in 2008. I am immensely grateful to C. Fred Bergsten and the Peterson Institute for International Economics for giving me this opportunity, which in turn has been facilitated by generous financing from the Victor Pinchuk Foundation. I want to express my special appreciation to Victor Pinchuk and Elena Franchuk.

My special thanks are reserved for Hans and Märit Rausing, who have shown an inordinate interest in Ukraine and provided me with generous financial support for my Ukrainian studies over the years. I dedicate this book to them.

Olesya Favorska and Ivan Yuryk provided me with excellent research assistance, especially producing the figures and chronology. I have benefited from substantial comments on a previous draft from Leszek Balcerowicz, Keith Crane, Nadia Diuk, Olesya Favorska, Simon Johnson, Irina Paliashvili, Steven Pifer, Poul Thomsen, and Ted Truman. I am also grateful for useful comments from Fred Bergsten, John Fox, Pradeep Mitra, and John Sullivan.

The publications department at the Peterson Institute for International Economics under the directorship of Edward Tureen swiftly and expediently produced this book. Madona Devasahayam edited the book with sense and elegance.

Finally, and most of all, I want to thank my wife, Anna, and my children, Carl and Marianna, for being so patient with my spending so much time poring over the manuscript.

ANDERS ÅSLUND
Washington
December 2008

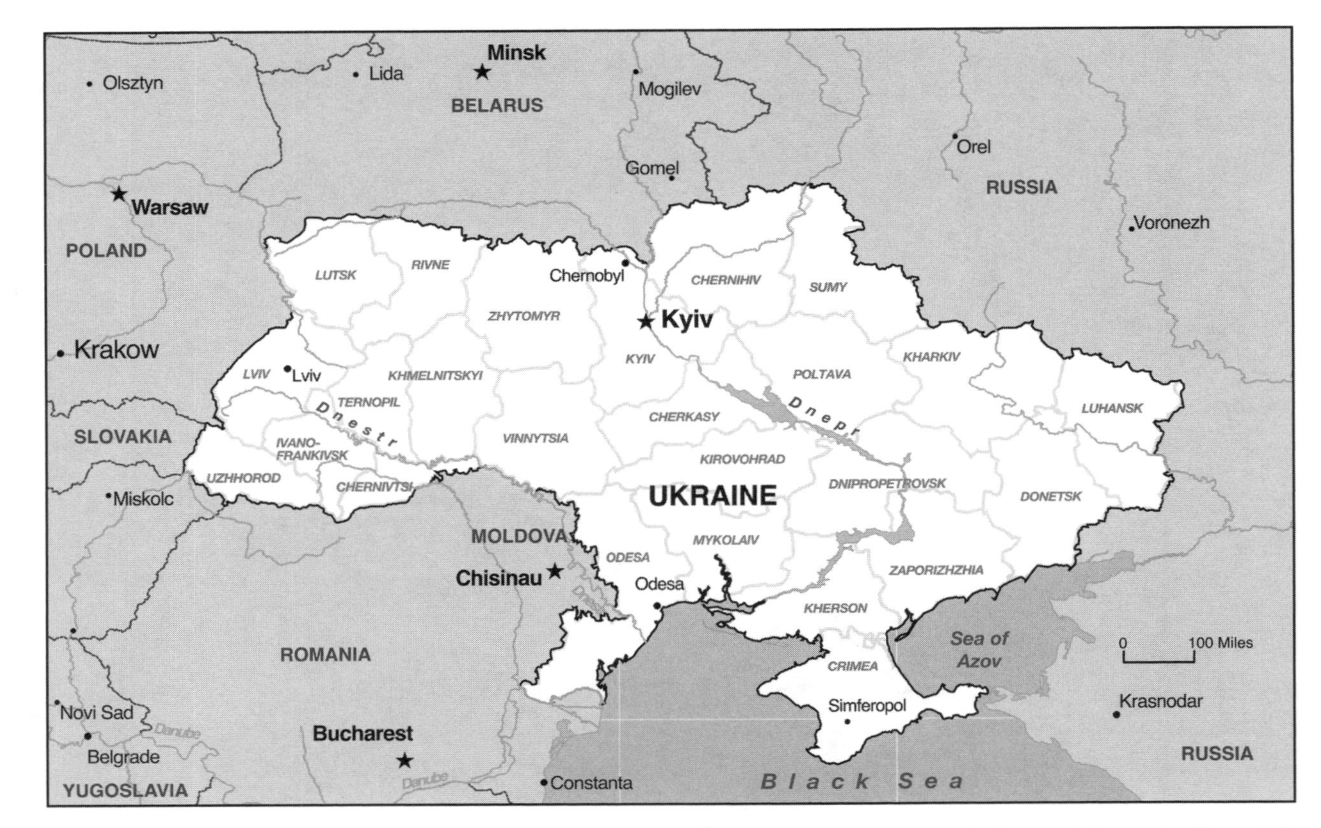

Reprinted with permission of the publisher of *Revolution in Orange* edited by Anders Åslund (Washington, DC: Carnegie Endowment for International Peace, 2006, p. ix, www.carnegieendowment.org).

Key Facts

Ukraine has been an independent state since December 1991. It first declared its sovereignty on July 16, 1990 and then outright independence on August 24, 1991, its national day. Its independence was reconfirmed in a referendum on December 1, 1991, and became effective with the collapse of the Soviet Union later that month.

Government

Ukraine is a unitary republic with a single-chamber parliament (the Supreme Rada), which has 450 members. The president is the directly elected head of state, while the cabinet of ministers is led by a prime minister.

People

Population: The official population has decreased from 52 million in 1991 to 46 million in 2008.

Languages: Ukrainian in the official language, but about as many speak Russian. Both languages are East Slavic, and almost the whole population speaks both.

Religion: Ukraine has no state religion. It has many religious communities with several large competing orthodox and catholic churches.

Geography

Area: Ukraine's total area is 604,000 square kilometers or 233,000 square miles, which renders it the largest fully European nation.

Boundaries: Ukraine borders on seven countries, Belarus in the north, Russia in the east, Moldova and Romania in the southwest, and Hungary, Slovakia, and Poland in the west. Its longest border is with Russia. River Dnieper divides the country into west and east banks.

Terrain: The country is dominated by level plains with black soil and excellent agricultural conditions. The main mountains are the Carpathian Mountains on the western border and the southern Crimean Mountains.

Major Cities: Kyiv, the capital, is the largest city, followed by Dnipropetrovsk and Donetsk in the east. Odesa on the Black Sea is the biggest port.

Economy

Economically, Ukraine is quite diversified. It was the granary of the Russian Empire, and few places on earth have better preconditions for agriculture. The soil and climate are ideal of cultivating many kinds of crops, notably wheat, corn, sunflower, and sugar beet. In the south, extensive irrigation systems allow cultivation of tomatoes and melons. Vineyards are ample in Crimea. Although food processing was poor throughout the Soviet Union, it was better than in any other republic.

The most prominent traditional industry is metallurgy, which is concentrated in the east, especially Donbas. Ukraine has unique comparative advantages in steel production, with good iron ore and hard coal located close to large ports with steelworks. Steel has consistently been Ukraine's main export item, usually accounting for about 40 percent of its exports. Ukraine is a major importer of oil and natural gas from Russia. It has more oil-refining capacity than it needs and a substantial chemicals industry. Ukraine has built substantial nuclear power capacity.

During the Soviet era, Ukraine became the country's engineering workshop. The main centers of machine-building were Dnipropetrovsk and Kharkiv in the east, but most big cities in Ukraine had extensive machine-building industry. Several port cities had large shipyards. Ukraine also had a substantial consumer goods manufacturing industry.

After the collapse of the Soviet Union, many new industries have evolved or greatly expanded, such as banking, mobile phone systems, retail trade, breweries, food processing, and automotive production.

Economic development of the country after communism surprisingly has been regionally balanced, though the three big cities, Kyiv, Donetsk, and Dnipropetrovsk, have taken off in all regards. The west is traditionally more rural with many small enterprises, while the east is dominated by large industrial enterprises and contains a large working class (Åslund 2005).

Source: Encyclopedia Britannica.

Introduction

I visited Ukraine for the first time in October 1985 to attend an economics conference at the State Planning Committee in Kyiv organized by the United Nations. Coming from Moscow, Kyiv made a very nice impression on me. It was greener, cleaner, and more orderly. In the evenings, people strolled around Khreshchatyk, the main street, and they were surprisingly friendly compared with the rude and rough Muscovites. Although people predominantly spoke Russian in the street, one instantly felt that this was another country. I enjoyed the pleasant atmosphere and intriguing society and have returned numerous times.

The drawback, however, was that Kyiv was isolated from the outside world and provincial. People turned around in the street at the sight of a foreigner. The Ukrainian economists were renowned as the most orthodox Marxist-Leninists in the Soviet Union. The intellectual night was deep. A peculiarity was that Ukraine had the liveliest religious life, with more active churches than any other part of the Soviet Union.

Today, everything has changed. One of Europe's old nations steeped in history, Ukraine is now an unquestioned independent nation and an open society. All Westerners can travel to Ukraine without a visa. It is the largest purely European country by size and the fifth largest by population.

This book offers a political and economic history of Ukraine from 1991 until 2008 meant to be accessible to a wide range of readers. It focuses on how and why key policies were made. At the time of its writing, it is the only book covering the whole period of Ukrainian independence that discusses both politics and economics. I hope it contributes to the understanding of what happened in Ukraine after 1991.

Main Arguments of the Book

Ukraine's postcommunist transition has been one of the most protracted and socially costly, but it appears to have taken Ukraine to a desirable destination. I offer below a brief summary of the main arguments in this book.

No Revolution, but National Independence

"Ukraine is not Russia," as President Leonid Kuchma (2003) named his book, is an insight that is as simple as it is profound. Unlike Russia, Ukraine did not experience a revolution when the Soviet Union collapsed. For Ukraine, the all-dominant goal was national liberation and nation-building, which was spearheaded by Ukrainian nationalists, the Ukrainian communist establishment, and the Soviet collapse. Russia, by contrast, needed to abandon its empire, while going through a liberal revolution against communism. Though similar in many ways, these two countries encountered completely different challenges, so their transformations had to be different.

On the one hand, it meant that Russia did more market economic reform at an early stage, which limited its social costs of transition. On the other hand, Ukrainians were prepared to accept higher social costs because their project was to build a nation, while the Russians had to reconcile themselves with the loss of empire.

Ukraine's Main Goal Was Nation-Building

Ukraine's aim was the building of a Ukrainian state and nation. Since it is a large state with a thousand-year history, this was a natural choice for the vast majority of the population. The Ukrainian nation builders were acutely aware of prior failures. The Ukrainian Cossack autonomy of the 17th century never resulted in an independent state. From 1917 to 1920, the burgeoning Ukrainian nation had several governments, which were all rash and radical, but the state succumbed to the Red Army. This time, national unity was crucial, which meant that the dominant groups had to be accommodated to accept the new independent state.

Therefore, the new Ukrainian state was formed by an alliance of Ukrainian nationalists organized in Rukh mainly in the west and Kyiv, national communists led by Leonid Kravchuk, and pragmatic state enterprise managers headed by Leonid Kuchma. The formation of this broad alliance had many consequences. Nearly the whole population was mobilized for the new nation: Over 90 percent of Ukrainians voted for independence on December 1, 1991, and separatism was surprisingly subdued.

The broad unitary approach of nationalism allowed a certain emphasis on the revival and extension of the Ukrainian language, but Russian and various minority languages were respected. Democracy-building, though, was put on the back burner. Initially, economic reform was sacrificed altogether. The nationalists thought Ukraine's main economic problem was exploitation by Russia, which would cease with Ukraine's independence. They did not realize that the main stumbling block was the inefficient Soviet economic system, because discussion of economic reform before independence was rudimentary. The national communists preferred to rule in the old way, while the state enterprise managers used new opportunities to enrich themselves.

Kravchuk led Ukraine during the most intense phase of nation-building. He was a jovial man who moved with amazing ease from the top of the Communist Party of Ukraine to become the new nation's first democratically elected president. His strength was his ability to find a consensus among people with little in common, while his weaknesses were an inability to act and a lack of intellectual clarity.

Ukraine Has Maintained a Strong Emphasis on Peace

Ukraine's independence has been remarkably peaceful for many reasons. The attempts at independence from 1917 until 1920 were foiled by blood. The many Ukrainian nationalists who had fought independently in World War II achieved nothing. The Soviet Empire imploded on its own, arousing no need for military action. Russian President Boris Yeltsin peacefully dissolved the Soviet Empire from within and guaranteed the existing borders between the Soviet republics.

The new Ukrainian nation had no reason to resort to violence and every reason to avoid it. In addition, the meltdown of the Chornobyl nuclear power station just north of Kyiv on April 26, 1986 convinced a broad Ukrainian opinion to oppose nuclear arms and opt for the new nation's denuclearization. Peacefulness became a source of national pride.

The Long Delay in Economic Reforms Led to Hyperinflation, Extreme Rent Seeking, and Output Collapse

In the early 1990s the government ignored economic policy. As a consequence, Ukraine was hit by hyperinflation of 10,155 percent in 1993, suffering the greatest official decline in output of any country not ravaged by war. Total confusion prevailed in economic policy.

The little thought devoted to economic policy derived from nation-building and took exception to Russia's attempt at radical economic reform. In order to strengthen the Ukrainian state, the National Bank of Ukraine was established, but it started issuing virtually unlimited amounts of ruble credits at low interest rates, which guaranteed hyperinflation. In another attempt to strengthen the Ukrainian state, a state-controlled Soviet-type foreign trade system was established, replete with quotas and licenses. For a few years, the prices of Ukraine's main export goods—steel, chemicals, and agricultural goods—were kept at a fraction of the world market price. Traders with good official connections made fortunes on privileged arbitrage between low domestic prices and high world market prices.

The greatest boondoggle was the importation of natural gas from Russia, whose natural gas monopoly, Gazprom, exported gas at low prices to an intermediary trading company, which shared its ample profits with top Russian officials and Ukrainian gas traders. The names of the intermediaries and beneficiaries varied, but gas trade was the dominant revenue source of the truly rich in Ukraine throughout the 1990s.

The long delay in market reforms generated no benefits. This made it more difficult to carry out market reforms because the vested interests that thrived on rent seeking had grown so strong that they were almost invincible. Since the most successful businessmen made their money by rent seeking, they ignored production. Officially, output continued to fall until 2000. Only after a full decade were the main sources of rent seeking blocked, and economic growth reemerged. The economic crisis caused social disruption through the miners' strikes in the summer of 1993 and also prompted the only serious secessionist threat in Crimea in 1994. The sustainability of the Ukrainian state was widely questioned because of its miserable economic performance. Ukraine's delayed economic reforms could have destroyed the budding state.

President Leonid Kuchma Brought about Financial Stabilization and Privatization, but Not Growth, in the Mid-1990s

The election of Leonid Kuchma to president in July 1994 offered Ukraine a badly needed break. Initially, Kuchma focused on salvaging the country from the rampant economic crisis. He advocated a normal market economy with private property and stable prices.

His first goal was to defeat inflation, which turned out to be the easiest task. The foundation stone was Ukraine's first International Monetary Fund (IMF) agreement, which was concluded in October 1994. Inflation never rose to triple digits again.

A second major achievement in the early Kuchma period was a successful program of mass privatization. As a consequence, since 1996, most of Ukraine's GDP has come from the private sector.

While these two reforms were successful, deregulation of prices and trade remained insufficient and was substantially reversed after a couple of years by the strong vested interests that lived on arbitrage between regulated and free prices, especially in the energy and commodity sectors. A market economy of sorts emerged, but it was hampered by red tape. Thus, rent seeking persisted and precluded economic growth. Ukraine was stuck in an underreform trap until 2000. Palpable corruption and the absence of growth provided fertile ground for communist agitation against a normal market economy. Ironically, both oligarchs and communists favored excessive regulation and state subsidies to enterprises, jointly blocking market reforms and economic growth.

Viktor Yushchenko's Reforms in 2000 Moved Ukraine from Rent Seeking to High Growth and Completed the Market Economy

At the end of 1999 the dominant oligarchs became truly worried. Ukraine faced an evident danger of external default, and Russia's financial crash of August 1998 had devastated many Russian oligarchs. They saw only one way out: Ukraine needed a reform government that could salvage the country. Therefore, a broad coalition of center-right party factions came together in parliament and appointed as prime minister the well-respected chairman of the National Bank of Ukraine, Viktor Yushchenko. In a few months, his government cleaned up Ukraine's state finances and energy trade. It also undertook several large privatizations and significant measures against corruption. As a consequence, Ukraine swiftly turned to high and steady economic growth. Yet the old establishment paid the price of the new economic growth. Upset over the elimination of so many rent-seeking schemes, it ousted the Yushchenko government in April 2000.

The European Union recognized Ukraine as a market economy in December 2005 and the United States did so in February 2006. In their antidumping legislation, the United States and the European Union define market economies in a similar fashion as the opposite of state-trading countries. The US Customs Code defines a nonmarket economy as "any foreign country that the administering authority determines does not operate on market principle of cost or pricing structures so that sales of merchandise in such a country do not reflect the fair value of the merchandise."[1] In making that assessment, the US Department of Commerce considers six criteria: (1) currency convertibility; (2) free bargaining for wages; (3) the "extent to which joint ventures or other investments by firms of other foreign countries are permitted in the foreign country"; (4) the "extent of government ownership"; (5) the "extent of government control over the allocation of resources and over the price and output decisions of enterprises"; and (6) other appropriate factors.

For the purposes of this book, however, the definition above is too slanted toward trade to be adequate. A market economy is best understood as the opposite of a socialist economy, as János Kornai (1992, 360–79) outlined it. First, the economic actors must be independent from the state

1. United States Code [19 U.S.C.1677(18)], available at the US Government Printing Office website, www.access.gpo.gov (accessed on August 9, 2007).

and act freely without state commands. Second, private ownership of enterprises should dominate, and property rights need to be reasonably safe. Third, prices and trade should be predominantly free, and fourth, state subsidies must be limited. A fifth criterion could be that transactions are largely monetized. Price stability, however, is not a condition. None of these criteria is absolute because all states distort their economies somewhat (Åslund 2007b). Ukraine attained these standards and became a market economy in 2000.

Competitive Oligarchy Bred High Growth and Pluralism

The Yushchenko reforms created a market economy and went far enough to become irreversible. After his departure, similar policies persisted. A new market economic consensus had been formed.

As a consequence, the oligarchs—as the few very wealthy were popularly called— changed qualitatively. Until 1999, all the richest people in Ukraine made their money on gas trade, but from 2000 on, they became steel producers. The country had traversed the crucial hurdle from arbitrage to export production. The oligarchs were no longer courtiers who made their money on intrigues in the corridors of power, but owners of large factories with well-defined and lasting interests. Their specialization allowed new big businessmen to evolve in other industries, such as machine-building, banking, retail trade, real estate, and agriculture.

Ukraine remained an oligarchic state, where a club of big businessmen dominated the government, parliament, and media, but intense competition prevailed among them. Their focus was no longer state subsidies but the privatization of lucrative companies and their production. The more private property rights were accumulated, the stronger was the political support for property rights.

Major oligarchs had their own factions in parliament to further their causes. Their competition was not fair but vibrant, and it bred pluralism and high economic growth. While this system was corrupt and unjust, it represented a considerable advance from the parasitical rent seeking and continuous decline of the 1990s. Power was not consolidated but divided.

The Orange Revolution Represented Ukraine's Democratic Breakthrough

The Orange Revolution of December 2004 was Ukraine's moment of euphoria. After many years of semidemocratic rule, the nation achieved its democratic breakthrough. All desirable underlying conditions had accumulated. Thanks to impressive economic dynamism, breeding greater pluralism, Ukraine had outgrown its semidemocratic system. The business elite was divided through increased competition and rebellious big businessmen could persevere. As a consequence, the millionaires rose against the billionaires. The divisions among the business elite were also reflected in law enforcement.

The March 2002 elections had given the opposition about half the seats in parliament, providing it with a strong, legal platform. As head of the largest opposition party, Our Ukraine, Yushchenko was its leader. Although the regime controlled most media, the opposition possessed a minor TV channel, several serious weekly newspapers, and excellent internet news. Civil society developed a strong nongovernmental organization to monitor the presidential elections, and when the election rules were tampered with, over a million people took to the streets. European politicians intervened at roundtable negotiations to maintain peace and reach a compromise.

The Orange Revolution brought about a neat democratic breakthrough and peace was maintained. The existing rules were accepted by all parties and were judged by Ukraine's highest courts. In the end, orderly presidential elections were held and their outcome was respected. The winner did not take all but left the vanquished side intact. An agreement was reached on a new constitutional arrangement. Thereby Ukraine complied with Juan Linz's (1978, 5) definition of democracy:

> Legal freedom to formulate and advocate political alternatives with the concomitant rights to free association, free speech, and other basic freedoms of person; free and nonviolent competition among leaders with periodic validation of their claim to rule; inclusion of all effective political offices in the democratic process; and provision for the participation of all members of the political community, whatever their political preferences.

Yet there were two serious institutional shortcomings. First, the democratic breakthrough should have been immediately followed by a parliamentary election that reflected the profound political transformation. Instead, politics became one long election campaign lasting until the parliamentary elections already scheduled for March 2006, and the revolutionary momentum was never used for reforms.

Second, the constitutional changes reduced the powers of the president but did not go far enough to create a viable parliamentary system. The new constitutional order was so inconsistent that the country became nearly ungovernable. Severe conflicts between the president and prime minister led to frequent government changes, early parliamentary elections, and minimal legislative activity.

Is Ukraine Moving toward a Parliamentary System?

Ukraine's political system has evolved very gradually. It started out as a dysfunctional post-Soviet system comprising a sovereign parliament and an equally sovereign president, with an indeterminate prime minister hanging in between.

The electoral system to the parliament has been transformed in steps from one-man constituencies with majority election to purely proportional elections with a threshold for representation of 3 percent of the votes cast. Considering the notorious sale of seats on party lists, personal choice within a proportional system would be a positive evolution.

The distribution of power between president and prime minister has always been problematic. At present, the president has minimal power to be constructive but plenty of power to block decisions, as he mainly exercises power through his veto. In Ukraine, as in other post-Soviet countries, the presidential administration resembles the Central Committee of the Communist Party, in whose buildings it is housed. The presidential administration has reproduced the "telephone rule," with officials giving oral commands beyond any legal order, which was characteristic of communist parties.

A persistent gridlock might be bearable if the existing legislation were appropriate, but Ukraine needs to adopt scores of new laws to establish normal rule of law. Therefore, a functioning legislature is vital. Given that the presidential system has never worked well, a transition to a full parliamentary system appears desirable. Parliamentary control facilitates transparency and accountability, which Ukraine needs to combat pervasive corruption. Not surprisingly, democracy and parliamentary rule are closely correlated in postcommunist countries. Yet the president may stay popularly elected, as in the parliamentary systems of Finland and Lithuania.

Also, at the regional and local levels, no clear division of power exists between councils and executives. Ukraine still suffers from extreme overcentralization characteristic of communism. Regional and local councils, as well as mayors, are elected, while regional governors are appointed. Logically, they should all be popularly elected. As a matter of both democracy and efficiency, regional and local governments should also be allowed to raise their own taxes and be responsible for their own expenditures rather than being subject to detailed tutelage by the central state administration.

Ukraine Is Turning to the West

Ukraine is increasingly turning to the West rather than to Russia. Russian President Boris Yeltsin tried to accommodate Ukraine and maintain friendly relations. He always expressed his respect for Ukraine's borders and independence. In response, President Kuchma developed his "multi vector" foreign policy, oriented to both the West and Russia. Ukraine participated in the post-Soviet Commonwealth of Independent States (CIS) as well as the Council of Europe. The high point of Russia-Ukraine cooperation was reached in 1997, with the Treaty on Friendship, Cooperation and Partnership and the agreement to lease the naval base in Sevastopol on Crimea to Russia for 20 years.

President Vladimir Putin broke with Yeltsin's policy of respect for Ukraine's sovereignty, making his infamous statement in April 2008 that "Ukraine is not even a state." The peak of Russian interference in Ukraine occurred during the presidential elections in the fall of 2004 that prompted the Orange Revolution, compelling Ukraine to turn to the West. Putin's ensuing aggressive policy has driven Ukraine further in that direction. Russia is Ukraine's only security threat, leaving it with little choice but to seek closer relations with the West.

On May 16, 2008, Ukraine became a member of the World Trade Organization (WTO), which is set to mold its trade policy. It is already negotiating a European Association Agreement with the European Union, which will include a wide free trade agreement. The United States should follow suit.

Russia, by contrast, has erected so many trade barriers that the share of trade between the two neighbors has declined. The basis for trade between Russia and Ukraine is a bilateral free trade agreement concluded in 1993, but it is impotent because it lacks arbitration and enforcement mechanisms, and Russia has failed to join the WTO. Ukraine did accept the Russian Common Economic Space initiative of 2003, but it was stillborn because Russia demanded more ambitious cooperation than Ukraine could accept. Repeated squabbles over gas trade and multiple Russian import embargoes on Ukrainian agricultural goods and steel pipes have harmed bilateral trade.

Commercial interests are increasingly attracting Ukraine to the European market. If Ukraine complies with the strict criteria of the EU legal rule book, the *acquis communautaire*, the European Union can hardly refuse Ukraine membership in the long term because the EU founding document, the Treaty of Rome, guarantees all European countries the right to apply for EU membership, and the recent EU eastern enlargement has clarified the rules and procedures for accession.

Structure of the Book

The structure of the book is chronological-thematic. It consists of seven chronological chapters, one chapter of background, and one concluding chapter with overall analysis. Within each chronological chapter, the main themes are analyzed in sections.

Chapter 1 provides Ukraine's background, discussing implications of its history, the awakening of society because of Mikhail Gorbachev's reforms, the early democratization, and the impact of the ill-fated Soviet economic reforms. Chapter 2 discusses the reign of President Leonid Kravchuk from 1991 to 1994. The only salient achievement of this time was nation-building, while the economy collapsed in the midst of hyperinflation. Chapter 3 deals with the first two years of Leonid Kuchma's presidency, from 1994 to 1996, which were characterized by substantial achievements, notably financial stabilization and mass privatization. Chapter 4, which covers the period 1996–99, is devoted to a miserable period of policy stagnation, rent seeking, and continued economic decline. In 2000 hope returned to Ukraine, as discussed in chapter 5. Viktor Yushchenko became prime minister and launched energetic reforms to cleanse the economy of corruption. Finally, economic growth returned. Chapter 6 considers the ensuing period, 2001–04, which amounted to a competitive oligarchy. It was quite pluralist, although repression increased. Economic growth was high. Chapter 7 is devoted to the Orange Revolution of 2004, which was the most joyful period, representing Ukraine's democratic breakthrough. Chapter 8 discusses the confusing period after the Orange Revolution, which has been characterized by great political instability but also democracy and a broadening social consensus. Chapter 9 offers major conclusions.

Transcription is a major problem when writing about Ukraine. Most people use both Ukrainian and Russian versions of their names, and they use both languages to various extents. Similarly, all places have both Ukrainian and Russian names. I have attempted to use Ukrainian names and transcription unless it becomes odd or outright confusing. There are no agreed transcription rules from Ukrainian to English, so I try to use the most common standards. The variations are considerable, and I have taken the liberty of standardizing the transcription of names of authors in the bibliography, even when they have been transcribed differently, so that all works by one author are found in one place.

1

Ukraine: Nation, History, and Soviet Reforms

In late 1987 I went to Canada to see the Ukrainian Catholic lay activist Iosyf Terelia. He had just been expelled from the Soviet Union after having spent 18 years, nearly half his life, as a political prisoner in the Gulag. Terelia told me matter-of-factly, "You know, in western Ukraine everybody looks upon the Soviet Union as something temporary." His insight was simple: What you believe is true.

A Proud but Tragic National Legacy

Ukraine is one of Europe's old, historical nations, which was squeezed between the Polish and Russian Empires, as well as the Hapsburg and Ottoman Empires. It did not gain national independence for centuries. Kyiv was the capital of Rus, which adopted Eastern Orthodox Christianity from Byzantium in 988. Both Russia and Ukraine saw Rus as their origin, and it was too early to talk about a distinct Ukrainian nation.

According to the outstanding historian of Ukraine Orest Subtelny (2005, 23), the word "Ukraine" has been used since the late 12th century. Even though its origin is unclear, most historians derive it from *okraina*, which means borderland. As Russia, much of Ukraine fell under Tatar rule in medieval times. The Polish-Lithuanian Commonwealth controlled most of present Ukraine's territory in the 15th and 16th centuries. Ukraine's national formation occurred in the 17th century. Many Ukrainians were Cossacks, free, Orthodox men roaming the steppes, and they were famously independent minded.

The Cossack leaders left two contradictory legacies, anti-Russian and anti-Polish. In 1648, just as the Thirty-Year War ended, Ukrainian Hetman Bohdan Khmelnytskiy led a Cossack uprising against the Polish-Lithuanian Empire, which was weakened by the war, and his Hetmanate acquired quasi-independence. In Ukrainian historiography, this is referred to as "a war of national liberation" (Wilson 2002, 61). In 1654 Khmelnytskiy concluded the Treaty of Pereyasliv, a military union with Russia. Khmelnytskiy's intention with this union is in dispute, but eventually eastern Ukraine became an integral part of Russia. Ukraine was divided into an eastern Russophone part and western Ukraine, which stayed Polish and Western-oriented.

While national independence remained elusive, the Cossacks faced the critical choice of fighting Russia or Poland. Unlike Khmelnytskiy, half a century later Hetman Ivan Mazepa took exception to Russia and leaned to the West instead. In the midst of the Great Nordic War, Mazepa abandoned Russian Tsar Peter I to forge an alliance with Sweden's King Charles XII, who invaded Ukraine with Swedish and Polish troops. However, the army of Tsar Peter I dealt them a devastating defeat in the epic battle at Poltava in June 1709, about which Voltaire, Alexander Pushkin, Lord Byron, and Victor Hugo wrote books and poems. It marked the emergence of Russia as a great power and the long-term subordination of Ukraine to the Russian crown. Russia and the Soviet Union celebrated Khmelnytskiy for having brought Ukraine to Russia, while Ukrainian nationalists see him as the father of the Ukrainian nation but also cherish the ultimately tragic Mazepa. Both decorate Ukrainian banknotes.

In the mid-19th century, Ukrainian nationalism rose around national myths, language, and culture, characteristic of budding European nations at the time. Ukraine's national poet, Taras Shevchenko (1814–61), formulated lasting national ideas. He wrote in Ukrainian and identified Ukraine with its language, idealizing the Cossacks as free men with a natural inclination to popular democracy, since they elected their hetmans. By contrast, Shevchenko identified the Poles as aristocrats and the Russians as autocrats. The Ukrainians were orthodox, standing up against the Catholics of the West (Wilson 2002, 90–95).

Few nations suffered as much as the Ukrainians during the bloody 20th century. Parts of Ukraine were a battleground during World War I and terrible bloodshed took place during the Russian Civil War from 1917 to 1921. Russia's imperial power collapsed through the February 1917 revolution. In Kyiv, nationalists formed an assembly that soon became the Ukrainian People's Republic and declared Ukrainian independence in January 1918. It elected historian Mykhailo Hrushevskiy president of the republic in March 1917 and established four national symbols that were adopted anew after independence in 1991: the currency, the hryvnia; the trident, the coat of arms of the Rurik Dynasty of ancient Rus; the blue-and-yellow flag, sky over corn; and the national anthem.

But several separate Ukrainian republics declared independence in 1917 and 1918. The Bolsheviks invaded Kyiv three times. In 1920 Poland occupied most of Ukraine, but it was beaten back by the Red Army. The Bolsheviks did not fully subdue Ukraine until the peace in Riga between the Soviet Union and Poland in March 1921. As Andrew Wilson (2002, 124) puts it, the existence of the Ukrainian People's Republic "was brief, its boundaries variable and its power limited, but still it left a durable mythology behind it. . . ." The period 1917–20 offered Ukraine its greatest moment of national revival, and the Ukrainian People's Republic started building democratic institutions, but without a regular army the state could do nothing but fail. Its failure was also seen as caused by excessive internal divisions, leaving democracy with a dubious reputation.

The Stalinist terror was particularly severe in Ukraine. The brutal collectivization of agriculture in 1932–33 is commonly assessed to have caused 5 million to 7 million deaths, about a quarter of the population, in what became known as *Holodomor*, the Famine or Hunger Death. Most people died because of imposed starvation as NKVD troops sealed the borders to the region condemned to die of hunger (Conquest 1986). Ukraine demands that this act be condemned as genocide. During the Great Terror in 1937, tens of thousands of Ukrainians were executed.

In August 1939 Joseph Stalin and Adolf Hitler concluded the Molotov-Ribbentrop Pact. It granted the Soviet Union western Ukraine, which then belonged to Poland. Similarly, Hitler promised Stalin the three Baltic states, Estonia, Latvia, and Lithuania. On September 1 Hitler invaded Poland from the west, and on September 17, Soviet troops attacked eastern Poland and annexed western Ukraine, executing and deporting a large part of the population. The Soviet occupation of western Ukraine through the Molotov-Ribbentrop Pact left the western Ukrainians deeply convinced that their belonging to the Soviet Union was unjust. Western Ukraine became the center of Ukrainian nationalism. A large part of the population fled to the West, mainly Canada and the United States, preserving a strong Ukrainian nationalist opposition to the Soviet Union. However brutal Soviet repression of western Ukraine was, the opposition was never defeated.

The western Ukrainian reaction left a complicated legacy for a future Ukrainian state. The strongest Ukrainian resistance organization was the Organization of Ukrainian Nationalists (OUN). The Ukrainian Insurgent Army (UPA) had as many as 90,000 men under arms at the end of World War II, though far more Ukrainians—2 million—fought in the Red Army. The Ukrainian Insurgent Army battled against Germans and Soviets. Alexander Motyl (1980, 167) labels it a "national liberation struggle." The guerilla war continued intensely until 1947 and persisted until the mid-1950s (Wilson 2002, 131–34, 143). This radical nationalism has survived within a small but vocal minority.

Ukraine has a vibrant religious life characterized by more diversity than in any other European state. It has four major churches: The Moscow Orthodox Church, the Kyiv Orthodox Church, the Autocephalous Orthodox Church, and the Greek Catholic Church. Through the Union in Brest in 1595, the Polish king persuaded the Ukrainian (Ruthenian) Orthodox Church in Poland to break with the Orthodox patriarch in Moscow and acknowledge the pope in Rome, forming the Ukrainian Greek Catholic Church. It primarily exists in western Ukraine. In 1946, after western Ukraine had been incorporated into the Soviet Union, Stalin forcibly merged the Ukrainian Greek Catholic Church with the Russian Orthodox Church. Its priests were jailed and many were executed while the Russian Orthodox Church seized its property, but the church persisted underground. In 1921 the Ukrainian Autocephalous Orthodox Church was founded in the wake of the collapse of the Russian Empire. Since it did not recognize the Moscow patriarch, Stalin prohibited it, and the Soviet secret police severely persecuted its priests and adherents. In addition, the Ukrainian Catholic Church was a large clandestine church. All these churches persevered as underground mass organizations and reemerged in the late 1980s.

After Stalin's death in March 1953, repression eased. Nikita Khrushchev's secret speech about Stalin's many crimes to the 20th Soviet Communist Party Congress in 1956 augured a thaw that was to last until his ouster in 1964. The thaw also affected Ukraine, where the intelligentsia reacted as the Moscow intelligentsia did. This was a time to believe in the reform of socialism, and its optimistic supporters were called *shestidesyatniki*, or Children of the 20th Party Congress in Kyiv as in Moscow, where their foremost representative was to be Mikhail Gorbachev. This generation of the 1960s took advantage of the more relaxed political atmosphere, and in Ukraine *shestidesyatniki* naturally also explored Ukrainian culture and language. Not all were nationalists and dissidents, but many were, notably Vyacheslav Chornovil and Levko Lukyanenko. The Ukrainians once again seized the opportunity to raise their nationalist cause.

Khrushchev was ethnically Russian, but he had spent his early career in Ukraine and led much of the repression. In 1963 Khrushchev promoted Petro Shelest to first secretary of the Communist Party of Ukraine (CPU). Shelest was a man of Khrushchev's cue, acting within the communist system but showing some common sense. As Taras Kuzio (2000, 45) puts it: "Shelest was never a separatist but he did lobby for Ukrainian cultural and economic rights. . . ." More specifically, he demanded more investment in Ukraine and favored the Ukrainian language. In 1972 Shelest was accused of Ukrainian nationalist deviations and duly sacked. The Kremlin unleashed serious repression targeting nationalist intellectuals in Kyiv. Hundreds of Ukrainian dissidents, including Chornovil and Lukyanenko, were sentenced to long prison sentences in the 1970s and 1980s.

Khrushchev's successor as general secretary of the Communist Party of the Soviet Union (CPSU), Leonid Brezhnev, instigated the new wave of repression. He was born and raised in the Dnipropetrovsk region in eastern Ukraine. In 1972 he replaced Shelest with his loyal friend from Dnipropetrovsk, Volodymyr Shcherbytskiy, as first secretary of the CPU. Kuzio (2000, 43) summarized: "Shcherbytskiy's rule was characterised by repression, economic and spiritual stagnation, and a determined campaign for the Russification of Ukrainian language and culture."

Because of his strong hold over the Ukrainian party apparatus, Shcherbytskiy stayed in power until September 1989, being one of the last Brezhnevites to go. As a consequence, among the European republics of the Soviet Union, Ukraine endured the most severe repression in the 1980s. Gorbachev's perestroika, glasnost, and democratization were long strange phenomena announced in Moscow and seen on Soviet television but lacking local roots in Ukraine, least of all in the CPU.

Society Wakes Up under Gorbachev

On March 11, 1985, Mikhail Gorbachev was elected general secretary of the CPSU after a standard but very fast-paced party career.[1] He had been first party secretary of the Stavropol region in southern Russia, close to Ukraine, and the Central Committee secretary for agriculture and ideology as well as a member of the politburo (Åslund 2007b).

Yet Gorbachev was no ordinary man. Three months before his coronation, he made a major speech on ideology in which he mentioned all the catchwords that became popular later: perestroika, glasnost, and democratization (Gorbachev 1987a). What was missing, however, was a nationality policy. However radical and knowledgeable Gorbachev was, unlike his hardened predecessors, he had no clue about nationality policy but harbored the naïve thought that the Soviet Union had solved the national dilemma. His 1987 book *Perestroika* illustrates his delusions:

> The Revolution and socialism have done away with national oppression and inequality, and ensured economic, intellectual and cultural progress for all nations and nationalities. . . . If the nationality question had not been solved in principle, the Soviet Union would never have had the social, cultural, economic and defense potential as it has now. (Gorbachev 1987b, 118–19)

It was long before the deep-frozen Ukrainian society woke up. The first year of glasnost and perestroika passed without particular notice in Ukraine. On April 26, 1986, a nuclear reactor in Chornobyl just north of Kyiv melted down. The radioactive cloud went north over Belarus, but

1. The two main sources of this section are Wilson (2002) and Kuzio (2000).

Ukraine suffered as well. On May 1, 1986, the CPU held its usual May Day parade without considering the radioactivity. No popular protest was recorded, but people were aware and shocked. The Chornobyl scandal enhanced glasnost in Moscow but had much less impact in Ukraine.

Even so, the Chornobyl catastrophe left serious legacies. People were upset that they had not been informed about the disaster. One of Ukraine's first popular movements was the environmental movement *Zelenyi Svit*, or Green World, which held the first officially sanctioned popular demonstration with 10,000 participants in Kyiv on November 13, 1988 (Banaian 1999, 12). The republican authorities were angry because they neither received information nor possessed any influence over all-union companies managed from Moscow. The Ukrainization of such enterprises became an issue. The shock of the disaster also bred popular dislike of nuclear arms.

In April 1987 Gorbachev declared a general amnesty for prisoners of conscience, most of whom were Ukrainians. Hundreds of them returned from Siberia to Ukraine. Some were religious, others democratic activists, but they were predominantly Ukrainian nationalists from western Ukraine or Kyiv. Hardened by many years in the camps, they were no longer afraid and naturally seized the leadership of budding popular movements.

Chornovil and Lukyanenko, who were returning after many years in prison camps, became nationalist opposition leaders, usually in competition with each other. In August 1987 Chornovil wrote an open letter to Gorbachev, which became the first major Ukrainian opposition document of the era. Lukyanenko was elected the leader of the Ukrainian Helsinki Group (later renamed the Ukrainian Helsinki Union), which became the mainstay of former political prisoners (Kuzio 2000, 66–71).

In 1988 each of the three Baltic states, Estonia, Latvia, and Lithuania, established powerful national fronts, which were soon demanding full independence. Ukrainian nationalists looked to the Baltic national fronts as examples to follow. In early 1989 many popular Ukrainian movements, including the Writers' Union, the Ukrainian Helsinki Group, and Green World, joined to form *Rukh*, which simply means movement. It was designed as a broad association and was originally called the "Popular Movement in Support of Perestroika." Its leaders were primarily intellectuals from Ukraine's cultural establishment, such as writers Ivan Drach and Dmytro Pavlychko, but also former political prisoners. Rukh was to lead Ukraine's national awakening and its focus was the revival of the Ukrainian language, culture, and national symbols. To remain legal, it did not call for full independence initially. It largely ignored economics. It criticized the old regime for being "totalitarian-communist" or "imperial-totalitarian," while the Russian liberal critique of communism also attacked the "command-administrative" system. Rukh's supporters came almost entirely from western and central Ukraine, limiting its potential support to one-quarter of the population (Wilson 2002, 156–60).

Rukh had to contend with a small but hard and well-organized nationalist movement on its right, which opposed compromises with the communist authorities and demanded outright independence. These hard-liners were significant only in the western-most regions, but they comprised Rukh's home turf, so these local right-wingers drove Rukh into a nationalist corner. One right-wing movement drew on the interwar nationalist organization, the Organization of Ukrainian Nationalists, which reemerged as the Congress of Ukrainian Nationalists in 1992. It attracted anti-Soviet war veterans and its rallies looked like gatherings of pensioners. Another right-wing challenge came from a student movement, which in September 1991 formed UNA-UNSO (the Ukrainian National Assembly and the Ukrainian National Self-Defense Force). It preached the greatness of the Ukrainian state, mobilizing militant men, who were repeatedly accused of resorting to violence. Although these two movements were marginal, attracting only a couple percent of voters, they forced Rukh to show its nationalist fervor, which deterred other voters (Wilson 2002, 181–82).

Rukh was prone to splits inspired by the Ukrainian People's Republic. Lukyanenko chose to go his own way with his nationalist Ukrainian Republican Party. Its leaders were former political prisoners, who demanded the annulment of the 1922 Union Treaty with Russia, which had formed the Soviet Union. Within Rukh, Chornovil won the leadership struggle against the more moderate Drach. Gradually, Rukh's emphasis moved from human rights and democracy to nationalism. As a consequence, Rukh failed to appeal to the country as a whole (Prizel 1997, 339–41).

Gorbachev's speeches and meetings riveted the whole world, but ironically because of the tight political control in Ukraine they had limited impact on its public. In June–July 1988, Gorbachev organized the 19th Party Conference in Moscow to promote democratization in the Soviet Union.

Eventually, this process also reached Ukraine through the all-union elections of a new Soviet parliament, the USSR Congress of People's Deputies, on March 26, 1989. These were the first elections offering some choice, but freedom was limited. The Communist Party and other Soviet organizations appointed one-third of the deputies. The remaining deputies were supposed to be elected, but in Ukraine only one-third of the candidates were accepted for registration, and almost one-third of the seats were not contested in the election. As many as 87.6 percent of the new deputies were members of the CPU, and only a handful belonged to the opposition, but a larger number were liberals. Even so, shockingly, several top communist officials lost, namely the first party secretary of Kyiv, the chairman of the Kyiv City Council, and four regional party leaders (Kuzio 2000, 96–98; Birch 2000a, 46, 53; Prizel 1997, 338).

In May–June 1989, the first session of the USSR Congress of People's Deputies in Moscow marked the breakthrough of freedom of speech in Russia. Its impact in Ukraine was more limited, but old-style communism had become untenable.

In the summer of 1989, the workers awoke. Coal miners went on strike throughout the Soviet Union, notably in Kuzbass in Siberia and Karaganda in Kazakhstan. These strikes also spread to the huge coalfields in Donbas in eastern Ukraine between July 18 and 24. Upset about massive shortages of goods and the impending collapse of the Soviet economy, the coal miners focused on economic demands. Their most moving demand was guaranteed supplies of soap so that they could wash themselves. These strikes gave rise to independent coal miners' unions, partially inspired by Poland's Solidarity. For the first time, the workers started playing a role and organizing themselves; they had coordinated their protests with coal miners in other parts of the Soviet Union. They spoke Russian, and Rukh with its Ukrainian nationalist agenda was alien to them (Banaian 1999, 13).

These strikes persuaded Gorbachev to finally sack the hard-line Ukrainian first party secretary, Volodymyr Shcherbytskiy. He was replaced by Volodymyr Ivashko, another Ukrainian party official of the same hue, but at least there was some change. Shcherbytskiy's ouster showed that the CPU had weakened, but it took some time before reformers emerged within the party ranks.

On March 4, 1990, Ukraine held its first semidemocratic republican elections to Ukraine's Supreme Rada, also imposed upon Ukraine by Gorbachev. These elections were much freer than the all-union elections a year earlier but far from free and fair. Administrative manipulation and ballot tampering were widespread. While independent candidates were allowed, opposition parties were not. Possibilities for campaigning were very limited. Voters could not know much about the candidates. Rukh staged one of its largest demonstrations in January 1990 by forming a human chain from Kyiv to Lviv to symbolize the unity of western and eastern Ukraine, following the example of the Baltic nationalists the previous year.

The March 1990 republican elections marked a breakthrough for democratization in Ukraine. The communists won no less than 373 seats out of the 450, that is, 83 percent, but many communists were no longer loyal to the party. The Democratic Bloc, which included Rukh, Lukyanenko's Ukrainian Republican Party, and others, won 108 seats, one-quarter of the vote, compared with 239 loyal communists, who formed the majority. The Democratic Bloc captured most seats in the western regions and did well in Kyiv and central Ukraine, while the communists maintained overwhelming control in the east and the south as well as in the countryside (Prizel 1997, 339–40; Wilson 2002, 160). This regional division of Ukraine has lasted. Rukh would never do better than how it did in this early election; one-quarter of the votes was its ceiling (box 1.1). This election

Box 1.1 Ukraine: A country of regions

Ukraine cannot be understood without its regional peculiarities and tensions. The divisions are many, between east and west, between Ukrainian and Russian speakers, as well as between countryside and towns.

Ukraine's fundamental division is between the east-south and the west-center, between the Ukrainian-speaking and Russian-speaking parts of the country. Roughly half the population prefers Russian and the other half Ukrainian. Ukraine's luck is that the division is not clear cut. Many people speak Ukrainian at home and Russian at work or vice versa. Quite a few converse in Russian with one parent and in Ukrainian with the other. An estimated one-fifth of the population speaks a mixture of Russian and Ukrainian, called *surzhyk*. Ethnically, the population also displays an amazing mixture of Jewish, Polish, German, Greek, Romanian, and Tartar blood.

By historical origins, Ukraine and its 27 regions can be divided into five territories. First, in the far west, five oblasts (regions) belonged to the Hapsburg Empire: Lviv, Ternopil, Ivano-Frankivsk, Chernivtsi (formerly Bukovyna), and Transcarpathia. The second region consists of Volyn and Rivne oblasts, which were long part of Poland but were gradually taken over by the Russian Empire. All these seven western oblasts were incorporated into the Soviet Union in 1944. Third, six oblasts around Kyiv on the right bank of the Dnieper River belonged to Poland until the partition of 1793, when they became Russian, but most of the land was owned by Polish landlords until the Russian revolution. Fourth, the left bank of the Dnieper is the most populous, industrial, and urban part of Ukraine. It consists of ten oblasts, including Dnipropetrovsk and Donetsk. It was also the cradle of Cossack Hetmanates but became Russian in 1654 through the Treaty of Pereyasliv. The fifth territory consists of former Ottoman lands at the Black Sea, notably Odesa and Crimea (Birch 2000b, 1019–20).

Hard-core Ukrainian nationalists, who comprise at most a quarter of the population, always oppose the Russified near half of Ukraine, but this division is so diffuse that it is unlikely to lead to a partition of the country as occurred in Czechoslovakia in 1992 or in Sweden-Norway in 1905. In those cases, the divide between two nations was much more clear cut, however close the languages. In both cases, the dominant nations (Czechs and Swedes) accounted for two-thirds of the population, making the minority feel that it could never win. In Ukraine, by contrast, election victories have wandered between the west-center, Dnipropetrovsk, and Donetsk.

(box continues on next page)

Box 1.1 Ukraine: A country of regions *(continued)*

Unlike countries such as the United Kingdom, France, Russia, or Austria, Ukraine is not dominated by its capital. Its circumstances are more reminiscent of the Federal Republic of Germany, Italy, or the United States. Until 1934, Kharkiv was the capital of Soviet Ukraine. In Soviet times, Dnipropetrovsk, the city of Brezhnev, Shcherbytskiy, and Kuchma, was the leading light. Donetsk produced prime ministers Yukhym Zviahilskiy and Viktor Yanukovych. These two cities represented the industrial wealth of Ukraine and became the seats of the wealthiest business empires. Meanwhile, Kyiv gained importance as the capital of the country. These three cities were to play against one another. As if to make that point, each city has its own soccer team. Yet other cities are also important. Lviv is the predominant western Ukrainian center, while Odesa is the main port and trading city. In the east, Kharkiv and Zaporizhe remain alternative centers.

In 2006 a top representative of one of Ukraine's biggest business groups told me: "In this country, the west and east always oppose and balance each other. We are four oligarchic groups, each of which is stronger than the state, and we all hate one another so we cannot agree on anything but balance one another. Therefore, Ukraine is bound to be a democracy."

marked the limits of both Rukh and the CPU, which energized the political center.

The parliament elected in March 1990 was to last until 1994, and the electoral order was formative for Ukraine's future parliamentary elections. On the positive side, reserved seats for the CPU and related organizations were abolished. The whole parliament was elected in direct elections. Many formal obstacles for nomination were removed. However, this order left several negative legacies. Political parties played a minimal role because all deputies were elected through majority vote in one-man constituencies, breeding weak and fractured parties and many independent deputies. Onerous demands for an absolute majority of the voters turning out made it nearly impossible to fill all seats in parliament. Elections were rerun repeatedly because of the failure to fill empty spots, exhausting voters (Birch 2000a, 55–67; D'Anieri 2006).

Local elections were also held on March 4, 1990. The Democratic Bloc won absolute majorities in the three western-most oblasts (regions), Lviv, Ternopil, and Ivano-Frankivsk, and Chornovil became chairman of the Lviv oblast council. For the first time, the opposition had acquired formal executive power (Kuzio 2000, 132).

After the March 1990 elections, liberalization finally encroached upon the hard-line CPU. Three kinds of moderate left emerged. As in Russia, a democratic platform was constituted within the CPU. It evolved into the Party of Democratic Rebirth of Ukraine, which favored privatization and the creation of a market economy, while maintaining a belief in socialism. State enterprise managers, commonly called "red directors," formed a second group of moderate communists. From the summer of 1990, they lobbied for the Ukrainization of all-union enterprises in Ukraine, effectively demanding personal ownership of the factories. A third group of moderate communists recast themselves as nationalists under the leadership of Leonid Kravchuk, who as second secretary of the CPU responsible for ideology had been Ukraine's ideological policeman. These three groups were amorphous and often overlapped (Prizel 1997, Wilson 2002).

In July 1990 Gorbachev called Ukraine's party chief and parliamentary speaker, Volodymyr Ivashko, to Moscow to become second secretary of the CPSU, ending his career in Ukraine. His two posts of party leader and parliamentary speaker were separated, which led to a division of the CPU. Stanislav Hurenko, a communist hard-liner, became first party secretary. He maintained a dogmatic Soviet line, marginalizing himself. Kravchuk assumed the position of chairman of the Ukrainian parliament in July 1990, and he swiftly transformed himself into the father of national communism, moving with remarkable ease and credibility in a nationalist direction.

All the Soviet republics held semidemocratic parliamentary elections, and almost all the newly elected parliaments declared their republics either independent or sovereign. Although these words are usually synonymous, "independent" was much stronger than "sovereign," which was understood as autonomous. On June 12, 1990, Boris Yeltsin persuaded the Russian State Duma to adopt the Russian declaration of sovereignty. Ukraine cautiously followed Russia. Under Kravchuk's leadership, the Ukrainian Supreme Rada adopted a declaration of state sovereignty on July 16, 1990, with an overwhelming majority of 355 to 4. Kravchuk had already accepted most of Rukh's agenda (Kuzio 2000, 137).

The summer of 1990 was hot. New strikes in Donbas preceded Ukraine's declaration of sovereignty. The workers demanded the resignation of the republican government. On September 30, 1990, Rukh organized its biggest demonstration ever with 200,000 participants in Kyiv, finally dropping its reference to perestroika and demanding full independence. In early October, students forced through a hunger strike the ouster of Prime Minister Vitaliy Masol, an old-style apparatchik, but he was replaced by Vitold Fokin, who was hardly better as the former chairman of Ukraine's State Planning Committee. Fokin focused on Ukrainizing all-union enterprises (Kuzio 2000, 161; Banaian 1999, 14–15). Meanwhile, the Five-Hundred-Day Program for transition to a market economy was the rage in Moscow, but this discussion hardly echoed in Ukraine.

In the fall of 1990, a first attempt at a Ukrainian economic policy was made. The new prime minister, Vitold Fokin, and the chairman of the

Parliamentary Commission on Economic Reform, Volodymyr Pylypchuk, wrote a program of economic reforms, which the parliament adopted on October 1, 1990. The inspiration came from the Russian Five-Hundred-Day Program. But Pylypchuk's program was very different. It focused on Ukraine acquiring control over its own economy and an orderly withdrawal from the USSR but did not prescribe a transition to a market economy. Rationing coupons were introduced so that Ukrainian goods were not diverted to Russia. In October 1990 Gorbachev turned against the reformers and to the hard-liners for support, and politics also cooled down in Ukraine.

Fokin tried again in the fall of 1991 with a program called "Fundamentals of Ukraine's National Economic Policy under Conditions of Independence." The parliament failed to adopt it, presumably because of both its disinterest in economic policy and the poor quality of the proposal. Ukraine adopted an enterprise law and elementary laws on privatization in 1991, but little was done. Although the old command economy was falling apart, no attempt was made to build a new market economy (Kravchuk 2002, 48–50).

On March 17, 1991, Gorbachev organized a referendum on the Soviet Union with multiple aims. He wanted to contain separatism but transform the Soviet Union into a real federation. He aspired to undermine Boris Yeltsin's political standing by formulating a question Yeltsin could not say no to and by gaining a large majority. The question, however, was just about impossible to understand: "Do you consider the preservation of the Union of Soviet Socialist Republics necessary as a renewed federation of equal sovereign republics, in which the rights and freedom of an individual of any nationality will be fully guaranteed?" (Dunlop 1993, 33).

Yeltsin could do nothing but accept it, but he cleverly avoided making this referendum a political issue. In Russia, 71 percent of voters answered yes, but the three Baltic republics (Estonia, Latvia, and Lithuania), Georgia, Armenia, and Moldova boycotted the referendum, which led to the independence of these six republics. In Ukraine, 70.5 percent of the voters said yes, and turnout was high. However, two alternative votes were tagged on. In the three western-most oblasts, a referendum on Ukrainian independence from the Soviet Union received the overwhelming support of 88 percent of voters. To another question, which Kravchuk added throughout Ukraine—"Do you agree that Ukraine should be a part of the Union of Sovereign States on the basis of the Declaration of State Sovereignty of Ukraine?"—80.2 percent answered yes (Wilson 2002, 164–65). Thus, he transformed the vote to one for greater Ukrainian independence.

Gorbachev won the referendum, but this was another Pyrrhic victory because nobody understood the question. Yeltsin retained his strength; six republics refused any further discussion of a new union. Ukraine had taken an ambiguous but distinct step toward full independence.

Impact of Soviet Economic Reforms and Crisis

A curious contrast exists between the historiography of Russia and Ukraine during the end of communism.[2] Books on Russia discuss economic crisis and reforms at great length, while studies of Ukraine mention economics just in passing. Much of the Russian political debate was devoted to economics, while the Ukrainian political debate focused on independence and the nation's relations with Moscow. Before independence, economic reform programs played no role in the Ukrainian debate, and the criticism of the socialist economic system that was rampant in Moscow barely reached Kyiv.

To the extent that economic issues entered the agenda, they were limited to those that Shelest had embraced in the 1960s: demands for greater republican powers and a larger Ukrainian share of total Soviet resources. Ukrainians did not oppose market economic reforms and privatization, but few paid attention. The idea was to build national institutions rather than undertake market economic reforms. The introduction of a national currency was much discussed as a powerful manifestation of national independence, while macroeconomic policy was all but ignored.

Ukraine faced the same economic problems as the rest of the Soviet Union, but Ukrainians predominantly saw Russia as the root cause of their economic misfortunes. Therefore, they sought to isolate themselves from the destruction coming from Russia. However, the economic problems conditioned Ukraine's future. Ukraine was richly endowed. Traditionally, it was one of the most developed parts of the Soviet Union, with a GDP per capita that was 10 percent higher than Russia's in 1990 (Goskomstat SSSR 1991, 12). Ukraine had an extensive machine-building industry and a large advanced military-industrial sector. It was known as the breadbasket of the Russian Empire with its vast wheat and corn fields. Ukrainians were better educated than average Soviet citizens. It also had large coal mines and iron ore mines in Donbas.

Like the rest of the Soviet Union, Ukrainians experienced a sense of stagnation from 1980 onward, a general sense that nothing would change any time soon. People paid no attention to early perestroika with its many minor economic experiments.

The Ukrainians' first experience of Gorbachev's perestroika was his campaign against alcohol, which he unleashed in May 1985. Alcoholism was a great concern, but the campaign was carried out with administrative means as an old-style communist campaign. Gorbachev intentionally cut alcohol production by half, destroying the finest wineries in Crimea. Since prices were not raised to balance the market, the outcome was horrendously

2. Åslund (2007b) is the main source of this section.

long queues. Soviet men were forced to sober up, increasing their life expectancy by two years, but they did not like it at all. The halving of alcohol sales led to plummeting sales tax revenues, which enlarged the budget deficit. To finance the gap, the government printed more rubles, accelerating inflation and aggravating the already bad shortages.

In the summer of 1986, the CPSU launched another vicious neo-Stalinist campaign, this time against "unearned incomes," that is, any private earnings. In practice, it was directed against poor pensioners who grew vegetables or fruit on their small household plots and badly needed this income for their subsistence. One effect was that private food supplies shrank, and prices on the relatively free *kolkhoz* markets soared.

For a long time, actual reforms were too minor to have any popular impact. In November 1986 the USSR Law on Individual Labor Activity was adopted; it came into force in May 1987 (*Pravda*, November 21, 1986). It legalized acceptable forms of individual labor activity. Economically, it was of minor significance, because the conditions offered were not very attractive, but it did legalize some forms of private enterprise.

The USSR Law on Cooperatives, which was enacted in May 1988, had quite another impact. Its content was amazingly liberal, delivering the real breakthrough for private enterprise. It was the first legal act consistent with a market economy. Any three adults could open a cooperative and hire an unlimited number of employees. These cooperatives were truly self-managing, self-financing, and profit-oriented, operating freely on the market without plans, centralized supplies, or price regulation. The law explicitly permitted cooperatives to engage in any kind of activity not forbidden by law, a sensational novelty. They could even set up banks and pursue foreign trade, and they benefited from very low tax rates, even if tax practices were unstable. Importantly, they were allowed to transform the abundant "noncash" money on enterprise accounts into cash. Most current big Ukrainian businessmen started their career by setting up a cooperative in 1988.

One of Gorbachev's first reforms was a partial liberalization of foreign trade, which began in August 1986, long before domestic liberalization. Its goal was to break the foreign trade monopoly of the USSR Ministry of Foreign Trade to the benefit of large state enterprises. This liberalization was very popular among the managers of big state corporations, who could make money through arbitrage on the difference between low domestic prices and much higher world prices.

In parallel, up to 3,000 so-called currency coefficients were introduced, as every significant foreign trade good was assigned its own exchange rate. The ratio between these currency coefficients varied from 1 to 20, offering extraordinary opportunities for arbitrage. In late 1990 a unified commercial exchange rate replaced these coefficients, but even so, the Soviet Union had one official rate, one commercial rate, and one plummeting black-market exchange rate, permitting ever greater arbitrage gains.

In June 1987 Gorbachev legislated comprehensive economic reform. Its centerpiece was the Law on State Enterprises, which came into force in January 1988, but this was a badly misconceived reform. It deprived the state of its rights to command state enterprises, but it did not give state enterprises freedom. Nobody could direct state enterprises. The Soviet economy fell into a deep chasm between two systems. After a couple of years, the managers seized control over "their" state enterprises without being accountable to anybody. They possessed the cash-flow rights but not the control rights, which meant that they could tap money from the enterprises but not sell them.

Unwittingly and unintentionally, Gorbachev had created a perfect rent-generating machine. The liberalization of foreign trade allowed state enterprises to carry out arbitrage between low domestic prices of raw materials and high world market prices and between greatly varied exchange rates. The Law on State Enterprises permitted enterprises to keep the remaining profits, previously confiscated by the state at the end of each year. The new cooperatives made it possible for enterprise managers to transfer the profits of their state enterprises to their private companies and to transform "bank" money to real cash. The new commercial banks provided them with cheap state credits to finance their businesses.

In practice, state enterprise managers, or red directors, sold commodities they produced at official state prices to an intermediary, a cooperative they owned together with other well-placed people who could provide them with export licenses and permits. At the end of 1991 the domestic Soviet price of one ton of crude oil was 50 cents, while the world market price was about $100, so an exporter's margin was 200 times the cost of a product. Yegor Gaidar (1999, 122) has noted that, at the end of 1991, someone with an official export quota for oil could pay as little as one ruble for one dollar when the free exchange rate was 170 rubles per dollar. Few understood this at the time, but those who did made fortunes at the expense of their neighbors.

From 1989 the Soviet economic crisis was turning into collapse. As part of the Soviet Union, Ukraine suffered as the rest of the country. Ukrainians experienced aggravated shortages of goods, rising inflation, and output collapse. The chronic shortages prompted extensive rationing. People hoarded whatever they could buy, and the only good in surplus was money. Every Soviet home was packed with staples such as sugar, soap, and toilet paper.

In 1986 the Soviet budget deficit rose to 6 percent of GDP because of the leadership's neglect and incompetence, expanding to 9 percent of GDP in 1988–89. Meanwhile, annual wage increases more than doubled as a consequence of the Law on State Enterprises. Managers concentrated on products with large profit margins, which boosted hidden inflation. They passed on some inflationary gains to their workers as wage hikes.

Toward the end of 1990, the Soviet macroeconomic crisis turned terminal, with populist social policy as a new driver. The USSR Congress of People's Deputies hiked social benefits by 25 percent, in competition with the republican legislatures, and in 1991 those benefits surged beyond control by 133 percent in Ukraine. The communists foolishly tried to maintain power and hold the Soviet Union together by opting for populism, sacrificing any remnant of fiscal sanity. Income increases accelerated to 85 percent in 1991 (Ministry of Statistics of Ukraine 1994, 12).

In 1991 Soviet state finances broke down. After the union republics had declared themselves sovereign or independent, they refused to deliver their revenues to the union treasury. Nor did they honor Soviet legislation, competing with the union in cutting taxes. As union revenues collapsed, the Soviet budget deficit skyrocketed to 31 percent of GDP (EBRD 1994). By the summer of 1991, the Soviet Union was no longer financially viable. The republics had established their own central banks, issuing ample credits in Soviet rubles. In 1991 the Soviet Union had no less than 16 mutually independent central banks issuing ruble credits in competition with one another. This monetary competition guaranteed the collapse of the Soviet Union.

Net Soviet foreign debt was not all that large at $56.5 billion at the end of 1991 (UNECE 1993, 289), but starting at the end of 1989 Soviet foreign trade enterprises failed to pay on time. By 1990, foreign debt service became alarming because it was increasingly short term (Gaidar 2007). Irresponsibly, the Soviet government refused to act until the country had run out of foreign currency reserves. The outside world saw the mounting economic crisis and the country's creditworthiness declined.

The official exchange rate became increasingly irrelevant as market forces gained momentum. The public perceived the black-market exchange rate ever more as the "real" exchange rate. For years the standard black-market exchange rate had been 5 rubles to the dollar, but from the end of 1988 to the end of 1990 it rose to 30 rubles. As the ruble lost all value, the public hoarded cash dollars. By 1991 the economy had become extraordinarily dollarized.

In 1990 the national income started declining, officially by 3.6 percent; in 1991 output plunged officially by 13.4 percent, approaching a free fall (Ministry of Statistics of Ukraine 1994, 12). Because people had to spend ever more time waiting in line to use their money, it made little sense for them to earn more worthless money, so they reduced their work hours. Factories suffered from shortages of all inputs, harming production.

In the second half of 1991 the Soviet Union faced financial ruin. Soviet economic policy had evaporated. A universal economic collapse was under way.

The economic crisis baffled the Ukrainian elite and public. They knew little about economics and did not understand what was happening to them. The enlightened public was preoccupied with nation-building, while the business elite indulged in rent seeking. The dominant economic policy demands remained rudimentary and confused: the introduction of a Ukrainian national currency, as if that on its own would salvage them from inflation, and the creation of a national bank. Inflation aroused people to call for more effective price controls, and nobody cared about macroeconomics. Privatization was discussed at length, but little was accomplished. Ukrainization of Soviet property was one of the strongest demands because a conviction prevailed that Ukraine was rich, but Moscow had exploited it.

2

Leonid Kravchuk: Nation-Building and Hyperinflation, 1991–94

At the request of philanthropist George Soros, Professor Oleh Havrylyshyn and I went to Kyiv in the second week of August 1991 to evaluate Ukrainian thinking on economic reform. He opened all doors for us.

In the fall of 1991, Ukraine was quite an absurd place. It was still a part of the Soviet Union, but the Soviet government had effectively lost control of most things that mattered: wages, tax revenues, and money supply. As a result of these dismal fiscal and monetary policies, shortages prevailed, and prices on the free private market were skyrocketing. The dominant state shops were literally empty because of artificially low regulated prices. Output was plummeting because nobody had any real incentive to work. The strange thing was that Kyiv was exceedingly normal. People were courteous and nice. It was not dangerous to walk in the streets late at night. Flowers were still planted in public parks. Yet, by the end of 1991, the average salary at the free exchange rate of the Soviet ruble was $6 a month. The old Soviet system replete with state control was still in place, but it had stopped producing. The economy was collapsing before our eyes, but Ukrainians were preoccupied with their nation's forthcoming independence.

Everybody was upset over the infamous "Chicken Kiev" speech[1] that US President George H. W. Bush had made when he visited Kyiv on August 1, 1991. He had told the Ukrainians to stay in the Soviet Union: "We will maintain the strongest possible relationship with the Soviet Government of President Gorbachev . . . as a federation ourselves, we

1. *New York Times* columnist William Safire nicknamed it so.

want good relations . . . with the Republics. . . . Americans will not support those who seek independence in order to replace a far-off tyranny with a local despotism. They will not aid those who promote a suicidal nationalism based upon ethnic hatred" (Bush 1991). But the Soviet Union could no longer be saved.

Finding qualified economists in Kyiv was not easy in August 1991. Throughout their rule, the Soviet leaders had feared Ukrainian nationalism, imposing far more severe repression on this republic than on Russia. Talented Ukrainians regularly moved to Moscow, which offered the best careers as well as more intellectual freedom. Ukraine, with 52 million people, had only one economics journal, which was dogmatic and mediocre. The curious consequence of this repression was that opposition in Ukraine focused on one issue: national revival. Secondary topics such as democracy attracted little attention and the building of a market economy even less.

We met three memorable economists. Volodymyr Pylypchuk, chairman of the influential parliamentary Economic Reform Committee, was a leading reform economist of nationalist inclination. He was convinced that Ukraine was rich and its economy would flourish only if Russian exploitation ceased. We tried to inform him that Ukraine enjoyed highly beneficial terms of trade with Russia and that a transition to market prices would cost Ukraine several percent of its GDP (Orlowski 1993, Tarr 1994, IMF 1994). Pylypchuk listened incredulously. He did favor a market economy, but his conception of it was vague.

During my first visit to Ukraine in 1985, I met Academician Oleksandr Yemelianov, director of the Institute of Economic Research of the State Planning Committee of Ukraine. He was the most dogmatic communist economist I have ever met. Now Yemelianov was President Leonid Kravchuk's chief economic adviser. When I met him again in 1991 he reassured us of his support for market economy and private enterprise, but his new vision did not match his (lack of) economic knowledge. As long as the formidable Yemelianov was chief economic adviser to the president, no market reform was possible. Curiously, he was soon ousted because of a sordid corruption scandal.

Our third meeting was positive. Oleksandr Savchenko was a leading Rukh economist. He was young and bright, spoke English, and had some training from Harvard University. Yet he was hardly strong enough to storm the fortifications of the collapsing command economy.[2] The building of a market economy would evidently be postponed until Kravchuk and Yemelianov were gone.[3]

2. Savchenko is currently deputy chairman of the National Bank of Ukraine.

3. Oleh Havrylyshyn drew a more optimistic conclusion and became deputy minister of finance in 1992.

As was necessary in Soviet days, I flew out through Moscow, where I met Pilar Bonet, a long-time Spanish correspondent in Moscow, on August 17. The stalemate in Moscow was untenable, and we speculated whether a hard-line coup would take place, as Gorbachev's former top associates Eduard Shevardnadze and Aleksandr Yakovlev had warned in December 1990. We agreed that a coup was possible, but it was impossible to say whether or when it would take place. The next day all hell broke loose.

National Independence

In April 1991, at his residence in Novoe Ogarevo outside Moscow, Gorbachev had instigated negotiations for a new looser "union of sovereign states" to replace the Soviet Union. From the outset, the Balts, Georgians, Armenians, and Moldovans had refused to join these talks, since they insisted on full independence. Soon the Azerbaijanis also withdrew. Thus, only 8 out of the 15 union republics participated, rendering Ukraine pivotal. Without Ukraine, the Soviet Union no longer appeared viable. As Zbigniew Brzezinski (1994, 80) later put it: ". . . without Ukraine, Russia ceases to be an empire, but with Ukraine suborned and then subordinated, Russia automatically becomes an empire."

The new union treaty was ready to be signed in Moscow on August 20, upon Gorbachev's return from a long summer holiday in Crimea. But, the party hard-liners felt betrayed by him. All Gorbachev's closest collaborators ganged up on him, organizing a coup and setting up the State Committee for the State of Emergency (GKChP) on August 19, 1991. The GKChP issued a manifesto, "An Appeal to the Soviet People," the first goal of which was to stop "the liquidation of the Soviet Union" (Dunlop 1993, 194–99).

In Ukraine little happened. The Ukrainian communist leadership quietly subordinated themselves to the putschists. Kravchuk equivocated, neither supporting nor opposing the GKChP. By August 21 the coup in Moscow had failed. Then Kravchuk took the lead. On August 24 the Ukrainian parliament declared Ukraine independent by an overwhelming majority of 346 to 1. As the eminent historian of Ukraine Roman Szporluk (1994, 1) has observed: "it is essential to remember that the independent Ukraine proclaimed in August 1991 did not define itself as an ethnic state. It was a jurisdiction, a territorial and legal entity, in fact, a successor of the Ukrainian SSR. Its citizens were of different ethnic backgrounds and spoke Ukrainian and Russian to varying degrees, but also other languages." Importantly, the Ukrainian identity was defined as civic and political and not as ethnic or linguistic.

The Ukrainian Soviet Socialist Republic was renamed Ukraine. August 24 became Ukraine's National Day. Formally, Ukraine remained a part of the Soviet Union. Only the three Baltic republics became universally recognized independent states at this stage. On August 30 the presidium of the Ukrainian parliament banned the Communist Party of Ukraine (CPU) and later confiscated its property, as in Russia, but nobody was held responsible for CPU deeds and the communists were not purged or prosecuted (Kuzio 2000, 185). The old state apparatus replete with communists remained in place.

With amazing skill, Kravchuk had transformed himself within less than two years from communist ideological policeman to national communist leader and now to Ukraine's first president and national leader. He had become the symbol of national independence, so nationalists could not attack him effectively, but the communists still trusted him, and so did Russian-speaking Ukrainians (Prizel 1997, 343).

A large number of state-building measures followed the Declaration of Independence. The parliamentary majority voted to form a Ukrainian Ministry of Defense and take control over all armed forces on Ukrainian territory. It decided to introduce a Ukrainian currency and passed a Law on State Frontiers. All references to Ukraine as "socialist" were deleted from the constitution (Kuzio 2000, 183–89).

The parliament decided to reconfirm its decision on national independence with a referendum on December 1, 1991. No less than 90.3 percent of the population voted for independence, and participation was high, at 84 percent. A majority voted for Ukrainian independence in each region, with the minimum being 54 percent in Crimea.

On the same day, Ukraine's first presidential elections were held. Kravchuk won with 61.6 percent of the votes, followed by Vyacheslav Chornovil, who received 23.3 percent (table 2.1). Characteristically, the left gathered behind one candidate, Kravchuk, while the right was divided between five candidates. Yet Kravchuk's support was quite evenly distributed across the country, and he won in all regions but western Ukraine (Kuzio 2000, 194–201).

Ukraine's greatest challenge was to break out of the Soviet Union. The overwhelming verdict in the referendum on independence facilitated that effort. Ukraine was lucky because Russian President Boris Yeltsin also desired to end the union as fast as possible, and he acted instantly and decisively (Åslund 2007b). In complete secrecy, Yeltsin organized a summit one week later with Kravchuk and the reformist chairman of the Belarusian parliament, Stanislav Shushkevich. The relationship between Yeltsin and Kravchuk was good. As Kravchuk (2001) commented: "Both Yeltsin and I needed one another. He was interested in me as an ally in his run for power. I was trying to use him to ensure the full independence of Ukraine without a painful split of economic ties and without more undesirable conflicts with Moscow."

On December 8–9 they met with only a handful of aides at a desolate Belarusian hunting lodge in Belovezhskaya Pushcha. Kravchuk (2001)

Table 2.1 Results of presidential election, December 1, 1991

Candidate	Percent of votes
Leonid Kravchuk	61.6
Vyacheslav Chornovil	23.3
Levko Lukyanenko	4.5
Volodymyr Grynyov	4.2
Ihor Yukhnovskiy	1.7
Others, against all, or not valid	4.7
Total	100
Voter turnout (percent)	84.2

Source: Uryadovyi Kur'er, 1991, no. 38–39.

appreciated Yeltsin's choice of time: "The principal difference of this meeting compared to previous meetings was that I came there armed with the popular vote of the Ukrainian referendum. In addition, at this time I was already President." Together these three heads of state agreed to dissolve the Soviet Union. As Yeltsin (1994, 113) saw it: "In signing this agreement, Russia was choosing a different path, a path of internal development rather than an imperial one." He insisted that this was "a lawful alteration of the existing order" because it "was a revision of the Union Treaty among the three major republics of that Union." The Treaty of the Soviet Union of 1922 had been invalidated. Kravchuk (2001) concurred: "The Belovezhskaya Pushcha accord gave us two chances: to bury the dead empire in a civilized and Christian fashion and to preserve the half-destroyed economic ties. Unfortunately, we used only one of them."

On December 21, 1991, the other remaining union republics (apart from fiercely nationalist Georgia) reconfirmed this decision in Kazakhstan's capital, Alma-Ata. In place of the Soviet Union, 11 former Soviet republics created the Commonwealth of Independent States (CIS).[4] The CIS was reminiscent of the British Commonwealth, even though various Russians tried to make something more of it, but with little success. On December 25 the Soviet Union ceased to exist. Russian President Yeltsin replaced Soviet President Gorbachev in the Kremlin, and the Soviet flag was lowered for the last time and replaced with the Russian flag. All the remaining Soviet republics, including Ukraine, became fully independent and replaced the Soviet flag with their new republican flags. Soon the whole world recognized their independence.

Suddenly Ukraine had achieved the full independence that some had dreamed of for centuries, while most had not dared to hope for it, and no

4. They were Armenia, Azerbaijan, Belarus, Kazakhstan, Kyrgyzstan, Moldova, Russia, Tajikistan, Turkmenistan, Ukraine, and Uzbekistan.

state questioned its sovereignty. National liberation had been fast and perfectly peaceful. The new nation's borders were secure, and it had a democratically elected and undisputed president in Kravchuk. This was Ukraine's moment of euphoria.

Kravchuk as President

Kravchuk was an amazing politician. Andrew Wilson (2002, 182) has caught his character:

> Always a consummate opportunist, Kravchuk became Ukraine's preeminent figure in the build-up to independence by skillfully constructing a public persona that was most things to most people. As president, he sought to delay any final act of self-definition for as long as possible by maintaining the broadest possible consensus amongst elites.

As chairman of the parliament, Kravchuk was already perceived as president. He realized that Soviet power was collapsing. As he later wrote: "We understood that the USSR was doomed and had to be replaced with a looser super-national structure. Such a union would allow the former Soviet republics to survive during their process of building their own institutions and national economies" (Kravchuk 2001). He was a jovial, clubbable, and understated man. It was easy to like him but difficult to think of him as a leader. He said little worth quoting, but his political intuition was superb, and he seemed to find a compromise with everybody. A popular anecdote had Kravchuk turning down an offer of an umbrella when he went out into the rain, because "I just walk between the drops."

Kravchuk cleverly switched from communism to Ukrainian nationalism without a hitch, gaining popular credibility with surprising talent. He realized where history was taking him: "Collapse was in progress for a long time and the end of it could be disastrous. The head of each republic just wanted to exit this geopolitical construct with minimal loss" (Kravchuk 2001).

He established Ukraine's independence swiftly and successfully. His nationalism was so moderate that he convinced the east and south to vote for independence. He happily adopted the three important national symbols: the blue-and-yellow flag, the trident, and the old national anthem. Ukrainian became the official state language, but Russian was generally accepted. Kravchuk also led the national communists, who opted for independence because they wanted the old communist establishment to stay in power.

The president's second success lay in foreign policy. Ukraine had few institutions of a sovereign state, but it had a rudimentary Ministry for Foreign Affairs with a small corps of able diplomats and an original membership of the United Nations. The small Ukrainian diplomatic corps comprised some of the brightest and most able people at that time.

Kravchuk masterfully managed the breakaway from the Soviet Union as well as Ukraine's control over the Soviet armed forces in the country. Crucially, Kravchuk insisted on all servicemen swearing an oath of obedience to the Ukrainian state, which made quite a few soldiers depart. He persistently pursued Ukraine's denuclearization.

His shortcoming, however, was that he had a minimal political agenda, essentially consisting of the establishment of the Ukrainian state and amicable foreign relations as well as his maintenance of power. Besides, he was very indecisive. Kravchuk had no clue about economic policy. Like Yeltsin in Russia, he started his term with substantial powers to legislate with decree, but unlike Yeltsin, he barely used his powers. He defended himself: "The president should be responsible for building the state, while the prime minister should manage the economy."[5] Ukraine's economy was descending into chaos with galloping inflation and plummeting output.

Nor was Kravchuk interested in political institution-building. His view of politics was to compromise with everybody within the existing political system. After the vote of independence and the election of Kravchuk as president on December 1, 1991, Rukh leader Vyacheslav Chornovil advocated the dissolution of the predemocratic parliament and early elections, but Kravchuk opposed early elections. Thus, he missed his chance to build a ruling party, and his national communism was never constituted as a party. Ukraine's parliament remained fractured and dysfunctional for over a decade. Its old Soviet constitution from 1978 persisted with amendments. Still, his ultimate virtues were that he stuck to the democratic rules and peacefulness in both domestic and foreign affairs.

I had the privilege of assisting Kravchuk for two days at the World Economic Forum in Davos in January 1991. I was surprised by his friendliness and humility, but it was difficult to believe that he would become the leader of a big country. When I met him a few years later and complained about his failed economic policies, he did not defend himself but looked down unhappily.

Liberation from Russia

Ukraine's first challenge was to form new relations with Russia.[6] Although Ukrainian historiography paints a bleak picture of Moscow, Yeltsin's desire to rid Russia of the burden of empire greatly helped Ukraine (Yeltsin 1994).

5. Quoted in Prizel (1997, 345).

6. Overall sources of this section are Olcott, Åslund, and Garnett (1999) and Garnett (1997).

The Ukrainian authorities took over government and enterprises from Russia with ease. Since the real state was the Communist Party, the simultaneous prohibition of the Communist Party of the Soviet Union (CPSU) and the CPU resolved much of this task. With independence, Ukraine faced five major issues in its relations with Russia, namely, the integrity of its borders, military (denuclearization and the division of the Soviet Black Sea Fleet), economic (mainly the breaking up of the ruble zone and credits), energy (gas prices and the payment of gas purchases), and CIS integration.

Of these assignments, the most important was the recognition and security of Ukraine's state borders, which Yeltsin appreciated. Dankwart Rustow (1970) emphasized the importance of securing the borders of a state, because otherwise the state could not be stable and no democracy could be built. On November 19, 1990, on behalf of the Russian Federation, Yeltsin and Kravchuk signed a Treaty on the Basic Principles of Relations between Russia and Ukraine (Sherr 1997). This treaty "acknowledged and respected the territorial integrity of the Ukrainian Soviet Socialist Republic," although it remained a part of the Soviet Union. Through his consistent policy of no border revisions, Yeltsin kept such issues off the agenda, but only in 1997 was a final treaty concluded.

An old saying runs that, while the United States had a military-industrial complex, the Soviet Union was a military-industrial complex. However complex the dissolution of the military was, it passed amazingly easily because of goodwill on both the Russian and Ukrainian sides, with keen engagement of the United States, especially Secretary of State James Baker (Goldgeier and McFaul 2003). With amazing ease, Ukraine took command over the conventional forces on its territory.

The big and lasting military dispute was the status of the Soviet Black Sea Fleet and its base, Sevastopol, on Crimea. One concern was the division of the Black Sea Fleet; another was Ukraine's sovereignty of Crimea and Sevastopol. It was subject to numerous partial agreements and remained the dominant topic of negotiations between Ukraine and Russia from 1992 until 1997; a series of bilateral agreements gradually generated a solution. The demarcation of the border in the Black Sea was never undertaken but was left in limbo.

An initial agreement was concluded in January 1992, awarding Ukraine 30 percent of the ships (excluding nuclear vessels). Yeltsin and Kravchuk reached a more specific agreement in June 1992 about dividing the Soviet Black Sea Fleet into equal halves, while Ukraine would sell a substantial number of ships from its share to Russia. At a summit in Moscow in June 1993, the two presidents provisionally agreed that Russia could lease Sevastopol. The Russians insisted that Sevastopol be the headquarters of the Russian Black Sea Fleet, but the Ukrainian constitution prohibited foreign bases. In 1992–93, the Russian parliament vehemently opposed Yeltsin, claiming that the 1954 transfer of Crimea to Ukraine was illegal and that Sevastopol belonged to Russia (Sherr 1997). As a result, Yeltsin could not conclude any agreement with Ukraine because the Russian parliament would have refused to ratify it. The Russian communists and populist nationalists loved antagonizing Ukrainians, many of whom perceived such provocations as Russia's "real" foreign policy. Since Ukraine's economic crisis was worse than Russia's in 1992–94, its negotiating position gradually weakened.

The greatest economic problem after the dissolution of the Soviet Union was the persistence of the ruble zone. The Soviet ruble and the CIS nuclear command were the only surviving common institutions after December 1991. Fifteen central banks were issuing ruble credit, that is, money, in competition with one another. The more money a country issued, the larger the share of the common GDP it extracted. Russian imperialists, conservatives, and rent seekers wanted to maintain the ruble zone because they were benefiting from its seemingly free money. The International Monetary Fund (IMF 1992) sought to find a working arrangement, so that the ruble zone countries would agree on how much money to issue, and it refused to condemn the ruble zone as a moral hazard (Odling-Smee and Pastor 2002), while the Russian reformers who realized its detriment were too weak to defeat it (Gaidar 1993). The three fiercely independent Baltic states swiftly abandoned the ruble zone, saving themselves from hyperinflation. The countries most closely allied with Russia (Belarus, Kazakhstan, and Tajikistan) hoped it would survive.

Ukraine, however, wanted to have its cake and eat it too. Ukrainian officials hoped to exploit the ruble zone for continued access to cheap Russian raw materials and credits, therefore postponing their long-declared introduction of a national currency. Ukraine's departure from the ruble zone occurred in fits and starts, with its exit being declared repeatedly but not really happening. Ukraine introduced its own coupon, which was called *karbovanets*. At one time, it was only legal tender in state shops. Then it functioned as cash, while bank transfers remained in the ruble zone. It was a mess, and the National Bank of Ukraine (NBU) continued to issue ruble credits. Because of this uncontrolled monetary regime Ukraine experienced hyperinflation in 1993. Finally, by September 1993, the Central Bank of Russia ended the ruble zone. At that time, Ukraine had accumulated a large debt to Russia for goods delivered through state trade but never desired by any consumer. The persistence of the hyperinflationary ruble zone until the fall of 1993 was the single biggest blow to Ukraine (Åslund 1995; Dabrowski 1995; Granville 1995, 2002).

Another economic problem was the distorted foreign trade system. Ukraine established a Soviet-type Ministry of External Economic Relations, which started regulating foreign trade with licenses, quotas, and permits in the old Soviet fashion. For years Ukraine remained completely dependent on trade with the other former Soviet republics, which was dominated by state trade with fixed quotas and prices that were far below the market level until 1994 (Michalopoulos and Tarr 1996). Trade within the former Soviet Union became the privilege of old State Planning Committee officials, who conducted it in their old fashion. Ukrainian ministers were so lost in the new situation that they continued traveling to Moscow, as they had in Soviet days, asking for all kinds of goods. They increasingly realized that nobody in Moscow wanted to see them as state trade faded away. From 1995 Ukraine's trade with former Soviet republics started becoming reasonably market-oriented, with the important exception of gas trade.

For Ukraine the old Soviet external debt was not a real problem but a confusing irritant. As the Soviet Union was breaking up, the US Treasury had one concern. It wanted the future Soviet republics to guarantee their "joint and several" responsibility to service the Soviet debt, which they willingly did in November 1991. In practice, this would not have worked, which the Russian reformers understood. They magnanimously offered to take over all the debt but on the condition that they also received the assets, which were worth much less (Åslund 1995). All former Soviet republics but Ukraine accepted these conditions. The Ukrainians, however, suspected that the Russians were cheating them and that the Soviet assets were much more valuable. They demanded an account of the Soviet assets, which the still-disorganized Moscow was unable to provide. Ukraine then demanded certain Soviet properties abroad, mainly embassies. This discussion lingered but was in effect resolved as Russia had suggested. For Ukraine, this agreement was highly advantageous, allowing the country to start afresh without external debt.

The CIS was supposed to manage multilateral relations among the former Soviet republics. It concluded many agreements, of which only a few were of significance. Ukraine's relationship with the CIS was ambivalent. It signed the CIS treaty but never ratified it. Even though Ukraine was one of the founders of the CIS and regularly attends CIS meetings, as if it were a full member, formally it is not because Ukraine objects to CIS claims to supernational authority. Ukraine's long-standing policy has been to go along with purely technical and economically beneficial decisions but stay away from foreign and security policy.

The CIS Agreement on the Creation of a Free Trade Zone in 1994 was supposed to form the basis of trade between the CIS countries, but it never came into force because Russia did not ratify it. Instead a bilateral free trade agreement on June 24, 1993 regulated trade between Ukraine and Russia. Trade among the CIS countries has never been particularly free. Whenever a company or industry in one CIS country successfully exports to another CIS country, the importing country clamps down with a sudden quota or prohibitive import tariff. For example, Russia restricted imports of vodka from Ukraine in 1996. The CIS lacks a conflict-solving mechanism, so the countries concerned can settle trade disputes only through bilateral negotiations. Without the guidance of principles, many conflicts remain unsolved. This trading system is highly inefficient, and the number of trade disputes only accumulates. As a consequence, the share of Ukraine's trade with the former Soviet Union has dwindled (Åslund 2003a).

Little is known about cooperation between the security police. Unlike the situation in the communist parties and the military, these links were neither disrupted nor revealed. They presumably remain strong and substantial. A case in point is the attempt to poison Ukrainian presidential candidate Viktor Yushchenko in September 2004.

On the whole, the Soviet Union was dissolved with surprising ease. The greatest problem was the monetary disorder that resulted in hyperinflation, in much the same way as most of the successor states of the Hapsburg Empire were hit by hyperinflation because they did not withdraw fast enough (Pasvolsky 1928). This was all the more disturbing because some of the great economists of the day had recently revived those insights (Sargent 1986, Dornbusch 1992). The Black Sea Fleet remained a persistent irritant. Yet Dominic Lieven's (2000) verdict holds true that no empire passed away as peacefully as the Soviet empire did.

Ukraine's Denuclearization

The all-dominant American concern about Ukraine was its nuclear arms. Ukraine was the third largest nuclear power in the world, after the United States and Russia but before China. The Americans wanted the Ukrainian nuclear arms transferred to Russia and destroyed, but Russia played only a secondary role in these negotiations. Incredibly, US Secretary of Defense William J. Perry regarded Ukraine's reluctance to give up its nuclear missiles as "the single biggest threat to international peace and security that we faced anywhere in the world" (quoted in Goldgeier and McFaul 2003, 166).

From the outset, Kravchuk committed himself and his country to a complete destruction of Ukraine's strategic and nuclear weapons (Goldgeier and McFaul 2003, 49). In December 1991 Kravchuk accepted the destruction of all its 176 intercontinental ballistic missiles (ICBMs) with 1,180 warheads (Wolczuk 2002, 35). After the Chornobyl catastrophe, a broad Ukrainian popular opinion wanted to get rid of them. Another early ambition was a policy of neutrality, which was even enshrined in its Declaration of State Sovereignty of July 16, 1990, but it was soon ignored (Larrabee 1996, 143). Still Ukrainians held a strong urge to stay out of US-Russian rivalry.

The United States demanded that Ukraine sign and ratify the Treaty on the Reduction and Limitation of Strategic Offensive Arms (START I) and the Nuclear Non-Proliferation Treaty (NPT) as a nonnuclear power. On May 23–24, 1991, the ministers for foreign affairs of the United States,

Belarus, Kazakhstan, Russia, and Ukraine met in Lisbon and signed the START protocols. Kravchuk committed Ukraine to becoming nonnuclear "in the shortest possible time," which he specified to seven years after START had come into force (Goldgeier and McFaul 2003, 56).

Ukraine wanted economic assistance, help with its denuclearization, and security guarantees, but the United States was not very forthcoming. This was a time when the United States seemed to get everything for free, and it was reluctant to pay real money or make serious commitments. A diplomatic breakthrough came at the Group of Seven (G-7) meeting in Tokyo in July 1993, when President Boris Yeltsin proposed that he, President Bill Clinton, and Kravchuk sign a trilateral accord on Ukraine's denuclearization.

In 1994 Ukraine's denuclearization was resolved with three important international treaties. First, on January 14, 1994, Yeltsin, Clinton, and Kravchuk signed the Trilateral Accord in Moscow, in which Ukraine committed itself to "the elimination of all nuclear weapons, including strategic offensive arms, located in its territory." The accord contained several paragraphs of American-Russian security guarantees. The United States and Russia stated that they would

> reaffirm their commitment to Ukraine, in accordance with the principles of the CSCE [Conference on Security and Cooperation in Europe] Final Act, to respect the independence and sovereignty and the existing borders of the CSCE members states and recognize that border changes can be made only by peaceful and consensual means; and reaffirm their obligation to refrain from the threat or use of force against the territorial integrity or political independence of any state, and that none of their weapons will ever be used in self-defense or otherwise in accordance with the Charter of the United Nations.[7]

In a private letter to Clinton, Kravchuk promised that Ukraine would be nuclear free by June 1996. When Kravchuk visited Washington in March, Clinton promised Ukraine an aid package of $750 million, which was quite a small amount.

The second important step was that the Rada ratified START I without conditions in February 1994. In return, the United States offered special security guarantees to the three countries that agreed to give up their nuclear arms, Belarus, Kazakhstan, and Ukraine.

In November 1994 the Rada took the final step toward formal denuclearization by ratifying the NPT as a nonnuclear country. Ukraine fulfilled Kravchuk's promise and completed its transfer of nuclear arms by June 1996, and much of its denuclearization was carried out with the help of American military experts and financing (Goldgeier and McFaul 2003, 170).

7. US Department of State Dispatch: Trilateral Statement by the Presidents of the U.S. Russia and Ukraine in Moscow on January 14, 1994.

Ukraine had behaved perfectly responsibly and fulfilled its substantial commitments. Although some Ukrainian nationalists regretted that their country had given up its nuclear missiles, the policy of denuclearization enjoyed strong popular support, and no Ukrainian government has revisited it. A lasting stricture, however, was that Kravchuk had given up the country's nuclear arms too cheaply.

The Grand Bargain of Ukraine's New Political Forces

Just before independence, Ukraine's politics had assumed a structure that was to last throughout the 1990s. Three broad forces formed Ukraine's politics: national democrats, the hard left, and an amorphous center. The national democrats were the driving force. Their main organization was Rukh, with 20 to 25 percent of the electorate. Their opponents were the hard left, dominated by the communists, who together with allies could gather up to 40 percent of the votes. As a consequence of this stalemate between the right and the left, the fluid center came to dominate the government.

Rukh set the political agenda with its goal of Ukraine's independence. However, from the elections in March 1990 Rukh's leaders understood that they were not strong enough to gain power on their own. Therefore, they sought what Wilson (2002, 174) calls "a grand bargain" or "historical compromise" with the national communists, whom Rukh accepted in power as long as they supported Ukraine's independence. Rukh was a movement of western and central Ukraine, which was both nationalist and democratic, but its emphasis on nationalism grew more dominant over time, hindering it from reaching out to other democrats.

Throughout the 1990s, Ukraine's hard left remained remarkably strong, with some 40 percent of the votes in the parliamentary elections of 1994 and 1998. The dominant left-wing group was the unreformed CPU, which did not even change its name. The CPU was prohibited on August 30, 1991, but it was allowed to reconstitute itself under the same name in June 1993, though without any legal claim to its predecessor's property. During its formal absence, it neither changed nor lost much support. It was the main advocacy group of the Russian-speaking population in Ukraine, demanding that Russia become a second state language. It favored "the voluntary creation of an equal Union of fraternal peoples . . . on the territory of the former USSR" (Wilson 2002, 191). Retirees dominated the CPU, which functioned as a trade union for pensioners. Petro Symonenko became the first party secretary of the CPU when it reemerged, and he has remained so.

In October 1991 communist leader Oleksandr Moroz founded the Socialist Party slightly to the right of the CPU. He stayed close to the communists but appeared more democratic, and although he cherished the cause of Ukraine's Russian speakers, he spoke Ukrainian. Moroz styled himself as a social democrat, but his economics remained communist. He favored state ownership, price controls and rigorous protectionism. Politically he was a realist: "Anybody who does not regret the collapse of the USSR has no heart; anybody who wants to restore the Union has no head" (Wilson 2002, 191–92).

To the left of the CPU, Natalia Vitrenko set up the vitriolic Progressive Socialist Party, which specialized in attacking the IMF and international capitalism. A characteristic statement of hers in 1995 was: "The deindustrialization, the de-intellectualization, and the degradation of Ukraine, all can be attributed to the recommendations of the IMF, since it is they who proposed to us, as the means of reform, to decontrol prices, to liberalize currency exchange, to deregulate foreign economic activity, and to have forced-march privatization. The IMF, together with the Soros Foundation, trained the personnel who came to carry out these policies."[8]

These three parties were to dominate the left. They remained communist on economics, favoring predominant state ownership, including of agricultural land, central planning, and far-reaching autarky. All three were too extreme to participate in a rational economic discussion.

The standoff between the national democratic right and the hard left served power to the center on a silver platter throughout the 1990s. Unlike the two ideological forces, the center was pragmatic and formative, driven by self-interest. To quote Oscar Wilde, they knew "the price of everything and the value of nothing." The center reacted swiftly to economic changes and altered nature ever so often. The transformation of this nebulous political center explains Ukraine's political development, which was usually fractured in about 10 party factions and many independent deputies.

The political center emerged in July 1990, when Leonid Kravchuk as newly elected chairman of the Ukrainian parliament adopted a national communist platform. He embraced independence, with the implicit condition that the old communist Nomenklatura would stay in power. The national communist program was completed with the independence of Ukraine, and from 1992 the movement started dwindling because of its lack of purpose.

Instead, another pragmatic part of the old communist elite came to the fore: the state enterprise managers, or "red directors." Unlike Kravchuk, they focused on the economy, but their aims were ambiguous. Two factions rose to prominence. One group of red directors came from coal mines and steelworks in Donetsk, led by Yukhym Zviahilskiy. They were pure rent seekers.

---

8. Rachel Douglas, "Flattened by IMF, Ukraine in Geopolitical Crosshairs," *Executive Intelligence Review*, December 10, 2004.

Another faction was formed by managers of military machine-building in Dnipropetrovsk, headed by Leonid Kuchma. They were driven by self-interest as well, but they also wanted a functioning market economy, although they did not quite know what that meant. These two forces were confusingly similar, but they opposed one another. Kuchma promoted gradual market reforms, while Zviahilskiy rejected them.

The missing force in Ukrainian politics was liberalism. Liberals were few and split into Ukrainian and Russian speakers. The most prominent early representative was probably Volodymyr Lanovyi. The government usually contained a couple of liberal economic reformers, whose ungrateful task was to stave off the complete collapse of the economy, while being scorned by the united left.

Thus, the political center mastered power and action, but it had no strategic goal. The national democrats set the political agenda, although they formed a minority. The hard left was little but a reactionary force. It never gained executive power, but it held a blocking majority in parliament, since the right and the center were split into multiple feuding factions. The unfortunate consequence was that minimum legislation was promulgated in the 1990s. The dysfunctional constitutional arrangement hindered both the president and prime minister from promulgating legislation, but the parliament could oust neither. The result was stalemate and frequent political crises. A positive effect, however, was pluralism with strong checks and balances.

A caricature of this time showed a number of apparatchiki with the caption "Ukraine's old communist rulers." The next picture was identical, but its caption read "Ukraine's new democratic rulers." Ukraine's old elite had their cake and ate it too. They were no longer supervised by anybody, neither the KGB nor Moscow nor the Communist Party, and they could quietly appropriate Soviet state property.

Nationalist Economic Policy with Little Thought

Kravchuk's chief economic adviser Oleksandr Yemelianov dominated economic policymaking in newly independent Ukraine. He presented an economic program called Fundamentals of National Economic Policy, which the parliament adopted on March 24, 1992. This program reflected nationalist sentiments, calling for Ukraine's immediate exit from the ruble zone and the introduction of a Ukrainian currency, the hryvnia. Alas, it contained few details and did not suggest a transition to a market economy (Kravchuk 2002, 48–50).

A young liberal economist, Volodymyr Lanovyi, entered new prime minister Vitold Fokin's government as deputy prime minister for the economy. He looked like Ukraine's answer to Poland's Leszek Balcerowicz,

Vaclav Klaus of the Czech Republic, or Russia's Yegor Gaidar. In opposition to Yemelianov, Lanovyi presented his own Plan for Economic Policy and Market Reform in March 1992. This was Ukraine's first program calling for a transition to a market economy. It contained standard reform prescriptions, such as monetary stabilization, sharp budget cuts, tax reform, price liberalization, deregulation of foreign trade, and rapid privatization. Lanovyi's program was used to facilitate Ukraine's entry into the IMF and the World Bank in the spring of 1992, but it went nowhere. Lanovyi was isolated and lacked the necessary political support. In July 1992, when price increases caused discontent, Kravchuk sacked him. On September 30, 1992, Fokin fell, which prompted a complete change of government (Kravchuk 2002, Prizel 1997).

By the summer of 1992, half a year after its independence, Ukraine had no economic program or even a budget. The ignorance of economics was astounding, and international interaction was minimal, as foreigners found few Ukrainian economic policymakers to whom they could talk. The Soviet economic system remained the only known game in town. Suspicious of both Poles and Russians, Ukrainian nationalists objected to their "shock therapy." A national consensus favored gradual reforms promoting a socially oriented market economy, but that became a pretext for doing nothing. In the constitutional chaos, the president, prime minister, and parliament liberally blamed the rampant economic crisis on one another.

National institution-building dominated the economic agenda as well. Ukraine already had many ministries, but some were added, and the NBU had been established in July 1991. The old Soviet bureaucrats stayed at their posts. Economic policy was painfully absent, but nature abhors a vacuum. As the Russian reformers liberalized most prices in Russia in January 1992, Ukraine was forced to go along, which led to a price rise of 285 percent that month.[9] For the rest, old-style state orders, which were remnants of central planning, persisted.

Ukraine's early economic policy amounted to the issue of massive ruble credits and budgetary subsidies to industry and agriculture, while the government tried to restrict sales through rationing and prices and exports through administrative controls. As Pynzenyk (2000, 79–80) lamented: "The main argument for a soft monetary policy was the idea that an increase in the money supply would stimulate an increase in nominal GDP. Additional arguments were the purported need for government purchases of agricultural goods and the social protection of the population from growing consumer prices. The Ukrainian way of 'saving' the national economy and 'protecting' the population through inflation resulted in serious economic decline and falling real living standards."

9. National Bank of Ukraine, State Statistics Committee of Ukraine online database, www.ukrstat.gov.ua (accessed on August 31, 2007).

Prime Minister Kuchma: Aborted Reform

On October 13, 1992, the Ukrainian parliament confirmed Leonid D. Kuchma as prime minister.[10] Unlike his predecessors, Kuchma was no apparatchik but the country's foremost red director, the director general of the world's biggest missile factory, Pivdenmash (Russian: Yuzhmash), in Dnipropetrovsk, which produced SS-18, the world's largest intercontinental ballistic missiles. Kuchma was Ukrainian but a Russian speaker. He was a no-nonsense man, stating that "Ukraine was on the verge of collapse," but his economic insights were limited. He began with a parliamentary coup against President Kravchuk, persuading the parliament to transfer to him for half a year the president's rights to rule over the economy by decree.

Kuchma established an economic reform team that was to last. He made Viktor Pynzenyk, a liberal Rukh deputy and sophisticated economist from Lviv, his deputy prime minister for economic reform, who mobilized a group of young liberal reformers. In January 1993 the agrarians in parliament lobbied for the appointment of the young deputy chairman of the Agro-Industrial Bank, Viktor Yushchenko, as chairman of the NBU. He was an economist and former *kolkhoz* accountant from a village in Sumy oblast in eastern Ukraine. In 1993 Kuchma appointed another reform economist, Roman Shpek from Ivano-Frankivsk in western Ukraine, minister of economy. Strangely, nobody noticed that Kuchma, the classical red director, assembled a team of three nationalist liberal economists.

In December 1992 and January 1993 Pynzenyk's reform team composed Ukraine's first serious program of market reform, Basic Principles for a National Economic Policy. Although it amounted to a big step forward, it was a mixed bag. The primary task was to curb inflation to 2 to 3 percent a month by improving budgetary discipline but also through wage and price controls and more progressive taxation. The program advocated faster privatization and the introduction of private ownership of land. It favored breaking up monopolies and promoting competition, ending the state's monopoly on retail trade; simplifying registration of new small enterprises; and making restrictions on foreign investment less onerous. Yet the program was protectionist, favoring stringent quantitative controls on imports and export controls for scarce goods. Kuchma supported better trade relations with Russia, which was not reflected in the program.

Many of these reforms were implemented, as the government issued dozens of significant decrees and the parliament promulgated reform laws. The Law on Privatization was improved, social welfare payments were pruned, and retail trade was opened to private competition. These

10. The main sources of this section are Kravchuk (2002, 52–56) and Prizel (1997, 346–48).

measures were market-oriented but neither radical nor comprehensive. Most of the program was not implemented for lack of commitment or the inflationary crisis. However decisive Kuchma sounded, he shared Kravchuk's disdain for radical market reform and preferred to talk about a special Ukrainian model introduced through evolutionary change. When Kuchma tried to advance privatization, the parliament blocked it.

In May 1993 Kuchma's half-year of special powers expired. Neither Kravchuk nor the parliament had any desire to prolong them. In the summer of 1993, the tenuous balance of power between the three branches of government broke down, and the specter of economic collapse was frightening. Once again, the coal miners in Donbas went on a crippling ten-day strike, threatening politics and the economy with chaos. The strike made Kravchuk call for early presidential elections in July 1994, although his five-year mandate expired in December 1996. At the same time, early parliamentary elections were scheduled for March 1994.

Kuchma, who was a fighter, reacted by issuing a more hard-hitting and detailed economic reform program with five major components: tax reform, energy price agreement with Russia, fast privatization of all enterprises, promotion of exports, and restriction of NBU credits to industry. Since it ran counter to the left-wing majority in parliament and his own constituency of state enterprise managers, it could not fly, but Kuchma had shown his mettle to the Ukrainian public. When he received no parliamentary support, he submitted his resignation, which the parliament repeatedly refused to accept, but on September 21 he quit. He made a dramatic exit to prepare himself for presidential elections.

Pynzenyk (1999, 30–31) later commented: "A few sensible politicians spoke of monetary emission as unacceptable and the need to undertake absolutely necessary but not always pleasant decisions, but their voices were lost in the choir of those who spoke of the uniqueness of the Ukrainian situation and the opportunities to get out of it with special, purely, Ukrainian methods."

Kuchma did not achieve much during his brief premiership, but he was the first Ukrainian executive who seemed to care about the national economy. He initiated some elements of market reform and advocated standard financial stabilization and privatization, even if deregulation was barely conceived. Three fixtures had emerged in Ukraine's political scene: Kuchma, Pynzenyk, and Yushchenko.

Prime Minister Zviahilskiy: Unabashed Rent Seeking

Kravchuk drew three lessons from the Kuchma intermezzo: He wanted a weaker prime minister, he should be in charge of the economy himself, and it was better to return to a command economy. All these three conclusions helped to finish off Kravchuk.

On September 22, 1993, Kravchuk appointed Yukhym Zviahilskiy acting prime minister.[11] One week later, he abolished the post of prime minister, demoting Zviahilskiy to acting first deputy prime minister never to be confirmed by parliament. Kravchuk also attempted to merge the presidential administration with the cabinet of ministers, but the forceful Zviahilskiy functioned as prime minister.

Overtly, Kuchma and Zviahilskiy appeared to be similar, as leading state enterprise managers and Russian speakers from eastern Ukraine, but Kuchma came from Dnipropetrovsk and Zviahilskiy from Donetsk. Kuchma's industry was sophisticated machine-building, while Zviahilskiy managed Ukraine's largest coal mine (which he privatized to his own advantage) and was a prominent commodity trader. The key difference was that Kuchma cared about the national interest, whereas Zviahilskiy was preoccupied with his personal affairs.

Together Kravchuk and Zviahilskiy tried to rebuild a command economy, although their aims were very different. Kravchuk, who knew nothing of economics, opposed a market economy, while the clever Zviahilskiy realized that more regulations bred more rents to the privileged few. They tried to reestablish the former Soviet central planning system with state orders for important goods. As in the old days, they commanded guaranteed state supplies to state enterprises producing on state orders. Prices were controlled, and state subsidies covered differentials between controlled prices. They, however, stopped short of setting plan targets for the production of individual enterprises.

This attempt at revived central planning failed miserably. Output continued to fall, and hyperinflation peaked at 10,155 percent in 1993.[12] The old communist control system was gone, and the red directors pursued their own interests. Regardless of the government's aggravated regulations, businessmen started to adjust to the market.

The only winners of this policy reversal were Zviahilskiy and his business partners. They made money on foreign trade arbitrage between low domestic prices of energy, metals, and chemicals and much higher world market prices. Since they controlled foreign trade licensing, they ensured that profits stayed in their circle. Zviahilskiy went too far. After Kuchma was elected president in the summer of 1994, Zviahilskiy was prosecuted for embezzling state-owned aviation fuel that he had sold for exports for $25 million. The sum was paid into his personal offshore bank account. Zviahilskiy fled to Israel for three years until he negotiated his return to Ukraine with the new authorities in 1997 (Wilson 2005, 9). Since

11. The main source of this section is Kravchuk (2002, 56–58).

12. The standard definition of hyperinflation is 50 percent a month or more (Cagan 1956).

his return, he has thrived as one of the leading businessmen in "old Donetsk" and been a steady member of Ukraine's parliament, being one of the powerbrokers in the Regions of Ukraine.

Hyperinflation and Economic Disaster

By 1994 neither plan nor market governed the Ukrainian economic system. The old centrally planned economy had stopped functioning, but no market economy had arisen. Enterprises remained predominantly state-owned. By the end of 1993, the European Bank for Reconstruction and Development (EBRD 1994) assessed that only 15 percent of Ukraine's GDP originated in the private sector. The government tried to control deliveries between state enterprises, but largely failed to do so. However, the state strictly controlled foreign trade. Prices of most essential goods were controlled, although most prices were free.

It was close to impossible to produce in a system ridden with overregulation and understimulation. Output fell like a stone from 1990 to 1994 (figure 2.1). Officially, the total decline in GDP in these five years was no less than 48 percent (UNECE 2004, 80). To a considerable extent, though, the growth of the underground economy compensated for this drop. Daniel Kaufmann and Aleksander Kaliberda (1996) pioneered assessments of the underground economy in Ukraine and found it to have expanded from 12 percent of total GDP in 1989 to as much as 46 percent of actual GDP, or almost as large as the official economy, in 1995 (figure 2.2). Compared with other postcommunist countries, Ukraine's underground economy was very large because it expanded the most in countries without either plan or market. The situation was similar in Russia but not quite as bad, while the Polish underground economy declined sharply after 1991 because more of the economy was legalized.

Officially, investment remained high at 24 to 27 percent of GDP during the first three years of independence. The explanation is that the investment was publicly financed, and the denominator is official GDP, which means that the real investment ratio might have been half as high. Vito Tanzi and Hamid Davoodi (1997) have established in a cross-country comparison that corruption and public investment often go hand in hand, while being negatively correlated to growth.

All Ukrainian statistics from this time are of very poor quality. With the old command economy, its recording system also collapsed, and no new system was built, leaving many activities unregistered. The Ukrainian Ministry of Statistics has been inert and reluctant to adopt modern statistical methods, and it loathes transparency. As alternative statistics rarely are available, one has no choice but to use the official statistics, while occasionally lamenting their poor quality and pointing out evident biases.

Figure 2.1 Decline in Ukraine's GNP, 1990–94

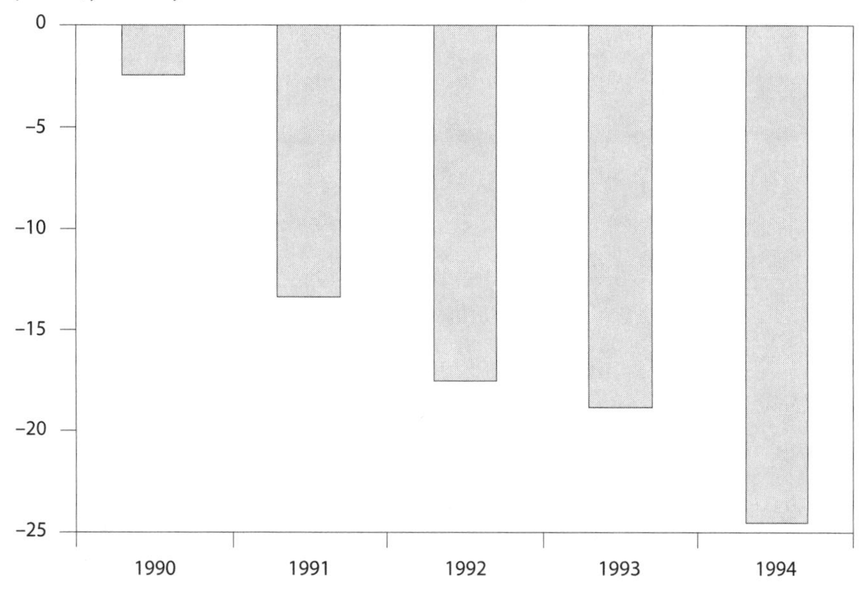

Source: Ministry of Statistics of Ukraine (1994, 10).

The main explanation for this output collapse was high inflation, which reached 2,730 percent in 1992 and 10,155 percent in 1993. After price liberalization, monthly inflation peaked at 91 percent in December 1993. Ten post-Soviet countries recorded hyperinflation, as did Poland, Yugoslavia, and Bulgaria, so Ukraine was not alone, but only war-ridden Armenia had higher hyperinflation than Ukraine (EBRD 1994). Hyperinflation disrupts all economic life and demoralizes society, as only a few insiders know how to make money on the many distortions, while the general public suffers.

Hyperinflation had three main causes: maintenance of the ruble zone, excessive monetary expansion, and too large public expenditures.[13] Monetary expansion was relentless. As early as February and March 1992 Ukraine's monetary base increased by about 50 percent a month, virtually guaranteeing hyperinflation (figure 2.3). The NBU was new and weak, and it was subordinate to the parliament, which every so often decided to issue huge credits. The NBU pursued no interest rate policy, issuing most credits at a subsidized rate of 20 percent per annum, a huge negative real interest, rendering any loan from the NBU a state subsidy.

13. Major sources to this section are Dabrowski (1994) and De Ménil (1997, 2000).

Figure 2.2 Underground economy, 1989–95

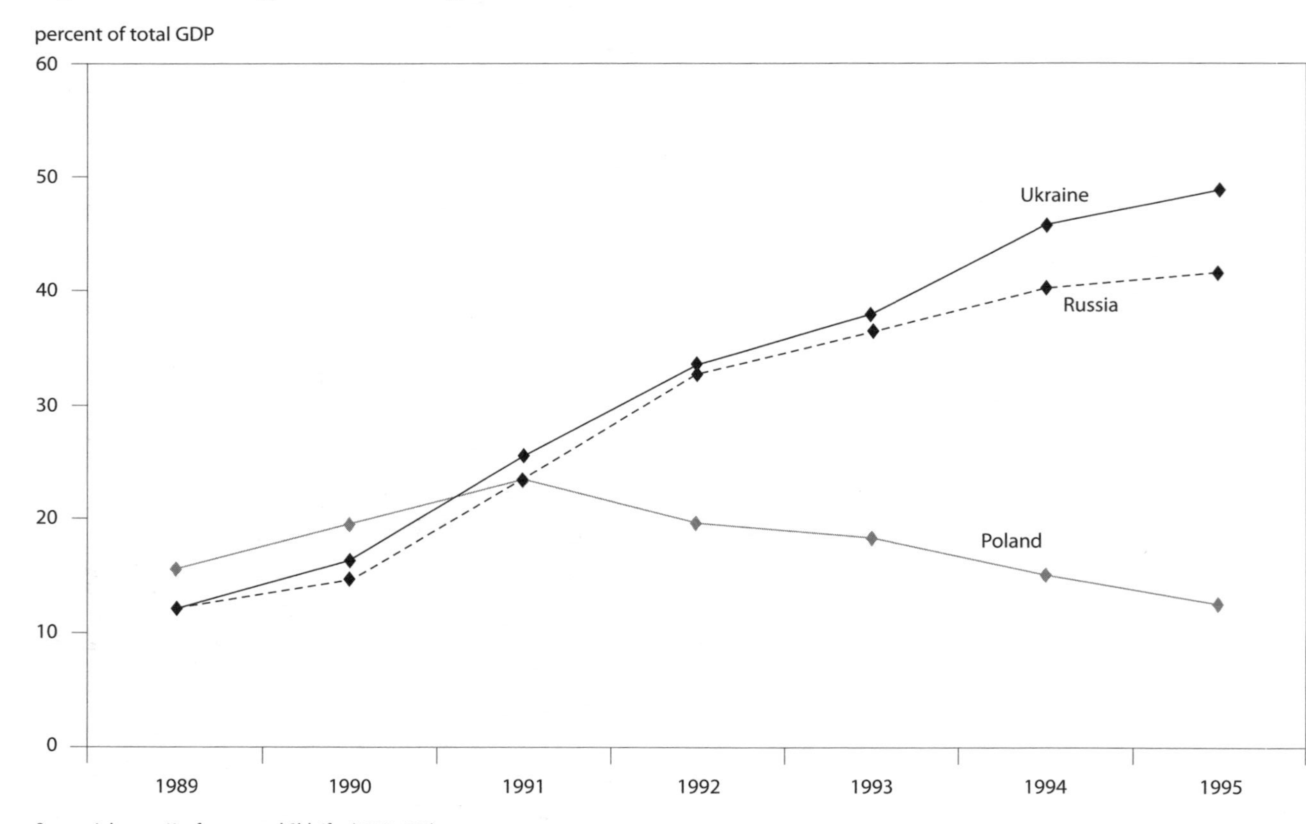

Source: Johnson, Kaufmann, and Shleifer (1997, 183).

Figure 2.3 Monthly inflation and monetary expansion in Ukraine, 1992–94

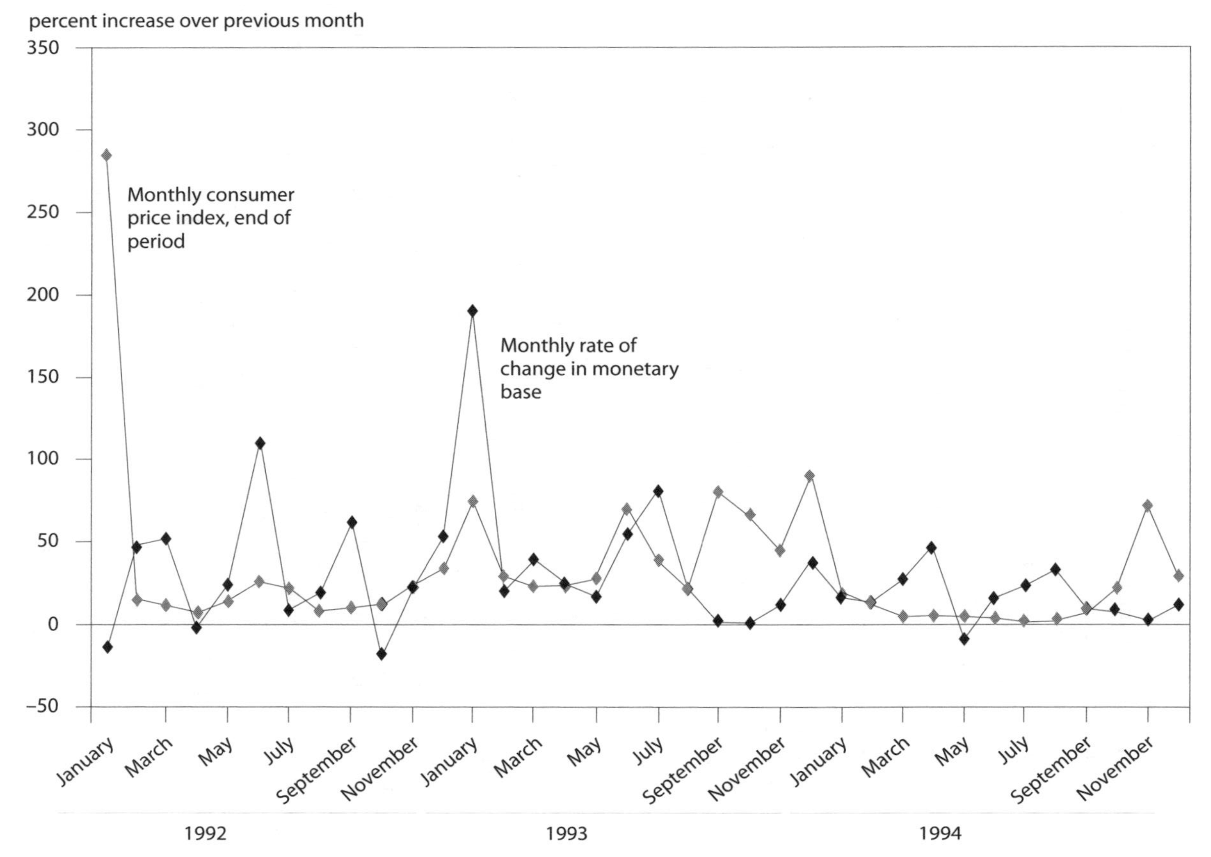

Source: National Bank of Ukraine, State Statistics Committee of Ukraine online database, www.ukrstat.gov.ua (accessed on August 31, 2007).

When Ukraine was forced to liberalize prices in January 1992, prices skyrocketed, which led to demonetization, as the volume of money in relation to GDP fell sharply. The velocity or speed of circulation of coupons (*karbovantsy*) increased because nobody wanted to hold money and thus pay the inflation tax. By 1996, broad money had shrunk to a miserly 8 percent of GDP, about one-tenth of what it had been in late Soviet days.

The predominant post-Soviet view was that real money supply had to be restored, which justified massive new emissions. Large interenterprise arrears piled up, because the payment system was rudimentary and enterprises had no incentive to pay in the absence of bankruptcy or other penalties. The NBU periodically cleared the arrears through additional issuance of money. The biggest peaks in the issue of base money occurred in June 1992 (110 percent) and January 1993 (191 percent). Every summer, the agriculture lobby demanded and received large subsidized credits to finance the harvest. The rational response would have been to minimize the issue of money to achieve financial stabilization.[14]

Ukraine started off with a colossal budget deficit without any constraint on public expenditures. The Ministry of Finance was very weak in the Soviet system, being the state accountant rather than a policymaking unit. It did not have full financial oversight and it was not supposed to deny expenditures. A large number of extrabudgetary funds, such as the Chornobyl Fund, the Pension Fund, the Social Insurance Fund, and the Road Fund, had revenues and expenditures beyond the purview of the ministry. The ministry remained inordinately weak for many years, as the main reformers tended to be a deputy prime minister for the economy and the minister of economy rather than the minister of finance, which was the case in most other transition countries.

State finances were nothing but chaotic. Ukraine had adopted a law on its budget system in December 1990, but budgeting was irregular and the parliament disregarded the state budget. It spontaneously ordered huge additional expenditures, mostly subsidies to industry and agriculture. Under the unclear constitutional arrangement, the government could hardly refuse expenditures. Initially, the lone voice of budget restraint was Deputy Prime Minister Lanovyi, for which he was quickly sacked. The parliament adopted the budget for 1992 as late as June that year and the budget for 1993 in April 1993 (Dabrowski, Luczyński, and Markiewicz 2000).

The 1992 budget prescribed a deficit of 2 percent of GDP, but the parliament added a variety of expenditures, expanding the deficit to an untenable 29 percent of GDP (figure 2.4). It was financed through the issuance of money, breeding hyperinflation. Officially, the budgets for 1993

14. See Banaian (1999, 43–44), Dunn and Lenain (1997, 41–42), Rostowski (1993, 1994), and Sachs and Lipton (1993).

Figure 2.4 Ukraine's total state revenues, expenditures, and budget deficit, 1992–94

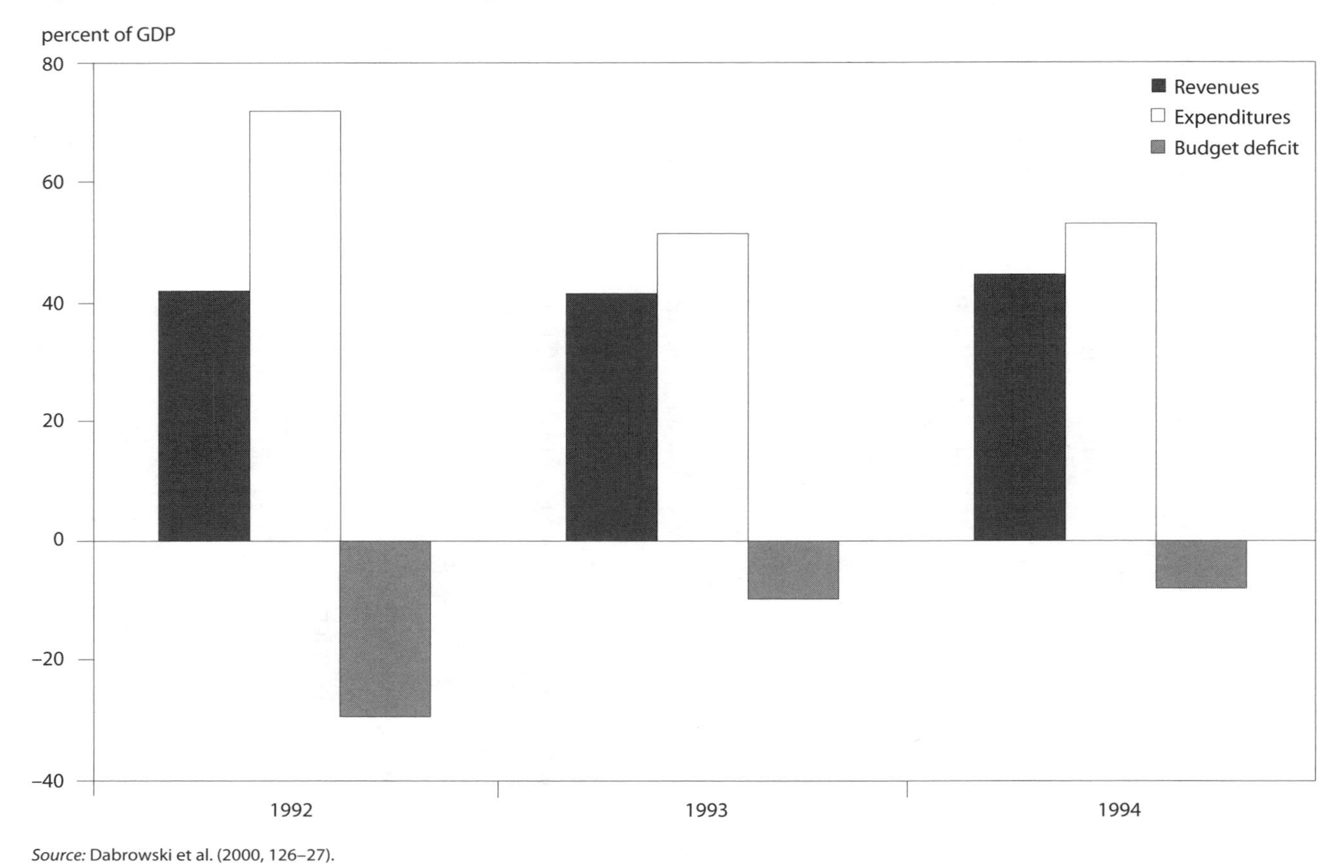

Source: Dabrowski et al. (2000, 126–27).

and 1994 were close to balance but only because of absurd assumptions of increased revenues. The budget for 1994 was officially balanced with revenues and expenditures reaching 86 percent of GDP. This would have been by far the highest in the world. When the illusory revenues did not materialize, Deputy Prime Minister Pynzenyk started sequestering expenditures, withholding payments for all but the most urgent aims. As a consequence, wage and pension arrears became a bane of the 1990s but often the real reason was that enterprise managers took the opportunity to blame the state and refused to pay their workers the wages they had earned (Banaian 1999; Dabrowski, Luczyński, and Markiewicz 2000).

A wide expectation was that Ukraine's state revenues would collapse with the Soviet system and hyperinflation. Oddly, total state revenues stayed nearly constant at 41 percent of official GDP in 1992 and 1993 and rose somewhat in 1994. The main explanation was that state enterprises paid most of the taxes, from which state banks collected taxes in advance. Another reason was statistical: Official GDP was only half of the real GDP, since the tax system had driven half the economy underground.

The most important taxes in the Soviet system had been a payroll tax of 38 percent, a sales tax that varied by good, a high corporate profit tax, and foreign trade taxes, while personal income taxes were tiny at a flat rate of 13 percent. The old turnover tax had to be changed with partial price liberalization, and a very high value-added tax of 28 percent was introduced as in Russia, but it was perforated with loopholes, exempting agriculture, energy, and services. The flat personal income tax was replaced with ever higher progressive income taxes, which peaked at 90 percent in early 1994 for as modest an income as $100 a month. The payroll tax was increased for various social purposes to a total of 60 percent. The profit tax was replaced by a corporate gross income tax, which in effect became confiscatory because no deductions were allowed (Dabrowski, Luczyński, and Markiewicz 2000, 121–23).

Ukraine had established a tax system that was formally confiscatory, but two escape routes existed. One was huge loopholes and the other was massive tax evasion. Needless to say, nobody paid these confiscatory taxes. As a countermeasure, Ukraine built a formidable State Tax Administration, which soon employed 70,000 people. It was to become the independent fiefdom of the Donetsk politician Mykola Azarov and a state within the state. It was considered massively corrupt and became a major impediment to business.

Ukraine's foreign trade remained quite limited in absolute terms and concentrated on the former Soviet republics, but in 1992 exports alone were actually larger than the deflated GDP, which was as small as $10 billion in current US dollars in 1992.[15] Trade was patently imbalanced, but

---

15. EBRD online database, www.ebrd.com (accessed on July 1, 2008).

the deficit was limited by the absence of financing since Ukraine was not creditworthy.

Rent Seeking: Rationale of Ukraine's Early Economic Policy

There was reason for this madness.[16] The small communist elite remained in power and designed the postcommunist transition to make money on economic distortions (Åslund 1996, 1999; Hellman 1998; Shleifer and Vishny 1998). To maximize their rents, they needed a slow transition. Much public attention was devoted to the country's excessive dependence on Russia, while the harmfulness of the inherited communist economic system, though universally recognized, attracted little public interest.

Radical reforms were initially discarded as characteristic Russian rashness, incompatible with Ukrainian peacefulness and moderation. As a manifestation of the Ukrainian state, a cumbersome bureaucracy and regulatory system were being built. These conditions bred severe corruption and rent seeking. In particular, the Zviahilskiy government maximized its personal revenues by intentionally introducing cumbersome foreign trade regulations. A mixture of state enterprise managers, new entrepreneurs, government officials, commodity traders, bankers, and outright criminals thrived on the resulting extraordinary rent seeking. From 1991 to 1993 four forms of rent-seeking dominated.

The first method was to buy metals and chemicals at home, where their prices were kept low through price regulation, and sell them abroad at the world market price. This required access to metals and export permits. In 1992 about 40 percent of Ukraine's exports were commodities (IMF 1993, 113), and their average domestic price was about 10 percent of the world market price. Hence, the total export rents amounted to some $4.1 billion, or 20 percent of the country's GDP in 1992. The beneficiaries were managers of state metallurgical companies, commodity traders, foreign trade officials, and some politicians.

The second trick was to import certain commodities, notably natural gas from Russia at a low subsidized exchange rate, and resell them at a higher domestic price. If the government paid for the deliveries because of state guarantees for gas imports, it was even more profitable. The beneficiaries were a small number of gas importers and their government partners, who shared the profits with their Russian partners in Gazprom.[17]

The third way was subsidized credits. In 1993, when Ukraine experienced 10,155 percent inflation, huge state credits were issued at an

16. This draws on Åslund (2000).

17. We lack the numbers for an estimation for these early years.

interest of 20 percent a year. State credits were therefore sheer gifts, given to a privileged few. Net credit expansion to enterprises was no less than 65 percent of GDP in 1992 and 47 percent of GDP in 1993 (calculated from IMF 1993, 109; IMF 1995, 73, 105).

The fourth form of rent seeking was straightforward budget subsidies, which amounted to 8.1 percent of GDP in 1992 and 10.8 percent of GDP in 1993. They were concentrated on agriculture and energy, that is, gas and coal, which became totally criminalized by a struggle over these subsidies (IMF 1995, 94).

In comparison with Russia, export rents were lower, import rents much higher, subsidized credit significantly larger, and direct enterprise subsidies about the same. In total, these Ukrainian rents approximately equaled Ukraine's GDP compared with Russian rents, which equaled 81 percent of GDP in Russia in 1992; rents were higher in Ukraine than in Russia in 1993 as well (Åslund 1999). These rents were largely accumulated abroad in tax havens through capital flight.

In this way, a small group of privileged insiders usurped a huge share of GDP in the early years of transition and grew even stronger. Their wealth was not based on property but on arcane financial flows. For society, the result was untold social suffering and sharply rising income differentials. Ukraine reached a Gini coefficient of 47, about as much as Russia or the Latin American average (Milanovic 1998, 41).

By 1994 the social consequences were becoming untenable, and the very cohesion of Ukraine was in danger, as it was approaching state bankruptcy. In 1994 the US Central Intelligence Agency (CIA) even issued a shocking National Intelligence Estimate entitled "Ukraine: A Nation at Risk," postulating that Ukraine might fail as a state and that there might be no Ukraine in 5 to 10 years (Pifer 2004). Moreover, the inflation tax no longer benefited rent seekers, as it had declined with demonetization (Åslund, Boone, and Johnson 1996). The rent-seeking elite started accepting the idea of low inflation and could contemplate financial stabilization.

Crimea: Threat of Secession

Ukraine had a few border territories on the west and the east that could claim special national treatment, but the only region that aroused serious concern was Crimea, which was the newest Ukrainian territory and completely Russified.

Crimea was the ethnic homeland of the Crimean Tatars, whom Stalin deported collectively to Central Asia in 1944 for alleged collaboration with the Germans. In 1954 Nikita Khrushchev transferred Crimea from the Russian Soviet Federated Socialist Republic to the Ukrainian Soviet Socialist Republic to celebrate the 300th anniversary of Ukraine's union with Russia. Russians saw this as capricious extravaganza, especially as Crimea was the favorite Soviet vacation spot and entirely Russian speaking. Before the collapse of the Soviet Union, the Soviet authorities allowed Crimean Tatars to return, and soon a quarter of a million arrived. For tactical reasons, the Crimean Tatars joined hands with Ukrainian nationalists, since their common enemy was Russian nationalism.

Russian nationalists who controlled the regional Crimean council exploited the approaching collapse of the Soviet Union. In November 1990 this council condemned Crimea's 1954 transfer to Ukraine. In January 1991 they organized a referendum that raised Crimea's status from autonomous oblast to an Autonomous Soviet Socialist Republic, which the Ukrainian parliament confirmed.

The referendum on Ukraine's independence on December 1, 1991, however, was a big blow to the Russian nationalists, since 54 percent of the residents on the peninsula voted for Ukrainian independence and even 57 percent in Sevastopol, the base of the Soviet Black Sea Fleet (Kuzio 2000, 202–24).

Yet, the Russian nationalists continued to strengthen Crimea's autonomy in several small steps. Its regional council declared Crimea a republic, announced self-government, and adopted a constitution. These events were spread out, and the Ukrainian government and parliament fought each step. The Russian nationalists in Crimea were also held back by the lack of official Russian support, as Yeltsin insisted on the inviolability of the borders of the former union republics.

As the Ukrainian economic crisis deepened, the Russian nationalists were reinvigorated and instituted the post of president of Crimea, and on January 30, 1994, pro-Russian Yuriy Meshkov was elected the first president. He invited a group of relatively liberal Russian economists from Moscow to operate his government and intensified Crimea's ambitions at ever greater autonomy. Curiously, Meshkov entered into endless quarrels with the Crimean parliament like Kravchuk with the Ukrainian parliament, but Meshkov went too far by disbanding the Crimean parliament.

Deftly, the Ukrainian government waited for the locals to fail to govern Crimea. The Crimean economy fell into complete chaos and criminalization, while in late 1994 Ukraine launched financial stabilization, making Crimea look more dysfunctional. In March 1995, on President Kuchma's initiative, the Ukrainian parliament scrapped the Crimean constitution as well as the post of president of Crimea. The peak of Crimean separatism was over, and it was brought under control. After Crimean separatism had been contained, all other separatist aspirations looked all the more futile. Ukraine had secured its integrity, even though Russian nationalists have remained active with steady support from some Russian politicians, notably Moscow Mayor Yuriy Luzhkov.

Kravchuk: Father of the Nation

After his election defeat in July 1994, Kravchuk and his staff departed without protest from the presidential administration, which was located in the old Central Committee building on Bankova. This was Ukraine's first democratic transition of power. Kravchuk remains a public personality in Kyiv, sometimes a centrist member of parliament. His achievements and failures can be summed up in five points.

First, as Robert Kravchuk (2002, 58; no relation) notes, President Kravchuk deserves to be called the Father of the Ukrainian Nation. He convinced 90 percent of the population to vote for independence, and he was elected new Ukraine's first president. He managed to take Ukraine out of the Soviet Union peacefully and swiftly.

Second, Kravchuk instigated Ukraine's denuclearization in agreement with Russia and the United States, and he prepared the ground for international guarantees of Ukraine's national sovereignty.

Third, Kravchuk failed to improve Ukraine's dysfunctional Soviet constitution. The rising tensions between president, prime minister, and the capricious, disorganized parliament rendered Ukraine close to ungovernable. However, Kravchuk did not undermine democracy and freedom and set a high democratic precedence by leaving power without protest.

Fourth, economic policy could hardly have been more disastrous. No postcommunist country was hit by such hyperinflation and such a huge decline in output without war as Ukraine. This enormous cost was brought upon the Ukrainian population for no good purpose. No market economy was built, and a sheer minimum of privatization was undertaken. An entrenched machine of rent seeking was established.

Fifth, the economic collapse was so severe that it threatened the nation's integrity. The worst specter of secession was Crimea's attempt in 1994. It failed because Boris Yeltsin opposed separatism and Crimea's economic failure was even greater than Ukraine's.

Ukraine had become independent peacefully, but for it to be a viable state, the constitutional order and the economic system had to be fixed. Kravchuk lacked the ability to fix these problems, but to his great credit he bowed out after losing the presidential elections in July 1994.

3

Leonid Kuchma's Reforms, 1994–96

The period of romanticism is over.
—Dmytro Tabachnyk,
Kuchma's chief of staff[1]

On July 10, 1994, Leonid Kuchma won the runoff against Leonid Kravchuk in Ukraine's second presidential elections. The elections were peaceful and orderly, free and fair. The challenger won, and the incumbent left the presidential office with his staff, allowing the newly elected president to move in. Ukraine had gone through its first democratic transition of power. Kuchma had run his campaign on change and economic reform, although his economic views remained somewhat hazy.

In November 1993 a friend and I drove through western Ukraine from Uzhhorod to Lviv. It was a dismal experience. To get into the right mood, we played Polish crisis songs from the 1930s. While crossing the border from Slovakia, we encountered a few hundred car thieves in track suits and sneakers or black leather jackets and blue jeans, who were prepared to bribe customs officials on both sides of the border to get through with their newly stolen German cars. I had never seen so many evident professional killers before. Since we were the only people in jackets and tie, we were quickly let through as long-forgotten remnants of an old civilization, or perhaps we just resembled the old Nomenklatura. In Uzhhorod, where Hungarians, Roma, and Russians are more common than Ukrainians in the streets, there was hardly any electricity and minimal heating. The shops were empty. Strangely, it was quiet and peaceful in misery.

1. Quoted in Kuzio (1997, 90).

While traveling through Transcarpathia we made three observations. First, all the shops were just about empty. It was incomprehensible how people were surviving. Second, outside every little town single-family houses were being built. Some new businessmen were clearly making money. Third, in every village, two more churches were being built in addition to the traditional one, as people turned to competing churches, while they quietly gave up on politics and economics. In Lviv, we stayed at Grand Hotel, whose owner, a Ukrainian-American entrepreneur, had just been murdered in some business dispute. People quietly went about their routine. Order prevailed. But people were evidently becoming ever poorer.

The situation looked as precarious economically as promising politically. Three days after Kuchma's installation, I contacted George Soros, who financed a network of foundations in Ukraine. I told him that if he wanted to provide a team of international economic advisers to Kuchma, I would be happy to assist. One week later, Soros called back. He had an appointment with President Kuchma in Kyiv the ensuing week. He asked if I would like to accompany him. I said yes.

In mid-August 1994, Soros, his outstanding policy director John Fox, and I met Kuchma in his office in Kyiv, together with his chief of staff Dmytro Tabachnyk and Minister of Economy Roman Shpek. Soros and Fox had met Kuchma before the elections hoping that he would bring the badly needed determination to reform Ukraine. Kuchma appreciated this moral support, especially as the US administration and the North American Ukrainian diaspora preferred Kravchuk.

Soros praised Kuchma's economic reform plans and offered support with a team of international advisers. Kuchma answered curtly: "I am ready." Soros asked: "With whom should we work?" Kuchma pointed at Shpek. We had received a mandate. We sat down for a few hours and discussed what needed to be done. In the evening, Soros asked me to come to his hotel suite. As I had expected, he said: "You do what you think is necessary. I pay."[2]

In the next year, Kuchma was deeply engaged in economic reforms and shepherded the necessary legislation through with great tenacity (in sharp contrast with Yeltsin). He was surprisingly accessible and did not mind an argument, which tended to be challenging but worthwhile.

The economic policy environment in Ukraine differed greatly from Moscow, where we had worked previously. In Moscow the active players were many. Reformers and conservatives formed well-defined ideologi-

---

2. Three days later, the International Monetary Fund mission arrived. At the same time, four economist-friends of mine flew in: Peter Boone and Simon Johnson, with PhD degrees from Harvard University and MIT, respectively, who had been involved in advisory activities in other postcommunist countries, and two of my graduate students from Sweden, Eva Sundquist and Elisabeth Hopkins. We freed ourselves from our ordinary jobs and worked intensely together with the Ukrainian reform team. Michael Zienchuk from Canada joined us.

cal camps, and they had staunch international supporters. Disputes sprouted everywhere, and competition was knife-sharp. Preemption was key: Your camp had to get a decision made before the rivals did.

In Kyiv, Kuchma and his reform team were the only game in town. Initially, they worked hard and fast, with great determination and little apparent opposition. Every reformist minister had a couple of close advisers, while the rest of the government staff seemed uninvolved, neither opposing nor supporting reforms, which few understood. It was peaceful and friendly. The issue was not rivalry or even what decision to make but rather to get the obvious decision made. Views were fluid. At a high-level internal government meeting I was struck by a deputy minister of economy initially opposing price liberalization but half an hour later concluding that it should be done instantly. Few policymakers had a clear ideology.

Ukrainian attitudes toward foreigners were amazingly positive. We were thanked ever so often. Senior officials were not bashful about asking us what they did not know and we tried to assist as we could, writing brief policy memos, which was not done much in the old Soviet system that administered rather than formulated policy. We received an office in the cabinet of ministers building and passes with liberal access, a world of difference from the security preoccupations that had taken hold in Moscow by 1993.

The Stalinist cabinet of ministers building was in a deplorable state. The parquet floors were falling apart. Computers, copiers, or fax machines were nowhere to be found except in ministers' offices. The staff was dignified and correct but poor. Years would pass before enrichment from corruption became noticeable. In the winter, Russia regularly cut off gas deliveries for alleged Ukrainian arrears, and the temperature in the government offices often fell below freezing, but the plucky staff worked in their warmest overcoats, drinking plenty of hot tea.

When Ukraine became independent, hundreds of Ukrainians from the diaspora hastened back to their motherland. Most were full of idealism to rebuild their native land from communist and Russian devastation, while others were hapless golddiggers. By 1994 they were disappointed, having realized that their idealized compatriots were often corrupt and not very truthful. They were politically not as prominent as the Baltic diaspora, although Roman Zvarych became minister of justice after the Orange Revolution. Bohdan Hawrylyshyn was a prominent adviser to President Kravchuk, and Oleh Havrylyshyn became deputy minister of finance. Yet the diaspora formed an invaluable network of competent professionals in all walks of life, and many prominent members have stayed in Ukraine since 1991. They were most helpful to us.

By 1994 many Western organizations and embassies were in Kyiv, but they still had the idyllic sense of pioneers. The slogan was public education on market reform. Through its resident representative Daniel Kaufmann, the World Bank took a public lead with weekly seminars for journalists.

George Soros was all dominant. Some of the leaders of the diaspora and the Ukrainian intelligentsia had approached him early on, and by 1994 he had developed a full network of institutions. The fund-giving International Renaissance Foundation was the centerpiece. Soros sponsored two of the best business schools (the International Management Institute and the International Institute of Business), later a graduate school of economics (Kyiv School of Economics), and several think tanks (the International Center for Policy Studies and the Legal Reform Foundation). Much of the new policy thinking arose from his institutions. The problem was his uniqueness. We set up the Soros International Economic Advisory Group as a complement to this Soros family of institutions.

The two biggest technical assistance donors were the United States and the European Union. The US Agency for International Development (USAID) was very active in Ukraine, especially engaged in privatization and the drafting of laws. Like most donors, it suffered from a lack of Ukrainian government counterparts for desired reforms, for example, social and agricultural reforms, but USAID was ever-present and relatively agile.

Through its Technical Assistance to the Commonwealth of Independent States (TACIS) program, the European Union spent a lot of money on Ukraine, but its mandate and procedures were construed in such a way that it could hardly do anything useful. For example, after Ukraine finally managed to break out of the ruble zone and bring inflation under control, TACIS sent a French Trotskyite into Kyiv with a project to restore a currency union with Russia and Belarus. The demand for such a proposal was limited and it quietly died.

From August 1994, the International Monetary Fund (IMF) played a central role in economic policymaking. The German government set up a qualified, ambitious, and well-connected German Advisory Group on Economic Reforms with the Ukrainian Government, which focused on supporting the National Bank of Ukraine (NBU) and its chairman, Viktor Yushchenko. In effect, it took the place of our Soros group when we wound down, and it remains active. By and large, cooperation was excellent between the foreign assistance projects. With the odd exception of TACIS, the question was not what to do but how to get the obvious tasks of postcommunist transition done.

One of the most auspicious chapters in Ukraine's history of independence was opening. The parliamentary elections in March 1994 did much to cement democracy. In July Kuchma won the presidential elections over Kravchuk, but no euphoria followed the election. Kuchma was determined to get things right and exploit his political honeymoon, which lasted from July 1994 until April 1995. On October 11, 1994, Kuchma made his great reform speech to parliament and declared his aim of radical market economic reform. By the end of September 1994 Ukraine had concluded its first IMF agreement that would lead to financial stabilization, and in November 1994 Ukraine undertook its great trade and price liberalization. In March 1995 the Ukrainian parliament invalidated the Crimean constitution, ending its move toward separatism. In June 1996 Ukraine finally adopted a new constitution through consensus in parliament. In September 1996 the Ukrainian national currency, the hryvnia, was successfully introduced as a manifestation of completed stabilization. Simultaneously, Ukraine's long-stalled mass privatization program finally took off. But from June 1995 Kuchma had altered his tone. He no longer spoke of radical but evolutionary reform, and change slowed down.

Parliamentary Elections, Spring 1994

Ukraine's parliament had been elected in March 1990, and its five-year mandate period was supposed to run out in March 1995, but the coal miners' strikes in the summer of 1993 led to a compromise on calling for early parliamentary and presidential elections.[3] The parliamentary elections were held on March 27, 1994.

That Ukraine's predemocratic parliament of 1990 was not dissolved earlier reflected the absence of revolution in Ukraine, which allowed the old establishment to stay in power. Initially, 83 percent of the deputies had been members of the Communist Party of Ukraine (CPU), but most had become independent, though they wanted to maintain their privileges. Their desires of personal comfort coincided with President Kravchuk's aspiration to render the parliament weak and fractious. These establishment forces favored minimal change of the electoral rules and deliberate discrimination against political parties. By contrast, Rukh and other reformers sought to strengthen political parties by advocating proportional elections with party lists for at least half the parliamentarians.

The establishment prevailed on electoral procedure. As before, all the 450 parliamentarians were to be elected through majority elections in single-member constituencies. The only improvement from the 1990 elections was that political parties were allowed, but the nomination process discriminated against parties. The elections were deliberately made almost indeterminate because of high turnout requirements. In each constituency, a participation of 50 percent of the voters was required, and a candidate needed to obtain an absolute majority of the votes to win. Otherwise an infinite number of runoffs ensued. President Kravchuk expressed the not very democratic hope that he might be forced to introduce presidential rule if the elections failed because of less than 50 percent voter participation.

Due to these demands for a hypermajority, only 338 out of 450 seats were filled in the first two rounds on March 27 and early April. Tedious

3. Sources of this section are Birch (2000a, 82–91) and Kuzio (1997, 11–38).

repeat elections were held in July, August, November, and December 1994, December 1995, and April 1996, aggravating voter fatigue. Twenty-five seats remained vacant because of ever lower participation. This election system was clearly not viable.

The election results produced three surprises. First, 76 percent participation was far higher than anybody had predicted, which was a rebuke to Kravchuk. Ukrainians showed they wanted their parliament, but they gave short shrift to the incumbents, throwing them out. Only 17 percent of the deputies were reelected. This was a vote for democracy and change.

Second, the reborn CPU became by far the biggest party with 84 seats, or 25 percent, while the Socialist Party of Ukraine with merely 14 seats saw its ambition to replace the CPU thwarted. Altogether, the hard left parties won 34 percent of the seats, forming a blocking minority. This was a protest against the disastrous economic performance and social suffering. The left won the economic votes, and public support for the as-yet-nonexistent market economy remained weak (table 3.1).

Third, Rukh and all nationalists were badly beaten. Rukh was decimated to only 20 seats. The extreme right received a paltry 2.4 percent of the votes, rendering it completely marginal for good. Only 50 percent of the seats went to parties, while the rest were taken by largely independent centrists, who were the real winners.

The parliamentary elections were held in the midst of hyperinflation. They amounted to a protest vote against the disastrous economic mismanagement and overly nationalistic policies by the odd combination of the left and the business community, which had mobilized the east and the south. These forces also wanted to improve the economic relationship with Russia to mitigate the economic crisis.

It took some time for the parliament to configure itself, but by the spring of 1995, 12 party factions had been formed. The three leftist factions—communists, agrarians, and socialists—held one-third of the seats, while an unwieldy center of six factions comprised 39 percent and three moderate right factions had 22 percent, leaving a balance of 34 unaffiliated deputies. In the end, this was a victory not for the left but for the centrists, as a result of their design of the electoral law. Yet the leftists were better organized and often attracted a couple of the centrist factions for specific votes. In May 1994 the clever socialist leader Oleksandr Moroz was elected to the powerful position of chairman of the new parliament.

The parliament represented insiders. No less than 29 percent of the deputies were senior state officials. Many deputy ministers had been elected deputies and could pass one vote in parliament and another in their ministry, creating considerable confusion among the branches of power. According to the amended Soviet Ukrainian Constitution of 1978, the only government executive with the right to be a member of parliament was the prime minister, but it took years before this rule was enforced (Kuzio 1997, 30).

Table 3.1 Results of election to the Supreme Rada, March–April 1994 (after first and second rounds)

Party	Vote share, first round (percent)	Seats won	
		Number	Percent
Total Left	18.6	116	34.3
Communist	12.7	84	24.9
Socialist	3.1	14	4.1
Rural	2.7	18	5.3
Total Center	3.4	12	3.6
Total National Democrats	9.2	32	9.5
Rukh	5.2	20	5.9
Total Extreme Right	2.4	8	2.4
All parties	33.5	168	49.7
Independents	66.3	170	50.3
Total seats filled in two rounds		338	100
Voter turnout (percent)			75.6

Sources: Birch (2000a, 84); official transcript of the first assembly of the Supreme Rada of the Second Convocation (1994–98), available at www.rada.gov.ua (accessed on July 2, 2008).

Businessmen comprised another rising group, accounting for nearly 20 percent of the seats. Many greeted their surge as a positive sign, presuming that Ukraine's long-suffering entrepreneurs had finally decided to go into politics to promulgate sound market economic legislation. Soon, however, these businessmen showed that they were more interested in rent seeking and blocked market economic legislation. The parliament had become a trading forum for the country's wealthy businessmen, who abrasively called it Ukraine's real stock exchange. State officials and businessmen, who were largely apolitical centrists, held the balance in the new Supreme Rada.

Foreign observers reported many violations of election procedures. Shockingly, a leading Rukh official, Mykhailo Boychyshyn, disappeared and presumably was murdered, but the crime was never solved. Yet, systematic fraud was not apparent. Ukrainians were proud of their peaceful democratic process and the high voter participation, which they compared with the shootout of the parliament in Moscow on October 3–4, 1993, when some 150 people were killed. Ukrainian democracy seemed to progress.

Kravchuk's soft attempt to get rid of the parliament failed, but the old establishment successfully captured it. The threat of the hard left persisted but was contained, though the combination of a fractured center and a hostile disciplined left made legislative work close to impossible. Rukh had been severely weakened, never to recover. This parliament was close to dysfunctional and was unable to adopt the hundreds of laws that the newborn state and budding market economy needed.

Presidential Elections, June–July 1994

The 1994 presidential elections became an epic battle. The first round took place on June 26 and the runoff on July 10, 1994.[4] The two dominant candidates were Kravchuk, the incumbent, and Kuchma, his former prime minister. They were both middle-aged members of the old Nomenklatura, but they held contrasting views on the defining issues of Ukrainian politics, nation-building, and economic reform.

Kravchuk presented himself as the father of the Ukrainian nation and a master of peace, a unifier and conciliator. By so doing he appealed to Ukrainian nationalists, who were heartened because he was a native Ukrainian speaker from a west Ukrainian village, and he marked his distance to Russia. His shortcoming was that he had no economic policy and seemed unlikely to develop one. Just before the presidential elections, Kravchuk surprisingly appointed Vitaliy Masol prime minister, the old Soviet stalwart who had been ousted after a hunger strike by students in October 1990. This seemed a concession to the communists in the east, but it was too late and not consistent with Kravchuk's electoral appeal.

Kuchma built on his agenda as prime minister. He attacked Kravchuk's economic policies, calling the economy "catastrophic" and Ukraine "bankrupt." He demanded change and sounded as if he contemplated radical market economic reform without quite saying so. Instead, like Kravchuk, he spoke vaguely of the need for a "socially oriented economy." His second theme was the need for better relations with Russia, calling for a strategic partnership focusing on the economic rationale. His election slogan was: "Russia and Ukraine: Less walls, more bridges."[5] After his stint as prime minister, Kuchma became chairman of the Ukrainian Union of Industrialists and Entrepreneurs, which he built as the bulwark of the state enterprise managers, following the pioneering example of Arkady Volsky's powerful Union of Industrialists and Entrepreneurs in Russia. He campaigned as the leader of Ukraine's state enterprise managers and Russian speakers, but for political reasons he had learned Ukrainian, which he consistently used in public.

Yet, the similarities between Kravchuk and Kuchma prevailed. They were both former senior party officials. Their economic and political out-

4. The main source of this section is Kuzio (1997, 39–66).

5. Anton Kriukov, "Ukraine-Russia: The Process Has Started," *Zerkalo nedeli*, October 15, 1994.

look was postcommunist as distinct from communist. Both favored stronger presidential powers. They advocated a strong, independent Ukrainian state and the retention of Ukrainian as the sole state language with Russian as a second official language. In the end, their differences boiled down to Kravchuk having established independence and being a Ukrainian speaker from western Ukraine and Kuchma being a Russian-speaking red director from the east focused on the economic crisis.

Two other candidates of note contested the first round, Oleksandr Moroz and Volodymyr Lanovyi. Socialist leader and speaker Moroz ran as the sole candidate of the hard left because communist leader Petro Symonenko yielded to him. His economic views were quite communist: He aimed for a "state-regulated market" with more state control than market forces. Yet Moroz also understood that the Soviet Union was gone and campaigned for an independent, socialist Ukraine.

Lanovyi was Ukraine's first significant liberal politician. He advocated radical market economic reform and Ukraine's withdrawal from the Commonwealth of Independent States. Although he was a Russian-speaking economist from Kyiv, Rukh supported him, opting for liberalism over nationalism.

The election excitement was unbearable. In the first round on June 26, Kravchuk won as expected, with 38 percent against Kuchma's respectable 31 percent. Surprisingly, the sole left-wing candidate, Moroz, received a paltry 14 percent compared with the 33 percent the hard left had won in the parliamentary elections three months earlier (table 3.2). The east and south preferred Kuchma, who seemed friendlier toward Russia and the Russian language than Moroz was. This was the first indication that the east and south cared more about Russian issues than about socialism. Although Rukh supported Lanovyi, it was remarkable that a free marketeer could win so many votes (9.4 percent). The contrast to the parliamentary elections three months earlier was baffling.

The runoff on July 10 was quite different. To general amazement, Kuchma won a clear victory with 52 percent of the votes over Kravchuk's 45 percent in an election that was considered free and fair. Ideology was thrown out. The country was mobilized into two linguistic camps: Ukrainian speakers in the west and center voted for Kravchuk and Russian speakers in the east and south for Kuchma. Rukh as well as the Ukrainian diaspora in the West supported Kravchuk, while the communists tacitly favored Kuchma.

Not having learned his lesson from the parliamentary elections, Kravchuk again hoped that participation would fall below 50 percent so that the presidential elections would be declared null and void. As if to calm his citizens, Kravchuk clarified that he would stay on as president in case of such a calamity. The Ukrainians were mortified by his threat and stormed to the ballot boxes with such enthusiasm that turnout exceeded 70 percent in both rounds.

Table 3.2 Results of presidential election, June–July 1994 (percent of votes)

Candidate	First round, June 26, 1994	Second round, July 10, 1994
Leonid Kravchuk	37.7	45.1
Leonid Kuchma	31.3	52.2
Oleksandr Moroz	14.0	
Volodymyr Lanovyi	9.4	
Valeriy Babych	2.4	
Ivan Pliushch	1.2	
Petro Talanchuk	0.5	
Against all	3.4	2.8
Total	100	100
Voter turnout (percent)	70.3	71.6

Sources: Central Election Commission of Ukraine, www.cvk.gov.ua (accessed on July 7, 2008); Prizel (1997, 357).

The natural interpretation of the runoff was that Ukraine suffered from a serious linguistic division, but an alternative interpretation is that the westerners were consumed by state symbols and language, while the easterners cared more about the economy.[6] The election result could be seen as evidence of a centrist national consensus, since the two ideological candidates lost badly in the first round.

Kuchma Proclaims Radical Economic Reforms

After his inauguration on July 19, President Kuchma could start with a clean slate. His victory had surprised most Ukrainians, so few had extracted any preelection promises from him.

The world looked at Ukraine with alienation, paying little attention to its elections. Yet on July 10, before the election results were announced, the Group of Seven (G-7) largest industrialized democracies concluded its summit in Naples, Italy, promising Ukraine financial support of $4 billion, which helped focus the minds of the Ukrainian leaders.

Besides George Soros, the other great international activist for Ukraine was Michel Camdessus, the managing director of the IMF, who saw a possibility of reform with the election of Kuchma. He was the first international official to fly to Kyiv to see Kuchma immediately after his inauguration. Camdessus promised to send an IMF mission to Kyiv in mid-August to try to conclude an IMF program with financing.

6. I owe this insight to Oleksandr Paskhaver.

Kuchma assembled the best reform team he could find in Ukraine. He kept Minister of Economy Roman Shpek, who became the initial reform leader, and Viktor Yushchenko remained chairman of the NBU. Yuriy Yekhanurov, who had been Shpek's deputy, became chairman of the State Property Fund or minister of privatization. Soon Viktor Pynzenyk came back as deputy prime minister for economic reform, overtaking Shpek's role as reform leader. Ihor Mitiukov was appointed deputy prime minister for international financial cooperation. All these men were well-educated professionals of about 40 years of age, trained in Ukraine with limited international experience. At his side, Kuchma had a senior economic adviser, Professor Anatoliy Halchynskiy, a rare professor of Soviet political economy who understood the need for full-fledged market economy. He authored Kuchma's economic speeches and played an important, largely positive, role, even if radical reformers complained about his moderating influence.

However, Kuchma could not get rid of the old-style communist Prime Minister Vitaliy Masol, whom the parliament had just appointed, and Kuchma did not want to antagonize the left immediately. A striking anomaly was that the minister of finance was not part of the reform team, and that ministry continued to function as the agency for the distribution of public funds rather than as a policymaking entity.

Kuchma was soon accused of bringing in too many people from his home town, Dnipropetrovsk, but such allegations were always exaggerated, as he brought few collaborators from Dnipropetrovsk, and his government was geographically diverse. The dominant group was civil servants from Kyiv.

Kuchma was preoccupied with Ukraine's economic problems, focusing on its inability to finance its public expenditures and foreign payments. Unlike his predecessor, he faced these problems straight on. The budget deficit arose from excessive public expenditures on import subsidies, enterprise subsidies, subsidized credits, and price subsidies, which were of no social benefit. The foreign trade deficit was caused by dubious loans and arrears, and Ukraine's international reserves were minimal. A persistent problem was Ukraine's nonpayment of nontransparent purchases of natural gas from Russia and Turkmenistan, which were largely paid for with barter, such as agricultural produce and steel pipes. The European Union had delivered "food aid" to Ukraine in the form of large agricultural credits, which were not cheap and had to be repaid soon. This unnecessary "humanitarian aid" aggravated Ukraine's payments crisis. Kuchma realized that Ukraine had to cut public expenditures, discipline its imports, attract foreign grants and credits to form international reserves, defeat inflation, and introduce its national currency, the hryvnia (Kuchma 1994a, 1994b).

Today it is difficult to imagine how the Kyiv elite spoke about international financing in the summer of 1994. The dearth of international financing was so devastating that Ukrainian officials dreamed of obtaining funds from the pope or the Maltese Order. The only evident alternative to the international financial institutions was Russia, but such financing approached treason. To cut public expenditures was declared impossible and contrary to the Ukrainian economic model that everybody talked about but nobody knew what it was.

Kuchma looked through this haze and saw the IMF as his savior. The Fund's mission had arrived to help Ukraine formulate a stabilization program, and it was backed by the G-7 promise of $4 billion. The Ukrainian government, however, did not know what to ask for. Shpek asked our group to help, and Peter Boone, who had worked on IMF negotiations for the governments of Poland, Russia, and Mongolia, quickly wrote a two-page memo proposing which IMF demands Ukraine should accept and refute and what financing the government should ask for in return. Shpek took this memo to Kuchma, who made it an instruction to the government. The ministers now had a mandate from which they could negotiate with the IMF, and six weeks later Ukraine signed its first IMF agreement.

In the quiet months of August and September, Kuchma, his reform team, the IMF mission, and our group worked hard on putting together a stabilization program, which would also be a market economic reform program. The public and parliament were not involved at this stage, and Kyiv was very quiet. A harbinger of what was to come was an article by Kuchma himself in the *Financial Times* on September 30 (Kuchma 1994a), in which he laid out his reforms in considerable detail. The purpose of this article was partly to coordinate the domestic reform process in its final programmatic stages and partly to make the case for Western aid for the Ukrainian reforms.[7]

On September 29, the IMF mission and the Ukrainian government signed off on a Systemic Transformation Facility Program. It was a soft IMF program, especially designed for post-Soviet countries in transition, allowing them a budget deficit of as much as 10 percent of GDP. For the rest, Ukraine's stabilization program was sound and standard. An immediate target was to abolish import subsidies for oil and natural gas from Russia. Most prices were to be liberalized, which eliminated price subsidies. The prices of some sensitive goods and services, notably coal and rents, would be hiked only gradually. An important plank of Kuchma's reform program was privatization. At this stage, he focused on the privatization of small enterprises and the mass privatization of large enterprises, while he considered the privatization of land too politically sensitive.

Kuchma understood that Ukraine had no choice but to opt for a market economy and that Western financial assistance was important:

7. I drafted this article on instructions from Shpek, who in turn received his instructions from Kuchma, and both significantly edited it. Kuchma, of course, approved the final version.

"Ukraine has taken a resolute step toward reform, and the west took a step toward Ukraine. . . . Without this help Ukraine will not overcome crises."[8] Since Russia had taken over the entire Soviet debt, Ukraine was encumbered only with its new foreign debt of a limited $7 billion in the fall of 1994. But most of this debt was instantly due because it consisted of unregulated arrears on energy deliveries from Russia and Turkmenistan and some short-term bilateral loans ("food aid"), which required years of tedious debt relief negotiations.

In a way, Kuchma looked upon his duty as president as that of a responsible national accountant. He wanted expenditures and revenues to match both for the government and for the country. He was committed to a market economy but favored extensive state regulation, particularly in foreign trade. In early 1995 the IMF failed to persuade Kuchma to abolish export controls on grain, whose prices were fixed at a low level on the domestic market. Since this was the main stumbling block for the forthcoming stand-by agreement with the IMF, I went to see Kuchma to try to convince him. The usually nice president was not happy with my plea for price and export liberalization. He shouted at me: "Don't you understand that the whole country will be empty!" Kuchma eventually accepted the liberalization of grain exports but presumably only because the IMF made it a condition of financing.

On October 11, 1994, Kuchma gave his first presidential address to parliament. He decided to take this opportunity to present his full reform program in an hour-long speech. I managed to get a seat on the full balcony in the Rada. I could not believe my ears. The title of Kuchma's address was "On the Road of Radical Economic Reform." He explained that Ukraine needed radical market economic reform to survive as a state: "The overwhelming majority of the voters showed their commitment, not to fruitless talks about reform, but to their decisive and effective completion. . . . The acceleration of the market transformation of the economy is the only possible way out of the crisis and to economic stabilization. . . . Ukraine can confirm itself as a really independent and sovereign state only on the basis of a strong economic and social policy." He specified his reform program in all its details (Kuchma 1994b).

It was the greatest speech Kuchma ever made. To a considerable extent, it corresponded to Boris Yeltsin's great reform speech three years earlier, but Kuchma provided more specifics and less rhetoric, reflecting the differences between their personalities. The chief author was Halchynskiy, who had invited contributions from the reformers in the government, but Kuchma had approved its details. The Ukrainian parliamentarians were stunned, but they greeted Kuchma's oration with thunderous applause. Liberal Deputy Serhiy Holovatiy commented: "We've

8. "New Chief in Ukraine to Toughen Austerity," *New York Times*, October 31, 1994.

just heard a revolutionary speech of the first leader of Ukraine who really cares about our future."[9]

Kuchma mastered the moment and put his reform program to a parliamentary vote. The Rada delayed its decision, but on October 19 it approved the presidential reform program by a majority of 231 votes (Kravchuk 2001, 64). This was a comprehensive market reform and financial stabilization reminiscent of the Balcerowicz program that Poland launched in January 1990 and the Yegor Gaidar program of Russia in January 1992. The IMF endorsed the program it had already negotiated, and so did the G-7 nations. Kuchma had established a firm base for his economic reform.

Pynzenyk commented: "Skeptics may ask if society can handle more reforms. . . . But for the last seven months, when inflation started to fall, there were no strikes or other social outbursts. When we started fixing the economy the social tension appeared to ease. It is dangerous when the illness starts to sore, but it is much more dangerous to keep it inside your body without a cure. . . . Our only chance is tight monetary policy with restructuring of economy and liberalization of wages."[10]

In the fall of 1994 Kuchma seemed unstoppable, and he passed a large number of reform decisions. Most were issued as presidential or governmental decrees, but some required legislation. The most important law, on the unification and freeing of the exchange rate as well as the liberalization of almost all prices, was promulgated on November 9 with a small majority of 216 votes (Kravchuk 2001, 64).

Although Kuchma won these parliamentary votes, each was a struggle. The parliament put up the greatest resistance in two areas. It blocked the privatization of most large enterprises and intermittently decided to increase public expenditures, usually large state-subsidized credits to industry or agriculture or increased public wages and pensions. No parliamentary coalition in favor of reform had been formed, and the parliament remained as floating as ever, so it could capriciously vote for or against a proposal.

The Ukrainian economic reforms in the fall of 1994 were undertaken under the immediate direction of Kuchma, who conscientiously scrutinized and approved every significant reform. His reform team ably assisted him with their preparation. Prime Minister Masol was largely bypassed by Kuchma because Masol openly opposed the reforms and sometimes mobilized the parliament against them. Kuchma used First Deputy Prime Minister Yevhen Marchuk, who was a KGB general and former chairman of the Security Services of Ukraine, as his ally and counterweight to Masol.

9. Aleksandr Makarov, "Leonid Kuchma Suggested to Follow New Way Avoiding the 'Right Direction'," *Zerkalo nedeli*, October 15, 1994.

10. Viktor Pynzenyk, "We Have No Choice," *Zerkalo nedeli*, October 8, 1994.

The population and public opinion played no role in this reform drama, although Ukrainian public opinion favored market reforms because people realized that Russia was much better off with its market reforms and that poverty was becoming devastating in Ukraine.

Financial Stabilization and Liberalization

In December 1993 Ukraine's hyperinflation peaked at 91 percent a month.[11] The chairman of the NBU, Viktor Yushchenko, had just issued money as requested by the parliament. He suddenly realized that this was wrong and that he could stop it. He halted issuing credit without explanation or policy declaration. Monthly inflation fell to 2.1 percent in July 1994. In August 1994 the mischievous parliament realized what was going on and forced the NBU to issue large credits to agriculture as it had done every August, and these credits boosted monthly inflation to 23 percent in October.

Yushchenko's credit squeeze was a curious incident. No public or major political discussion preceded it, but it lasted for seven months. It was a silent act by one powerful individual. High inflation could be defeated, and the dwindling inflation tax had been dissipating the interests favoring high inflation (Åslund, Boone, and Johnson 1996). Otherwise Yushchenko would not have been able to beat them single-handedly. Yet to last, a stabilization program had to be comprehensive, with liberalization and fiscal adjustment (De Ménil 2000). Yuschenko had made his political reputation as the first hero of Ukrainian stabilization.

Kuchma's stabilization, initiated in November 1994, was a logical follow-up. The biggest step was the liberalization of almost all prices. Until November 1994, Ukrainian shops were nearly empty because of unrealistically low regulated prices. To buy something one usually had to go to one of the free markets. As everywhere else, the population calmly accepted price liberalization, although prices skyrocketed by 72 percent in November 1994. Prices that were socially very sensitive were hiked gradually, namely rents, energy prices for households, and public transportation. By 1996 these prices had been raised 15 times to a cost recovery ratio of 60 percent. The liberalization was so far-reaching that shortages ended almost instantly, and the agricultural market was reinvigorated (Shpek 2000, 31). Domestic trade was basically free, even if the old state-owned wholesale organizations persisted and initially reduced competition.

Another important step was to unify the exchange rate and liberalize currency exchange. Kyiv was suddenly full of exchange booths. In old

11. Major sources of this section are De Ménil (1997, 2000), Kravchuk (2002), Kuzio (1997), Pynzenyk (2000), Shpek (2000), and Yushchenko (2000).

Soviet fashion, as Shpek (2000, 31) put it, "Ukraine had a number of widely differing exchange rates, with large subsidies going to those least in need, in particular to major importers of energy." Incredibly, the state subsidized natural gas imports from Russia, which boosted imports and Ukraine's foreign indebtedness, and the subsidy went into the offshore accounts of a few gas traders. The abolition of this subsidy also reduced the budget deficit. In the absence of significant reserves or any stabilization fund, the exchange rate was allowed to float, and the currency was traded daily on the Ukrainian Inter-Bank Currency Exchange. Money came alive.

Formally, Ukraine already had a rather liberal import regime without any quantitative restrictions on imports because, as in other postcommunist countries, everybody yearned to overcome the dearth of goods, and the very low exchange rate was an effective barrier to imports. However, Kuchma liberalized imports further through a presidential decree that created the Commission on Import Regulations, which was authorized to change import rules. The average import tariff was only 5 percent, although tariffs for a few goods were as high as 60 percent. Unfortunately, this regulation of customs tariffs through decree allowed for arbitrary and frequent changes in tariffs.

As in other postcommunist countries, export tariffs and quotas were far more difficult to abolish because powerful rent seekers exploited them for their foreign trade arbitrage, particularly in the important steel exports. The government issued a decree on the liberalization of export operations, which drastically reduced the number of goods subject to export quotas and licenses, but export controls were maintained for such essential goods as grain, coal, scrap metals, and pig iron. These few remaining export barriers have remained persistent bones of contention. The export quota for grain was eliminated in the fall of 1995, but it was repeatedly resurrected. The new Ministry of External Economic Relations was a fortress of rent seeking and corruption. Its senior staff were reportedly charging private commissions for the issuing of quotas and other services. It responded to the liberalization of exports by introducing bureaucratic and unjustified registration of export contracts, but it was abandoned at the request of the IMF at the beginning of 1996.

Tax rates were untenably high. Through a presidential decree, on September 13, 1994, Kuchma reduced the maximum personal income tax from 90 to 50 percent, which was still too high. As nobody paid this confiscatory tax, the revenue effect of the tax cut could only be positive. At the end of 1994, as the parliament promulgated a Law on the Taxation of Enterprise Profit, the equally confiscatory tax on the gross income of enterprises, which did not allow any deductions, was replaced with a moderate corporate profit tax of 30 percent for most enterprises. Yet the profit tax remained confiscatory because few business expenditures were deductible. On March 22, 1995, the parliament reduced the value-added tax rate from 28 percent (the highest in the world) to 20 percent, but it maintained exemptions for the large privileged sectors, agriculture and energy (Dabrowski, Luczyński, and Markiewicz 2000, 123). These tax rates were still far too high for such a poor and corrupt state.

Reforms, however, did not touch the social sector. Education and medical care costs kept up as a share of GDP, but no structural reforms were undertaken, so the overcentralized, inefficient Soviet system persisted. The intention was to introduce a targeted social safety net, but because of the near absence of reformers in the social sphere, little could be done. Kuchma tried to hold back on social expenditures, but the parliament hiked wages by four to six times, doubled pensions, and tripled social security payments in opposition to him in October 1994 (Kravchuk 2002, 64; Malysh 2000).

Kuchma exceeded all expectations with this reform. He was elected on the same day that Aleksandr Lukashenko was in Belarus, and some Western commentators drew parallels between them, arguing that they reflected pro-Russian and populist sentiments in the region, but they chose different paths. Kuchma's liberalization of trade and prices went further than that in Russia in January 1992. His deregulation of November 1994 marked Ukraine's decisive transition to a market economy.

The budgetary adjustment was impressive. Public expenditures declined by no less than 11 percent of GDP from 1994 to 1996, and the budget deficit shrank from 8.7 percent of GDP in 1994 to an acceptable 3.2 percent of GDP in 1996 (figure 3.1). Inflation declined substantially but slowly from 401 percent in 1994 to 182 percent in 1995, 40 percent in 1996, and finally 10 percent in 1997 (figure 3.2). In effect, price stabilization was attained in June 1996, one-and-a-half years after its start. It could have been done faster, but it was accomplished.

The financial stabilization had multiple positive effects on the economy. Although the output contraction did not end, it slowed down. From late 1994, the real exchange rate of the national currency rose steadily, and in 1996 the nominal exchange rate stabilized. By March 1995 the financial credibility of the Ukrainian government had improved sufficiently to enable the Ministry of Finance to issue treasury bills, which partially financed the budget deficit (Pynzenyk 2000).

Currency Reform, September 1996

The Ukrainian dream of a national currency, the hryvnia, remained unfulfilled, but the primitive printed coupon, the *karbovanets*, had in effect become a national currency. In the Kuchma team, NBU chairman Yushchenko and Deputy Prime Minister Pynzenyk conceptualized the currency reform. They wanted the hryvnia to be introduced as proof of the completion of Ukraine's financial stabilization.

Figure 3.1 Ukraine's consolidated state budget deficit, 1994–99

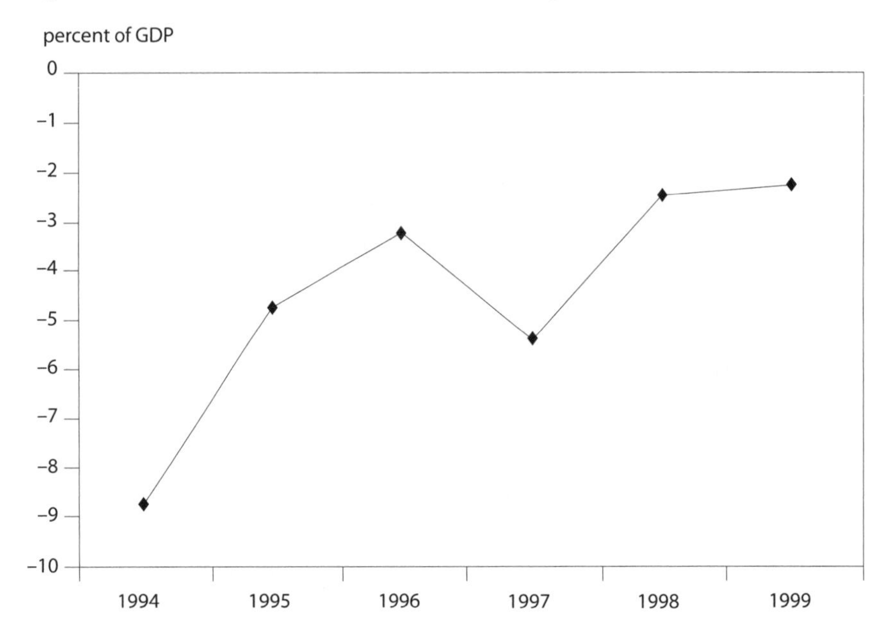

Source: European Bank for Reconstruction and Development online database, www.ebrd.com (accessed on August 31, 2007).

To imbue confidence in Ukrainians about their national currency, it had to be ensured that money exchange was not confiscatory and that people had sufficient time to exchange all their money, whether on bank accounts or in cash. Ukrainians had repeatedly suffered from confiscatory currency reforms, in January 1991 and again in July 1993, when the ruble zone really ended. New, elegant hryvnia bank notes with historical Ukrainian personalities had already been printed in Canada in 1992 and were ready for use.

In July 1995 Kuchma announced that Ukraine would introduce the hryvnia no later than that October. The NBU had already accumulated international reserves of $2 billion, which was considered sufficient. Inflation was still high but falling. However, Kuchma's statement was premature. It unleashed panic selling of existing *karbovantsy* as people bought dollars, presuming that not all *karbovantsy* would be exchanged for hryvnia. In order to calm the panic, the authorities had to delay the introduction of the hryvnia until 1996.

In the summer of 1996 monthly inflation approached zero, and the situation appeared ripe. On August 24, Ukraine's fifth anniversary of independence, Kuchma announced the introduction of the hryvnia and instantly issued a presidential decree that clarified all the details of its introduction to avoid new panic. From September 2–16, all cash *karbovantsy*

Figure 3.2 Ukraine's inflation rate (consumer price index), 1994–99

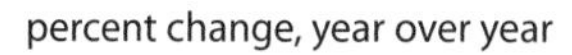

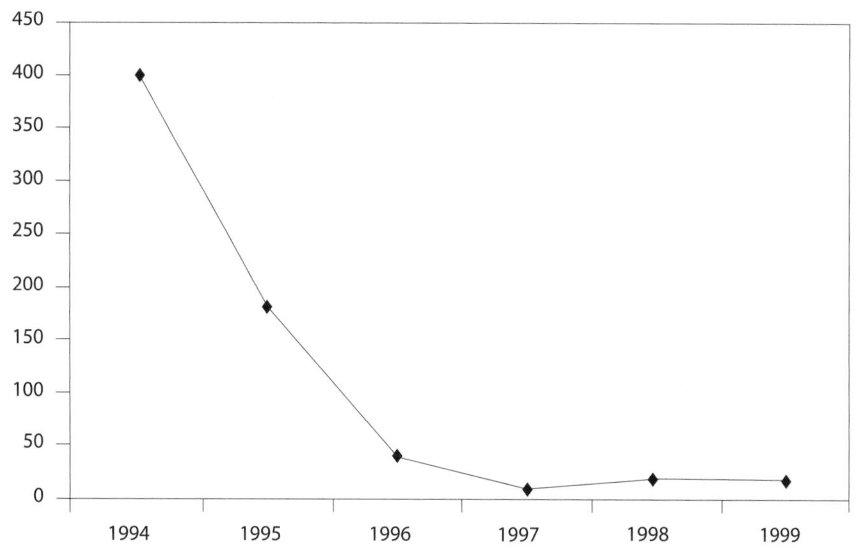

Source: European Bank for Reconstruction and Development online database, www.ebrd.com (accessed on August 31, 2007).

could be exchanged in unlimited amounts at a rate of 100,000 *karbovantsy* for one hryvnia. Bank accounts were given two weeks of extra time. The exchange rate was chosen so that $1 would purchase almost 2 hryvnia. The NBU had planned the distribution of the new currency well. It undertook a major propaganda campaign to make sure that everyone knew what to do, and the currency exchange took place perfectly (Kuzio 1997, 150–51; Kravchuk 2002, 71).

Economically, this exchange of currency meant little because the *karbovanets* had already assumed all the properties of a national currency, but the public perceived it as provisional. Like the *karbovanets*, the hryvnia was convertible on current account but not on capital account. Psychologically and politically, however, the introduction of the hryvnia was important. It showed that Ukraine was a permanent nation with a lasting national currency, not to be absorbed by the ruble zone.

At the same time, the exchange rate regime changed. Ukraine moved from a free float to a currency band within which the hryvnia was supposed to stay stable in relation to the dollar in order to moderate exchange rate fluctuation. The arrangement had been agreed with the IMF in line with the Russian example, and it was to last until the fall of 1998. Yushchenko emerged as the national hero who had given the country its national currency.

Privatization Takes Off

Privatization aroused more popular interest and controversy than any other reform, and no reform was more complex.[12] As elsewhere, the public initially favored all kinds of privatization because they wanted to acquire public property at little or no cost, but popular expectations were exaggerated and contradictory.

People wanted privatization to be just, by which most meant egalitarian, transparent, and comprehensible, and they aspired to substantial personal revenues. Many enterprises had sharply reduced their production after the fall of the Soviet Union. The popular view was that privatization would raise their productivity and utilize their full production capacity, although an essential objective of privatization was structural change through bankruptcy and liquidation of obsolete, value-detracting factories. Finally, privatization was supposed to end the economic crisis within a couple of years and develop a new middle class of entrepreneurs. With such high expectations, people could be nothing but disappointed, and they were (Paskhaver and Verkhovodova 2006).

The first task was actually to nationalize all Soviet or all-union enterprises, transferring them to the Ukrainian state. It was quickly and effectively accomplished through the early adoption, on September 10, 1991, of the Law on Enterprises, Institutions and Organizations of Union Subordination Located on the Territory of Ukraine.

Privatization was subject to more early legislation than any other economic issue, but poor and contradictory legislation impeded privatization. In early 1991 two basic laws on private enterprise were promulgated. The Law on Entrepreneurial Activity was passed on February 7, 1991. The important Law on Enterprises of March 27, 1991 replaced a prior Soviet law and guaranteed state enterprise managers independence and quasi-property rights of "their" enterprises, so that all privatization had to be negotiated with managers.

On August 19, 1991, the first day of the abortive August coup in Moscow, the cabinet of ministers of Ukraine adopted a resolution to set up the State Property Fund of Ukraine, which was Ukraine's ministry of privatization. It was given broad authority on both policy on and procedures for privatization. But since the State Property Fund was subordinate to both president and parliament, it was caught in a tug of war, which persists. The president appoints the chairman of the fund, but the parliament must confirm the appointment. This double subordination left the chairman accountable to nobody, which impeded privatization and generated corruption scandals.

12. Major sources of this section are Frydman et al. (1993), Yekhanurov (2000), Paskhaver and Verkhovodova (2006), and Kuzio (1997, 153–64).

On September 19, 1991, the Law on Economic Partnerships (Associations and Organizations) was enacted and remained the only corporate law in Ukraine until the adoption of the civil code in 2003. It laid down the rules for joint stock companies and other legal entities but did so in a rudimentary and partially flawed fashion, which later facilitated corporate raiding. For example, a minority shareholder with one single share was entitled to all information about an enterprise, which could be used for blackmail.

In the spring of 1992 the Ukrainian parliament adopted a series of key laws on privatization. The fundamental Law on the Privatization of Property of State-Owned Enterprises was passed on March 4. It was followed on April 12 by the Law on the Privatization of Small State Enterprises. Another essential law was the Law on Leasing of State-Owned Enterprises and Organizations of April 10.

In July 1992 the parliament approved the first State Program for the Privatization of State Enterprises, which became the main policy directive. It stated three major goals of privatization: to change the ownership of the means of production, create a social group of property owners, and foster competition. The program divided enterprises into six categories depending on their book value and character, prescribing different methods of privatization for each category. It stipulated that privatization certificates or vouchers be issued for mass privatization, and the Law on Privatization Certificates was promulgated.

Despite all this legislation, little happened. Ukraine had no strong privatizer. The State Property Fund had little authority, and it took a long time for it to develop its regional and local administration. The parliament regularly interfered in privatization decisions, usually blocking them. Rules were complex and contradictory. The managers who controlled the state enterprises preferred to privatize firms through "leasing" to their own advantage. If no formal privatization took place, the managers gradually appropriated everything. Privatization was slow as a result, and most of it was *prikhvatizatsiya*, the grabbing of enterprises by their managers (Yekhanurov 2000).

Meanwhile, privatization vouchers were distributed through the state savings bank. About 50 million people, or 94 percent of the population, were entitled to receive privatization certificates, but they showed little interest. Most vouchers were distributed in 1995, but by the end of the year only 28.5 million or 55 percent of the population had received them (State Property Fund of Ukraine 1996). Citizens could either use these certificates themselves to bid in a privatization auction or transfer them to an investment trust licensed by the State Property Fund. Like the Czechs, but unlike Russians, Ukrainians were not allowed to sell their vouchers but could transfer them to a trust or investment fund. By 1996 the State Property Fund had licensed over 600 trusts, which eventually accounted for 40 percent of all privatization certificates invested in privatization.

The corporatization of state enterprises proceeded, and in 1993 the regional privatization administration was established. A momentum was building, and in 1994 privatization speeded up. Only 30 enterprises were privatized in 1992, 3,600 in 1993, and 8,000 in 1994, but State Property Fund Chairman Yuriy Yekhanurov assessed that 80 percent of these privatizations occurred through leasing at minimal cost. Curiously, privatization evolved faster in the more left-wing east than in the west, contrary to expectations, and relatively few small enterprises were privatized, which reflected the dominating insider privatization by managers (Kuzio 1997, 156–57; Yekhanurov 2000).

One of Kuchma's main goals was to expedite privatization, and Yekhanurov was his answer to Russia's Anatoly Chubais. During the following two and a half years, Yekhanurov secured the success of Ukraine's privatization.

Yekhanurov (2000, 194–95, 209–13) analyzed the main sources of resistance against privatization. The parliament was ardently left-wing, with a minority opposed to privatization. Local authorities were reluctant to privatize because of insufficient incentives, as most revenues went to the central government. The branch ministries were inevitable enemies, since privatization deprived them of their enterprises, so they had to be weakened and steamrolled. The state enterprise managers formed the most powerful and intricate force. They did not oppose privatization, but they wanted it to be slow to reap the maximum wealth from it. Yekhanurov tried to align the powers in favor of privatization.

On July 29, 1994, the parliament passed a moratorium on privatization out of spite, which lasted until December 7, when it instead issued a list of some 5,400 enterprises exempt from privatization. Yekhanurov argued that the communists had been emboldened by their success in the parliamentary elections. For the next few years, the government tried to slim this list down, but the parliament resisted, extending it to 6,000. Even in 1999, no less than 1,600 enterprises were excluded from privatization (ICPS 1999b, 42).

Privatization really took off in 1995, when privatization of 16,265 enterprises was started, 80 percent of which were small firms. Of the over 3,000 large and medium-sized enterprises that started selling shares, 1,445 sold more than 50 percent (State Property Fund of Ukraine 1996). After the resistance against the privatization of small shops was broken, it was quickly completed in 1996, as everybody wanted to get their piece of the action, which facilitated its completion. Employees bought predominantly small shops and workshops for a symbolic amount, though a significant share was auctioned to the highest bidder.

With considerable political skills and good technical assistance from numerous Western advisers financed by USAID and the World Bank, Yekhanurov untangled the many knots that hindered privatization. His foremost adviser was Oleksandr Paskhaver. As Yeltsin did in Russia,

Kuchma moved privatization forward through presidential decrees rather than legislation.

The privatization of large and medium-sized enterprises was technically more difficult and politically controversial. These privatizations occurred mainly through three methods: insider privatization, voucher privatization, and external sales. Most of the property was given away for next to nothing to managers and employees. In 1998 managers owned 17.5 percent of the stocks of privatized industrial enterprises and employees 47 percent, which was more than in Russia. In reality, the managers controlled a large chunk of the workers' stocks. The initial Ukrainian privatization did not promote new or strong owners intent on serious restructuring but nebulous insider ownership. As a result, even in 1999, no significant difference in performance between privatized and state-owned industrial enterprises was apparent (Estrin and Rosevear 1999, ICPS 1999a).

Voucher privatization officially ended in mid-1997. It was followed by cash privatization, with enterprises being sold to outside investors, domestic or foreign. Such privatizations were always slow and controversial, accused of intentionally too low prices and kickbacks (Åslund 2007a).

The European Bank for Reconstruction and Development (EBRD) assessed that the share of Ukraine's GDP originating in the private sector rose from 15 percent in 1993 to 55 percent in 1997 (figure 3.3). The predominance of private enterprise in Ukraine was secured. Ukrainian privatization started two to three years later than in Poland and Russia, and it persistently lagged behind, reaching Russia's level only in 2005, when Russia reverted to renationalization. This was no stellar performance, but a great catch-up started from 1994.

In the end, privatization worked. According to the EBRD, the private sector has accounted for 65 percent of Ukraine's GDP since 2002; the real number is probably significantly higher, on the order of 80 percent (Paskhaver and Verkhovodova 2006, 3). The Ukrainian government claimed that its privatization made 15 million citizens into shareholders. Yet, most of this ownership was illusory, consisting of only a few shares that could not be traded, returned no yield, and offered no influence. As in other postcommunist countries, privatization of large enterprises has steadily become less popular, while privatization of small enterprises is more endearing, and private entrepreneurship is increasingly appreciated. The investment trusts disappeared with few traces, but many scandals, enraging their victims. Privatization alone could not resolve the economic crisis but was a precondition for its resolution.

In the summer of 1994 many feared that Ukraine would fail in its efforts to privatize, as neighboring Belarus did. Three years later, however, the victory was evident. Through his exquisite political and administrative skills, Yekhanurov secured privatization, and unlike most ministers of privatization in the postcommunist world, he has not been seriously

Figure 3.3 Share of GDP from private enterprise, 1991–2007

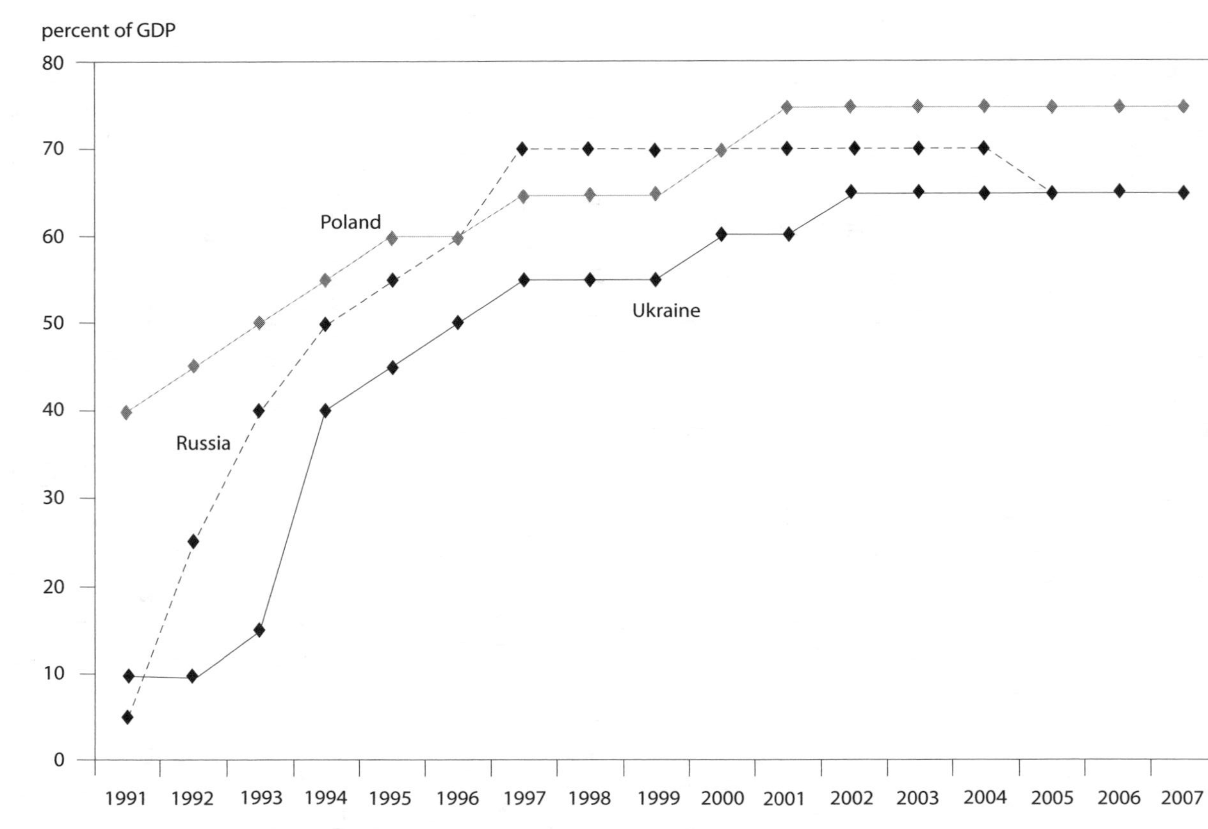

Source: European Bank for Reconstruction and Development online database, www.ebrd.com (accessed on September 16, 2008).

accused of corruption. He proved himself to be a major politician who was effective and a capable negotiator rather than a rousing orator.

Yet, enterprise restructuring did not take off for years. The main beneficiaries initially were the red directors, who mostly did not know how to run their enterprises under market conditions. We conducted an enterprise survey and found that many factories had lost both electricity and telephone connections, but substandard old managers remained.

In July 1996 I traveled around and looked at enterprises in Kherson oblast. It was a sad sight. Old managers had gained ownership control in most cases. I especially remember one old juice factory. It looked like a ruin and barely worked. The manager had ample stocks of unsold goods. His storage was divided into two parts, and in one of them he had stored salaries in kind for his poor staff, which they had not taken out. He also had ample uninstalled expensive Western equipment lying for years, but he refused to sell it, claiming it was the factory's future.

The saddest scene was in a village with a factory that produced construction elements of reinforced concrete. A concrete element as large as a room's wall stood in front of literally every house in the village, as compensation for unpaid wages, and the impoverished villagers hoped to hawk these elements to rare passers-by. No real restructuring could start until these useless owners sold the factories or were forced into bankruptcy.

In 1996 the Ukrainian government tried to innovate by killing two birds with one stone. A persistent public complaint was that bank savings had been inflated away from 1990 to 1993. At the same time, the demand for enterprises was limited. On November 24, 1995, inspired by Pynzenyk, Kuchma attempted to resolve both problems by issuing a decree that promised citizens of Ukraine a new kind of privatization vouchers—compensation certificates—for their lost savings. These certificates would be distributed starting in February 15, 1996. They would be freely tradable and could be used for the privatization of state property. However, these compensation certificates never gained popularity, and the actual compensation every year was minuscule. The government attained neither objective. Instead, it reinforced people's conviction that the state should reimburse their lost savings.

Adoption of the New Constitution, June 1996

Since independence, Ukraine has suffered from an acute constitutional dilemma.[13] Its constitutional development has been path-dependent, determined by the starting point, the Soviet Ukrainian Constitution of 1978.

13. D'Anieri (2006) offers an excellent analysis of Ukraine's constitutional order and evolution, while Kuzio (1997, 99–136) provides ample details.

In 1977 the Soviet Union adopted its new "Brezhnev" Constitution. Like other Soviet republics, Ukraine received a similar constitution designed in Moscow the next year. Since communism was contemptuous of law on ideological grounds, the exact provisions of the constitution were given little thought and were arbitrary. After the republican elections in 1990, the Ukrainian parliament assumed real life, and its rule book was the 1978 Soviet Ukrainian Constitution.

This constitutional design was quite peculiar. It confused legislative, executive, and judicial powers and rendered the parliament sovereign. In these regards, the Soviet constitution was reminiscent of mid-18th century aristocratic European constitutional order in Poland or Sweden, which led to corruption and paralyzed decision making. In Poland, the paralysis ended with the country's partition in 1772, while corruption in Sweden led to a popular royal coup. Charles de Secondat Montesquieu [1748] resolved this dilemma through a clear division of powers, but Leonid Brezhnev ignored his wisdom.

Nor was the constitution stable, as two-thirds majority could change the constitution instantly. The salvation was that no group ever enjoyed a constitutional majority (unlike the Russian parliament under Speaker Ruslan Khasbulatov in 1993).

In the fall of 1991, the introduction of the offices of president and prime minister changed the situation. The two new posts brought about some checks and balances, and the political strife became a struggle between president, prime minister, and parliamentary speaker, although the dominant feud raged between president and parliament.

As a consequence of the strategic compromise between Rukh, which focused on independence, and the Nomenklatura, which nurtured its own power, Ukraine did not experience any revolution, only national liberation. The centrist Nomenklatura under Kravchuk maintained power. Apart from the president, the main elected officials were the parliament of March 1990, and that predemocratic election determined the nature of Ukraine's post-Soviet polity (Roeder 1994).

The literature on democratization emphasizes the importance of early founding elections with a strong role of political parties to strengthen political parties, parliament, and democracy (McFaul 2001). Unfortunately, Ukraine held no new parliamentary elections until 1994. As Paul D'Anieri (2006, 72) notes: "This gave existing elites plenty of time to make the transition to the new system, and to put rules in place that would make it more difficult to oust them." Consequently, the rules in the parliamentary elections in 1990 and 1994 remained essentially the same.

The outcome was a dysfunctional political order. After a political honeymoon in the spring of 1992, legislative ability dried up. The president, prime minister, and parliament ended up in an indeterminate quarrel that blocked both legislation and implementation. The same kind of strife was reproduced at the level of regional governments, and the relationship between the central and regional governments was confused.

Throughout the Kravchuk period, futile attempts were made at adopting a new constitution. For Kuchma, the constitution was his top priority. To strengthen his own power, he wanted strong presidential powers with vertical executive command also in the regions and a unitary state, as did the national democrats, who aspired to a mighty Ukrainian state. The communists, with their impressive standing in the parliament and the east, on the contrary, wanted potent parliamentary and regional powers.

Kuchma was determined to bully the parliament into a constitutional compromise, and he persisted with repeated attempts. In November 1994 he presented a draft Law on State Power and Local Self-Government, which the parliament finally adopted after multiple amendments on May 18, 1995. In the process, two contentious clauses were removed—the right of parliament to impeach the president and the president's prerogative to dissolve parliament—but the law did not solve much. In June 1995 Kuchma escalated his conflict with the parliament by issuing a decree on a referendum, but the parliament immediately vetoed his decree because Kuchma enjoyed greater popularity than the parliamentary majority. Some centrists resolved the impasse by pursuing a constitutional agreement, which was adopted by parliament and signed by both president and Speaker Oleksandr Moroz on June 8. It was described as a mini constitution.

Kuchma had recorded a minor victory, but he did not ease the pressure on the parliament because he wanted a real constitution. By threatening a referendum again, he managed to persuade the left-wing parliamentarians to compromise on a new constitution after an all-night session on June 28, 1996. No less than 316 deputies—that is, more than the necessary two-thirds majority—voted for the new constitution, although most communists and some socialists opposed it.

The 1996 constitution was a major victory for Kuchma. The cabinet of ministers was subordinate to the president, who nominated the prime minister, subject to approval by parliament. The president appointed all ministers and regional governors, while regional councils would remain elected. Controversially, the right to private property was inscribed in the constitution. The parliament maintained the right to legislate, but the president could issue wide-ranging economic decrees and veto laws. Ukraine would remain a unitary state. Russian was acknowledged as a minority language, but Ukrainian was the sole state language.

Russia's 1993 constitution was frequently referred to in the Ukrainian constitutional debate. Both constitutions were "superpresidential," concentrating powers with the president, but varied greatly. Unlike the Russian constitution, the Ukrainian one was referred to as "presidential-parliamentarian," leaving a stronger role for the legislature. Ukraine was a unitary state, while Russia was a federation, which meant that Ukraine was more centralized. In Ukraine, the president appointed regional governors, which President Vladimir Putin introduced only in 2005.

Kuchma claimed his main purpose with the new constitution was to intensify economic reforms but after his victory he lost interest in them. With reinforced executive power, he no longer needed to react to popular pressure. Moreover, executive control over law enforcement, especially the prosecutor general, was reinforced, and judicial reform received little attention. Nor was anything done to strengthen the weak political parties. Executive power was far too centralized in the old Soviet fashion, and Kyiv indulged in petty tutelage.

On the whole, Ukraine moved from political disorganization to excessive presidential powers. The country needed stronger checks and balances. A final problem was that the new constitution left many key questions to be determined by law. As a consequence, the parliament could change many constitutional conditions instantly through a two-thirds majority. Therefore they were never really resolved because the parliament could revoke any decision it made.

Economic Policy Reversal

On March 1, 1995 Kuchma finally managed to retire Prime Minister Masol, who had persistently opposed his reforms together with the communists. In his place, Kuchma appointed his ally, First Deputy Prime Minister Yevhen Marchuk, as prime minister, whom the parliament easily confirmed.

Kuchma gave his second annual address to parliament on April 4, 1995.[14] He had many reforms to be proud of. His reform team had hardened from principled battle for market economy, financial stabilization, and privatization, but his speech marked a policy reversal.

Kuchma broke with his line starting in October 1994, criticizing backers of a "blind monetarist policy." Instead, he returned to his old tune of "state-regulated transition to a social-market economy." The economic reforms must be state regulated and generate a social safety net. None of these ideas directly contradicted the reforms under way, but the emphasis had moved from finances and deregulation to production and social goals.

In June 1995 Kuchma specified his policy correction. The IMF target of 1 to 2 percent monthly inflation at the end of 1995 was dropped for 4 to 5 percent. Admittedly, the IMF targets had been overoptimistic, but Kuchma's weakening of the macroeconomic policy contributed to the de-

14. The main source of this section is Kuzio (1997, 144–49).

lay of financial stabilization and renewed economic growth. Once again, top officials started talking about that mythical Ukrainian economic model, which was supposed to deliver everything and demand nothing. On October 11, 1995, one year after Kuchma's great reform speech, the parliament celebrated by approving a new government program on evolutionary economic reform. It was an old-style program of 116 pages that covered every conceivable aspect without identifying priorities.

Kuchma's reversal surprised his reform team. Why would he abandon a policy when it was succeeding? Three factors drove him in this direction. First, Kuchma was never a free trader. He believed in financial stabilization, private enterprise, and certain deregulation, but he was a mercantilist. He had gone further in liberal rhetoric than he felt comfortable with to get the main tasks done. Once he felt convinced of market economic success, he could revert to his real beliefs. After having averted the immediate threats, it was all too easy to revert to complacency. Kuchma (2003, 190) explained:

> Sometimes I had to apply "manual management" to the economy and finances. It is not normal in theory, but it was a savior in reality. For example, to eliminate debts in pension payments we had to increase the tax burden on expensive and luxury consumer goods substantially. After a careful analysis I understood that it was the only way out and signed a decree.
>
> After direct regulation was abandoned, the Ukrainian government couldn't find any tools to affect the economy that would be accepted in a market economy for a long time.

A second factor was corruption. When Kuchma took over power in July 1994, the profoundly corrupt Kravchuk administration marched out. Notable departures from the circle of power were Yukhym Zviahilskiy, the gas trader Ihor Bakai, and the metals trader Vadym Rabinovich, probably the richest people in Ukraine at the time. Soon, however, these corrupt characters returned, and Bakai became a pivotal power player. The substantial presidential powers aggravated corruption in Kuchma's circle as well, which was particularly noticeable in commodity trade.

A third reason for Kuchma's policy reversal was that the political pressure overwhelmingly came from the left in the parliament, which constituted the best organized and publicly most vocal group. Kuchma fought them but did not want to alienate them altogether and so compromised from time to time, thus finding his powers constrained. After most of the economic reform was done, Kuchma could turn his attention to constitutional reform, which required a compromise with some left-wingers.

This sudden policy reversal revealed five flaws in Kuchma's economic reforms. First, Kuchma's attitude toward market reforms was not an ideological commitment but a pragmatic one. He saw himself as a man who solved one problem after the other, and market reforms formed one set of tools. Therefore, he was not really concerned with the consistency of the new economic system, which is most evident in his treatment of foreign trade.

Second, the reforms were undertaken by a small group of technocrats without major changes of the government or policymakers. The old *apparat* just waited for a moment of peace when they could reverse the reforms.

Third, many of the reforms were undertaken by decree and not legislated. Unlike laws, decrees lacked consistency and could easily be changed. Many were (Protsyk 2004; Remington, Smith, and Haspel 1998).

Fourth, the Ukrainian legislature remained a marsh that could be swayed in any direction, and its main director was not Kuchma but socialist speaker Oleksandr Moroz, who exploited any opportunity to take Ukraine to the left.

Fifth, the reforms had not been accompanied by any major public education campaign or broader public discussion. Kuchma had utilized his political capital from his presidential election victory, but nobody had really explained the reforms to the population. The World Bank and USAID actually undertook the main public education campaigns. The public neither understood nor believed in a market economy.

To conclude, the problem was not only Kuchma's wavering conviction but also that consistent market economic thinking stayed marginal and the political and constitutional foundation for comprehensive reform remained weak. Capitalist ideology was too weak, though no real alternative was apparent, and all along corruption was a dangerous underlying force.

Limited but Effective International Assistance

Kuchma's rise enabled the Ukrainian government to utilize the international assistance on offer, but for international assistance organizations, Ukraine was a challenge. Few Ukrainian officials spoke foreign languages, and few foreign officials spoke Ukrainian or Russian. For most foreigners but the Ukrainian diaspora, Ukraine was terra incognita. Many Ukrainian officials did not know their new jobs very well—which was why they needed assistance—but few knew how to interact with foreign officials. The first three failed years of Ukrainian independence had left many Westerners cynical, but Kuchma's reform team revived Western interest.

The IMF took the lead in macroeconomic policy and liberalization through Managing Director Michel Camdessus's trip to Kyiv in July 1994 and his ambition to conclude an early stabilization program. The IMF provided substantial financing, disbursing $356 million in 1994, $1.2 billion in 1995, and $777 million in 1996. Altogether the IMF disbursed no less than $3.5 billion from 1994 to 1999, and it became the financial guardian of Ukraine (Åslund 2002, table 10.7).

The United States paid great attention to Ukraine for at least three reasons. First, Ukraine was a loose pawn geopolitically, which could go in any direction, and it was a potentially powerful country strategically located in Europe. Second, Ukraine was a nuclear power that reneged on its nuclear forces to the enormous gratitude of the Pentagon. Finally, the Ukrainian diaspora comprised an important constituency in the United States, whose members were concentrated in the so-called swing states in the midwest that could vote either for a Republican or a Democratic US presidential candidate.

Hence, Ukraine received more top-level American than European visitors. US Vice President Al Gore took a special interest in Ukraine and visited it repeatedly, being the second major international visitor after Camdessus to go to Kyiv after Kuchma's election. The United States and Ukraine formed a high-level Gore-Kuchma Commission on the model of the Gore-Chernomyrdin Commission with Russia, signifying the great US official attention to Ukraine.

The United States gave priority to economic assistance to Ukraine, establishing a huge USAID mission in Kyiv. From 1994 through 2000, USAID committed nearly $1.5 billion in grant assistance to Ukraine, slightly more than $200 million a year (Åslund 2002, table 10.5). In 1995–96, Ukraine was the third largest recipient of US foreign assistance after Israel and Egypt. The main success of USAID in Ukraine was the revival of the privatization program under Yekhanurov, which required extensive Western consultancy and which the World Bank also assisted. Another major achievement of USAID was the drafting of hundreds of laws, most of which are still lying in the archives of the Rada. Yet when any draft law was requested, USAID had usually already produced one, which was quite convenient.

The World Bank was the key actor in Ukraine's structural reforms, but apart from privatization, not much happened. One odd exception was an electricity reform that was carried out before vested interests woke up (Lovei 1998b). The World Bank was supposed to provide the international lead in social reforms, but little could be done because of the absence of Ukrainian counterparts with any interest in reforms. By and large, officials in the social sector just asked for more money and no structural changes. The World Bank committed loans of $2.8 billion from 1996 through 1999, but its disbursements might have been half that amount (Åslund 2002, table 10.8).

Ukraine also developed a substantial number of nongovernmental organizations, most of which were started with seed money from George Soros, who also cofinanced most major education and training initiatives.[15]

15. I represented George Soros on the International Advisory Board of the Economics Education and Research Consortium from the outset in 1996, and I am currently co-chairman of its continuation, the Kyiv School of Economics. Soros has expressed his reasons for assisting postcommunist countries, for example, in Soros (1991).

Surprisingly little foreign government aid went into serious education, while many short courses for policymakers and legislators were undertaken. As a result, Ukraine suffers from a great scarcity of qualified labor.

The European Union could have been expected to play a major role in its backyard, but it did not. From 1991 until 1998, the European Union committed 422 million euros in technical assistance to Ukraine, though actual disbursement might have been about half that amount (Åslund 2002, table 10.6). Moreover, EU assistance was oriented toward political idiosyncrasies in EU member states and almost entirely spent on European consultants. Therefore, EU assistance was of minimal value to Ukraine.

Four entities assisted Ukraine with its international finance gap: the IMF, the World Bank, Russia, and Turkmenistan. The IMF and the World Bank organized Ukraine's debt rescheduling and assisted it with new financing, while Russia and Turkmenistan kindly accepted the rescheduling of substantial arrears of natural gas payments.

Kuchma Saved His Country

In July 2008 I asked Kuchma to characterize himself. True to his personality, he answered with one word, "pragmatist." Oleksandr Paskhaver has elegantly summarized that Kuchma's greatest strength was what people did not like him for. He saw people exactly for what they were, neither worse nor better. His great realism helped him to act rationally, but people regretted that he did not think more highly of them.[16] Kuchma was no visionary but a deadpan realist, while Kravchuk appeared as a jovial romantic.

Kuchma has summarized his wisdom: "I know the history of Ukraine and I know the character of its people—both the strong and the weak sides. Ukrainians in general know themselves very well. We praise ourselves less than we curse ourselves. And what do we curse ourselves for most? For the fact that there are three bosses for every two Ukrainians. You know the old saying—in a struggle for power, people are ready to destroy one another and everything around them."[17]

"What was your greatest deed?" I asked. Kuchma responded: "I saved the integrity of our country." When Kuchma was democratically elected president in July 1994, Crimea was toying with separatism. Through complex negotiations in many small steps, Kuchma peacefully exhausted this disorganized attempt at secession.

---

16. Conversation in Yalta, Crimea, July 12, 2008.

17. Radio Free Europe/Radio Liberty (RFE/RL), "Ukraine: Former President Observes 'Ukraine without Kuchma'," August 7, 2006, available at www.rferl.org (accessed on August 6, 2008).

"What else are you most proud of?" I queried. Kuchma stated the obvious: "The construction of a market economy in Ukraine and we brought about financial stabilization."

Kuchma had a clear idea of what was important and what was not. When he became president in July 1994, he focused on five major goals: financial stabilization, privatization, the integrity of Ukraine, the adoption of a new constitution, and improved relations with Russia and the United States. Impressively, within two years he had accomplished all five goals, which looked almost unattainable in July 1994.

In the summer of 1996, Ukraine had no inflation, and in September 1996 the hryvnia was fortuitously introduced. However difficult privatization was, most Ukrainian enterprises were privatized. The separatism of Crimea was peacefully averted in 1995. In June 1996 Ukraine finally adopted the new constitution with a great parliamentary majority and without major political crisis. US President Bill Clinton devoted as much attention to Ukraine as it could possibly get, and President Boris Yeltsin, Ukraine's best friend in Moscow, was reelected in July 1996. Kuchma was not only pragmatic and focused but also a remarkably successful problem solver. The Ukrainian people rewarded Kuchma with persistent support in public opinion polls, and he was an all-dominant politician.

Curiously, Kuchma satisfied the western Ukrainian constituency of national democrats far more than his original eastern and left-wing constituency. He had strengthened presidential and central state powers, he had reinforced the unitary nature of the Ukrainian state, and he did nothing to enhance the official status of the Russian language. In his books, Kuchma (2003, 2007) emphasized what he did for Ukraine's nation-building and state-building. He secured the integrity of the nation more than what Kravchuk did.

Kuchma's problem was that his political agenda was too short. His strength was a clear policy focus, but he paid little attention to topics outside his agenda. He did not seem all too disturbed by the continued economic decline. Corruption did not abate but probably grew worse, and media freedom started being undermined. Kuchma needed to renew and broaden his political agenda to make it more ambitious, but he succumbed to the temptation to rest on his laurels.

4

Kuchma's Stagnation, 1996–99

By the summer of 1996 Leonid Kuchma's strategic outlook was clouded. He had introduced elementary market economic reform and the national currency, the hryvnia. Although he desired to pursue more privatization, his reformist endeavors had to a large extent been accomplished. After long and hard work, a Ukrainian constitution was finally adopted in June 1996. National integrity seemed safer. But Ukraine's foreign policy was not settled, and no great deed, such as membership of the European Union, was within reach. Kuchma started devoting a lot of time to foreign policy. Politically, he was at his peak, but he had no real vision or major goals to accomplish. His strategy seemed to have evaporated, and tactics took its place.

As so often happens with politicians who have enjoyed early success, Kuchma focused on his own political survival, which took five expressions, best summarized as standard divide and rule with limited policy ambitions. First, he checked the power and ambitions of his prime minister. Second, he devoted great efforts to both parliamentary and presidential elections. Third, he played different business and regional groupings against one another. Fourth, he also played different branches of law enforcement against each other. Fifth, the presidential administration increasingly disciplined and controlled media. These were tactics without strategy.

This period was not pretty. In 1996–97 Pavlo Lazarenko was prime minister but acted like a businessman. Deputy Prime Minister Viktor Pynzenyk undertook a brave but hopeless attempt at renewed economic reform for the sake of economic growth. Kuchma replaced Lazarenko with the passive bureaucrat Valeriy Pustovoitenko. Kuchma's main achievements lay in his foreign policy, notably the 1997 agreements with Russia.

The main boondoggle at this time was gas trade with Russia, which augured the rise of the oligarchs. Crime continued rising, which strengthened the political role of law enforcement. Worst of all, media freedom was reduced. The parliamentary elections of March 1998 largely mimicked the 1994 elections, though they were less free. Kuchma's reelection in October–November 1999 was designed on Yeltsin's reelection in Russia in July 1996. By 1999 Ukraine appeared to be stuck in an underreform trap.

As usual Kuchma attained his main goals. He survived the parliamentary elections of March 1998 and won the presidential elections of October 1999. The problem was that he hardly had any goals but power.

Lazarenko's Excesses

In September 1995, when Yevhen Marchuk was prime minister, Kuchma appointed Pavlo Lazarenko, a strong man from his home town, Dnipropetrovsk, first deputy prime minister responsible for energy. Yet, Lazarenko was never perceived as Kuchma's close ally but as an independent force. When he became first deputy prime minister, he was only 42. He was a bull of a man, and his eyes blinked nervously, giving him a rather frightful look. He was a crude, uneducated man who had spent his first 15 years of professional life on a collective farm.

Before entering government, Lazarenko made a fortune on the natural gas trade in the Dnipropetrovsk region, and he was considered the richest man in Ukraine. He was also regional representative of the president, in an egregious conflict of interests.

As first deputy prime minister, Lazarenko's primary task was to allocate gas quotas to private companies. He gave priority to two gas trading companies: Itera, which was connected with the management of Gazprom, and United Energy Systems of Ukraine (UESU), which was headed by his diminutive business partner from Dnipropetrovsk—Yuliya Tymoshenko, only 35 years old and nicknamed the gas princess—and which he partly owned himself (Global Witness 2006, 22).[1]

He also fought successfully for the right to supervise the environmental inspection. When I investigated why, I learned that environmental inspectors extorted the largest bribes because of Ukraine's exceedingly strict Soviet environmental standards, which had been established for show and were never supposed to be applied. Ukraine's inspectors used them to extort large bribes.

---

1. In November 1996 I had the honor of hosting Yuliya Tymoshenko at a seminar at the Carnegie Endowment for International Peace in Washington during her first trip to the United States. She made a strong impression on the audience and defended her business eminently, but she argued that complex barter schemes were necessary.

On May 27, 1996, Kuchma, complaining about the absence of economic reforms, fired Marchuk and nominated Lazarenko in his place. On July 10, the parliament approved Lazarenko's appointment. When he became prime minister, the humble Volga cars outside the cabinet of ministers building were replaced by large, expensive, black Mercedes Benz cars. The previously rudimentary security was beefed up, indicating that a major clan leader had moved in.

On July 16, 1996, just six days after Lazarenko became prime minister, someone tried to blow up his car in the middle of his convoy when he was heading to Kyiv airport to fly to Donetsk. Despite its sophistication, the attempt failed. Lazarenko came out roaring, accusing the Donetsk clan of trying to murder him, which made many suspect a setup. He instantly sacked about 50 state enterprise managers in Donetsk. On November 3 Yevhen Shcherban, a leading shady businessman and parliamentarian from Donetsk, was murdered at Donetsk airport. Ukrainians reckoned that organized crime had taken over government.

Lazarenko's year-long tenure as prime minister became the epitome of corruption. He acted without inhibition, reintroducing multiple regulations which facilitated the extortion of money from businesses. His dominant business remained gas trade, which he pursued through UESU, whose regional gas monopoly was greatly extended under Lazarenko's executive power (Lovei 1998a). As an offshore company, UESU was not subject to Ukrainian taxation.

Grain export was another lucrative business. Kuchma had liberalized grain exports, but nothing could stop Lazarenko. A Ukrainian minister told me that the prime minister had written on ordinary paper to all regional governors that they were entitled to prohibit grain exports from their oblasts if they considered it necessary. Although these letters had no legal status and contradicted Ukrainian law, all governors obeyed and blocked all grain exports. Lazarenko also issued statutes prohibiting the railways and ports to export grain. The state-controlled grain procurement agency Khlib Ukrainy purchased grain surpluses at low, regulated domestic prices and exported the grain at great profit.

Lazarenko considered the privatization of big enterprises too serious to be done by anybody but the prime minister. In a nontransparent fashion, big enterprises were privatized to favored purchasers. Needless to say, apart from privatization, Lazarenko stalled all reforms and some liberalization, while he allowed public expenditures and the budget deficit to grow sharply (figure 3.1). He made any kind of policy statement.

Lazarenko harbored great political ambitions. He set up his own party, *Hromada* (Ukrainian for community), in evident opposition to Kuchma, with Yuliya Tymoshenko as its leader. Ideologically, *Hromada* was another centrist business party that desired extensive state regulation to generate rents for its business owners.

As long as Lazarenko was prime minister, he was hyperactive and appeared to have taken over from Kuchma as Ukraine's top leader. He had certainly taken charge of economic policy. Nobody could understand their mutual relationship. They both hailed from Dnipropetrovsk and their paths had crossed before. On June 19, 1997, Kuchma surprised everybody by sacking the seemingly omnipotent Lazarenko purportedly for "health reasons." In addition, he complained that Lazarenko had failed to pursue tax reform and had done nothing to enact an anticorruption program.

Lazarenko went into direct opposition to Kuchma and mobilized for the March 1998 parliamentary elections. Kuchma's associates used all means to beat Lazarenko and *Hromada*. He was subsequently accused of corruption, and a tragicomedy began.

In December 1998 Swiss police arrested Lazarenko at the border, when he tried to enter the country with a Panamanian passport. They charged him with laundering millions of dollars through bank accounts in Switzerland. He was freed on $2.6 million bail.[2] But Lazarenko escaped bail and returned to Ukraine. On February 17, 1999, the Ukrainian parliament voted by a large majority to lift his parliamentary immunity,[3] and he left the country in haste. On February 20, 1999, he tried to enter the United States through John F. Kennedy airport in New York. A *New York Times* article reported, "Lazarenko held an expired diplomatic passport and a valid tourist visa. But he was detained after immigration officials interviewed him and concluded that he had not come to the country merely for a casual visit, as the rules governing visitor visas require. . . ."[4] His lawyers claimed that he applied for political asylum, and they fought successfully against his extradition to Switzerland.

Instead, Lazarenko was arrested for laundering $114 million in the United States and accused of unlawfully receiving over $200 million from various Ukrainian businesses as prime minister. He was eventually sentenced in California in 2006 to nine years in prison for money laundering, wire fraud, and transporting stolen goods. He was also fined $10 million.[5]

When Lazarenko left the country, *Hromada* split. His right-hand woman, Yuliya Tymoshenko, left the party and founded her own

---

2. Timothy L. O'Brien, "A Palace Fit for a Fugitive and Ukraine's Ex-Premier," *New York Times*, September 1, 1999, available at www.nytimes.com (accessed on September 25, 2008).

3. Pavel Polityuk, "Ukrainian Parliament Votes 310–39 to Strip Lazarenko of Deputy's Immunity," *Ukrainian Weekly* LXVII, no. 8, February 21, 1999, available at www.ukrweekly.com (accessed on September 25, 2008).

4. Michael Wines, "Ex-Ukraine Premier, Accused of Corruption, Detained by U.S.," *New York Times*, February 23, 1999, available at www.nytimes.com (accessed on September 25, 2008).

5. Jesse McKinley, "Ukraine: 9 Years in U.S. Prison For Ex-Premier," *New York Times*, August 26, 2006; Global Witness (2006, 23).

Batkivshchyna (Fatherland) Party to distance herself from Lazarenko. She continued to lead the opposition against Kuchma, but her opposition was no longer irreconcilable as Lazarenko's had been. Meanwhile, she wound down her business and became a professional politician.

Lazarenko stands out as the greatest parasite in the history of independent Ukraine, and the only surprise is that he was so appropriately punished. I once asked socialist leader Oleksandr Moroz how that could have happened. Moroz answered: "Lazarenko made only one mistake: He did not share."

Pynzenyk's Abortive Program for Economic Growth

A basic market economy with financial sanity had been established, but economic growth remained elusive. In 1994, the year of confiscatory taxation and economic chaos, GDP plummeted by no less than 23 percent. Market economic transformation usually led to the closure of value-detracting production lacking real demand, which was reflected as a decline in official output. Therefore, a continuous fall in official GDP of 12 percent in 1995 could have been anticipated (figure 4.1).

In early 1996, however, it became evident that GDP would continue to contract by 10 percent. Lazarenko's regime had not abolished the market economy, but it had encumbered the economy with extraordinary red tape. The State Planning Committee had not reemerged, but numerous inspection agencies troubled and extorted productive business. At this time, the Polish economy was long booming with growth of 7 percent, and even the Russian economy was slowly approaching growth. Ukraine's persistent economic decline was truly shocking, but few leaders were concerned, with the exception of Viktor Pynzenyk, deputy prime minister, and Viktor Yushchenko, chairman of the National Bank of Ukraine (NBU).

The reasons for the absence of growth were all too evident: Government bureaucracy paralyzed the economy. Ukraine was mired in all conceivable and inconceivable inspections, which made entrepreneurial work just about impossible. In a pioneering work on corruption, Daniel Kaufmann (1997), the resident representative of the World Bank, found that in 1996 Ukrainian enterprise managers spent over one-third of their time with government officials, the highest in the world.

Tax inspections were outright comical. While visiting a modern Western factory in Kyiv I learned that they had seven to eight permanent tax inspectors on their premises throughout the year, who demanded office space and food. A vodka factory suffered even worse, hosting four inspectors round the clock. The resident representative of the International Monetary Fund (IMF) in Kyiv, Alexander Sundakov, explained it to me: In order to reduce the number of tax inspections, the government allowed

Figure 4.1 GDP growth, 1990–99

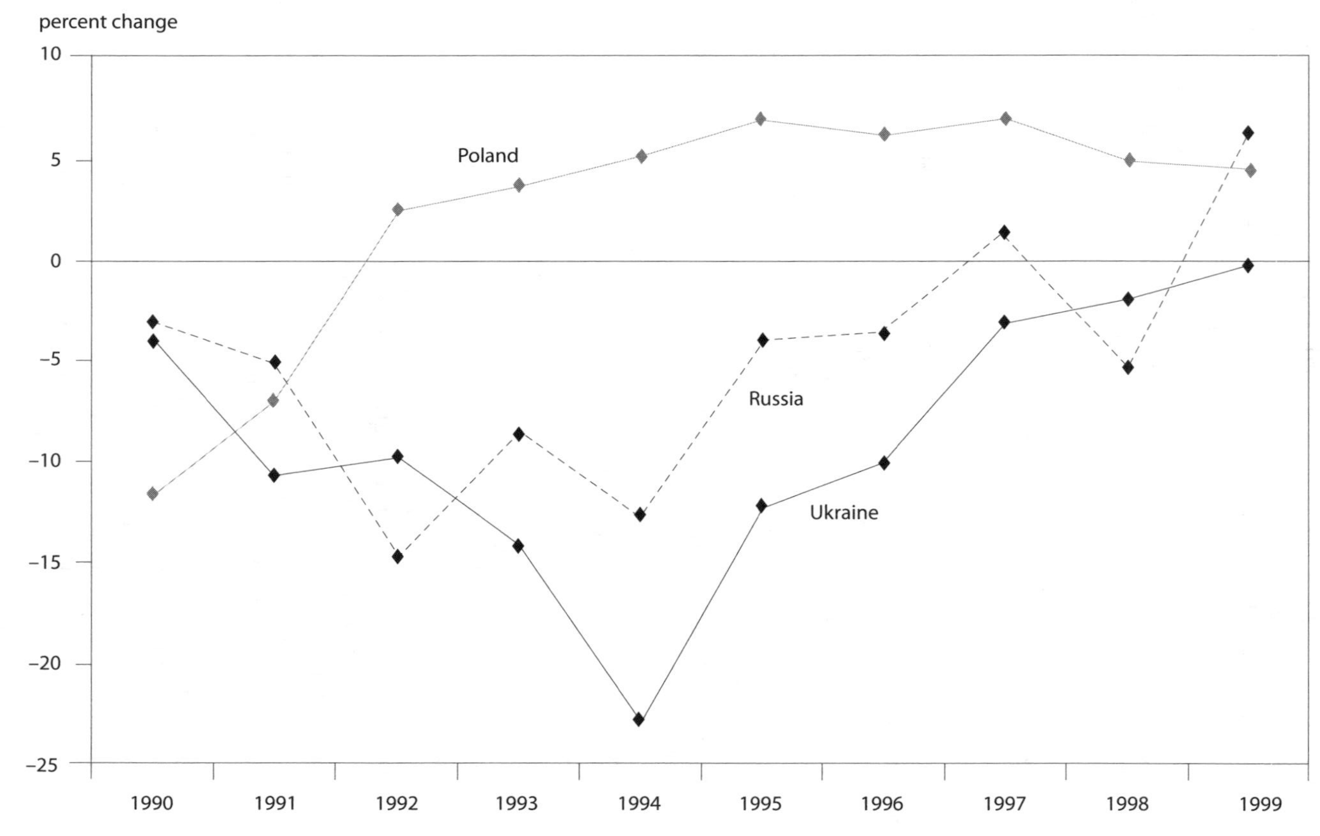

Source: European Bank for Reconstruction and Development online database, www.ebrd.com (accessed on September 16, 2008).

only one tax inspection a year, but its length was not specified. Ukraine had about 10,000 enterprises that paid significant taxes and 70,000 tax inspectors, which meant an average of 7 tax inspectors per taxpaying enterprise throughout the year.

Almost all prices had been liberalized in November 1994, but the powers of the Anti-Monopoly Committee to control monopolies had been reinforced, though its definition of monopolies was far too broad. Ukraine had four large champagne factories, and all Ukrainian champagne bottles had the same price because the Anti-Monopoly Committee regulated their prices. Every page of the menu at any restaurant was signed by both the accountant and the manager of the restaurant because the Anti-Monopoly Committee demanded it. Thus the committee was the reincarnation of the old Soviet State Price Committee, and its inspectors were as numerous as activist, extorting bribes whenever they could. Dozens of control agencies conducted similar harmful inspections. Little surprise that price stabilization had not brought about economic growth.

In the summer of 1996, desperate for the lack of concern among his colleagues, Pynzenyk initiated a reform program he called Economic Growth '97. He received overt support from President Kuchma and Prime Minister Lazarenko. Although this support was evidently not sincere, Pynzenyk went into battle. He organized dozens of Ukraine's best experts, who wrote a 134-page program for three years of reform.

Economic Growth '97 was Ukraine's most comprehensive and radical reform program to date, with detailed structural and social reforms. A large part of the program was fiscal. The tax system was supposed to be simplified with fewer and lower taxes, as well as fewer unjustified exemptions. Most of all, the high payroll tax would be cut. The treasury and payment systems would be reinforced to avoid arrears. Pynzenyk let his experts scrutinize the large social expenditures, which more often than not turned out to be pure Nomenklatura benefits. The poorest 20 percent of the Ukrainians received as little as 8 percent of all nonpension cash transfers in 1995, showing that Ukrainian social benefits were starkly regressive, giving more to the wealthy than the poor (Milanovic 1998, 113). For example, the widow of a colonel was entitled to four weeks of paid vacation at a nice resort in Crimea. The Pynzenyk package also called for a modern pension reform with part of the pension going into private accumulative savings accounts. The reform package prescribed substantial deregulation of business, especially of licensing, as well as the reduction of inspections. It advocated stricter regulation in one area, energy monopolies.

On October 15, 1996, Lazarenko presented the program to parliament. As was its habit, the parliament adopted the program itself but refuted the many draft laws that ensued. Pynzenyk realized that neither Kuchma nor Lazarenko supported him. Nor did his ministerial colleagues. Instead of giving up, Pynzenyk went on the offensive with a public relations campaign, but the parliamentarians were more interested in their own incomes than in their voters and turned down the package. Only minor changes to the value-added tax and the corporate profit tax were legislated. On April 2, 1997, Pynzenyk accepted *fait accompli* and resigned.

Although Pynzenyk failed miserably, he had formulated a strong, detailed reform agenda that became a fixture. He had become the country's leading economic reformer. Kuchma, who had done little to support his old brother-in-arms, used Pynzenyk's failure as an excuse to sack Lazarenko.

Serhiy Holovatiy, the high-profile reformist minister of justice from 1995 to 1997, experienced a similar fate. Soon after he became minister, he had Ukraine's first law on organized crime adopted, and in April 1997 he launched a program called Clean Hands, directed against corruption, not least among parliamentarian deputies. Within the elite, that was not a popular theme, and in September 1997 Kuchma sacked Holovatiy for his exuberant promotion of this program.[6]

Pustovoitenko: Passive Loyalist

On July 16, 1997, Kuchma replaced Lazarenko with Valeriy Pustovoitenko. Shockingly, a man with a seriously tainted reputation was succeeded by Ukraine's arguably greatest bureaucrat as prime minister, while corruption and bureaucracy were the country's two most severe ailments.[7] But Kuchma remained the political master.

Lazarenko was as colorful as Pustovoitenko was gray. Lazarenko was frightening; Pustovoitenko was boring. Yet both came from Dnipropetrovsk, where Pustovoitenko had been mayor, but his comparative advantage was absolute loyalty to Kuchma. After having appointed two strong prime ministers who had betrayed him to succeed him, Marchuk and Lazarenko, Kuchma desired a completely reliable prime minister. Moreover, Kuchma's goal was no longer reforms but to win the parliamentary elections in March 1998 and the presidential elections in October 1999, which was Pustovoitenko's task. Pustovoitenko returned to a government dominated by civil servants. He made no major changes, packing the government with older and grayer Soviet apparatchiki.

Once I had the misfortune to chair a dinner for Pustovoitenko with prominent international business leaders. This dinner should have been

---

6. Taras Kuzio, "Ukraine's Virtual Struggle against Corruption and Organized Crime," Radio Free Europe/Radio Liberty, Crime, Corruption, and Terrorism Watch, September 6, 2002, available at www.taraskuzio.net (accessed on October 2, 2008).

7. That day I decided to close down our Soros International Economic Advisory Group in Kyiv.

an opportunity for Ukraine's prime minister to promote his country. Instead, Pustovoitenko seemed absorbed by one salient idea: how to get out of this. He refused to talk to anybody but Yeltsin's amicable chief of staff, Yuri Petrov, who had been mayor of Sverdlovsk (now Yekaterinburg), a city confusingly similar to Dnipropetrovsk.

Kuchma's Foreign Policy

Kuchma loved foreign policy, and after he had settled crucial domestic concerns, he indulged himself in his favorite occupation. He traveled extensively, going on official visits to many countries that had had minimal contacts with Ukraine. In his election campaign, Kuchma had spoken about a multivector foreign policy, which others would call multipolar, with a desire to improve Ukraine's relations in all directions.

Ukraine's most important foreign partner was Russia, and two vital issues were outstanding: the division of the Black Sea Fleet and the status of its headquarters, Sevastopol, on Crimea. After Yeltsin's reelection in July 1996 and his prolonged treatment for a heart ailment in the fall of 1996, Yeltsin regained sufficient political and physical strength to return to his long-desired final settlement with Ukraine.

On May 28, 1997 the Ukrainian and Russian prime ministers signed three intergovernmental agreements on the division, basing, and cost of the Black Sea Fleet. By letting the prime ministers sign these controversial agreements, Yeltsin did not have to ask the Russian parliament for ratification. The fleet was finally divided, with Russia obtaining the lion's share. Formally, the fleet was divided in half, but Russia bought a large part of Ukraine's share. Ukraine leased the port facilities in Sevastopol to Russia for 20 years (until 2017) for $98 million a year. The lease could be prolonged for five more years by mutual consent. Sevastopol would remain the headquarters of the Russian Black Sea Fleet for at least 20 years. Ukraine's 1996 constitution allowed an exception for temporary presence of foreign bases on Ukrainian territory (Sherr 1997; Wolczuk 2002, 29–32, 36–38). Yet Crimea, Sevastopol, and the Black Sea Fleet are still rallying cries for Russian nationalists. In practice, Russia has paid its lease to Ukraine by netting out Ukrainian gas arrears.

As a follow-up, on May 31, 1997, Russia finally recognized Ukraine's borders by signing the Treaty on Friendship, Cooperation and Partnership between the Russian Federation and Ukraine. Repeatedly and in detail, this treaty clarifies the two countries' mutual respect for each other's territorial integrity and the inviolability of their borders. A territorial dispute that remained was the demarcation of the sea border on the Azov Sea and the Kerch Strait. Amazingly, the Ukrainian Rada did not understand that this was the best they could possibly obtain from Russia. Only on

December 25, 1998, one and a half years later, did the Rada finally ratify the treaty, after which the comparatively propresidential Russian Federation Council did the same (Rossiiskaya Federatsiya 1999). At the same time, Russia abolished all the many trade barriers it had raised against Ukraine.

These Russian-Ukrainian agreements were a great success for Kuchma and the high point of the Russian-Ukrainian relationship. Russia had accepted Ukraine's legal demand, although the Ukrainians had, of course, wanted a higher payment. Russia had reconfirmed its recognition of Ukraine's sovereignty of Crimea and Sevastopol in a ratified interstate treaty.

But Ukraine could not do much more with Russia. Cooperation with the Commonwealth of Independent States (CIS) led nowhere because Russia remained a bully, with covert neoimperialist agenda that could not appeal to any partner. As neither Russia nor Ukraine were members of the World Trade Organization (WTO), they lacked a rulebook for free trade (Olcott, Åslund, and Garnett 1999). Kuchma's view of Russia was simple: "We are doomed to live in friendship."[8]

Kuchma valued his excellent relations with the United States the most, and US-Ukrainian friendship flourished. In November 1994 Kuchma received the honor of an official visit to Washington. The *New York Times* (November 23, 1994) reported President Bill Clinton's compliments to Kuchma: "Your boldness in the face of daunting problems reminds us of one of our greatest leaders, Franklin Roosevelt, who provided leadership in a time of great hardship. You have blazed a path ahead on the two most critical issues for the future: economic reform and nuclear weapons." In May 1995 President Clinton responded with a visit to Ukraine, which became a lovefest. Vice President Al Gore was a frequent guest of Kuchma's.

The European Union was much more reserved. Its institutional cooperation with Ukraine was rudimentary. It treated Ukraine like any other CIS country, although it was a European country and thus entitled to apply for EU membership according to its founding Rome Treaty of 1957. The European Union offered partnership and cooperation agreements (PCA) valid for ten years to the CIS countries. The Ukrainian PCA was concluded in 1994 but did not come into force until 1997. Although it was comprehensive, covering political dialogue, goods and services trade, and economic, environmental, scientific, cultural, and legal matters, it contained little of substance. On trade, it codified WTO principles only for non-WTO members, while the European Union concluded free trade agreements with many other countries and association agreements with the EU candidate members in Eastern Europe. The European Union's

8. *Zerkalo nedeli*, October 16, 1998.

only subsequent trade policy for Ukraine was its conclusion of a textile agreement that eliminated its import quotas.

The contrast between the development of exports to the European Union from the 10 postcommunist EU candidate members in Central and Eastern Europe and Ukraine was huge in the 1990s. Barely half of the exports from Central and Eastern European countries went to the European Union in 1989, but they rose to 67 percent in 2000. By contrast, 33 percent of Soviet exports went to the European Union in 1989, but Ukraine's exports to the European Union comprised only 16 percent of its total exports in 2000, showing that Ukraine was especially disadvantaged. Given economic geography—Ukraine's location, transportation routes, and the relative size of adjacent economies—the European Union should be Ukraine's all-dominant export market, buying 60 percent of its exports (Åslund and Warner 2004). Ukraine suffered from extreme EU protectionism because two-thirds of its exports consisted of goods especially sensitive to protectionist measures, namely steel, chemicals, agricultural goods, and textiles.

Throughout the 1990s the main EU interest in Ukraine was to close down the Chornobyl nuclear power station, where one reactor melted down in April 1986. However, two other reactors continued to produce electricity. They were major energy assets to Ukraine, and the Ukrainian government demanded compensation through the completion of two almost-finished nuclear power reactors at other locations if Chornobyl was closed. The European Union engaged the European Bank for Reconstruction and Development, which did not trust the safety of the Soviet-designed reactors. The European Union wanted Ukraine to build other power stations, which would be much more expensive, but it was not prepared to pay. On April 19–20, 1996, Ukraine was invited to a nuclear safety summit with leaders of the Group of Seven (G-7) and Russia in Moscow and agreed to close Chornobyl. It closed one reactor in November 1996 and on December 15, 2000, the last reactor.[9] It completed two of the almost-finished nuclear reactors, which have worked well.

But Kuchma wanted to integrate Ukraine into Europe. The European organization that was open to Ukraine was the Council of Europe. It is separate from the European Union and has a larger membership. It is primarily an interparliamentary organization focused on human rights, election monitoring, judicial standards, and constitutions. Its Venice Commission is a major authority on the design of constitutions. In November 1995 Ukraine became a member of the Council of Europe, which has played a major role in Ukraine's democracy building. In a speech to the Parliamentary Assembly of the Council of Europe in April 1996, Kuchma stated that Ukraine's strategic goal was full membership

9. See the Nuclear Threat Initiative's website at www.nti.org (accessed on August 7, 2008).

in the European Union (Solchanyk 2001, 92). But his public request was followed by a deafening silence from the European Union.

Kuchma also favored Ukraine's integration into the North Atlantic Treaty Organization (NATO), pursuing a piecemeal approach suggested by NATO. In May 1997 Russia and NATO concluded their Founding Act on Mutual Relations, and Ukraine hastened to establish the NATO-Ukraine Commission two months later at the NATO summit in Madrid. The only serious domestic reaction against Kuchma's Western-oriented foreign policy occurred in 1999, when NATO bombed Yugoslavia in defense of the Kosovars. Most Ukrainians took a strong stand for their Orthodox brethren in Serbia, as did the Russians. Even so, in July 1999, Ukraine decided to deploy 800 soldiers in Kosovo. Ukraine has persistently provided peacekeeping troops to the various stages of Yugoslavia's partition.

An innovation was the formation of the regional grouping GUAM, an abbreviation of the four member states, Georgia, Ukraine, Azerbaijan, and Moldova. Cooperation between these four countries started during discussions about revising the Treaty on Conventional Forces in Europe in late 1996. The common denominators among GUAM's members are that they are all reluctant members of the CIS, wanting to keep a certain distance from Russia, and they are all Black Sea countries. GUAM was formed to safeguard their common security interests, which have been extended to energy, but they have always been careful to underline that their cooperation is not directed against Russia. In 1999 Uzbekistan joined the group, which then became GUUAM, but it withdrew in 2005 because it had little in common with the other members. After the massacre in Andijan in May 2005, Uzbekistan improved its relationship with Russia, which showed more understanding for the massacre than the United States did. In practice, GUAM is little more than a consultative forum (Olcott, Åslund, and Garnett 1999).

Not without reason, Kuchma took great pride in his foreign policy, which was his main preoccupation (beside elections) in the late 1990s: "I was criticized a lot for my multi-vector policies, but I'm proud of my foreign policy and consider it an important achievement. . . . It helped me preserve Ukraine's sovereignty."[10]

Intricacies of the Gas Trade

The gas trade was the greatest source of rent seeking in Ukraine, although Ukraine imported three-quarters of the natural gas it consumed, but it is

10. Radio Free Europe/Radio Liberty (RFE/RL), "Ukraine: Former President Observes 'Ukraine Without Kuchma'," August 7, 2006.

a major transit country.[11] Ukraine's energy intensity was even greater than Russia's. At the outset, both countries had equally low energy prices and were dominated by heavy industry.

At its worst in 1995, Ukraine used 28 times more energy to produce $1 of GDP than energy-efficient Italy.[12] The scope for energy saving was enormous. Ukraine's consumption of natural gas declined from 115 billion cubic meters in 1990 to about 80 billion in 1995, but it has stayed more or less constant at that level, as energy saving has proceeded, while production has picked up (Lovei 1998a).

The modalities for gas trading changed every few years, but prices were always greatly distorted, the trade nontransparent, and arrears substantial. The two dominant sources of gas have been Russia and Turkmenistan. Their weights have varied, but Russia has preferred to let Turkmenistan deliver gas to Ukraine because gas prices for Ukraine were lower than for Europe, and it was difficult to extract payments from Ukraine.

Most things about the gas trade were strange. Prices were low and subsidized, but even so, arrears were notorious and often forgiven by Gazprom or the Ukrainian state. The arrangements for gas trade changed almost every year between different state and private companies. The changes occurred because gross corruption was revealed, arousing political criticism. However, things rarely improved. All these companies were nontransparent, and top officials and select businessmen in Turkmenistan, Russia, and Ukraine seemed to cash in large corrupt revenues (Global Witness 2006).

Russia's Gazprom was amazingly tolerant with the Ukrainian arrears, but not out of benevolence. It transformed its arrears into Ukrainian bonds, for which it demanded debt-equity swaps, preferably acquiring gas infrastructure. Gazprom acquired large chunks of the gas pipeline systems in Georgia, Moldova, and later Belarus, and Ukraine was its prime target. In addition, the world's largest gas storage facilities were located in western Ukraine, and they were of great value to Gazprom (Lovei 1998a). The Ukrainian parliament responded in late 1996 by prohibiting the privatization of Ukraine's transit gas pipelines and its gas storage (Balmaceda 1998, 264).

From 1992 to 1995 the Ukrainian state company Ukrhazprom imported natural gas from Russia and Turkmenistan, and Ukraine accumulated about $6 billion of state debt/arrears for these gas deliveries (Lovei and Skonik 1997, 204). During these years, Ukraine received very substantial

11. Good overall sources are Balmaceda (1998), Lovei (1998a), and Von Hirschhausen (1999).

12. Measured at current exchange rates. See Energy Information Administration, "World Energy Intensity," table E.1g, available at www.eia.doe.gov (accessed on July 14, 2008). If measured in purchasing power parity, Ukraine and Russia were five times less energy-efficient than Italy.

oil and gas subsidies from Russia. Gregory Krasnov and Josef Brada (1997, 840–41) estimated them at approximately 1.3 percent of Ukrainian GDP annually from 1992 to 1995.

In early 1994 the Ukrainian state recruited a private company, Respublika, headed by Ihor Bakai, to pay Turkmenistan mainly with barter, but it failed to do so, and Kuchma ousted Respublika and Bakai (Global Witness 2006, 33). Instead, the Gazprom-related private trading company Itera and Lazarenko and Tymoshenko's UESU took over the gas trade from 1995 until 1997. In October 1996 Gazprom's CEO Rem Vyakhirev suggested that Itera receive monopoly on selling Russian gas to Ukrainian companies (Balmaceda 1998, 264). Prime Minister Lazarenko refuted the offer, but after his fall Itera sold all Russian gas to Ukraine. As was their habit, the gas traders did not pay Gazprom, which eventually forced the Ukrainian state to pay (Balmaceda 1998, 270–71; von Hirschhausen and Vincentz 2000).

In 1998, after the fall of Lazarenko, Kuchma brought together state oil and gas enterprises into the new Ukrainian state company Naftohaz Ukrainy to control Ukraine's gas trade. An obvious aim was to secure campaign financing for the presidential election in 1999. The company's first chairman, Ihor Bakai, stayed until 2000. Presumably, Kuchma thought he needed the most unscrupulous gas trader to recover full control after Lazarenko. For this period, Naftohaz Ukrainy did not release any financial information or audits (Global Witness 2006, 29). It was an obvious source of leakage of hundreds of millions of dollars every year. Within Ukraine, a number of regional distributors were given regional monopolies, aggravating the boondoggle. In the fall of 1998, Bakai, unabashedly stated: "All rich people in Ukraine made their money on Russian gas" (Timoshenko 1998).

The techniques of enrichment were many and varied. Most blatant but least prominent was theft of gas from the main pipeline through Ukraine to Western Europe. Another means was not to pay Itera/Gazprom, but as Itera happily continued the trade, suspicion lingers that it was paid. Yet Gazprom/Russia demanded that the Ukrainian state guarantee these payments by private Ukrainian importers. A third form of rent seeking was payment through barter and offsets, which usually brought about a discount of about 50 percent. In addition, Russia paid in kind for gas transit through Ukraine, which disappeared into private hands. Altogether, a few Ukrainian oligarchs netted at least $1 billion a year on this dubious gas trade, but their identity varied from year to year.

Rise of the Oligarchs

One of the most controversial topics is the oligarchs. In Russia, oligarch became a popular label for the wealthiest tycoons around 1994, when the first truly rich people emerged, and that notion was soon accepted in

Ukraine as well. Oligarch is an ancient concept, and an oligarchy is traditionally defined as "government in the hands of a few." In fact, it has been more applicable to Ukraine than to Russia.

In Ukraine an oligarch was understood as a very wealthy and politically well-connected businessman, a dollar billionaire, or nearly so, who was the main owner of a conglomerate of enterprises and had close ties to the president. The oligarchs were few, and it might be more appropriate to call them plutocrats, as their aim was to make money and they saw politics as a means to accomplish that goal.

Oligarchs are not unique to Russia and Ukraine but the international norm. Randall Morck, Daniel Wolfenzon, and Bernard Yeung (2005, 693) concluded in a survey of recent literature on ownership around the world: "Control pyramids effectively entrust the corporate governance of the greater parts of the corporate sectors of many countries to handfuls of elite, established families, who can quite reasonably be described as *oligarchs*." The United States and the United Kingdom are exceptions.[13]

In Ukraine, we may distinguish among three waves of oligarchs or big businessmen. The first group rose to prominence around 1994. In July 1994, when Kuchma was unexpectedly elected president of Ukraine, he disrupted the old corrupt networks. At least three people were already known as oligarchs: former prime minister Zviahilskiy, who was a coal and steel trader; media oligarch and steel trader Vadym Rabinovich; and gas trader Ihor Bakai. They had worked with Kravchuk and all fell out of favor with Kuchma. Zviahilskiy and Rabinovich were even prosecuted in an anticorruption drive. Yet the old oligarchs managed to mend their fences with the new president as the Kuchma regime succumbed to corruption.

A second wave of Kuchma oligarchs were gas traders. In 1996–97, the biggest gas trading group was Lazarenko and Tymoshenko's United Energy Systems of Ukraine, which branched out into other industries, becoming a conglomerate.[14] Another early big oligarchic group was led by Kyiv businessman Hryhoriy Surkis and his partner Viktor Medvedchuk. They formed a large conglomerate, trading gas and owning plenty of real estate in Kyiv. In the late 1990s they went into electricity distribution on a big scale. Surkis owned the famous Dynamo soccer club in Kyiv. Ihor Bakai, the tenacious gas trader, patched up his relationship with Kuchma and stayed an oligarch, uncharacteristically moving between private and state companies. Oleksandr Volkov was primarily a courtier and presidential adviser. He was a dealmaker, never identified with any company, although he was a major oil importer (Gongadze 2000).

---

13. For further general elaboration on oligarchs, see Åslund (2007a, chapter 10). I have provided more detail on the Ukrainian oligarchs in Åslund (2006).

14. It was a private Ukrainian company and had nothing in common with the eponymous company in Russia, which was the state-controlled utility company.

None of these early corporate beginnings has survived. They were all murky offshore trading companies, escaping taxation, being the masters of nonpayments and barter. UESU was a real enterprise, but Kuchma destroyed it in 1997–98 by pursuing it with the various arms of law enforcement. The Surkis and Medvedchuk group has probably broken up into different enterprises, whose ownership remains unclear. Bakai and Volkov never had serious corporate structures. Bakai fled to Russia after the Orange Revolution, and Volkov has been marginalized. These early oligarchs held high state positions: Lazarenko was prime minister, Medvedchuk first deputy speaker of the parliament, Volkov presidential adviser, and Bakai head of the state oil and gas company (Naftohaz Ukrainy), in 2003–04 responsible for real estate in the presidential administration. Surkis and Medvedchuk had regional bases in Kyiv and Transcarpathia in the west, and Lazarenko in Dnipropetrovsk, while Bakai and Volkov operated in the presidential circles in Kyiv.

A third wave of oligarchs emerged in the late 1990s and rose to prominence after 2000. They also had made their initial capital on commodity trading but they were all steel producers and developed substantial corporate structures. They had bought up the Ukrainian steel mills, which had been privatized in the 1990s, partly through voucher privatization and partly through insider privatization. The oligarchs restructured the steelworks to boost their production, rendering them highly profitable. Soon Ukraine was dominated by four large industrial groups, each with about 100,000 employees and worth more than $10 billion by the spring of 2008. They were all located in eastern Ukraine, two in Donetsk and two in Dnipropetrovsk.

The Industrial Union of Donbas (ISD), founded in 1995, has been the traditionally preeminent group in Donbas. It owns steelworks in Ukraine, Poland, and Hungary. Its main owners are billionaires Vitaliy Haiduk, Serhiy Taruta, and Oleg Mkrtchan. Haiduk and Taruta are engineers, former state enterprise managers from the metallurgical industry, and managing partner Taruta has a past in a Soviet foreign trade organization.[15]

The competitor of ISD in Donetsk is System Capital Management (SCM), by far Ukraine's biggest company, with about 160,000 employees. It was formed as late as 2000, and it is almost completely owned by Rinat Akhmetov (born in 1966), who in the late 1990s suddenly emerged as Ukraine's richest man. He comes from a poor Donbas coalminer's family. SCM is a holding company, with steelworks, iron-ore mines, and coal mines as well as heavy machine-building plants. Akhmetov rules as the king of Donetsk with control over the regional

15. Interview with Serhiy Taruta, December 2004; Zimmer (2003); Yevhen Dubohryz, "More-or-less Civilized," *Kontrakty*, January 17, 2005.

administration.[16] SCM and ISD previously shared ownership of many steelworks, but they have divided their properties. SCM got the bulk of them, and ISD claims to have been squeezed out.

Victor Pinchuk's Interpipe (renamed EastOne in 2007) in Dnipropetrovsk might be the second wealthiest company in Ukraine, but its employment is smaller. It was founded in 1990 and specializes in high value-added steel products, such as steel pipes and railway wheels. Pinchuk, who is a metallurgist with a doctoral degree, also owns three medium-sized TV channels (ICTV, Novy Kanal, and STB) and until early 2008 owned Ukrsotsbank.[17] Pinchuk married Kuchma's only daughter, Elena Franchuk, in 2002. EastOne and SCM pride themselves on having the most rationalized and Westernized corporate structures, both employing many westerners.

Privat Group in Dnipropetrovsk is probably the second biggest corporation in terms of employment and wealth after SCM. It was founded in 1992 and is headed by three billionaire partners: Ihor Kolomoiskiy, Gennadiy Bogoliubov, and Alexei Martynov. Kolomoiskiy, another engineer, is the managing partner. Privat Group controls Ukraine's biggest bank (Privatbank), a vertically integrated oil company (Sintoza and semi-state-owned Ukrnafta), a vertically integrated mining-and-steel company, large electricity holdings, and many other companies. It is a true conglomerate. Like the Surkis-Medvedchuk group, Privat Group does not have clear corporate structures, and much of its ownership is hidden in offshore companies. Privat Group and Interpipe are even fiercer competitors than ISD and SCM.[18]

Three cities dominate Ukrainian big business, Kyiv, Donetsk, and Dnipropetrovsk, but large enterprise groups also emerged in other regions, mainly in the east because of the inherited industrial structure. Ukraine had no less than 23 billionaires in the spring of 2008, and seven of the biggest oligarchic groups concentrate on steel and mining.[19] The transformation of big business from gas trade to steel production improved their

16. Interview with Rinat Akhmetov, December 8, 2004; Zimmer (2003); Adrian Karatnycky, "A Ukrainian Magnate Tries to Mend Fences," *Wall Street Journal*, January 14, 2005; Yevhen Dubohryz, "More-or-Less Civilized," *Kontrakty*, January 17, 2005.

17. Interview with Victor Pinchuk, March 2003.

18. Interview with Gennadiy Bogoliubov, March 2003. "Sekrety gruppy 'Privat'—mesta starta kar'ery Tigipko" ["Secrets of the Privat Group—the Starting Place of the Career of Tyhypko"], *Ukrainskaya pravda*, August 3, 2004; "Semeniuk suditsya za sobstvennost' Pinchuka, Akhmetova, Privata i Ruslana" ["Semeniuk Is Suing for the Property of Pinchuk, Akhmetov, Privat and Ruslan"], *Ukrainskaya pravda*, February 9, 2005.

19. *Korrespondent*, "List of 50 Richest Ukrainians," July 14, 2008. The seven biggest oligarchic groups are System Capital Management, EastOne, Privat Group, Industrial Union of Donbas, Ferrexpo (Konstantin Zhevago), Zaporizhstal, and MMK imeni Ilicha (Volodymyr Boiko). Kryvorizhstal was eventually bought by ArcelorMittal, but otherwise all the steel groups were owned by Ukrainian citizens.

business practices. The leading corporations could no longer hide as commodity traders can. They had to make their accounting official and legalize their business practices.

By 2000 the characteristics of oligarchs were easy to establish. Most of them were around 40 years of age and mostly engineers from Kyiv, Donetsk, or Dnipropetrovsk. They went into business in 1988, when the Soviet Law on Cooperatives was adopted, which allowed legal private enterprise and facilitated the transformation of dead noncash money into real cash. Nearly all the oligarchs manage huge companies themselves in a highly centralized manner. While the oligarchs of the 1990s were primarily courtiers and arbitrage traders, the current oligarchs are self-made entrepreneurs who have made their fortunes by reanimating existing Soviet mastodons.

The rise of Ukrainian oligarchs had much in common with that of oligarchs in other countries, such as America after its Civil War or Europe during the Industrial Revolution.[20] One cause of this generation and concentration of wealth was the sudden achievement of great economies of scale in certain industries, nota bene steel.

A second feature common to the Industrial Revolution and postcommunism was rapid structural change, which facilitated great accumulation of wealth among the few who knew how to take advantage of the convulsion. A third economic characteristic was the presence of rent, which is often difficult to distinguish from economies of scale, as the intricacies of the Microsoft antitrust case have taught us.

Fourth, US robber barons benefited from the free distribution of state assets, notably land around the railways, and cheap state credits, since multiple early railway companies went bankrupt because of insufficient state support to reach the desired economies of scale (De Long 2002). In Ukraine budding oligarchs bought up cheap steelworks that many thought were condemned to die as was the case in Central Europe.

Fifth, the absence of strong legal institutions required oligarchs. Even today, Ukraine has few relevant corporate and property laws. The judicial system functions poorly, and bailiffs barely exist. Such conditions breed poor corporate governance, impeding the evolution of financial markets. Without strong corporate legislation and a potent judicial system, partners find it difficult to agree or resolve conflicts. Nor can principals (owners) control their agents (executives), so they are compelled to manage their companies themselves. Therefore, businessmen with concentrated ownership tend to be more successful than those who have to deal with many minority shareholders, as has indeed proven to be the case in Ukraine (Grygorenko, Gorodnichenko, and Ostanin 2006). "When institutions are weak, doing business with strangers is dangerous and unreliable" (Morck, Wolfenzon, and Yeung 2005, 672). Businessmen

20. The ensuing section draws on Åslund (2007a, chapter 10).

escape concluding contracts that they cannot secure in court by rationally opting for vertical integration, choosing corporate hierarchies over horizontal markets (Williamson 1975).

Economically, the oligarchic systems have proven highly adaptive. The Ukrainian oligarchic corporations EastOne and SCM have excelled in buying international services of all kinds, notably auditing and management services, while the state companies resisted doing so. They have bought and sold companies at great speed, specializing and altering their corporate structures.

Only Ukrainian and Russian oligarchs appear able to restructure large Soviet industrial enterprises, which requires rather peculiar skills. Close relations with both the central and regional governments are necessary. In the absence of a functioning legal system, the owner/manager must be able to secure property rights and enforce contracts in an effective extralegal fashion. A prime task at a Soviet plant is to root out rampant theft by employees. Ukraine has plenty of social regulations, but only some are honored, and a businessman needs to know which. Soviet enterprises were chronically overstaffed, and only local businessmen have the guts to lay off workers as is necessary. Soviet factories were typically overloaded with equipment, most of which had to be scrapped. Foreign businessmen tend to gut the factories, using little but the premises. Local businessmen with less capital are anxious to utilize valuable physical capital and technology, thus preserving more value. Soviet management had its peculiarities, and in factories with thousands of workers, knowledge of the old management is necessary to successfully renew these factories, while outside financial and management skills can be brought in. Therefore, local businessmen tend to do better than foreign investors in the early stages of restructuring of Soviet metallurgy. Later on, other skills are likely to be more relevant, such as know-how and international networks, lending a new premium to foreign investors.

Yegor Grygorenko, Yuriy Gorodnichenko, and Dmytro Ostanin (2006) analyze a sample of almost 2,000 Ukrainian companies and found that oligarchs picked underperforming firms with large capital stock and sales and firms owned by oligarchs had much higher productivity growth than others. This finding tallies with that of an earlier empirical study of Russian financial-industrial groups in the mid-1990s, which found that these hierarchical groups were more efficient in their real investment than independent owners (Perotti and Gelfer 2001).

Two major conclusions can be drawn. First, only a few businessmen with concentrated private ownership and supreme knowledge of the informal rules could manage large Soviet enterprises in the early transition. The real alternatives were to keep them state-owned and unreformed until they collapsed or to sell them off to foreign investors, who usually closed them down not knowing how to manage them. The question was whether the state would allow big local businessmen to emerge or not, and only a few countries did so. The oligarchs have been more successful in restructuring large Soviet mining and metallurgical industries.

Second, the oligarchs were not guilty of the existing conditions that arose, but they responded rationally. Whenever state regulation created wedges between fixed state prices and market prices, businessmen arbitraged between these prices to their personal benefit. When privatization was launched, they transferred state property to themselves in the cheapest way. During mass privatization, they bought vouchers and stocks. Given that many enterprises were privatized unexpectedly and suddenly, they bought what they could until mass privatization had been completed, acquiring more assets rather than investing in already purchased enterprises. After mass privatization was completed, some oligarchs elaborated business strategies, streamlined their assets, specialized in a few industries, and invested heavily.

In the late 1990s, Kuchma was deeply engaged with the oligarchs, balancing three major oligarch groupings against one another—Medvedchuk-Surkis, Volkov-Bakai, and Pinchuk—but others were also in play. Kuchma and the oligarchs had a symbiotic relationship. The oligarchs needed state support for their businesses, while Kuchma desired ample political campaign financing. He checked the oligarchs through his skillful divide and rule strategy, making sure that no single force could consolidate power.

The oligarchy amounted to a "partial reform equilibrium," as Joel Hellman (1998) and Rosaria Puglisi (2003) have seen it. In Hellman's words, the winners took all, and the winners were the oligarchs. They maintained and reinforced their rents or state resources in return for political support through campaign financing, media, and mobilization of regional constituencies.

However, most of the big and powerful in 1999 would lose their privileges sooner than anybody had imagined because competition prevailed and offered a lifeline to this seemingly stagnant society. Kuchma avoided consolidating power and building a strong vertical command, which President Vladimir Putin and President Nursultan Nazarbayev did in Russia and Kazakhstan, respectively.

Crime and Law Enforcement

In the early postcommunist period, crime skyrocketed, as is typical during liberalization after a severe dictatorship, but society found defense mechanisms that shifted over time.[21]

21. The best analysis of post-Soviet crime and defense mechanisms is Volkov (2002), who in turn draws on similar observations in Sicily by Diego Gambetta (1993). I have elaborated on this in Åslund (1997a, chapter 9).

In Ukraine the number of homicides and attempted homicides more than doubled, from 2,100 in 1985 to a peak of 4,900 in 1996. The murder rate remained at this high level until 2000, after which it fell substantially (figure 4.2). The Ukrainian homicide rate was slightly higher than the US rate, but it has persistently been less than half the extraordinary Russian rate. Within Ukraine the rate was much higher in the urbanized east than in the more rural west.

Individual crime became unbearable. Every businessman was exposed to racketeering, but since multiple claimants competed over turf, they did not know whom to pay. Many never figured out but saw their premises burned and some were killed. A friend of mine attended the birthday party of Ihor Bakai on the banks of the Dnieper in 1995. He counted 72 bodyguards; a few were trying to enhance security by waterskiing with their Kalashnikovs. In hindsight, it may sound exotic, but it was frightening. In 1995 and 1996, two businessmen in Donetsk (Ahati Bragin, a.k.a. Alik the Greek, and Yevhen Shcherban) were murdered, presumably by their competitors, though their cases were never solved. Bragin was killed in the midst of 150 bodyguards at Shakhtyar stadium in Donetsk and Shcherban at Donetsk airport. Never before had bodyguards been so prominent and numerous in Kyiv's few good restaurants.

In response to this criminal anarchy, a second stage evolved in 1996, when crime was soon rationalized. Under Prime Minister Lazarenko (1996–97), organized crime appeared to have taken power. Organized racketeers had divided urban territories among themselves, and businessmen knew which racketeer they had to pay. Protection rates declined as did racketeering murders. I used to eat at a nice Italian restaurant, Di Mario, on Saksaganskogo Street in Kyiv. Every evening a group of four Chechen brothers would hang out there, working their mobile phones. Between them sat bored beautiful blond girls smoking their long, slim cigarettes. Reportedly, they comprised one of the city's two main racketeering groups, but police did not bother them.

By 2000 the oligarchs took over from organized crime. By establishing their own large armies of security guards, they freed themselves. Although the threat of bloodshed persisted, carnage among businessmen dwindled, as did the number of bodyguards, and the cost of protection declined.

Eventually, law enforcement recovered but became a law unto itself. In Ukraine, the four main law enforcement agencies are the huge and multifaceted Ministry of Interior, the elitist Security Services of Ukraine (SBU, the old KGB), the large new State Tax Administration, and the Prosecutor General. Three strong men loyal to Kuchma controlled the main branches of law enforcement. Minister of Interior Yuriy Kravchenko commanded Ukraine's 420,000 policemen, Leonid Derkach the SBU with only 28,000 officers, and Mykola Azarov the State Tax Administration, which,

Figure 4.2 Rate of homicides and attempted murders in Ukraine and Russia, 1990–2007

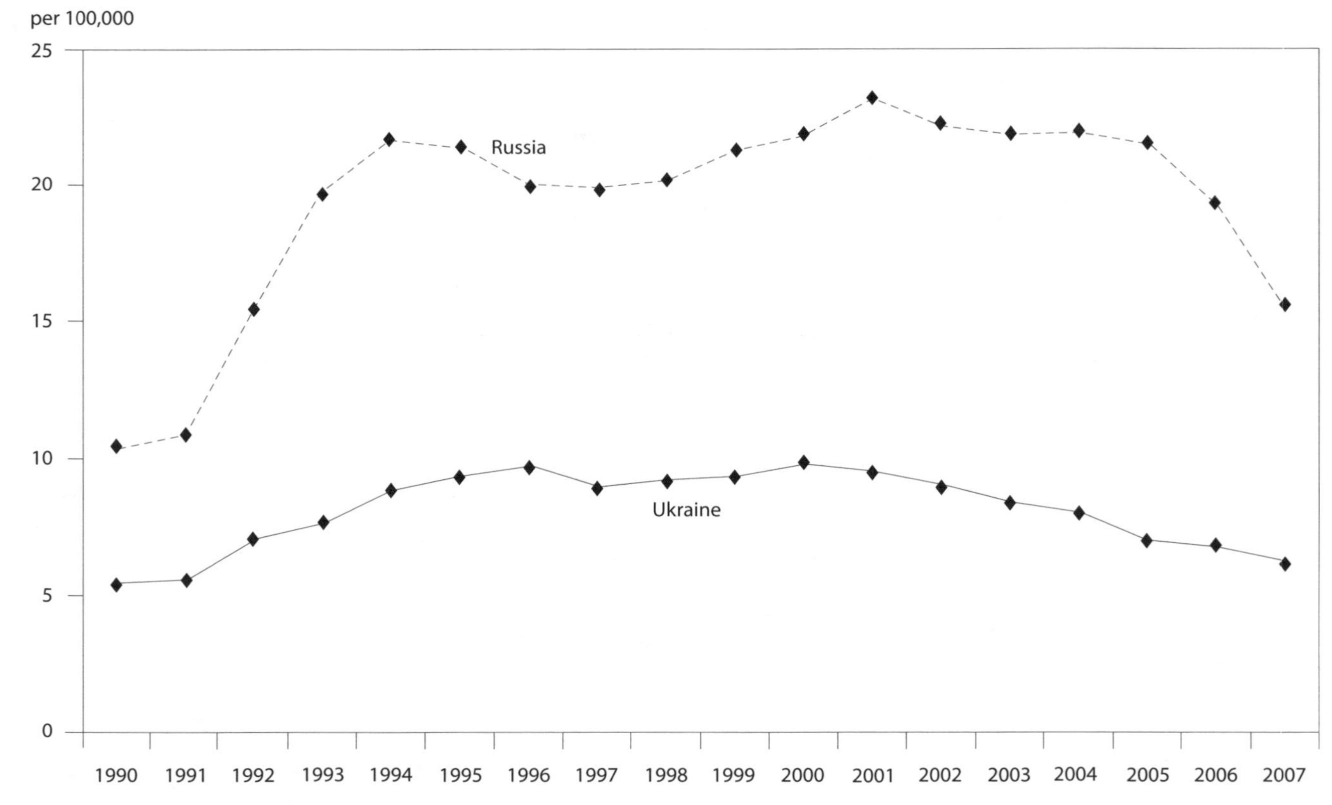

Sources: Ministry of Statistics of Ukraine (1994, 477; 1996, 514; 1997, 488; 1998, 515; 2000, 499); State Statistics Committee of Ukraine online database, www.ukrstat.gov.ua (accessed on July 18, 2007); European Bank for Reconstruction and Development online database, www.ebrd.com (accessed on July 1, 2008); Federal State Statistics Service of Russian Federation, www.gks.ru (accessed on July 22, 2008).

with its 70,000 inspectors, was the most politicized and dangerous repressive force. Azarov was also a major politician from Donetsk, usually a deputy in the Rada, and one of the leaders of the Regions Party, the regional party of Donbas. The three agencies became centralized, commercial organizations, competing among themselves as oligarchic groups. Justice was their least concern, but law entitled them to carry arms and arrest people.

Kuchma handled law enforcement as he did the oligarchs, playing them against each other, while making sure that strong and loyal men headed each service. The military with some 200,000 men in uniform played no political role.

Demise of Media Freedom

In the early 1990s, the Ukrainian media were in financial disarray, suffering from the general economic decline. State financing dried up and private advertising revenues did not become significant until after 2000. The transportation of newspapers became too expensive, eliminating national newspapers and rendering the press entirely regional. As the print media shrank, the vast majority of Ukrainians stopped reading newspapers, and television and radio became all the more dominant. Quality remained poor. Ukraine had relatively few trained journalists, since Soviet media were dominated from Moscow. Still, media were very free.

In the mid-1990s Kyiv had about 10 small daily newspapers, mostly owned by minor entrepreneurs, though the parliament owned one newspaper and the government another. The main TV channels were state-owned and poorly financed, while a few small private channels were emerging. Ukraine had one early media tycoon, Vadym Rabinovich, who was rumored to own one-quarter of Ukraine's media at his peak in 1994. He seemed to be Ukraine's response to Russia's Vladimir Gusinsky, but he was accused of being involved in organized crime and was barred from entering the United States. He never came as close to Kuchma as to Kravchuk. In 1999 Rabinovich fell out with Kuchma and fled to Israel (Wilson 2002, 198, 265).

The most viable television programming consisted of rebroadcasts of Russian programs, but direct broadcasts from Russia were banned in 1995 (Wilson 2002, 270). At the time, it was perceived as an act of boosting Ukrainian language broadcasts, but it also increased the government's opportunities to control television.

Soon the Kuchma administration began circumscribing media freedom. In 1995 one of Kyiv's small but good newspapers, *Kievskie vedomosti*, published that Minister of Interior Kravchenko had built a big private house with state money. Kravchenko, who was a Kuchma loyalist, did not suffer, and the president defended him publicly, but the newspaper was evicted from its premises because of a supposed fire hazard.[22] This was the first harbinger of a repressive media policy that flourished in 1997–98 before the parliamentary and presidential elections.

Later on, *Kievskie vedomosti's* competitor, *Vseukrainskie vedomosti*, published damaging revelations about Kyiv tycoon Hryhoriy Surkis. It was sued for libel and sentenced to pay confiscatory damages of more than $1.5 million. The general prosecutor closed down several other critical newspapers (Wilson 2002, 198). Media freedom had been severely curtailed, but repression remained limited to media that were an acute nuisance to the authorities. The main means were tax inspection, police, prosecutors, and the courts. Independent media survived, but they were marginalized.

Two big private channels, 1+1 and Inter, dominated television and fell under the control of Medvedchuk, who also commanded the main state-owned television channel, UT-1. In 1996 former prime minister Marchuk started a daily newspaper, *D'en*, which has survived as one of Kyiv's best newspapers, but it was not independent because Marchuk led Medvedchuk's party. Every big businessman had some media outlet, and before the parliamentary elections in March 1998, Ukraine's media were dominated by tycoons friendly with Kuchma. However, the media remained underfinanced and of poor quality, and their impact on Ukrainian public opinion was remarkably limited.

Because of the weak national media, foreign radio stations broadcasting in Ukrainian—BBC World Service, Radio Free Europe, and Voice of America—were important sources of information and analysis, but Russian television beat them all.

Parliamentary Elections, March 1998

On March 29, 1998, Ukraine held its ordinary parliamentary elections. These were Ukraine's lamest elections. Kuchma remained the most popular politician in the country. Overall he was still a centrist, but he had leaned to the right on economic reforms, state-building, and foreign policy. Therefore the main opposition came from the left, though it was neither inspired nor enthusiastic. The chief novelty was electoral reform.

Ukraine finally abandoned its pure majority elections with single-mandate constituencies.[23] The 1994 elections had not filled all seats, and the parliament had discredited itself by being too unstructured and fluid, rendering decisions exceedingly complex. A broad sense prevailed that political parties had to be reinforced. Ukraine largely adopted the Russian

---

22. I wrote a monthly column about economic policy in *Kievskie vedomosti* in 1995.

23. The main source of this section is Birch (2000a, 101–107).

Table 4.1 Results of election to the Supreme Rada, March 29, 1998

Party	**List votes** (percent)	Seats
Total Left	40.6	173
Communist	24.7	122
Socialist/Rural	8.6	34
Progressive Socialists	4.0	16
Total Center	30.8	102
Greens	5.4	19
People's Democrats	5.0	29
Hromada	4.7	23
Social Democrats (United)	4.0	17
Total Right	19.4	59
Rukh	9.4	46
Independents		116
Against all	5.3	
Total	100[a]	450
Voter turnout (percent)	71.2	

a. Total includes invalid ballots, not counted as votes.

Sources: Birch (2000a, 107); Central Election Commission of Ukraine, www.cvk.gov.ua (accessed on September 31, 2007).

semiproportional system, which was the main source of inspiration. The 1998 electoral law prescribed that half of the 450 members were to be elected in a proportional election with party lists, with a threshold for representation of 4 percent of the votes. The other 225 seats were elected as before in single-mandate constituencies, but through simple majority and without any turnout requirement.

Another novelty was that these elections were less free and fair than the 1994 elections. The regime-controlled television channels openly ridiculed opposition candidates, and so-called administrative resources were used extensively. The State Tax Administration undertook tax audits of those who financed Kuchma's opponents, and law enforcement pursued them as well.

The election results were confusingly similar to those of 1994. The hard left, represented by the communists, socialists, and the progressive socialists, performed somewhat better than in 1994, receiving 41 percent of the votes in the proportional vote and 38 percent of the total seats. The right was weakened, with only Rukh passing the 4 percent hurdle with 9 percent of the votes and 10 percent of the seats, presumably suffering from Kuchma's turn to the right. The victor was the oligarchic center, which had reinforced its party structures (table 4.1).

Four centrist parties scraped over the hurdle for proportional representation. The Popular Democratic Party was the party of power, led by Prime Minister Pustovoitenko. Their miserable showing was quite a shame, but initially many independents were persuaded to join that party faction. The Social Democratic Party (United) was formally headed by former prime minister Marchuk, and former president Kravchuk joined it, but the real leaders were Medvedchuk and Surkis. Despite its name, it was a corporate party, closely allied with Kuchma. The Greens sounded like an environmentalist party, but it had been bought by a group of businessmen owning the steelworks Zaporizhstal. They were in politics for opportunistic business reasons so they wanted to be close to power.

The fourth centrist party was Lazarenko's *Hromada*, which was a corporate party with support in the Dnipropetrovsk region that sharply opposed Kuchma. It suffered the most from repression during the preelection campaign, but this did not arouse major protests because Lazarenko's party was reminiscent of a criminal gang. Yet the persecution of *Hromada* undermined legal standards.

As is usual in initial proportional elections, far too many parties emerged. No less than 30 parties and electoral blocs contested the ballot. Of these, eight passed the 4 percent hurdle, and no less than 34 percent of votes were wasted on parties that failed to reach that threshold. Participation remained high at 71 percent.

Big businessmen swarmed into parliament. Many centrists and independents were businessmen, whose share of the seats rose from one-fifth in 1994 to one-third in 1998. A deputy jokingly told me that it cost about $1 million to enter the Rada, which was normal because it cost the same to become a member of the New York Stock Exchange, and the Rada performed the same function.

The centrists and independents organized themselves into eight centrist factions, Rukh split in two, and the electoral bloc of the Socialist Party and the Rural Party did so as well. Thus, in the spring of 1999, the Rada had four left-wing factions and ten centrist or right-wing factions, comprising a total of 14 factions (Wilson 2002, 186–87).

An informal alliance of four oligarchic factions supporting Kuchma became the driving force of the new parliament: the Social Democratic Party (United), whose leader Medvedchuk became first deputy speaker; the Democratic Council, led by Oleksandr Volkov and Ihor Bakai; Labor Ukraine, headed by Victor Pinchuk and Serhiy Tyhypko; and the Donetsk clan's party the Regions of Ukraine, which was still taking shape. The oligarchs had reinforced their political power.

Kuchma's Reelection, October–November 1999

The parliamentary elections were seen as a primary for the real elections, the presidential election in October–November 1999. Soon after Boris Yeltsin won the second round against Russian communist leader Gennady Ziuganov in July 1996, Kuchma and his advisers decided to do the same.[24] As Andrew Wilson (2002, 204) saw it: "Kuchma's strategists planned a Ukrainian version of Russia-96, and basically that is what they got, all rather too easily in fact."

The scenario was evident. Kuchma would stand as the incumbent, representing the least evil and not proposing any new program. He would run against a credible communist threat, so communist leader Petro Symonenko was needed for the second round. Huge financing from oligarchs would facilitate a massive media campaign and the ample utilization of "political technologies" and "administrative resources."

Unlike Yeltsin, Kuchma was in good health and reasonably popular, since he had been quite successful. He was usually the most popular politician in the country, although he trailed Moroz and Symonenko in one poll in late 1998. His first task was to eliminate any threat from the democratic right. Rukh was badly divided and readily accepted Kuchma's candidacy.

Viktor Yushchenko, the popular chairman of the NBU, had been toying with the idea of running for president, but he stopped doing so in April 1998 after his potential campaign manager and funder, Vadym Hetman, his predecessor as chairman of the NBU and a wealthy commercial banker, was murdered in a contract hit in Kyiv. The murder was never solved, but Yushchenko would hardly have had any chance of winning in 1999. The old Rukh leader Vyacheslav Chornovil died in a mysterious traffic accident that year, which was widely blamed on the Kuchma administration. These suspect political murders marked a degradation of political freedom and scared the opposition.

On the left, there were three potential candidates. Socialist leader Oleksandr Moroz had the greatest potential popularity, while communist leader Petro Symonenko had the highest opinion poll rating. Natalia Vitrenko of the Progressive Socialist Party was a wild, extreme leftist.

The Kuchma camp's tactical goal was to make Symonenko gain more votes than Moroz in the first round on October 31, 1999. Their first draw was to block the reelection of Moroz as speaker of the parliament. Their determined actions paralyzed the parliament for four months after the March 1998 elections, but finally Oleksandr Tkachenko, leader of the Rural Party, a leftist with views similar to Moroz but with less popular appeal, was elected speaker.

The leading Ukrainian oligarchs had gathered huge sums for the Kuchma campaign. The main cashier was Oleksandr Volkov. A public claim was that he held campaign funds of as much as $1.5 billion (Wilson 2002, 202). That seems an exaggeration, but the election funds surely amounted to hundreds of millions of dollars. The big Kuchma-friendly businessmen

24. The main source of this section is Wilson (2002, 200–206).

Table 4.2 Results of presidential election, 1999 (percent of votes)

Candidate	First round, October 31, 1999	Second round, November 14, 1999
Leonid Kuchma	36.5	56.3
Petro Symonenko	22.2	37.8
Oleksandr Moroz	11.3	
Natalia Vitrenko	11.0	
Yevhen Marchuk	8.1	
Yuriy Kostenko	2.2	
Gennadiy Udovenko	1.2	
Others, against all, or not valid	7.5	6.0
Total	100	100
Voter turnout (percent)	70.2	74.9

Source: Central Election Commission of Ukraine, www.cvk.gov.ua (accessed on July 17, 2008).

already controlled all major television channels. They also hired a large number of Russian "political technologists," who had proven their mettle in the Russian presidential elections in 1996. One of them happily told me that he had never seen so much money being spent on an election.

During the presidential campaign, the regime-controlled television was even more biased than during the 1998 parliamentary elections. Naturally, Kuchma received the most positive publicity, but Vitrenko and Symonenko were also favorably treated, while Moroz was denigrated.

In October 1999 a small bomb went off at a Vitrenko rally in Dnipropetrovsk but no one was injured. The state media blamed the local organizer of the Moroz campaign, but the purported perpetrators who later surfaced in Russia blamed Vitrenko herself. Thus this incident hurt both Vitrenko and Moroz (Wilson 2002, 201).[25]

The elections themselves were relatively free, and they panned out exactly as the Kuchma camp had planned. In the first round, Kuchma received 36.5 percent against Symonenko's 22.2 percent, with 11 percent each for Moroz and Vitrenko (table 4.2). Former prime minister Yevhen Marchuk, who had run as an alternative left-of-center candidate to Moroz, received 8 percent and was immediately offered the post of secretary of the National Security and Defense Council, a direct parallel to Yeltsin's appointment of General Aleksandr Lebed after the Russian 1996 elections.

In the second round on November 14, the communist threat was vivid, boosting voter participation to 75 percent. The Ukrainian population

25. A Russian political technologist told me that he recognized the people who carried out the attempt on Vitrenko. They were former Federal Security Service (FSB) officers who worked for Boris Berezovsky, who had thrown in his lot with the Kuchma camp but tended to work very independently.

mobilized behind Kuchma, who obtained 56 percent of the votes against 38 percent for Symonenko, much less than the 45 percent the united left had received in the first round. This time, Kuchma won primarily in the west, but the regional disparity was not as great as in 1994, and the fear of the country breaking up did not arise. Kuchma and his associates easily accomplished what they wanted with relatively limited violations of democracy, rendering Ukraine semidemocratic.

Underreform Trap

By the end of 1999 the picture of Ukraine was pretty clear but somber. At this stage, Kuchma's greatest successes were national integrity and foreign policy. The worries that had existed in 1994 about Crimean separatism and a division of Ukraine between east and west appeared a distant memory. Ukraine was whole and free. In 1997 Kuchma had settled the outstanding problems with Russia, rendering Ukraine more secure than ever.

The domestic situation, by contrast, appeared all the more disturbing. Ukraine seemed unable to solve its economic and political problems. Economically, Ukraine had ended up in an underreform trap, which had political causes (Åslund, Boone, and Johnson 2001). Ukraine shared this dilemma with Russia, Moldova, Bulgaria, and Romania. All these post-communist countries had started with slow and partial reforms because of lacking political support for radical and comprehensive market economic reform, which had proven to work so well in Central Europe and the Baltic countries (Åslund 2007a).

The big businessmen indulged in rent seeking, and the great economies of scale of rent seeking reinforced their wealth and political power (Murphy, Shleifer, and Vishny 1993). The unreformed but overregulated state imposed confiscatory taxes on, and extorted, ordinary entrepreneurs, driving them into the unofficial economy. The combination of a flourishing parasitical rent-seeking economy and a repressed productive economy caused a long-lasting decline in output and welfare.

The economic underreform trap had a political counterpart. Because of the miserable economic performance of postcommunism, the communist party remained popular and stayed orthodox. Their voters recognized the robber capitalism that Karl Marx had described so vividly, reinforcing their socialist mindset. The communists demanded high taxes and public expenditures, state ownership, more state regulation, and protectionism.

The big businessmen formed the political center. Paradoxically, they and the communists advocated similar policies. The oligarchs favored high taxes (because they paid fewer taxes than their smaller competitors), large enterprise subsidies (to themselves), and maximum regulation (which kept potential competitors down). The oligarchs opposed the rule of law out of convenience, while the communists did so on ideological grounds. The only major disagreement was private ownership, which the oligarchs favored for themselves, unlike the communists.

Ukraine's few true free marketers faced an impossible dilemma. They could not win on their own until a real market economy had come into existence, and they could not join hands with the communists who contradicted everything they stood for. Thus, classical liberals, such as Yushchenko, Yekhanurov, and Pynzenyk, were forced to compromise with the oligarchic center or stay in the political wilderness as Lanovyi. No electoral backlash could prompt the reforms necessary to break free from the underreform trap.

Paul D'Anieri (2006) has identified similar problems with Ukraine's constitutional design. Ukraine's persistent problem was that the parliament was a marsh of deputies floating between a dozen party factions, which made it almost impossible to form a parliamentary majority. First, "the stronger the executive, the less incentives for parliamentarians to compromise in order to form a majority coalition." Similarly, the "less power and privilege that accompanies the formation of a parliamentary majority coalition, the less reason there is to pay the costs. . . . In sum, then, the very existence of a strong presidency reduces the chances of maintaining a parliamentary majority." Kuchma did not help: "Several efforts to form a center-right majority were foiled through pressure by Kuchma on individual members, at the very same time that Kuchma was arguing that the absence of such a majority demonstrated the need for stronger executive powers" (D'Anieri 2006, 55).

Second, the weakness of the political parties made it more difficult to form a coalition, but electoral and constitutional arrangements had caused this frailty. Until 1998, political parties endured discrimination in the elections. The parliamentary rules still discriminated against large parties: ". . . because each party or 'faction' receives funding, staff, and membership on the presidium, parties that split into two receive more of those benefits as two small parties than as one big one. A strictly rational choice analysis would predict that parties would fragment to the smallest possible size in order to maximize the number of party leadership slots and staff funding available. Thus, the once-powerful Rukh split into three factions."[26] The weakness of the political parties caused a vicious cycle: "Because many parties are new, and have little to contribute in terms of money, organization, or reputation, individual politicians gain little from them. Similarly, prominent politicians have little to lose if they abandon their party" (D'Anieri 2006, 59).

The political and economic shortcomings of the semireformed postcommunist countries, typified by Russia and Ukraine, were connected.

26. Herron (2002) pursues the same argument.

Since these states were neither full market economies nor full democracies, they did not deliver the virtues of those systems. Their populations were left with two alternative conclusions: They could blame their suffering either on the new system or on insufficient reforms. The key was to find a lever that could lift society out of its political and economic underreform trap.

One option was to strengthen presidential power further, proceeding to full authoritarianism: "First, with the parliament ineffective, many people viewed increased presidential power as the only alternative to deadlock. Second, even when many in parliament became worried about Kuchma's behavior, the parliament was ineffective in checking his power" (D'Anieri 2006, 58). D'Anieri (2006, 53) takes this point to its logical extreme: "Simply put, both left and right . . . saw Kuchma's authoritarianism as a lesser threat than the success of their adversaries." Russia chose this option under President Vladimir Putin, but Russia had already returned to sound fiscal policy and high growth because of the financial crash of August 1998, which made the politically impossible feasible (Åslund 2007b). Similarly, financial crises in 1997 had taken Bulgaria and Romania out of their underreform traps (Åslund 2007a).

An alternative way out of the underreform trap was increased economic and political competition among the elite: "Economically, rents need to dwindle through competition and new entry, while political power needs to be dissipated as a consequence of competition within the elite. The policy goal should be to foster such competition" (Åslund, Boone, and Johnson 2001, 89). Effectively, Ukraine chose this road.

5

Viktor Yushchenko's Reforms, 2000

At the end of 1999, Ukraine looked miserable.[1] It was the only postcommunist country that had failed to achieve a single year of economic growth for a whole decade. With a registered cumulative decline of 61 percent of GDP from 1989 to 1999, it had suffered the greatest official slump of all postcommunist countries that had not been involved in war. Russia had suffered a comparatively moderate decline of 41 percent during the same period because of more far-reaching reforms. By contrast, Poland, the ambitious reformer, had recorded a growth of 22 percent (figure 5.1).

These large slumps should not be taken at face value. Considering the growth of the unregistered economy, the actual decline might have been only half of that recorded (Johnson, Kaufmann, and Shleifer 1997). The poor survived on moneyless subsistence agriculture on their small household plots, as neither pensions nor wages were paid on time or in full.

The titles of Oleh Havrylyshyn's analysis of the Ukrainian economy at the time are characteristic: "The Political Economy of Delayed Reform" (2000) and "What Makes Ukraine Not Grow?" (2003). Shockingly, by 2000 Ukraine's GDP per capita at current exchange rates was one-third of Russia's, although it had exceeded moderately reforming Russia's in 1990, and that was before the oil boom. Even worse, it was as little as one-seventh of radically reforming Poland's GDP per capita at current exchange rates, although the World Bank had ranked Ukraine as richer than Poland before the end of communism.[2] Naturally, this also reflects Ukraine's deflated

1. This chapter draws on Åslund (2001). An additional source is Deutsche (2001).

2. International Monetary Fund, *World Economic Outlook*, October 2008 (accessed on November 18, 2008).

Figure 5.1 Cumulative GDP change, 1989–99

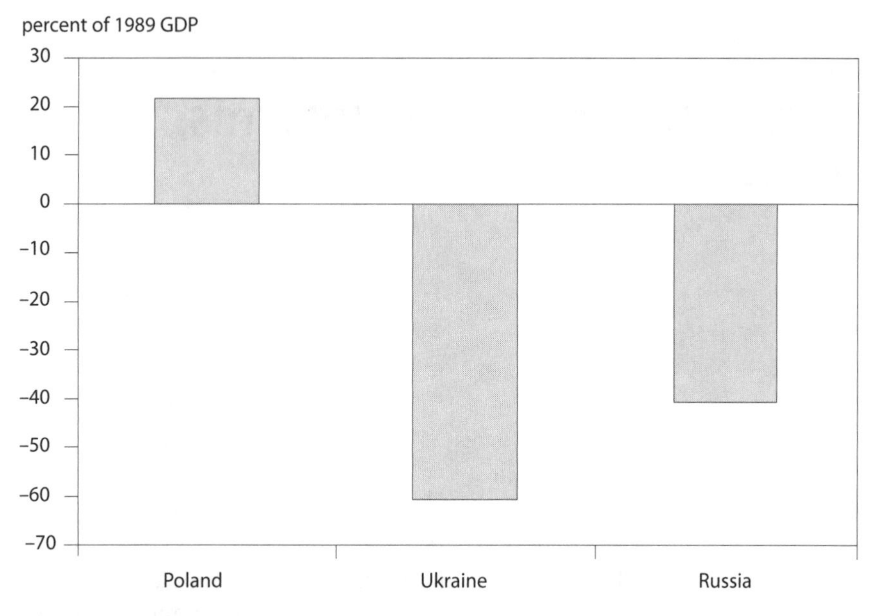

Source: UNECE (2004, 80).

exchange rate, and not only had the standard of living declined but also the social cost of delayed reforms had proven horrendous.

The decline and economic malaise could be seen in the streets. Until 2000 hardly any new construction took place in the cities. Soviet ruins and unfinished construction littered the city centers. On the outskirts, though, many new houses were being built by a budding bourgeoisie, and churches were being constructed all the time. Shops and restaurants were the first strong positive development, and the streets were filling up with imported cars, most of which were bought secondhand. Industry, however, was stagnant at best.

Market reforms had been tardy and half-baked, as the European Bank for Reconstruction and Development's composite transition index comparing Poland, Russia, and Ukraine shows (figure 5.2). Ukraine had not quite qualified as a full-fledged market economy, but the old socialist command economy was dead. Its cumbersome red tape bred ever more corruption. Inflation was high but under control, around 20 percent a year in 1998 and 1999 (figure 3.2). The budget deficit was small at 2.5 percent of GDP in 1998 and 1999, but larger than the financing and not planned (figure 3.1). Arrears were notorious, and barter rose until 1998. While the foreign debt was not large, much of it was nonpayments, mainly on natural gas imported from Russia and Turkmenistan.

Figure 5.2 EBRD transition index, 1994–2007

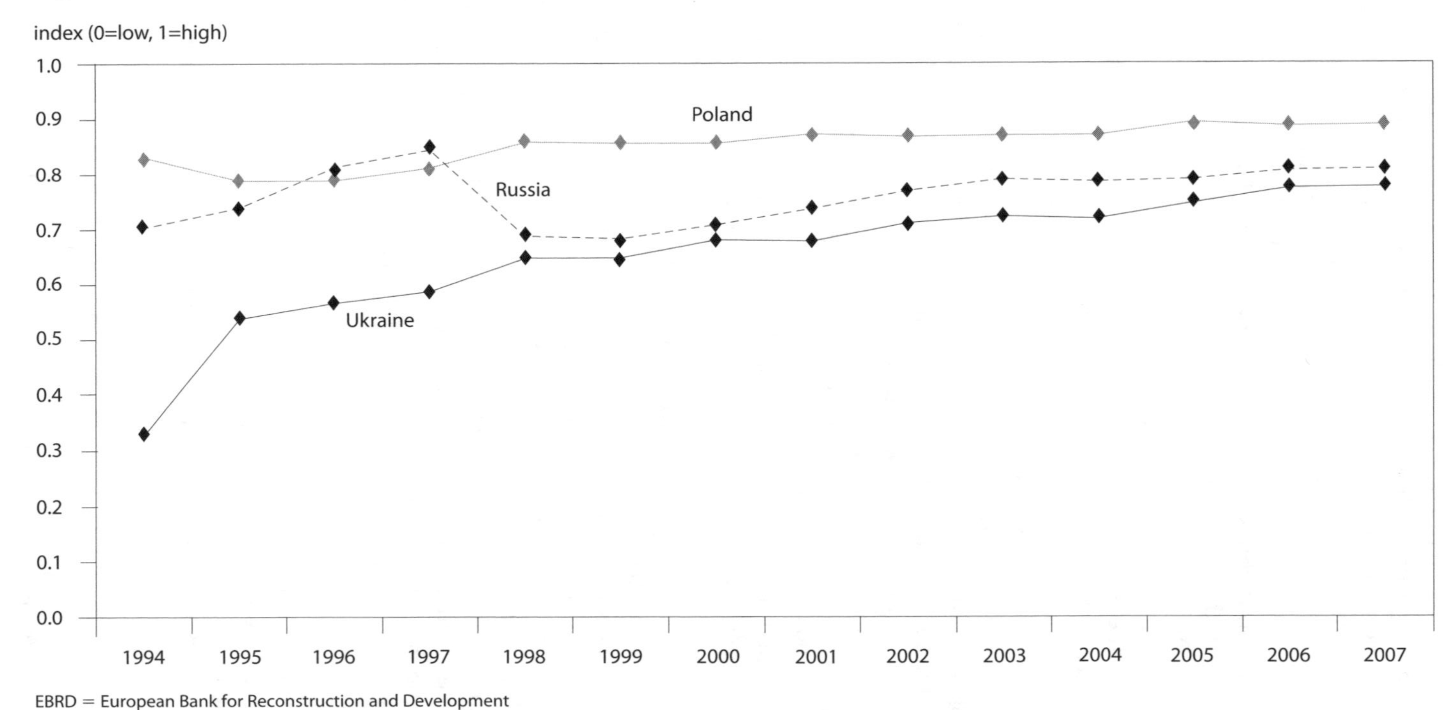

EBRD = European Bank for Reconstruction and Development

Note: The formula of this index is 0.3 times the EBRD index for price liberalization and competition policy, 0.3 times the EBRD index for trade and foreign exchange liberalization, and 0.4 times the EBRD index for large-scale privatization, small-scale privatization, and banking reform. Thus this index represents liberalization to 73 percent, while the rest is privatization.

Sources: De Melo, Denizer, and Gelb (1997); Havrylyshyn and Wolf (2001); author's calculations from the EBRD *Transition Report*, 1998, 1999, 2006, and 2007.

After the Russian financial crash of August 1998, investors and international financial institutions were suspicious of Ukraine, leaving the country on the verge of default. Its currency reserves covered less than one month of imports, and its export performance was poor. The International Monetary Fund (IMF) concluded repeated stabilization programs with Ukraine, but the government invariably violated them, prompting the IMF to stop disbursements from time to time. The social situation was dismal, with income disparity approaching Latin American levels (Milanovic 1998).

Ukraine had become an oligarchic economy, with a few tycoons dominating the economy and politics, as well-connected businessmen extracted tax rebates, subsidies, and regulatory privileges. A rent-seeking iron triangle of government, oligarchs, and parliament controlled the nation. They all favored extensive regulation and state interference to maximize rent seeking, while the population was of little consequence. This model of self-reinforcing rent seeking was close to equilibrium and thus stable.[3] Civil society was so frail that Ukrainians rarely stood up to defend their own interests (O'Loughlin and Bell 1999).

An archetypal rent-seeking society, Ukraine appeared stuck in a severe underreform trap. The prominent Ukrainian scholar Oleksandr Paskhaver (1999) argued that the Ukrainian system of "bureaucratic capitalism" implied that only private capital that had merged with the state bureaucracy could exist. President Leonid Kuchma had just been reelected because the situation was so bad that the threat of a communist *revanche* seemed credible. Democratic standards had slipped, and the country was semidemocratic at best.

Ukraine needed a radical break. The danger of default convinced the oligarchs that they needed a reform government, and they formed a center-right parliamentary majority to make the leading reformist of the day, Viktor Yushchenko, prime minister. He took the challenge without illusions and started 100 days of intense reforms, including the government itself, state finances, energy trade, agricultural land privatization, large privatizations, and deregulation of small firms. Ukraine swung to a substantial growth of 6 percent in 2000, primarily driven by industry, agriculture, and exports, and this broad-based economic expansion continued until the financial crisis of 2008.

In October 2000, however, the murder of journalist Heorhiy Gongadze became an all-dominant political scandal, which severely weakened Kuchma. In April 2001 Yushchenko was ousted, but Ukraine had been reformed, and its rent-seeking society had been transformed into a productive market economy.

3. Murphy, Shleifer, and Vishny (1993) have shown how such a model works.

On the Verge of Default

After the introduction of the hryvnia in September 1996, the Ukrainian economic drama calmed down.[4] Economic decline continued, but it moderated, and every year growth seemed to be around the corner.

The IMF cooperated closely with the Ukrainian authorities, and since Ukraine's international reserves stayed tiny, every IMF disbursement was vital for state finances. Ukraine also borrowed on the international market through eurobonds and domestic treasury bills, but because of its miserable payments standards, the latter had horrendous yields fluctuating around 70 percent a year, which was costly to the Ukrainian treasury (Pynzenyk 2000, 90).

In the fall of 1997 the Asian financial crisis shook the world through financial contagion, as foreign investors abhorred risk. By October its impact reached Ukraine. International portfolio investors refused to buy Ukrainian eurobonds or treasury bills, which drove up yields and thus the refinancing costs of Ukrainian debt. The National Bank of Ukraine (NBU) defended the hryvnia's exchange rate within the band of 1.8 to 2.25 hryvnia per US dollar, but Ukraine's international reserves plummeted from $2.3 billion in January 1998 to below $900 million, less than one month of imports, in September 1998 (figure 5.3).

As was revealed in early 2000, Ukraine's reserve situation was even worse. From late 1996 until 1998, the NBU had engaged in impermissible transactions with its international reserves. It had deposited reserves with a foreign commercial bank that bought Ukrainian government bonds and treasury bills, although international reserves were supposed to comprise liquid foreign assets. As a consequence, the Ukrainian reserves were exaggerated, overstated by $400 million to $700 million in September–December 1997, which deceived the IMF into giving Ukraine three unjustified disbursements. Yet a serious investigation by the auditing company PricewaterhouseCoopers, instigated by the IMF, did not reveal any misappropriations, and, with the exception of one bad loan of $15 million, all the money was recovered (IMF 2000a, 2000b).

The stable exchange rate of the hryvnia had become a matter of national pride, and since most of Ukraine's state debt was denominated in hard currencies, its domestic cost would rise with devaluation. The left-wing parliament aggravated the situation by refusing to adopt legislation that the government had agreed with the IMF, prompting the IMF to withhold financing during the first half of 1998.

On August 17, 1998, the Russian financial crash exploded. Russia devalued sharply and defaulted on $70 billion of domestic treasury bills,

4. An overall source of this section is Kravchuk (2002, 73–83, 219–21).

Figure 5.3 Ukraine's public debt and foreign exchange reserves, 1994–2007

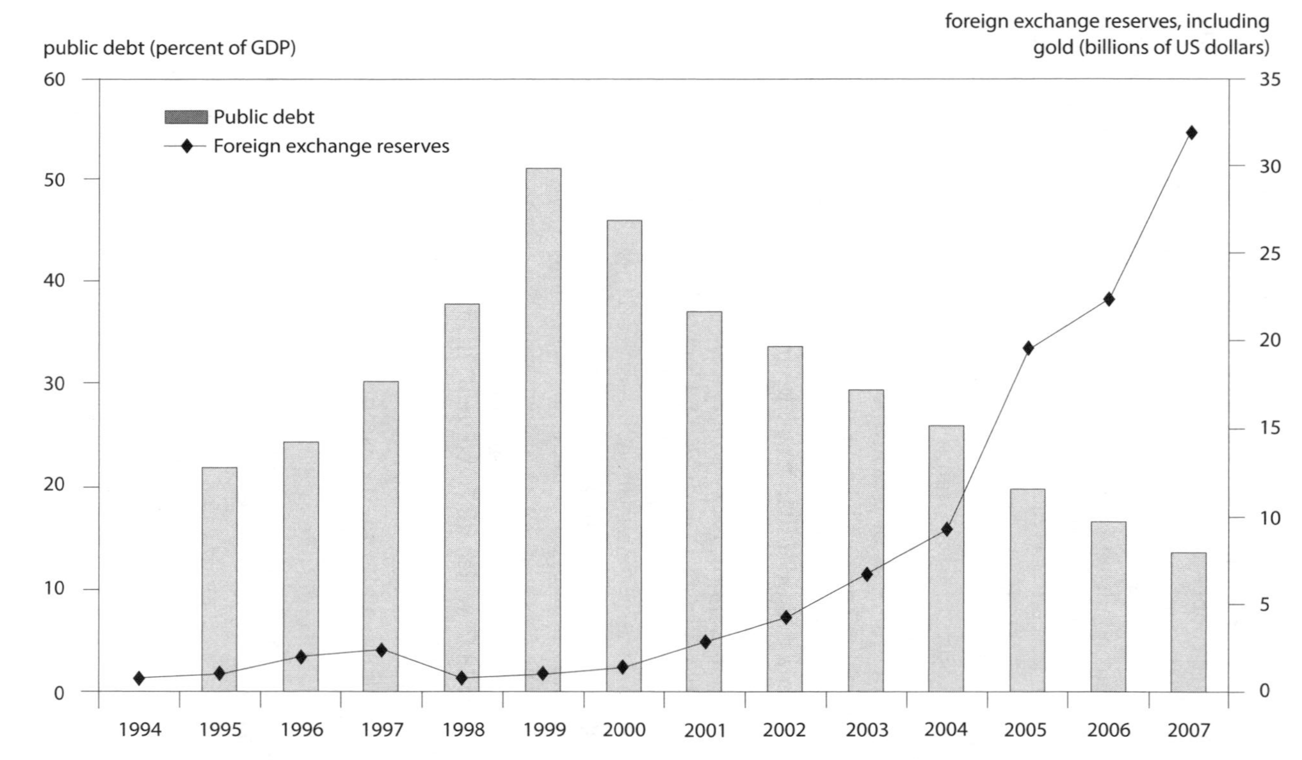

Sources: European Bank for Reconstruction and Development online database, www.ebrd.com (accessed on July 1, 2008); World Bank, *World Development Indicators* online database, www.worldbank.org (accessed on August 16, 2007).

while freezing the banking system for three months. International financial panic erupted, and the whole emerging financial world suffered. The NBU sensibly followed Russia's devaluation, depreciating the hryvnia by 60 percent on September 5. Further devaluations followed in fits and starts until the hryvnia stabilized at a historic low of 5.54 hryvnia per $1 in January 2000. The government enacted an anticrisis program on September 10, 1998. Its main measure was the forced conversion of 99 percent of the treasury bills held by nonresidents into eurobonds that were to mature in 2000. The purpose was to relieve the state budget from the enormous hryvnia bond yields.

For the moment, Ukraine had staved off external default, but the threat persisted, and financial worries gripped the population. From August until October 1998, 18 percent of all household deposits were withdrawn from the banks. Ukraine's foreign debt was rising as a share of GDP because of continuous depreciation of the hryvnia, although this share was never large. International reserves fell below $500 million (worth 14 days of imports) in February 1999.

Valeriy Pustovoitenko was so weak as prime minister that Kuchma had to do most of the heavy lifting himself, but his economic policy declarations became increasingly contradictory. In May 1998 he presented the Strategy for Economic Growth, 1999–2005, advocating a greater regulatory role of the state and more financial support for industry but also a smaller budget deficit. In early August Kuchma sensibly cut expenditures by decree. But in November 1998, in the midst of need for funding, he rejected the advice of the IMF, instead calling for stricter currency controls, monetary expansion, and the abolition of the NBU's limited independence. Not surprisingly, the IMF, the World Bank, and the European Union froze planned credits to Ukraine. Kuchma learned his lesson and stopped criticizing the IMF.

In the summer of 1999 Kuchma criticized the left-wing parliament for having failed to consider about 700 draft laws on economic and social issues that he had submitted to the Rada. In their place, Kuchma issued 39 decrees covering the most important economic issues, but the parliament vetoed nearly all of them. Legislation was deadlocked.

Kuchma seemed to have lost it, but he did not give up. According to the 1996 constitution, Prime Minister Pustovoitenko and his whole cabinet had to resign on the day of the presidential inauguration, November 30, 1999. Kuchma renominated Pustovoitenko, but the necessary parliamentary majority of 226 votes could not be mustered.

Ukraine's financial situation was untenable. In 2000 it faced a seemingly impossible repayment schedule of its foreign debts of some $3 billion, and no financing was on hand. External default was a distinct possibility. The Russian financial crash of August 1998 had sounded a stark warning to the Ukrainian oligarchs. They saw how their Russian brethren had suffered from financial chaos and realized that they had to tighten their belts for their own survival. Though protracted, Ukraine's payments crisis appears to have worked as an external shock. The top oligarchs came together and decided to act.

Oligarchs Opt for a Reform Government

Viktor Medvedchuk, who was first deputy speaker of the Rada and the foremost oligarch, took the lead. He formed an alliance of ten centrist and right-wing factions in the Rada for the financial salvation of Ukraine, which supported the candidacy of the liberal chairman of the NBU, Viktor Yushchenko, as prime minister. Kuchma accepted his candidacy, although he was not the first mover. At the request of the ten centrist and rightist party factions, he nominated Yushchenko on December 20, 1999.

Yushchenko, who knew Ukrainian politics far too well, demanded a free hand to appoint his own cabinet, guarantees from Kuchma for support from his presidential majority in parliament to legislate his reform program, and a mandate to carry out radical reform. Fearing financial disaster, the top oligarchs and Kuchma went along. The ten party factions voted overwhelmingly with 296 votes to confirm Yushchenko, and on December 24, 1999, they signed a government coalition agreement. This was quite a Christmas gift.

Yushchenko was an attractive political personality. He was young and handsome. His background offered an ideal political compromise. He came from the east, Sumy oblast, but he was a native Ukrainian speaker and an orthodox believer. He was a Ukrainian nationalist, though his father had fought in the Red Army during World War II. Yushchenko was a leading economic liberal, but he came from a village and owed his career to the agrarians, who had promoted him to chairman of the NBU. At a time of massive corruption and organized crime, Yushchenko had a clean reputation, although he had been in a high position of power for seven years. Yushchenko knew his political value, and he had chosen his moment.

After his confirmation, Yushchenko wasted no time. He appointed a strong and attractive government of reformist professionals. Yuriy Yekhanurov became first deputy prime minister with responsibility for administrative reform, privatization, and economic deregulation. Most surprising, Yushehenko named the former oligarch and now staunch oppositionist Yuliya Tymoshenko deputy prime minister for energy. The main reform endeavors rested on the shoulders of these three people. For the rest, Yushchenko appointed the best professionals at hand. Serhiy Tyhypko, who was Victor Pinchuk's top politician and had been deputy prime minister for the economy since 1997, became minister of economy. Ihor Mitiukov, Ukraine's most competent minister of finance since 1997, stayed on, though Yushchenko complained privately that he had wanted to appoint Viktor Pynzenyk, but Kuchma refused.[5] Yushchenko gathered Ukraine's best and brightest reformers as Kuchma had in 1994. They were more experienced and knowledgeable than in 1994 and ready to play hardball.

Yushchenko already had a reform program called 1,000 Days of Reform in Ukraine. It had been prepared in cooperation with the German Advisory Group on Economic Reforms with the Ukrainian Government (1999). This program summed up a consensus achieved in the market economic reform debate in Ukraine, calling for a retreat of the state from economic intervention through subsidies and tax privileges as well as administrative reforms and anticorruption measures. Yushchenko wisely realized that 1,000 days was more than he would get, so he opted for a shorter First 100 Days program, which became the real government program. Yushchenko boldly promised results on the 101st day.

Soon, Kuchma wanted to get back into the act. On February 28, 2000, he made a national address to parliament with a new long-term economic and social strategy for 2000–2004, which he labeled Ukraine Toward the XXIst Century. His policy prescriptions coincided with the Yushchenko program. He focused on regulatory reform for entrepreneurship, advocating that intrusive regulations be replaced with general laws and that administrative barriers to business development be eliminated. In mid-March, Kuchma followed up by presenting about 80 draft laws to parliament that were urgently needed to accelerate reforms. These drafts included many key laws that Ukraine was still missing, notably a tax code, a land code, a housing code, and a new criminal code.

The first four months of 2000 saw the greatest reform drive that Ukraine had seen since the fall of 1994. It was broader and more comprehensive, and it would put the market economy right. The main measures can be summarized as central government reform, fiscal reform, energy reform, land reform, large privatizations, and anticorruption measures. Yushchenko and his allies knew that the oligarchs would not tolerate them for long, so they struck while the iron was hot.

Government Reform

The first reform might sound surprising, but elementary order in government decision making was badly needed and was shepherded by Yekhanurov. Ukraine had been notorious for having no standardized

5. Personal communication with Yushchenko in 2002.

decision-making procedures. The state administration was too centralized and hierarchical, but responsibility was diluted as one decision often required a score of signatures. Top officials could sign hundreds of decisions in a day. No clear division of responsibility existed among the president's administration, the large cabinet of ministers apparatus, and the ministries. One could always blame someone else.

Extreme bureaucracy and anarchy characterized the Ukrainian administration. When I wanted to meet Yushchenko when he was chairman of the NBU, I would go to the NBU usually between 8 and 9 a.m. to make an appointment, because then Yushchenko's agenda was set for the day. I tended to opt for a meeting at 5 or 6 p.m. because I knew that he was often called to unexpected meetings between 10 a.m. and 5 p.m. One day, when I came for my 5 p.m. appointment, Yushchenko arrived at 6 p.m. He explained that in the morning my meeting had been the only one on his calendar that day, but some foreign prime minister was visiting Kyiv, and his schedule completely changed. In accordance with strict protocol, the president, the prime minister, and the speaker of the parliament called him to three two-hour meetings with this foreign prime minister. He thus lost almost his whole working day, which was a standard occurrence.

Senior officials did not respect their subordinates' time but demanded their presence at will. Consequently, nobody but the president could plan their day. As any conference organizer in Kyiv knows, ministers were reluctant to commit themselves to events, and, if they did, they often cancelled. Everywhere else in the world, cabinet meetings are held at a specific time every week. In Ukraine they were fixed ad hoc by phone the evening before the next morning meeting, obviously in the hope that key ministers would be absent. This system was typically Ukrainian. It was untenable, but it lasted until 2000.

The extreme voluntarism and collectivism meant that few had time to inform themselves about what they approved. Nobody was responsible, and no gatekeeper barred dubious decisions. The oligarchs, who were usually members of parliament, walked the corridors of the presidential administration and the parliament to extract formal decisions that granted them subsidies and regulatory privileges. The foremost master of this art was Oleksandr Volkov.

Government reform was simple and started from the top. At long last, Ukraine introduced regular weekly cabinet meetings. Four government commissions were set up within the cabinet, each headed by one of the four deputy prime ministers. Any government decision had to be prepared by one of these commissions, and the respective deputy prime minister was held personally responsible. In this way, the cabinet would only discuss well-prepared proposed decisions and be offered an orderly argument. An effort was also made to reduce the number of signatures needed on each decision and the number of documents senior officials had to sign. The number of state agencies was sharply reduced. Accountability was raised, and the president accepted that his administration lost operative power.[6]

Financial Cleansing and the Defeat of Barter

The second task was to clean up the fiscal system. Yushchenko had the draft state budget for 2000 revised. For the first time, the budget had to be balanced because of the complete absence of financing other than tax revenues. In addition, Ukraine had to service all its international financial commitments. Yushchenko emphasized cutting expenditures rather than raising revenues.

At the time, most payments in the Ukrainian economy were made through barter and offsets rather than with money. Russia suffered from the same problems. Many thought there was too little money in the economy. Yushchenko, however, understood that the problem was flawed incentives. Enterprises that did not pay their taxes extracted state orders at favorable prices by paying with services such as road construction. As a rule, the real monetary value of a service provided in barter was only half of the nominal price. Thus enterprises received both a tax rebate and state contracts by not paying their taxes. Barter benefited large corporations with extensive business and government contacts over small and medium-sized enterprises.

As a central banker, Yushchenko realized the importance of the remonetization of the economy, and the means of accomplishing that was not monetary emission but a change of incentives. Consequently, he requested that businesses pay all their taxes in real money and not through barter, offsets, or other monetary surrogates. A related reform was to put state payments in order. The key legislation was the budget code, which was adopted on June 21, 2001. Another important measure was the introduction of effective treasury control. A new Law on Procurement was enacted on February 22, 2000 to ensure competitive purchases and stop corrupt practices.

The combined effect of these measures was much greater than nominal budget statistics show, as they counted barter at face value, twice their real market value. Barter, which had risen for years until 1998, fell sharply, while monetization proceeded, rising steadily to 55.6 percent of GDP in 2007.[7] At the same time, the playing field was leveled and rents were eliminated, stimulating competition and thus economic growth. The

6. Interviews with First Deputy Prime Minister Yuriy Yekhanurov and Cabinet Secretary Viktor Lysytskiy in November 2000.

7. Statistics Committee of Ukraine, www.ukrstat.gov.ua (accessed on July 31, 2008); National Bank of Ukraine, www.bank.gov.ua (accessed on July 31, 2008); ICPS (1999a).

prevailing conventional wisdom was that barter could not be defeated, but Yushchenko did so in no time (Dalia and Schnitzer 2002).[8] Unjustified subsidies were eliminated, while the government budgeted so that it could honor all its commitments, notably pensions, and expenditures had to be adjusted to a lower level than revenue. One of Yushchenko's greatest claims to fame was that he eliminated Ukraine's persistent pension arrears from October 2000 and also paid public wages on time.

A large number of government and presidential decrees had awarded specific enterprises privileges in regulation or taxation, often tax exemptions and subsidies and sometimes monopoly rights. Yushchenko eliminated loopholes in taxation with great passion. He abolished numerous value-added tax (VAT) exemptions on imports and pharmaceuticals. The VAT would no longer be based on cash flow but on accounts, which eliminated the main tax advantage of barter. Overall, taxes were somewhat reduced. The main tax cut was that the 12 percent payroll tax for the Chornobyl Fund was abolished. Some of the least-justified expenditures came from the Chornobyl Fund, since the nuclear catastrophe in 1986 was used as a boondoggle by all kinds of privileged groups. Many enterprises and narrowly defined industries that had benefited from corporate profit tax exemptions saw their privileges eliminated. Similarly land tax exemptions and excise tax exemptions for goods manufactured in Ukraine were abolished. The oligarchs, who were the main culprits, were as stunned as they were furious.

On the expenditure side, the state had financed a large number of so-called categorical social benefits, which were primarily social transfers targeted at the Nomenklatura and paid out through the government budget. Yushchenko started his administration by instantly eliminating about 270 decrees awarding unjustified privileges for the well-connected. This action required little sophistication but a great deal of courage. Other important financial legislation comprised a law on banking and a law on promissory notes.

Although Ukraine has maintained relatively high public expenditures as a share of official GDP, this share declined by 10 percentage points from 44.2 percent in 1997 to a still high 34.5 percent in 2000, while the budget deficit shrank from 5.4 percent of GDP to 1.1 percent of GDP during the same period (figure 5.4). When the state possessed fewer resources, it caused less damage, and more people could break out of the stranglehold of the corrupt state. Yet this tax burden remained excessive (Tanzi and Tsibouris 2000).

---

8. For the corresponding situation in Russia, see Gaddy and Ickes (1998) and Pinto, Drebentsov, and Morozov (1999).

Figure 5.4 Ukraine's consolidated state revenues and expenditures, 1995–2007

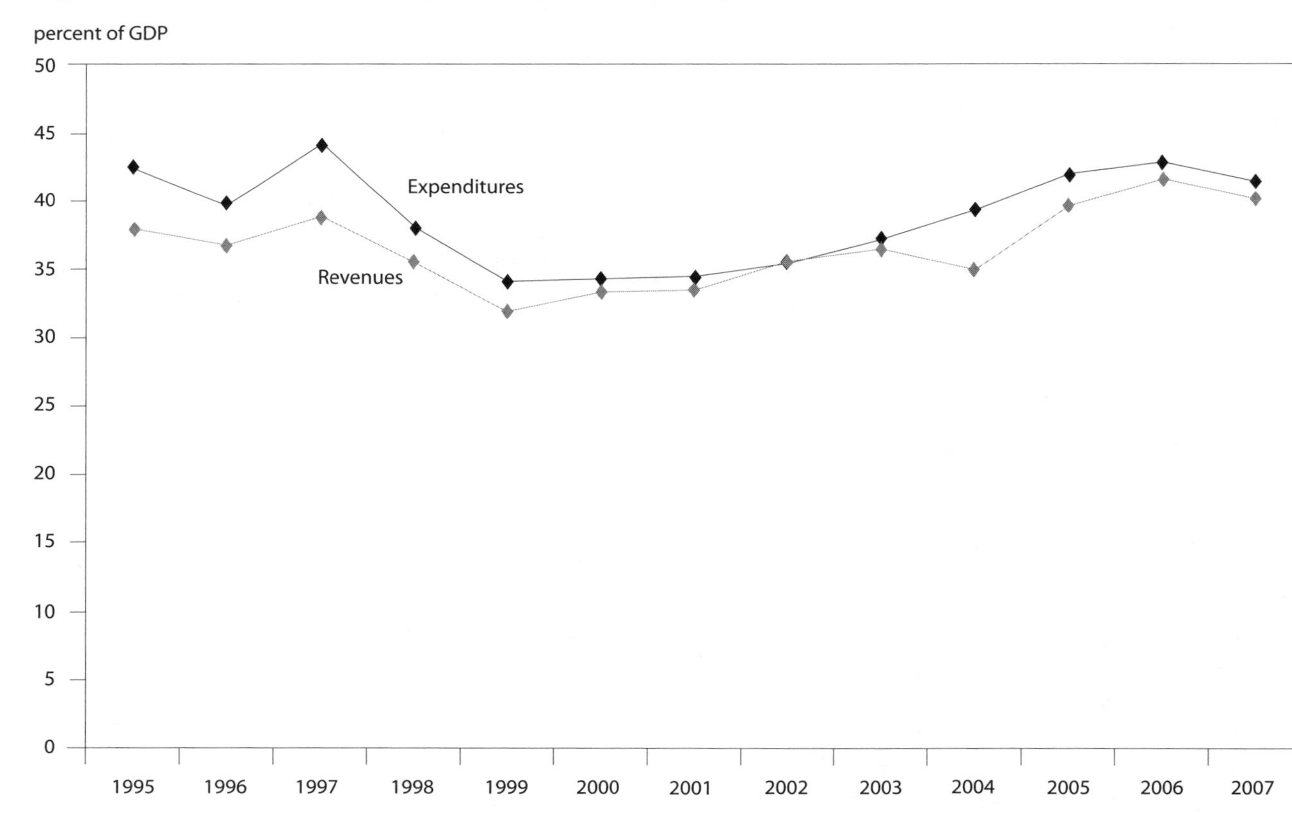

Source: European Bank for Reconstruction and Development online database, www.ebrd.com (accessed on July 8, 2008).

Energy Trade Cleaned Up

The politically most sensitive measure undertaken by the Yushchenko government was energy reform. It was vital, but since all the leading Ukrainian businessmen were commodity traders, energy reform was considered politically impossible.

Few dared to fight these ruthless giants, and even fewer understood their intricate schemes of subsidization and arrears. Yushchenko invited the dissident oligarch Yuliya Tymoshenko to battle her previous competitors as deputy prime minister for energy.[9] By 1999 she had left active business. The question was whether she would clean up the natural gas business or reestablish herself as gas princess. She relished her assignment, and no credible claims of self-dealing emerged.

Tymoshenko knew all the tricks of the gas trade and did her utmost to clean it up. She tried to enhance transparency and eliminate barter as payments for imports with support from Russia. She insisted on tax payments in cash rather than through offsets and tried to stop theft of gas from pipelines. She ended up in a vicious conflict with Ihor Bakai, whom she sacked from his post as president of the Naftohaz Ukrainy, the state oil and gas company, in March 2000.

Electricity was another major source of rents. Here the rent-seeking scheme was much simpler, namely nonpayment. State-owned generators produced electricity, which was distributed by regional monopoly distributors, one-third of which were owned or controlled by Hryhoriy Surkis. While the distributors extracted payments from the final customers, they paid for only 6 to 7 percent of the electricity they "bought" and even less in taxes. Tymoshenko insisted on full payment of both electricity and taxes in real money, and she assessed that she forced the distributors to pay $1.8 billion more for electricity and in taxes in one year. This reform was promulgated as a law in parliament, which made it more difficult to reverse.

Oil was a minor source of energy rents. One oligarch, Oleksandr Volkov, had the exclusive right to import oil at one price, but he could sell it for double the price because of personal tax exemption. The government easily eliminated Volkov's privilege. The oil market was leveled, and Volkov went out of business.

The coal industry received direct government subsidies of hundreds of millions of dollars every year, but Tymoshenko was ousted before she could take on the powerful coal industry in Donetsk, which she blamed for her fall.

The total energy rents that were eliminated probably amounted to some $4 billion a year, or about 13 percent of official GDP, which had

9. This section is primarily based on an interview with Yuliya Tymoshenko in May 2001.

many positive economic effects.[10] Payment discipline and tax revenues improved. Ukraine's energy consumption and energy import costs fell sharply, as enterprises had to pay real money for the energy; and, as the playing field opened up, foreign companies entered Ukraine's oil and electricity sectors. Bakai, Surkis, and Volkov, however, suffered big losses, and they were furious.

Agricultural Land Privatization

Reformers persistently aimed at introducing private ownership of land, but the left in the parliament vetoed all land reform (Lerman 1999). The reform coalition finally made land reform possible.

As an original villager himself, Yushchenko's great passion was to decollectivize agriculture, and in early 2000 he carried out comprehensive land reform. State and collective farms were formally disbanded, and the land rights were distributed to the people on the farms. A shortcoming, however, was that agricultural land could not be privately sold during a transition period, and the left in the parliament stayed strong enough to maintain this land sales moratorium for years.

Initially, most land was leased back to the old managers of the state and collective farms for minimal payment, but much of the land went to private plots, private farms, and increasingly to large commercial holdings. Agricultural land ownership became varied, and the mixed ownership facilitated the deregulation of agricultural trade, which had eluded the country for so long. While little could happen during the redistribution of land, a major supply response occurred in 2001–02. Big new businessmen went into agriculture with a vengeance, and commercial banks were happy to provide loans to farms.[11]

Ukraine traditionally had relatively large private household plots in agriculture, which comprised 15 percent of agricultural land. During hard times, most poor Ukrainians survived through subsistence agriculture. According to official statistics, the share of agricultural production from the small household plots rose steadily until 2000, when they accounted for as much as 62 percent of all agricultural production (State Statistics Committee of Ukraine 2004, 157). However, the household plots did not evolve into real farms, although the small private land holdings expanded to about one-quarter of all land.

Instead, big businessmen, not only Ukrainians but also foreigners, acquired large chunks of land through long-term leases of up to 49 years.

---

10. Tymoshenko's approximate numbers: $2 billion of gas rents + $1.8 billion of electricity rents + $0.2 billion of oil rents = $4 billion.

11. Interview with Peter Sochan, an agricultural expert in Kyiv, in October 2000.

They usually took over one *kolkhoz,* about 5,000 hectares of land, at a time. By 2008 several agrofirms had accumulated a few hundred thousand hectares of land, and they occupied about half of the agricultural land. Ukraine had become a country of large estates.

The remaining quarter or so of agricultural land was still controlled by the old state and collective farm managers. The land often lay fallow, while new agrobusinessmen scrambled to seize it. Ultimately the parliament maintained the moratorium on private land sales because big businessmen wanted to acquire as much land as possible cheaply through leases before land trade started. In early 2008 the moratorium formally lapsed, but legal sales could not take place until a couple of laws regulating such trade had been adopted.

The vital land code was adopted after Yushchenko's fall on October 25, 2001. The ensuing year Ukraine had a bumper harvest of 39 million tons of grain, of which 10.7 million tons was exported, more than the Russian empire as a whole exported in its peak year, 1913.[12] In 2008 the grain harvest reached 49 million tons, with anticipated exports exceeding 22 million tons.[13]

Yushchenko's land reform of 2000 was sufficient to get Ukrainian agriculture going. The breadbasket had been restored, even though harvests have fluctuated greatly because of still-neglected agricultural infrastructure, especially caused by the late privatization of grain elevators.

Privatization of Large Enterprises

The privatization of large enterprises received new impetus. The transformation of the oligarchs from commodity traders to industrialists had started, and two waves of large-scale privatizations were apparent in 1998–2000.

In 1998 and 1999 numerous large enterprises were privatized to a few major oligarchs, notably Surkis, who acquired nine regional electricity distributors. Most of Ukraine's many large steelworks were quietly privatized at this time. These privatizations were inspired by the loans-for-shares deals in Russia in late 1995 (Åslund 2007b, 161–64). The beneficiaries were Ukrainian oligarchs. Usually, they had already secured control over the enterprises in question by buying the incumbent managers. Kuchma's staff desired that the oligarchs raise funds for his reelection in October 1999. Although these were privileged insider privatizations,

12. "Eksport zerna iz Ukrainy sostavit 10,5-11,0 mln tonn" ["Ukraine's exports comprise 10.5-11.0 million tons"], www.gazeta.ru, March 3, 2005, (accessed on July 10, 2008).

13. Interfax—Food & Agriculture, Kyiv, Ukraine, September 10, 2008.

they improved the way these enterprises, big business, and the whole economy operated.

Another wave of large-scale privatization occurred in 2000, when several large enterprises were sold in tenders primarily to big private Russian enterprises, which could now win in competition with Ukrainian oligarchs because they had more money. Four major oil refineries were sold to four different Russian oil companies (TNK, Lukoil, Tatneft, and Alliance), a petrochemical factory to Lukoil, the big Mikolayiv alumina plant to RUSAL, and an aluminum factory to SUAL. Ukraine had huge but old refinery capacity. These refineries produced only a minimum in the 1990s, but privatization made them start working, boosting the country's GDP and allowing Ukraine to become self-sufficient in petroleum products, while it economized on its import bill.[14]

Later, other Russian companies expanded into Ukraine by buying private companies. The Moscow mobile telecommunications company MTS bought the leading Ukrainian mobile company UMC, while Alfa Group bought a large share of the competitor Kyivstar. Among the biggest "Russian" investors were Mikhail Fridman and Viktor Vekselberg, both from the Lviv region.

Yekhanurov also prepared the sale of six regional electricity distribution companies through open international tenders, which was carried out in 2001. This was the first truly open and fair international sale of big Ukrainian enterprises. Two of the companies were bought by American AES, while four were overtly purchased by the Slovak state utility company, which turned out to have acted as an intermediary for Aleksandr Babakov, a Russian businessman close to President Vladimir Putin's Kremlin and a business partner of Surkis and Medvedchuk.

By 2000 the EBRD (2000) assessed that the private sector generated 60 percent of Ukraine's GDP (figure 3.3). Until then, privatization had not had much impact (Estrin and Rosevear 1999). A critical mass had been formed, allowing the economy's mode of operation to change. Enterprises finally started adjusting and expanding.

Deregulation of Small Firms and Anticorruption Measures

The proliferation of low, simplified taxes for small entrepreneurs had started in the least reformist period. From 1986, Ukraine had fixed lump-sum taxes on the books for individual entrepreneurs, but these taxes had been set too high and given little bureaucratic relief (Åslund 2007b). This

14. Since 2005, however, these refineries have been working poorly again because Ukraine imposed close to confiscatory taxation on oil refining.

was how small enterprise was allowed to expand in Poland in communist times (Åslund 1985).

The idea was revived in 1998. The author was Yekhanurov, who was then chairman for the State Committee for Regulatory Policy and Entrepreneurship. A small fixed lump-sum tax was introduced for individual entrepreneurs to legalize them, minimizing their contacts with the authorities and prohibiting all inspections while making them official taxpayers. An individual entrepreneur had to interact with government officials only a few times a year when he or she paid this low fixed tax. No bookkeeping was required, and these entrepreneurs were completely excluded from the inspection rage.

For slightly larger enterprises with up to 10 employees, a low turnover tax of 10 percent was introduced as the single tax. It had similar advantages even if it did not altogether preclude inspections. As a consequence, the number of single entrepreneurs swiftly skyrocketed to an estimated 2.7 million by 1999, and 250,000 enterprises had 1 to 10 employees (Thiessen 2001).

Similarly, Ukrainian agriculture benefitted from a highly favorable fixed tax per hectare that corresponded to as little as 1.5 percent of the value of agricultural output, while being exempt from value-added tax and other taxes (Demyanenko and Zorya 2004). A consequence, however, was that many urban companies acquired huge tracts of land to be taxed as agricultural enterprises, ignoring the actual farming.

All kinds of services flooded the market at low prices. Businesspeople who had operated underground could legalize and intensify their trades, allowing them to raise their output and productivity. After three years of trial and error, deregulation started to bite.

The bureaucratic burden on medium-sized and large enterprises was also great. In a 1997 survey of new medium-sized entrepreneurs in Poland, Slovakia, Romania, Ukraine, and Russia, Simon Johnson, John McMillan, and Christopher Woodruff (2000) found that, in comparison with Central Europeans, Ukrainian entrepreneurs paid 50 percent more taxes as a share of their turnover and 75 percent more unofficial payments to officials. A World Bank survey established that inspections required more management time in Ukraine than anywhere else in the world (Hellman et al. 2000).

A large and intrusive state inspection apparatus of numerous competing agencies indulged in overgrazing of the same companies. The revenues went partly to underfunded public programs and partly to corrupt inspectors (Shleifer and Treisman 2000, Kravchuk 1999). The main scourges increasingly became law enforcement itself, the Ministry of Interior, the Ministry of Security, and the State Tax Administration, each of which was run by a loyal Kuchma strongman.

For long, medium-sized and large enterprises had not really opposed the inspection fury because it granted them monopoly rents. When it faced price competition from myriad small entrepreneurs, however, the established business community demanded lower regulatory costs as well, prompting a decline in inspections. In 2000 Yekhanurov instigated a series of laws to achieve a breakthrough in the conditions for small enterprises, state support for small enterprises, a program on the development of small enterprises, and a law on licensing.

Ukraine was the first postcommunist country where regulatory hazards were well analyzed,[15] and from 1997 onward a substantial reform agenda was gradually elaborated. The number of state agencies was cut, and the agencies were streamlined, while a special agency for the support of enterprises was instituted; licensing was reduced and simplified; inspections were registered and became subject to oversight; and underfunded public mandates were either eliminated or funded. Initially, little came out of changes such as the simplification of licensing and the control of inspections, as the fundamental problems of underfunded mandates and almighty corrupt inspectors persisted. As Iryna Akimova (2002, 168) summarized the situation: "the business environment in Ukraine . . . is characterized by a high level of corruption, insecurity about property rights, a weak legal system for contract enforcement, and extensive tax evasion." The tightening of public finance in 2000, however, brought about real success, as inspections fell off sharply (EBRD and World Bank 2002, 2005).

The Gongadze Murder and "Kuchmagate"

In the fall of 2000, one dramatic event brought about unexpected political change. Heorhiy Gongadze, an independent journalist, had launched an irreverent online newspaper called *Ukrainska Pravda* (*Ukrainian Truth*), which sharply criticized the authorities. On September 16, 2000, Gongadze disappeared in Kyiv. On November 2 his decapitated body was found in a shallow grave in a forest 120 km outside the city. From the outset, this looked like a political murder, but Ukraine had experienced a few other mysterious deaths of journalists, which had aroused no outcry.

Gongadze was a free spirit who had written many stories about corruption criticizing the authorities, but 11 days before his disappearance he had published a critical article called "Everything about Aleksandr Volkov," (Gongadze 2000) which was seen as a likely cause of his disappearance (Wilson 2005, 51–55).

On November 28, 2000, socialist leader Oleksandr Moroz made a sensational speech in parliament. He accused President Kuchma of being involved in Gongadze's murder, and he presented audiotapes as evidence.[16] One of Kuchma's bodyguards, Major Mykola Melnychenko, had

15. The pioneering work was Kaufmann (1995).

16. "Transcript: What Do Melnychenko's Tapes Say About Gongadze Case?" Radio Free Europe/Radio Liberty, March 3, 2005, www.rferl.org.

allegedly recorded hundreds of hours of Kuchma's private conversations in his office in the course of one year. As Adrian Karatnycky (2006, 33) writes: "In those conversations, Kuchma demanded Gongadze's abduction, discussed the criminal harassment of political opponents, engaged in high-level corruption, and revealed himself to be at the center of a criminal and corrupt system of rule."

Melnychenko released the recordings one after the other, discrediting Kuchma. When Moroz presented the tapes, Melnychenko was already in the Czech Republic under the protection of Ukrainian socialists. Later he received political asylum in the United States. However, his behavior aroused doubts about the veracity of the tapes and his intentions. He did not publish all the tapes but continued talking about his future extraordinary revelations, which never occurred, and he was trying to sell his tapes for millions of dollars. After receiving political asylum in the United States, he was sighted in Moscow. He alleged that he acted on his own, which was not altogether convincing. He and his intentions remain a mystery.

In March 2008 a Kyiv court convicted three former Ukrainian police officers from *Sokil* (Hawk), one of the many special units of the Ministry of Interior, for the Gongadze murder, but law enforcement officials were never able to identify who ordered the killing. The responsible lieutenant general of the Ministry of Interior was given the chance to flee abroad, while the key witness died in police custody. The chief suspect, Minister of Interior Yuriy Kravchenko, died in a suspicious suicide on March 4, 2005, just before he was supposed to testify in the Gongadze murder. The roles of Kuchma and his chief of staff Volodymyr Lytvyn in this drama remain unclear.

The Gongadze affair was nicknamed "Kuchmagate." Although the recordings were never fully verified, their impact was devastating for Kuchma. The picture of an administration regularly acting beyond the law was all too evident. The public blamed Kuchma, and their perception of him changed for good. His still respectable popularity rating fell to single digits, never to recover. For most purposes, this day made Kuchma a lame duck, but he had four years left in his presidency.

Kuchma appeared weaker than ever, and a protest movement against him, Ukraine without Kuchma, started. Thousands of people took to the streets in the middle of the winter, demanding his resignation and setting up a tent city in central Kyiv. Moroz and the Socialist Party initially led the movement, but it included protesters on the right as well. Anti-Kuchma protests continued for three months, but the demonstrations never exceeded 20,000 people. The organizers despaired because they had failed to reach a broader public. On March 9, 2001, violence broke out between protesters belonging to the hard nationalist right, UNA-UNSO (the Ukrainian National Assembly and the Ukrainian National Self-Defense Force), and the police. The protesters alleged that this was a provocation, but whatever the truth was, the incident led ordinary people to abandon the protests, which came to an abrupt halt.

Kuchma persisted, but he was forced to sacrifice his strong and long-serving head of the Security Services of Ukraine, Leonid Derkach, in February 2001 and his equally loyal minister of interior, Yuriy Kravchenko, in March 2001. Their departure seriously weakened the political strength of the law enforcement bodies and Kuchma's leverage against big businessmen. The presidential administration reinforced its control over the media (Prytula 2006; Wilson 2002, 32–36; Wilson 2005, 51–55).

A few other mysterious deaths of journalists followed. In July 2001, Donetsk regional television director Ihor Aleksandrov was beaten to death, and in December 2003 another journalist, Volodymyr Karachetsev, was murdered in a purported suicide (Pifer 2004).

The Melnychenko tapes also recorded that Kuchma had approved of the illegal sale of Ukraine's advanced Kolchuga radar to Saddam Hussein's Iraq, which was prohibited by a United Nations Security Council resolution. In September 2002 the United States claimed that it had authenticated this recording, but no Kolchuga radar was found in Iraq after the Western invasion there; it might not have been delivered (Pifer 2004).

These scandals curtailed Kuchma's hitherto extensive foreign travel. He was now considered persona non grata in the West, circumscribed to meetings with Russian President Putin and leaders of other countries in the Commonwealth of Independent States (CIS). The main exception was Poland's President Alexander Kwasniewski, who continued having frequent meetings with Kuchma. Kuchma loved travelling, and he intensified his exchanges with Russia and other CIS countries. Contrary to his desires, his multivector foreign policy had become a single-vector policy. Kuchma courted NATO by all means. In May 2002 he announced that Ukraine's ultimate goal was to join NATO (Pifer 2004). In November 2002 NATO held a summit in Prague, which Kuchma gate-crashed despite NATO having made clear that it did not invite him (Wilson 2005, 60).

Yushchenko's Ouster

Nobody had expected the Ukrainian reforms of 2000 to be so successful, but the elite considered them controversial. Yushchenko concentrated on priority measures and carried them out as planned during his first 100 days, while the elite still needed his economic reforms and international credibility to keep the country from defaulting.

In April 2000 the oligarchs perceived the danger of default had passed, and they began complaining about Yushchenko and Tymoshenko's high-handed rule, calling for consensus and a coalition government. In early April the Social Democratic Party (United), led by Medvedchuk and Surkis, and the faction led by Volkov and Bakai, now called Regional Revival, voiced concerns over the government's reform program. On

April 19, President Kuchma himself started criticizing the government quite sharply for being "insufficiently active." In particular, he disapproved of Tymoshenko's energy policy (Kravchuk 2002, 85).

During the early months of 2000, the *Financial Times'* stringer in Kyiv pursued a virtual campaign against Yushchenko for the incorrect reserve management at the NBU in 1996–98, with Medvedchuk as the apparent source. Because of these vocal complaints, the IMF could not give Ukraine any financial support during the first half of 2000. The consequence, however, was that the oligarchs became all the more dependent on Yushchenko for their own survival.

From the summer of 2000, the oligarchs stepped up their criticism of Yushchenko's economic policy and especially Tymoshenko's energy policies. The main critics were Yevhen Marchuk, Volkov, and Mykola Azarov, the head of the State Tax Administration, who also represented the Donetsk clan. Kuchma largely sided with the oligarchs, though wily as he was, not too obviously. His complaint now as always was that reforms were insufficient.

In September 2000 Foreign Minister Borys Tarasiuk was sacked for having offended Moscow and became the leader of Rukh instead. By November 2000 the Kyiv rumor mill asserted that the president would sack Yushchenko within weeks, but the Gongadze scandal delayed this decision.

On January 19, 2001, Kuchma dismissed Tymoshenko, and on February 13 she was arrested, accused of three crimes committed during her time as a gas trader in 1996–97. First, her company UESU had allegedly not paid VAT on gas sales amounting to $2.5 billion. Tymoshenko's response was that UESU was an offshore company that had been legally exempt from VAT. Second, she was accused of giving Lazarenko a bribe of $110 million when he was prime minister. Tymoshenko retorted that he was coowner of UESU so this was no bribe but dividends. The third accusation was that in a gas deal with the Russian Ministry of Defense she had not paid some $350 million in a barter deal. Tymoshenko stated that she would pay. On March 27 she was let out but not acquitted, as the legal case was only allowed to rest.[17]

In April 2001 four centrist oligarchic parties joined hands with the left and voted Yushchenko out of power. On April 19 they declared the work of the cabinet of ministers unsatisfactory with a large majority of 283 votes. On April 26 a majority of 263 deputies voted no confidence in Yushchenko and ousted him. The remaining center-right with about 170 seats continued to support Yushchenko. The old oligarchs were furious with Yushchenko and Tymoshenko for having deprived them of their old rents.

---

17. Interview with Tymoshenko in May 2001.

A Severe Break in the Rent-Seeking Society

For a decade, Ukraine had been one of the sickest economies in the former Soviet Union, seen as hopelessly corrupt and stagnant. The sudden substantial growth in 2000 was all the more surprising. Ukraine in 2000 offers a textbook example of how reforms can be successful even in adverse circumstances.

Yushchenko's reforms in 2000 were a stunning success in every relevant regard. The prime concern, external default, was soundly averted. Since 1999, Ukraine's public debt as a share of GDP has steadily fallen, and international reserves have risen (figure 5.3). Near fiscal balance was established and maintained for the next few years (figure 5.4). In 2000 Ukraine returned to economic growth after a decade of decline, and growth was substantial at 6 percent. It has proven sustainable and averaged at 7.5 percent a year in 2000–07 (figure 5.5). That is slightly more than Russia's growth despite its oil boom and almost twice Poland's growth. In comparison with Russia, Ukraine's growth has been more volatile.

For the electorate, Yushchenko's most important deed was probably that he started paying pensions on time from October 2000 onward, abolishing the chronic pension arrears, and soon afterward eliminating public wages arrears as well. All these achievements derived from his far-reaching structural reforms.

How could Yushchenko's government succeed so well after so many years of failure? Ukraine's fundamental economic problem was that it was an archetypical rent-seeking society, and the surprise was that this seemingly stable system could be disrupted without revolution, although the rule stayed oligarchic. The explanation is that this was highly sophisticated political economy, pursued by Prime Minister Yushchenko.

First, Yushchenko was given the chance to become prime minister with a strong mandate because the risk of external default was great, which the Ukrainian oligarchs understood well after the Russian financial crash. This complies with Allen Drazen and Vittorio Grilli's (1993) argument that a crisis can facilitate reform by undermining the finances and power of opposing vested interests. It also coincides with the Ukrainian national self-perception that Ukrainians go all the way to the precipice but then retract, while the Russians cross into the chasm.

A second factor was the parliamentary elections in March 1998. The new partially proportional electoral system structured the parliament in sufficiently strong party factions to make bargaining possible. The political representation of the oligarchs rendered their dealings more open and transparent. While not accountable, the public perceived them as responsible. The broad center-right coalition facilitated many decisions that had previously been politically impossible, when one or two oligarchic parties usually joined the left to oppose any market reforms for purely corporate

Figure 5.5 Official GDP growth, 1999–2007

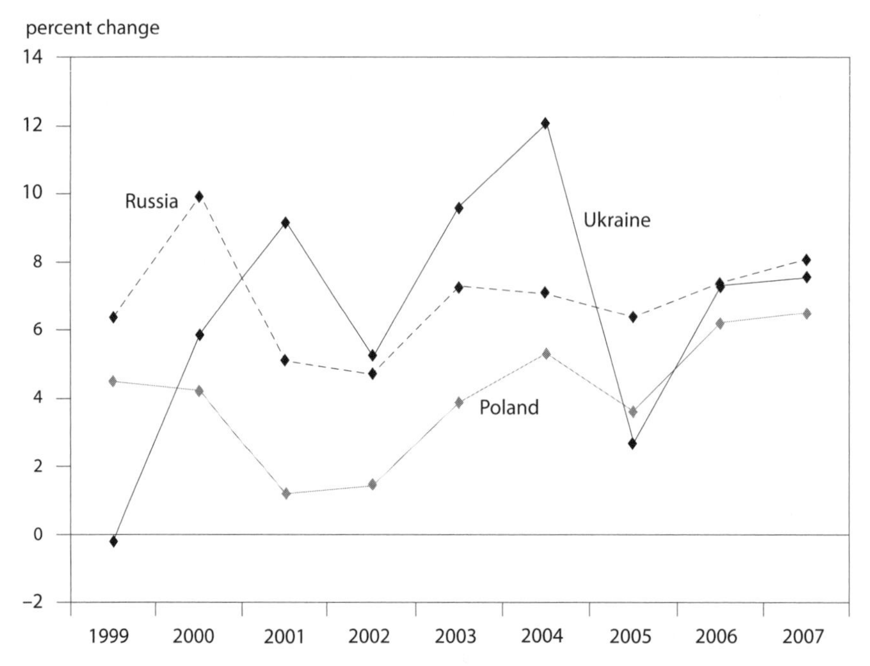

Sources: United Nations Economic Commission for Europe (UNECE) online database, www.unece.org (accessed on July 1, 2008). 2007 estimate from World Bank, *Ukraine: Economic Update,* April 2008, www.worldbank.org.ua (accessed on July 13, 2008).

interests. The coalition agreement impeded defection for a few months, which was sufficient.

A third reason for Yushchenko's political success was his political astuteness. He and his collaborators acted fast and hard. They knew that their time was short and that the oligarchs had brought them as an emergency measure to avoid default. Therefore they emphasized their first 100 days. In that brief window of opportunity, they promulgated all their controversial reform laws that had been discussed but blocked for years. Yushchenko wisely dealt the oligarchs an early devastating blow before they could oust him, taking his cue from Machiavelli. His daring stroke of genius was to invite the forceful Tymoshenko to diminish the oligarchs' energy rents. Her actions put two major oligarchs (Volkov and Bakai) out of business, while the others lost money. Since she dared to challenge the major oligarchs, both Tymoshenko and her husband were arrested and prosecuted. Yet, within a year, the nature of the oligarchs had changed. The worst rent seekers, the commodity traders (Volkov, Bakai, Surkis, and Medvedchuk), had lost money and power, while the steel producers (Akhmetov, Pinchuk, Haiduk, Taruta, and Kolomoiskiy) suffered little and gained wealth and power under the new economic conditions.

A fourth, related explanation was the transformation of Ukrainian big business through privatization. Regardless of how Ukrainian oligarchs had acquired property, their ownership of large producing enterprises changed their behavior. Traditionally, they had made their money through commodity deals secured in the corridors of power rather than through production. Because of their frequently shifting alliances, they had to maintain good relations with all. The privileged privatizations before the presidential elections in 1999 separated the oligarchs' interests by connecting them with specific industries. The pure commodity traders (Volkov and Bakai) lost out, while the others went into large-scale manufacturing. The emergence of millions of small legal entrepreneurs provided the market competition needed to reduce monopoly rents, although they played no apparent political role as yet. The creation of a larger private sphere outside of state influence thus contributed to political development (Boycko, Shleifer, and Vishny 1995).

A fifth lesson is much older than Machiavelli, namely, divide and rule. In energy, Tymoshenko took on one oligarch after the other. Robert Ekelund and Robert Tollison (1981) argued that mercantilism in Britain broke down in the 18th and 19th centuries because of protracted rivalry between the royal court and parliament over rents, leading to laissez-faire. Similarly, Andrei Shleifer and Robert Vishny (1993, 1998) advocated competition over bribes as the best way to drive them down. This seems to have cured Ukraine, although the legalization of the new state of affairs is not in sight.

A sixth explanation is that the public was ready. Many understood Ukraine's predicament and a broad consensus had evolved regarding what reforms were needed to cure the economy. The year 2000 brought execution. Hundreds of reform laws had been drafted and were ready to be adopted. Yet no popular pressure was apparent, not least because the oligarchs controlled the media.

Finally, external pressure was important. The IMF defined the threat of external default and made the rulers aware of the dangers. Paradoxically, its pressure was stronger when it provided no credit. The West strongly influenced the government's ideas, notably the German advisory group, but also the IMF and the World Bank. Ukrainian officials were anxious to be respected by the West, and Yushchenko greatly benefited domestically from being considered so highly in the West. That was why the oligarchs chose him.

To sum up, thanks to the right resolve, a great deal could be accomplished in 100 days. All these reforms were important, but the reduction of energy rents was key, followed by the cleaning up of the state budget and payments, because those reforms reduced rents and thus transformed the oligarchic stratum. Yushchenko provided a textbook case for how a rent-seeking society could be broken up through speed, determination, division, and hard hits, focusing on the most important rents, while taking on one oligarch after another. These reforms would not have been possible if they had been introduced more slowly or if consensus had been sought; the breaking up of the previously cohesive elite rendered them successful. Privatization had made the oligarchs more autonomous from the state and one another, which intensified competition among them.

The 2000 reforms were the second round of brief radical reforms in Ukraine, the 1994 reforms being the first. In many ways they were similar. They were comprehensive radical reforms suddenly imposed from above when people had given up hope. Although the reforms were delayed, they were not gradual or piecemeal but swift, radical, and concentrated. Otherwise, they could not have been carried out. International advice and financing were significant on both occasions.

Much of the deregulation in 1994 was reversed, while that was not the case with the 2000 reforms. One reason was that the 2000 reforms were largely legislated, while most of the 1994 reforms had been imposed through decrees. The tenacity of the reform laws was also reinforced by the existence of a majority coalition consisting of party factions rather than only individual deputies. Moreover, the reforms of 2000 led to economic growth, which made them self-reinforcing, especially as they were based on private ownership. Devaluation and rising international metal prices helped but were hardly fundamental causes. The new growth was also facilitated by a prior shakeout of value-detracting industry.

The breadth of the reforms should not be exaggerated, as the reform capacity stayed limited. No social reforms were undertaken, and no tax code has been promulgated as yet. Judicial reform is urgent. Yet the reforms undertaken in 2000 were probably those most needed.

6

Competitive Oligarchy with High Growth, 2001–04

The sacking of Prime Minister Viktor Yushchenko in April 2001 came as no shock. His departure seemed unfair as his government had done more for Ukraine than any other government, but at this stage Ukrainians were pessimistic and cynical. The surprise was that his government accomplished so much and survived for so long.

Ukraine's economy was finally taking off. In August 2003 I noted: "Anybody who comes to Kyiv is impressed by the frantic construction of big buildings in the city and the swift development of restaurants and shops, while its green beauty remains. With each visit to Ukraine, I am struck by the discussion being more open, intellectual and interesting."[1] The economic dynamism was stunning, especially in the three biggest cities: the capital, Dnipropetrovsk, and Donetsk.

Yushchenko was succeeded by Anatoliy Kinakh, who continued Yushchenko's reform policies at a more leisurely pace. The government continued to function far better than before the Yushchenko interlude, not least because society demanded more. The ensuing government led by Viktor Yanukovych maintained a focus on economic growth.

Intellectual and political liberation accompanied the novel economic boom. The old regime seemed too obsolete to last, and Leonid Kuchma was no longer without competition. For the first time, a strong center-right opposition organized around the two foremost leaders, Yushchenko and Yuliya Tymoshenko. Their first goal was opposition victory in the parliamentary elections scheduled for March 2002, and their ultimate aim

1. From my notes from a trip to Kyiv, August 19–22, 2003.

was victory in the presidential elections in October–November 2004. The strengthening of political parties in parliament laid the foundation for a full democracy. Yet Ukraine was at best semidemocratic (Freedom House 2008). The old regime was digging in its heels, gradually reducing the freedom of the media.

The oligarchs ruled. The greatest symbol of their might was the privileged privatization by Ukraine's two richest men, Rinat Akhmetov and Victor Pinchuk, of Kryvorizhstal, the country's largest steelworks. In July 2004 a real estate company put up posters on Shevchenko Avenue in central Kyiv, advertising a gated community with beautiful mansions on the outskirts of the city. The posters read: "The Rebirth of Aristocracy."

The Kinakh Government

Kinakh replaced Yushchenko as prime minister and was confirmed by parliament on May 29, 2001. He was a highly educated and intelligent man who had become chairman of the Ukrainian Union of Industrialists and Entrepreneurs after Kuchma. Kinakh had been deputy prime minister for industry a couple of times in Kuchma's world of musical chairs. He was a moderate reformer, though representing the old red directors he advocated some protectionism. Among the centrists, he was one of the most liberal, and he was not a businessman. Kinakh was the ultimate consensus seeker, and his main weakness was extreme caution.

His appointment was unexpected but ideal for Kuchma. First, he was a placeholder. The central theme of all political discussions was who would be the next president. Kinakh was too soft to be Kuchma's candidate and he did not represent any oligarchic clan. Second, as in 1997, Kuchma again needed a completely loyal prime minister. Kinakh still belonged to the Pustovoitenko's Popular Democratic Party, which was a leftover of Kuchma loyalists without more profitable connections. Third, in spite of his protestations, Kuchma appreciated Yushchenko's economic reforms and did not want them reversed.

Kinakh fulfilled his job description perfectly, following the Hippocratic oath: Do no harm! He maintained Yushchenko's strict fiscal policy and did not reverse any reforms. He continued promulgating acts Yushchenko initiated, notably the budget code and the land code. The important customs code was also adopted. Yushchenko had started the long-desired judicial reform with a new criminal code, and Kinakh followed up with a law on the court system and a program for the adaptation of Ukrainian legislation to EU legislation. Together, the Yushchenko and Kinakh cabinets promulgated more reform legislation than Ukraine had seen before. Yet the legislative speed slowed down under Kinakh.

Yushchenko had departed with only Yuriy Yekhanurov and his closest personal aides, and Kuchma had sacked Borys Tarasiuk and Tymoshenko earlier. The rest of Yushchenko's government stayed on. Yushchenko in turn had inherited most ministers from Valeriy Pustovoitenko. The government remained the high church of civil service, even if the odd big businessman intruded from time to time. A characteristic example is Ihor Mitiukov, who stayed as minister of finance from 1997 until 2001.

As expected, in due course Kuchma sacked Kinakh, citing his usual complaint about all his prime ministers: not pursuing enough reforms. This time, however, Kuchma's real purpose was evident. It was November 16, 2002, eight months after the parliamentary elections of 2002, a suitable time to choose a candidate for the presidential elections in October 2004. Yanukovych was elected with a slight majority of only 234 votes, only eight more than necessary (Wilson 2005, 83).

The absence of any policy reversal under Kinakh was the litmus test of the success of Yushchenko's reforms: They had proven irreversible. They had transformed the oligarchs from rent seekers to producers, and the producers needed a functioning market economy, although they did not mind tax privileges and some protectionism.

Organization of a Strong Center-Right Opposition

For years Ukraine had no organized center-right opposition of significance. Leading liberal or center-right politicians preferred to work within Kuchma's sphere rather than organize outright opposition. This was true of many prominent ministers, Yushchenko, Viktor Pynzenyk, Yekhanurov, Tarasiuk, Yuriy Kostenko (Rukh leader and minister of environment, 1995–98), and Serhiy Holovatiy. As a group, they had been too weak and individually sufficiently satisfied with cooptation by Kuchma. In 2001 the preconditions changed because the Kuchma regime had acquired three unforgivable flaws.

First, Kuchma had alienated Yushchenko, although the parliament formally sacked him.[2] Yushchenko and his associates remained ambiguous in their attitude toward the president. They did not enter the movement Ukraine without Kuchma, which Tymoshenko considered a betrayal, because she had joined it immediately after her sacking in January 2001. The

2. In his unique fashion of reconciliation, Kuchma himself went to Yushchenko's home the very evening of his ouster and commiserated with him. They drank, and Kuchma took out the guitar and sang melancholic songs. (Personal information from one of the few who attended this extraordinary event.)

Yushchenko group had many well-known leaders, including many former ministers, and numerous seats in parliament.

Second, the Mykola Melnychenko tapes had shown Kuchma's regime to be lawless and morally unacceptable. When media oligarch Viktor Medvedchuk took over from Volodymyr Lytvyn as Kuchma's chief of staff in June 2002, he imposed Soviet-style *temnyky* (theme papers) to instruct journalists what to write about and what to ignore (Prytula 2006, 106–107).

Third, several big Ukrainian businessmen had fallen out with Kuchma and his establishment. These businessmen were not necessarily more virtuous than the oligarchs, but they maintained substantial wealth. The Kuchma regime was sufficiently mild not to destroy them, but it did subject them to tax inspection and legal harassment. Most such businessmen made up with the regime, but four stood out as new opposition hardliners: Petro Poroshenko (nicknamed "chocolate bunny," as he was Ukraine's chocolate king), Yevhen Chervonenko (Ukraine's largest trucker and owner of a drinks company), David Zhvania, and Mykola Martynenko (both primarily engaged in nuclear power). These men were not billionaires, but each was worth a few hundreds of millions of dollars.

In 2001 a large number of right-wing and centrist forces founded the Our Ukraine bloc, which gathered together all the Rukh factions, other right-center party factions, and independents who supported Yushchenko. It was formed in opposition to Kuchma and its self-evident leader and future presidential candidate was Yushchenko. The formation of this bloc involved a great rethinking among the center-right, which was tired of losing. At long last, these forces were coming together rather than underlining their differences.

Yushchenko emphasized universal values, such as faith, family, clean government, and a liberal market economy, and he displayed his achievements as prime minister, notably the elimination of wage and pension arrears. Our Ukraine tried to reach out to the east and big businessmen, welcoming recent defectors from the Kuchma camp. Personally, Yushchenko was prepared to talk to everybody, including Akhmetov and Pinchuk, with only Medvedchuk being his absolute enemy. Yushchenko was determined to create a moderate image and move to the political and geographic center. Therefore he downplayed cultural and linguistic nationalism and excluded extreme nationalists.

Formally, Our Ukraine was an electoral bloc that included seven or eight small parties. It attracted many prominent personalities and enjoyed broad support in western and central Ukraine, especially among Kyiv's intelligentsia, while its attempts to appeal to the east largely failed. Thanks to its newly recruited businessmen, it had substantial financial backing. Its main weakness was media support, but strangely the government gave Poroshenko a license to establish his small cable television Channel 5.

Tymoshenko stayed outside Our Ukraine. She had her old *Batkivshchyna* (Fatherland) Party, which was a one-woman party without much ideology. Her first deputy was Oleksandr Turchinov, who had always been by her side but lacked popular appeal. No one else in her party was prominent. Nor did anybody pay much attention to her party program because only Tymoshenko herself mattered.

After she was sacked from the government in January 2001, Tymoshenko defined her party through staunch opposition to Kuchma. Her message was to fight against corruption and for democracy. Tymoshenko's original electoral base was Dnipropetrovsk in eastern Ukraine. She learned Ukrainian only in the late 1990s after becoming a politician, but even so, she swiftly turned around, nurturing western Ukraine and accepting hard right-wing nationalists, such as the UNA-UNSO (Ukrainian National Assembly and the Ukrainian National Self-Defense Force), whom Our Ukraine did not admit. Her politics, though subdued, appeared social democratic and populist. Together with the socialists, Tymoshenko formed the backbone of the Ukraine without Kuchma movement. As that action faded in March 2001, she renamed her movement the Front for National Salvation, making the ouster of Kuchma and his oligarchic circle in favor of democracy her goal. Eventually it became the Bloc of Yuliya Tymoshenko, suitably abbreviated BYuT to allude to her beauty.

In October 2001 Tymoshenko called for the creation of a broad political alliance that would link her front, the socialists, and Yushchenko's new Our Ukraine bloc. She claimed that this coalition would win the parliamentary elections in March 2002 (Karatnytcky 2006). Yet the Communist Party remained the largest party in parliament. It opposed Kuchma and the oligarchs but disliked Yushchenko and the national democrats more, so the opposition to Kuchma could not unite.

The March 2002 Parliamentary Elections

On March 31, 2002, the parliamentary elections took place as scheduled. The electoral system was the same as in 1998. In one single round, half the 450 seats were allocated through proportional party list elections and half through single-mandate majority elections. The politicians had learned their lesson from the first semiproportional elections in 1998 and ganged up in larger electoral blocs.

The center-right opposition united around Yushchenko and Tymoshenko, respectively. Similarly, most of the Kuchma oligarchs had merged into one electoral bloc called For a United Ukraine. Only Medvedchuk's social democrats ran as an independent oligarchic party because it was the best organized party, claiming 300,000 members, though the party paid the membership dues. On the left, the communists, socialists, and progressive socialists persisted as three independent parties.

The ruling group employed a large number of Russian political consultants before these elections. Their favorite trick this time was to set up

Table 6.1 Results of election to the Supreme Rada, March 31, 2002

Party	List votes (percent)	Seats[a]
Total Left opposition[b]	34.1	87
Communist	20.0	65
Socialist	6.9	22
Total Center/government[b]	28.2	148
For a United Ukraine	11.8	121
Social Democrats (United)	6.3	27
Total Right opposition[b]	31.4	134
Viktor Yushchenko's Our Ukraine	23.6	112
Bloc of Yuliya Tymoshenko	7.3	22
Deputies from other parties and independents		80
Against all	2.5	0
Total	100[c]	449
Voter turnout (percent)	69.3	

a. Seats won in list vote plus seats won by party members and party-endorsed independents in direct vote.
b. List votes include parties that failed to clear the 3 percent threshold (and did not win seats in the parliament).
c. Total includes invalid ballots, not counted as votes.

Source: Central Election Commission of Ukraine, www.cvk.gov.ua (accessed on July 2, 2008).

a dozen fake parties, labeled political twins, that were confusingly similar to the existing opposition parties. They were funded by businessmen close to the regime and given substantial television time.

The election results varied greatly between the proportional part and the single-mandate constituencies. In the proportional part, the four opposition parties (Our Ukraine, the Communist Party, the Socialist Party, and BYuT) won a landslide by no less than 58 percent of the votes cast against 18 percent for the two government parties. On the right, Our Ukraine became the biggest party with 23.6 percent, while BYuT received no more than 7.3 percent (table 6.1).

Our Ukraine had successfully mobilized the whole potential national democratic vote of one-quarter of the electorate. Could it proceed beyond this limit set by Vyacheslav Chornovil in the 1991 presidential election? Tymoshenko succeeded in her electoral makeover and won most of her votes in the radical nationalist western regions. On the left, communist support, which had been steady in the 1990s, fell significantly from 25 to 20 percent, while the socialists maintained their support at 6.9 percent.

For a United Ukraine received a paltry 11.8 percent, admittedly more than twice as much as Pustovoitenko's Popular Democratic Party had obtained in 1998 but still miserable. Medvedchuk's well-financed and superbly organized social democrats gained no more than 6.3 percent of the votes, even though he had spent large amounts and possessed Ukraine's

Table 6.2 Composition of the Supreme Rada, 2002 and 2004

Faction	List votes (percent)	Total seats (March 31, 2002)	Total seats (January 15, 2004)
Opposition	57.7	221	200
Our Ukraine	23.6	112	102
Communist Party	20.0	65	59
Bloc of Yuliya Tymoshenko	7.3	22	19
Socialist Party	6.9	22	20
Propresidential	18.0	148	229
For a United Ukraine	11.8	121[a]	
Party of Regions[b]			67
Labour Ukraine			42
Democratic Initiatives			18
People's Power			22
Agrarian Party			14
People's Democratic Party			16
People's Choice			14
Social Democratic Party (United)	6.3	27	36
Deputies from other parties and independents	21.8	80	20
Total	100[d]	449[c]	449[c]

a. Split after elections.
b. Joined by European Choice in November 2003.
c. One seat remained vacant.
d. Total includes invalid ballots, not counted as votes.

Source: Karatnycky (2006, 35).

strongest party organization. Much of those votes were captured in Transcarpathia with administrative resources, that is, fraud.

The political twin parties were surprisingly successful. Together they received no less than 13.5 percent of the votes, most of which would otherwise have gone to the opposition, but none of them entered parliament through the proportional elections (Wilson 2005, 65–67). As expected, the number of parties that passed the 4 percent hurdle declined—from eight in 1998 to six in 2002, and the share of the votes that did not result in representation shrunk from 34 to 24 percent.

But most of the individually elected seats went to oligarchic representatives. Altogether the opposition received 221 seats, while the government obtained 148 seats. In addition, 80 independents were up for grabs (table 6.2). It had proven cheaper and easier to buy individual seats than party list seats.

An independent exit poll indicated that some vote manipulation and fraud took place, but it was relatively limited, changing the results of the major parties by 0.5 to 1.5 percentage points, which amounted to a few percent of the total vote (Wilson 2005, 67). The speed with which the exit poll was announced might have prevented greater fraud by the government.

The social composition of the new parliament was quite extraordinary. Tymoshenko told me in October 2002 that no less than 300 of the 450 deputies were millionaires. Most of Ukraine's significant businessmen were deputies, and they were found in all parties, including the Communist Party. Their share had doubled from one-third after the 1998 elections to two-thirds. Ukraine's parliament had become a club of millionaires, as the US Senate was known under President Ulysses Grant, when the United States was at the height of its oligarchic era (Steele 2004). In these terms, the oligarchy seemed stronger than ever, but it was badly split and faced a strong and well-organized opposition.

An intricate situation had arisen. For Tymoshenko and Oleksandr Moroz, the situation was evident: The four opposition parties had to unite and form a government in opposition to Kuchma. For the presidential administration, the diagnosis was equally evident: It had to buy or bully the votes needed to maintain control over the parliament. Nobody was more skilled or better endowed at this art than Medvedchuk, and he acted fast and effectively.

Yushchenko, by contrast, faced a dilemma. He could try to mend fences with Kuchma or stay in opposition, but to him cooperation with the communists was precluded because he had nothing in common with them. These parliamentary elections were merely a test run for him. His focus was the presidential elections in October 2004. Consequently, he took a one-month holiday in Europe, Tymoshenko bitterly lamented. Conversely, the communists felt closer to the eastern oligarchs than to the western Ukrainian national democrats in Our Ukraine, so they made no attempt to oust the government. Tymoshenko and Moroz jumped in fury.[3]

Neither Kuchma nor the oligarchs were prepared to give up without a fight. Kuchma reacted to the poor election results by appointing Medvedchuk, his chief of staff, replacing Volodymyr Lytvyn, who was an intelligent intriguer playing politics like chess. Medvedchuk was a heavyweight. A lawyer by training, he was one of the big oligarchs and their leading politician. His big shortcoming as a politician was that his character was all too obvious, making it impossible for him to gain popularity.

Medvedchuk single-mindedly focused on two tasks. One was to persuade businessmen in parliament to join the regime. Since most of them were multimillionaires, they were not easily bribed, so the regime intimidated them instead. Most major businessmen in the opposition endured

3. Interviews with Tymoshenko, Moroz, Yushchenko, and several of Our Ukraine's leaders in October 2002.

raids by the tax police and arrests of their top managers for purported economic crimes, while parliamentary immunity of the deputies was respected. One after another, they gave in. After all, they were in politics for the sake of money. But several became so infuriated that they formed the backbone of holdouts, supporting Yushchenko.

Medvedchuk's second task was to subdue the already obedient media. The leading oligarchs owned most media outlets, and Medvedchuk himself controlled the three dominant television channels, which he had degraded to tabloid status. The same was true of nearly all daily newspapers. Disobedient independent newspapers were sometimes sued for libel and slapped with prohibitive fines, forcing them into bankruptcy. The State Tax Administration was the main means of repression. It inspected no less than 260 media outlets in 2002, adding insult to injury by complaining about their poor tax morals (Prytula 2006, Åslund 2003b).

After the parliamentary elections, two presidential candidates were evident. On the right, Yushchenko had proven to have much broader popular appeal than Tymoshenko, who still suffered from her prior status of an oligarch. Still young at 41, she decided to wait. On the left, the communists had gained three times more support than the socialists, so communist leader Petro Symonenko no longer saw any reason to yield to Moroz. Yet Moroz, never a shrinking flower, remembered Symonenko's poor second-round result in 1999 and insisted on being a third opposition candidate.

After the oligarchs had reassured themselves of their hold on parliament, they happily subdivided themselves into nine clan factions as was their habit. The three most powerful oligarchic factions each had around 40 deputies: Regions of Ukraine (controlled by Akhmetov of Donetsk), Labor Ukraine (Pinchuk of Dnipropetrovsk), and the Social Democrats (Surkis and Medvedchuk of Kyiv and Transcarpathia). The six other oligarchic factions had 14 to 20 deputies each.

The regime received a severe warning that it was likely to lose the presidential elections 17 months later, but it survived for the time being. The opposition had consolidated into four big electoral blocs or parties, while the regime was split into nine factions. As before, the parliament had 13 party factions. The stage was set for a monumental presidential election in October 2004.

The Yanukovych Government

Kuchma and the oligarchs also mobilized before the parliamentary and presidential elections. Their central question was who would become their presidential candidate. Several names were mentioned, but only two seemed plausible, Serhiy Tyhypko and Viktor Yanukovych.

Tyhypko had quite a good reputation. Until 1997, he had been one of the partners in Privat Group of Dnipropetrovsk, one of Ukraine's largest corporate groups involved in banking, metallurgy, mining, oil refining, and retail. When Tyhypko replaced Pynzenyk as deputy prime minister for economic reform in the Lazarenko government, he sold his share in Privat Group, showing an uncommon sense of avoiding conflict of interests. He had served in various governments, including as minister of economy in the Yushchenko government, and maintained good relations with most people. Tyhypko was sophisticated and a smooth talker. He was Pinchuk's foremost politician and the leader of his Labor Ukraine faction in parliament. His electoral drawback was that he was wealthy and elitist.

Yanukovych was quite another kettle of fish. He looked like the big and heavy apparatchik he was, but he was also a self-made man. Yanukovych was born into a poor working-class family in a mining village. His mother died when he was two, and he was left to grow up in youth gangs. The excellent investigative *Ukrainska Pravda* found out that he had been sentenced to prison twice in his youth for violent crimes, assault, and robbery and served jail time, but his records had been deleted. His nickname in prison was *kham* (boor). When he was out of jail, he worked as a laborer. But thanks to good connections, he got a new start. In the 1990s he advanced within the regional state administration in Donetsk, becoming the forceful governor of Donetsk oblast from 1997 until 2002. He befriended Rinat Akhmetov, Ukraine's richest businessman and the head of the Donetsk clan, and they rose together (Wilson 2005, 7–8, 12–13). While a conversation with Tyhypko was delightful, Yanukovych was an archetypical boss who hardly conversed but gave orders, and his authority bred popularity. Especially in eastern Ukraine, where many men had served jail time, the argument ran that jail service had made him a real man.

At the time, the three politically leading oligarchs were Akhmetov (Donetsk), Pinchuk (Dnipropetrovsk), and Medvedchuk (Kyiv and Transcarpathia). None of the members of Medvedchuk's group was electable—Surkis and Medvedchuk had tried repeatedly and failed miserably—so Medvedchuk had no candidate. Therefore, the competition was between Tyhypko and Yanukovych. Westerners rooted for the pleasant Tyhypko, but Yanukovych enjoyed support from Akhmetov and the Donetsk clan, which was richer and stronger in parliament than the other oligarchic clans. Finally, Yanukovych had the knack of a professional, popular politician. While Tyhypko's popularity rating did not rise from the low single digits, Yanukovych's popularity surged. When Kuchma made Yanukovych prime minister on November 21, 2002, he provisionally anointed him the presidential candidate.

The competitive Tyhypko did not give up. Yushchenko had built his authority as chairman of the National Bank of Ukraine (NBU). That position was occupied by Yushchenko's long-time first deputy Volodymyr

Stelmakh, a loyal civil servant with no particular qualifications for that job. One week after Yanukovych's appointment as prime minister, the parliament—contrary to the idea of central bank independence—tried to oust Stelmakh, but the first attempt failed. However, Tyhypko supporters maintained pressure on the nice, not very combative Stelmakh, and he resigned. On December 17 Tyhypko became chairman of the NBU. Although he was more qualified than Stelmakh, his maneuvers left a bad taste.

Yanukovych formed a new type of government. Since 1991, approximately the same group of civil servants had played musical chairs with government portfolios. Most of them had become reasonably competent over time, but they also grew older and less interested in reform, and many had become quite corrupt. Yanukovych undertook the first (nearly) complete change of ministers since independence. His new ministers were big new businessmen who had made large fortunes in their early thirties, mainly from the east but also from Kyiv. Most were parliamentarians and this was the first parliamentary coalition, formed by nine centrist, oligarchic factions. The new ministers loved to decide and hated to obey or compromise. Some of them wanted to do good, though most of them were more interested in doing well. Somewhat unexpected, the Yanukovych government proved dynamic in its legislation, mobilizing a legislative majority mostly to its right.

A stalwart was First Deputy Prime Minister and Minister of Finance Mykola Azarov, who had built the repressive State Tax Administration. He authored Yanukovych's most important reform, a tax reform, which was adopted on May 22, 2003. Its purpose was to liberalize and simplify the tax system. It had two major components. First, the previous progressive income tax peaking at 40 percent was replaced with a flat income tax of 13 percent starting in January 2004. Ukraine followed the example of Russia, which had introduced such a flat income tax in 2001 resulting in higher revenues from the personal income tax (Åslund 2007b). When I met him in March 2003, Azarov advocated a flat income tax of 20 percent, while the right-wing opposition wanted a progressive tax with two rates, 20 and 30 percent, but as in Russia sheer political momentum carried the day.

A second tax reform was a reduction of the corporate profit tax from 30 to 25 percent. In addition, some remaining loopholes in the value-added tax (VAT) were abolished, but the free economic zones that primarily benefited Donetsk businessmen were maintained. A new law on the registration of enterprises and entrepreneurs was also adopted, which eased the bureaucratic burden and arbitrariness on business.

The Yanukovych government legislated a new progressive three-pillar pension system on July 9, 2003, introducing mandatory private pension savings in line with the World Bank (1994) best practice. But no follow-up legislation was enacted, leaving the pension reform unimplemented.

Yanukovych had a rather liberal minister of justice, Oleksandr Lavrynovych, who originated from Rukh. He continued the judicial reform, adopting a criminal-procedural code and a civil-procedural code as well as a law legalizing private arbitration courts.

In other cases, different parts of the government promulgated contradictory laws. Ukraine had long needed a civil code with modern corporate legislation. The Yanukovych government sensibly adopted a civil code on January 16, 2003, but in a weird compromise it enacted a contradictory economic code on the same day. Both codes covered the same ground, but the economic code entitled the state to interfere in private corporate contracts. Ukrainian judges were given a free hand to choose which code to apply, facilitating lucrative bids from competing businessmen. This legal situation was absurd, but it persists (OECD 2004, EBA 2004).

Yanukovych's government did not reverse Yushchenko's reforms because its industrialists desired economic growth. As a strong minister of finance, Azarov maintained the fiscal balance until the presidential election campaign posed more pressing demands. Most disappointed was Minister of Economy Valeriy Khoroshkovskiy, who at 34 was one of the youngest ministers but a successful businessman in banking and retail trade. His liberal urge was to take Ukraine into the World Trade Organization (WTO), but his endeavor found little sympathy among his industrialist colleagues. Liberal trade legislation came to a halt.

A dominant concern of exporters in Ukraine was to recover their VAT refunds after export. By law, exporters were entitled to receive a refund of the 20 percent VAT on their exports from the state, but hardly anybody did. As a result, VAT functioned as a 20 percent penalty tax on exports. The International Monetary Fund (IMF) tried to sort out the VAT problems. Originally, one authority (e.g., the State Tax Administration) received VAT payments while another (e.g., the Customs Committee) was supposed to pay refunds, but the latter refused to do so because they had not received any funds for this purpose. Moreover, the government budgeted too little money for VAT refunds or crudely sequestered such funds. The government complained that widespread exemptions from VAT led to tax fraud, since many did not pay this tax but illegally claimed refunds. In particular, VAT was not paid on imports through Ukraine's 20 free economic zones, depriving the state of large tax revenues. Similarly, agriculture and much of the energy sector were exempt from VAT. The main cause, however, was that Ukrainian officials did not give businessmen money unless they were paid a commission. A system had developed where a central group of state officials demanded, and usually received, 20 to 30 percent of the VAT refunds in commission through a private intermediary (Åslund 2003a, EBA 2004).

When the weather conspired against agriculture in 2003, Yanukovych reacted in the old Soviet fashion, unleashing a major antimarket drive. He threatened grain traders with arrest because of price gouging and ordered regional governors to control grain trade and prices and the police to check grain transportation. The marketization of the countryside suffered a serious setback.

Controversial Privatization of Kryvorizhstal

Privatization of large enterprises proceeded slowly. Hardly any privatizations were open, and the main beneficiaries were usually big Ukrainian businessmen with good political connections. Although disadvantaged, Russian businessmen also knew how to please the authorities, while Western businessmen were lost.

By and large, state enterprises had been declining. They could cut costs and undertake purely defensive restructuring, but they were unable to develop new production or expand. As a consequence of privatization, the big Ukrainian businessmen successfully turned around neglected Soviet behemoths, and the Ukrainian capitalists grew stronger, more productive, and more multifaceted.

One privatization caught the public's imagination. On June 14, 2004, Ukraine's two richest oligarchs, Pinchuk and Akhmetov, bought Kryvorizhstal steelworks together. This privatization became a cause célèbre as the Russian loans-for-shares privatizations had in 1995 before Yeltin's reelection (Freeland 2000).

The reasons for the controversy were many. This was Ukraine's largest and most modern steelworks, considered the jewel in the crown, and it was the only state-owned steel mill left. Other metallurgical factories had already been revived so it was no longer seen as a white elephant. Akhmetov and Pinchuk were the richest oligarchs and the bulwark of the Kuchma regime. They usually competed with each other, but in this case they colluded. Several competitors had expressed interest, ranging from the Industrial Union of Donbas to Europe's Arcelor and Russia's Evraz group. The conditions for the tender were highly protectionist: "Only two of the six companies, both Ukrainian, which submitted tenders could meet the requirement of having produced at least one million tons of coke and two million tons of rolled steel for the last three years, two of them profitably, inside Ukraine" (Kuzio 2004).

The price was the highest paid for any Ukrainian company at $800 million, and it was in cash. Pinchuk argued that this was twice as much as had been paid for the privatization of all other Ukrainian steelworks. Yet at that time Kryvorizhstal might have caught a price of $3 billion in an open tender. Akhmetov and Pinchuk insisted that it was vital for Ukraine's future that Kryvorizhstal remain Ukrainian, because it was the backbone of the country's steel industry. Without it, Ukraine's steel industry would be parceled out among global giants, such as Arcelor, Mittal, and Russian steel corporations.

By Ukrainian privatization standards, the privatization was not all too shocking, but powerful competitors existed, and the conditions were more transparent than in any other major privatization, which facilitated criticism. Most important, this blatant underpricing occurred four-and-a-half months before the epic presidential elections, of which it became one of the main themes.

Economic Boom

The year 2004 was a strange time in Ukraine. The air held a tantalizing sense of the end of an era, a *fin de siècle*, but the elite was not worried but joyful. They seemed caught in hubris, thinking that they could get away with anything. The oligarchs made money as never before, and the economy developed at an extraordinary speed. Ukraine's growth hit 12 percent in 2004, the highest in the country's modern history (figure 5.5).

An underlying cause of this boom was the rise in international steel prices. Steel accounted for close to 40 percent of Ukraine's exports. In 2004 Ukraine's exports skyrocketed by 41 percent, as its volume and value surged (figure 6.1). Imports could not keep up in this race, and Ukraine achieved a large current account surplus of 7 percent of GDP in 2004, although it suffered from rising prices of imported oil (figure 6.2).

Ukraine's gross fixed investment had held up well at around 20 percent of GDP in the downturn (a normal European level) and started surging in 2003, reaching the respectable level of 27 percent of GDP in 2007 (figure 6.3).

Ukraine's workers had suffered from wage arrears, low wages, and underemployment rather than unemployment, which never became very high, though no appropriate survey measures were available before 1998. In the breakthrough year of 2000, unemployment was 11.6 percent. It fell to a reasonable level of 7.2 percent in 2005 (figure 6.4).

The long-depressed real wages started an impressive recovery of between 15 and 20 percent a year, peaking at an incredible 24 percent in 2004, the year of the Orange Revolution (figure 6.5).

This picture is full of irony. In most regards, Ukraine's economic development had never looked better than in 2004. In his famous book, *The Old Regime and the French Revolution*, Alexis de Tocqueville (1955 [1856], 176) noted that the French Revolution did not occur when things were getting worse but when they were improving. Likewise the Orange Revolution took place in the midst of an unprecedented economic boom. As in de Tocqueville's France, public concern was not the economic efficiency of the old system but its lingering injustices: "There was nothing new in these delinquencies on the part of the administration; what was new was the indignation they aroused" (178).

Figure 6.1 Ukraine's exports and imports of goods, 1992–2007

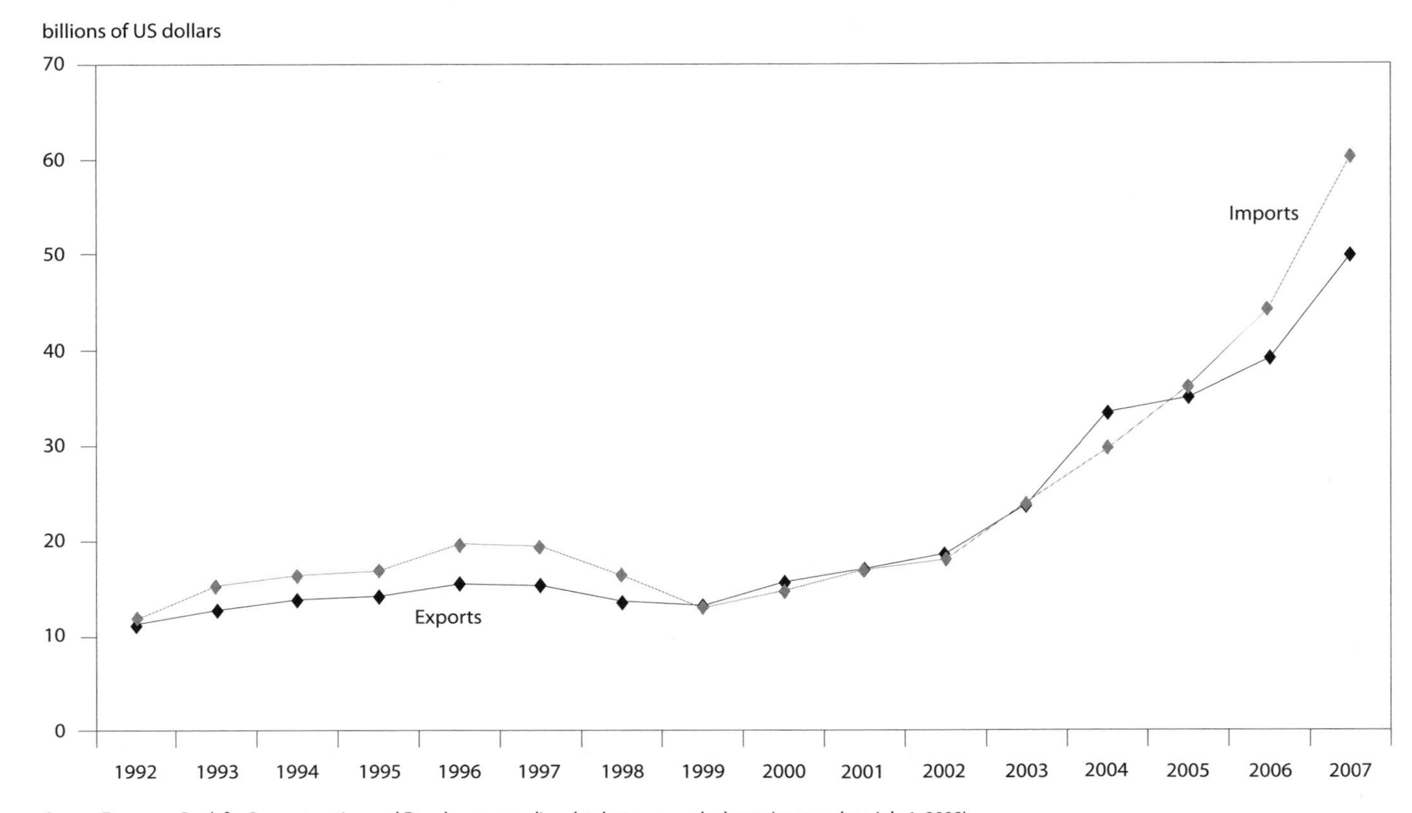

Source: European Bank for Reconstruction and Development online database, www.ebrd.com (accessed on July 1, 2008).

Figure 6.2 Ukraine's trade and current account balances, 1992–2007

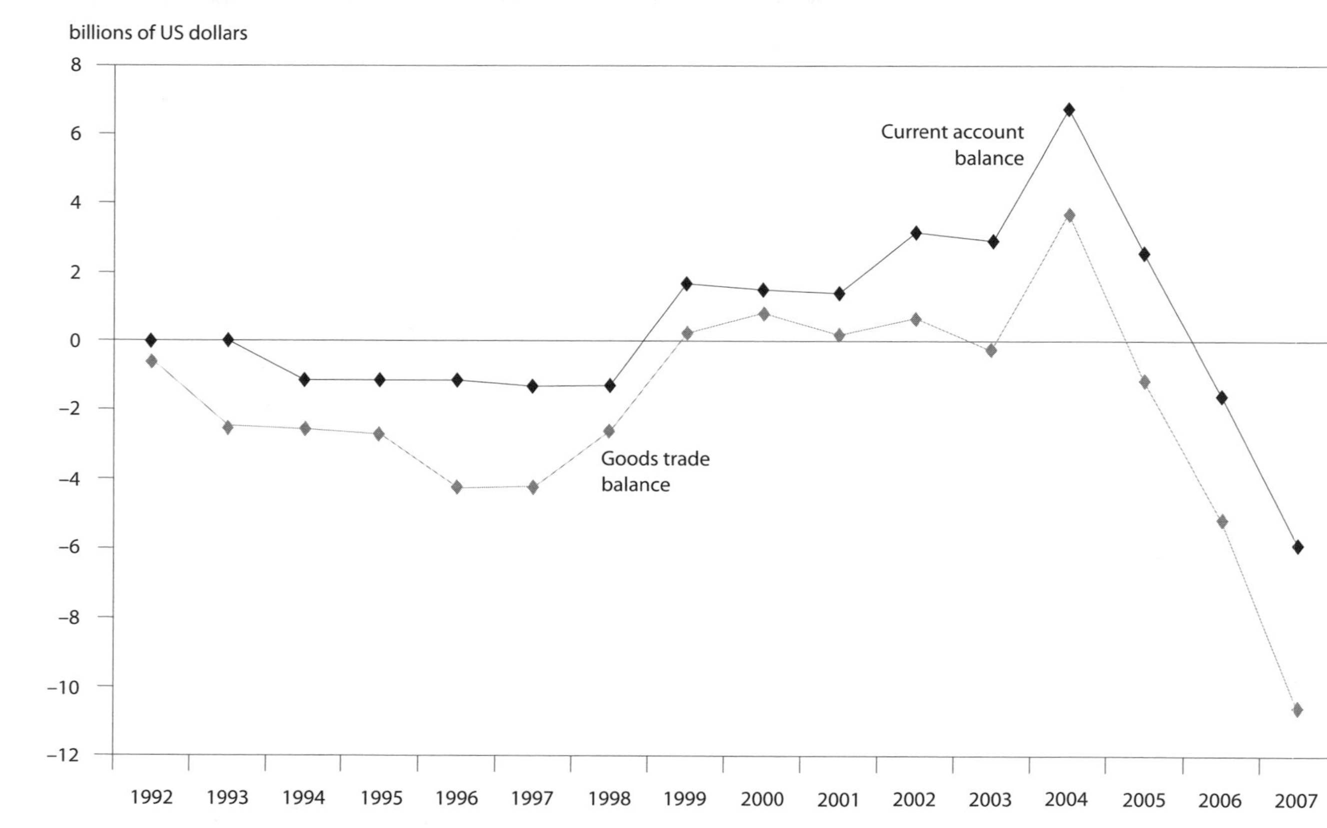

Source: European Bank for Reconstruction and Development online database, www.ebrd.com (accessed on July 1, 2008).

Figure 6.3 Ukraine's gross fixed investment, 1991–2007

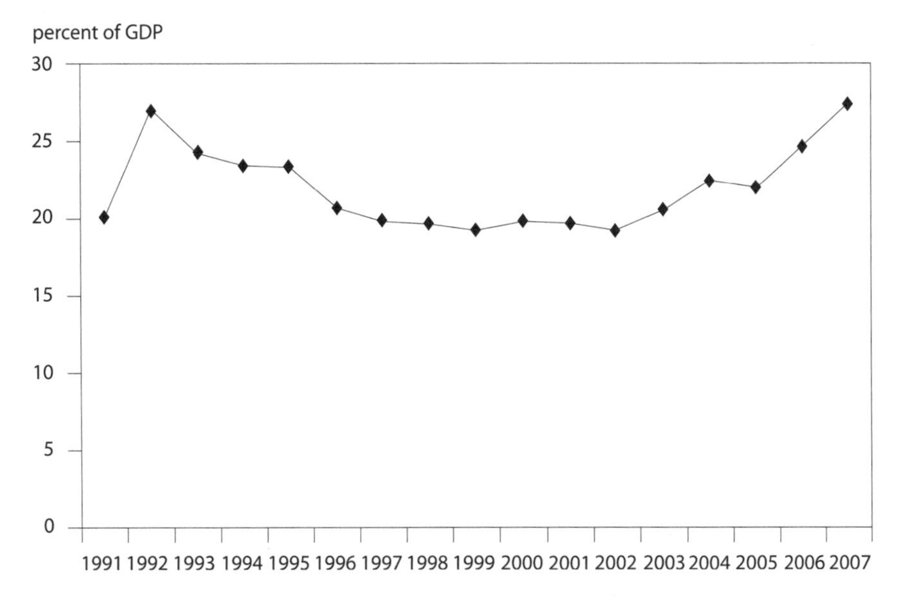

Note: Gross fixed capital formation at prices and purchasing power parities of current year.

Source: UN Economic Commission for Europe online database, www.unece.org (accessed on July 1, 2008).

The Ukrainians also acted in line with modernization theory (Lipset 1959). High economic growth and rising welfare convinced them that the political system was obsolete. A Marxist would say that the economic base had outgrown the political superstructure, and rising welfare undoubtedly enhanced the self-confidence of the surging middle class (Åslund 2006).

But were the statistics credible? Two caveats exist. First, VAT fraud in exports was rampant, and it skyrocketed in 2004, when Yanukovych's tax people decided to make a killing before the deluge. As a consequence, exports were substantially exaggerated that very year, which would also have overstated GDP. The two ensuing governments made several alternative assessments. The largest claim was 5 percent of GDP, but 2 to 3 percent of GDP is more likely, which would have been substantial but still not changed the overall picture of 2004 having been Ukraine's finest boom year.

A second statistical query is whether the sudden rise in growth rates reflected a gradual incorporation of the large unregistered economy into the official economy, but that was hardly the case. The Ukrainian Ministry of Statistics has been very conservative and inert, not revising its numbers much and using surveys and samples less than most statistical authorities. A careful study by Iryna Mel'ota and Paul Gregory (2001) found that the undetected shadow economy, revealed through statistical discrepancy, would raise the real Ukrainian GDP by as little as 12 percent in 1999. The popular perception, however, is that the unregistered economy is much larger.

Figure 6.4 Unemployment in Ukraine, 1998–2007

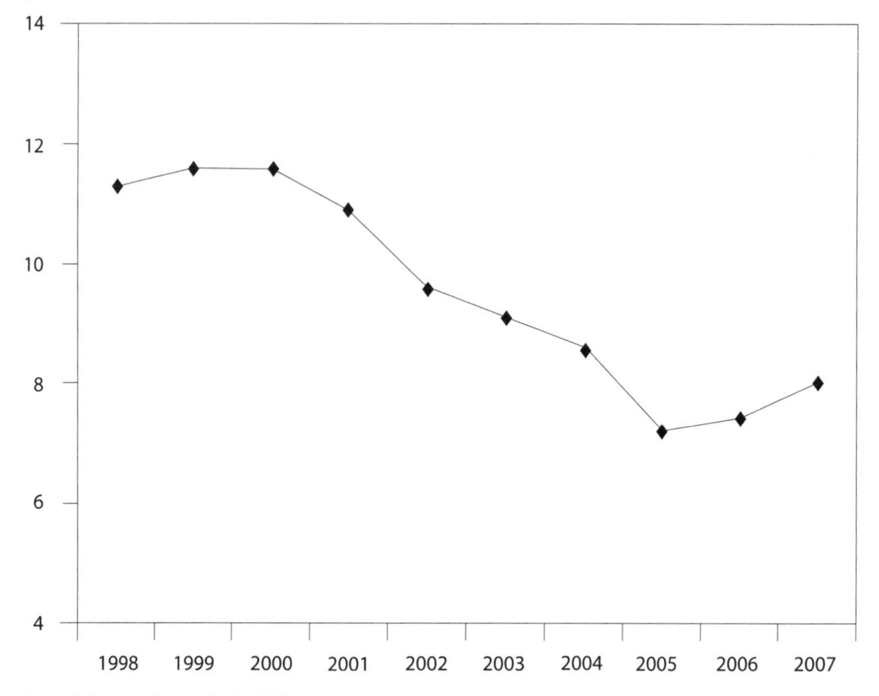

Note: 2007 statistics as of July 2007.

Sources: UN Economic Commission for Europe online database, www.unece.org (accessed on August 16, 2007); Statistics Committee of Ukraine, www.ukrstat.gov.ua (accessed on August 16, 2007).

Moreover, Yanukovych let the budget deficit explode in 2004, delivering a massive fiscal stimulus that boosted GDP. Economic growth in 2004 was great, but a significant part of the recorded growth might have taken place in 2005.

Putin's Policy on Ukraine: Gas Trade, Common Economic Space, and the Tuzla Incident

On December 31, 1999, Boris Yeltsin anointed Vladimir Putin president of Russia. Initially, Putin paid little attention to the former Soviet republics, but gradually his interest was aroused.[4] His foremost interest was

4. The main sources of this section are Stern (2005), Wagstyl and Warner (2006), and Åslund (2007b).

Figure 6.5 Real wages of Ukraine's population, 2000–2007

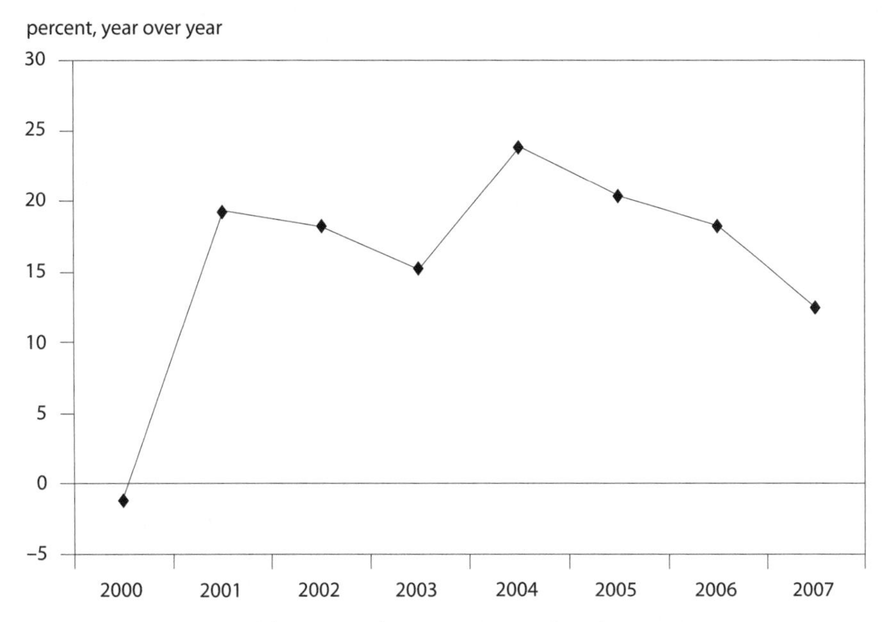

Source: Statistics Committee of Ukraine, www.ukrstat.gov.ua (accessed on July 28, 2008).

Gazprom, and he looked at Ukraine through its prism. His second policy focus was the Ukrainian presidential elections in October 2004. Third, he wanted to rope in Ukraine through the Common Economic Space. Finally, a strange border incident occurred in October 2003 on the unpopulated islet of Tuzla on the Kerch Strait.

In the spring of 2001, Putin carefully plotted the ouster of the Gazprom management, where the Russian government was majority owner. Former Prime Minister Viktor Chernomyrdin was chairman of Gazprom's supervisory board and the guardian angel of Gazprom CEO Rem Vyakhirev. In order to sack Vyakhirev, Putin first dismissed Chernomyrdin as chairman of its supervisory board and then sent him off as ambassador to Ukraine in May 2001. Days afterward, Putin personally ousted Vyakhirev at a meeting in the Kremlin. He appointed two of his closest collaborators to run Gazprom: His first deputy chief of staff Dmitri Medvedev became chairman of the supervisory board, and his former assistant Aleksei Miller was appointed CEO.

The change of Gazprom management was important also for Ukraine. The key issue for Ukraine was the gas trade regime—the usage of an intermediary trading company, the length of contracts, the system of pricing, and payment in barter or cash. In practice, little changed. Itera lost out to a new intermediary trading company, Eural Trans Gaz, which was established in December 2002, but the trading conditions remained as before.

In late July 2004 Kuchma and Putin met in Yalta and replaced Eural Trans Gaz with another intermediary, RosUkrEnergo. They oversaw the signing of its contracts with Gazprom and Naftohaz Ukrainy for gas deliveries to and through Ukraine. RosUkrEnergo was better formalized than Eural Trans Gaz. It was registered in Zug, Switzerland, and half-owned by Gazprombank. The other half was owned by Centragas Holding, a company whose Ukrainian owners remained a secret, but it was managed by Austria's Raiffeisen International Bank.

A coordination committee for RosUkrEnergo was appointed, which included Yuriy Boiko, Ukraine's deputy minister of energy and chairman of Naftohaz Ukrainy, and his deputy, Ihor Voronin, although the Ukrainian government and Naftohaz Ukrainy had no official ownership in RosUkrEnergo. In a blatant conflict of interests, these two Ukrainian officials represented a private trading company. The renewed trading system did not clean up the gas trade (Global Witness 2006, 51–52; Milov and Nemtsov 2008).

In return, Putin did not push for higher gas prices with Ukraine, and international oil price rises took off only in 2004. His dominant interest in this trade appears to have been to skim off profits and direct them to his men in the Kremlin. As before, the Russian officials concerned were happy to share their gains with their Ukrainian counterparts to facilitate their personal enrichment.

In early 2003 Putin turned his eyes on Ukraine because of the upcoming presidential elections. Russia had repeatedly tried to rope in Ukraine with attractive trade arrangements, but Ukraine was a hard flirt, and the Russian-dominated Commonwealth of Independent States (CIS) had a bad habit of setting up a new organization rather than solving the dysfunction of existing bodies.

True to style, Putin came up with a new scheme, the Common Economic Space (CES).[5] It was specifically designed to attract Ukraine. Therefore, it was not bilateral but multilateral, but without the Central Asian countries, which were of little interest to Ukraine, and it was exclusively economic.

On February 23, 2003, the CES was launched with great fanfare in Moscow, with a common declaration by the presidents of Russia, Ukraine, Kazakhstan, and Belarus. By September 2003 they concluded an agreement as planned, and all four parliaments ratified it. The CES was designed to be a customs union as well as a currency union, coordinating the four countries' entry into the WTO, which all four had been negotiating for years. However, as Russia's prior attempt at a customs union showed, it was not going to work because Russia insisted on dictating its own import tariffs on the other members, who naturally resisted. The spectacular collapse of the ruble zone in 1993 and the lasting double-digit

5. An overall source on the CES is Bukkvoll (2004).

inflation indicated that a currency union was premature. Any attempt at coordinating WTO accession was likely to delay entry for all countries concerned.

Even within Yanukovych's government, the CES was immensely controversial. Three major members of his cabinet protested publicly against the CES, namely Minister for Foreign Affairs Kostyatyn Gryshchenko, Minister of Economy Valeriy Khoroshkovskiy, and Minister of Justice Oleksandr Lavrynovich.[6] The minister responsible for foreign trade, Khoroshkovskiy, soon resigned. Kuchma accepted the CES with hesitation, as did Yanukovych, who was anxious to obtain Moscow's support for his presidential candidacy. The only enthusiastic supporter of the CES in the Yanukovych cabinet was First Deputy Prime Minister Mykola Azarov, who was considered most pro-Russian.

Thus, both economically and politically, this scheme looked even less viable than previous Russian ideas, and it was to be a drain on time, energy, and policymaking capacity. In September 2003, thanks to having gone along with the CES, Ukraine resolved many of its numerous trade conflicts with Russia as at the conclusion of the Russian-Ukrainian Treaty on Friendship, Cooperation and Partnership in May 1997. These trade disputes usually amounted to Russia prohibiting particularly successful Ukrainian export items, typically agricultural goods or steel. Ukraine, however, subscribed only to the free trade part of the CES, and then Putin was not interested. The scheme slowly died after the Orange Revolution.

On October 22, 2003, a Russian-Ukrainian conflict of a new type erupted without warning. Russian emergency troops unexpectedly stormed the uninhabited islet of Tuzla on the Kerch Strait. The border between Russia and Ukraine had never been regulated on these waters, and Tuzla was disputed territory. Surprisingly, Prime Minister Yanukovych vehemently protested against the Russian border violation, and without delay both Ukraine and Russia started substantial troop movements to the area. After a few days of excited public exchanges, the Russian troops withdrew, and the dispute died down. Apparently, Ukraine had responded with sufficient force to persuade the Kremlin to interrupt its surprise action.

NATO and the European Union's European Neighborhood Policy

After the Melnychenko tapes started being released in November 2000, the West began treating Kuchma as a pariah. As a consequence, and contrary to his desires, Kuchma's multivector policy collapsed into a single

6. Tom Warner and Stefan Wagstyl, "Ukraine Ministers Seek to Change Treaty," *Financial Times*, September 16, 2003.

Russia/CIS policy. Kuchma did whatever he could to break his isolation from the West, but nobody listened to him.

Kuchma courted the North Atlantic Treaty Organization (NATO) by all possible means, and Ukraine participated in all NATO cooperation that was offered and in all peacekeeping operations in former Yugoslavia. Most spectacularly, in May 2002, Kuchma announced that Ukraine's ultimate goal was to join NATO (Pifer 2004), but nobody seemed to take him seriously. He even gate-crashed the November 2002 NATO summit in Prague, despite NATO having made clear that it did not invite him (Wilson 2005, 60).When the United States contemplated invading Iraq in 2003, Ukraine became one of the original members of the coalition of the willing, sending no less than 1,700 troops to Iraq.

In 2003 the long-slumbering European Union finally took a new initiative toward Ukraine. The irony was that Russia desired to tie Ukraine closer to itself, while Ukraine resisted. The European Union, by contrast, wanted to keep Ukraine at arm's distance, but Ukraine aspired to get much closer to it.

For years, the European Union had been so preoccupied with the Central and Eastern European countries designated to become EU members that it had no time for other countries. However, by 2003, it was clear that eight former Central and Eastern European countries would become EU members on May 1, 2004 (Estonia, Latvia, Lithuania, Poland, the Czech Republic, Slovakia, Hungary, and Slovenia), with Bulgaria and Romania following on January 1, 2007. The EU bureaucracy had freed up time and capacity to look further, raising the question of how to regulate EU relationships with other adjacent countries.

In March 2003 the European Commission published a conceptual document, "Wider Europe Neighborhood: A New Framework for Relations with Our Eastern and Southern Neighbors" (Commission of the European Communities 2003).[7] It outlined the principles for a new European Neighborhood Policy (ENP). This policy was designed for both North African and Middle Eastern countries (Algeria, Morocco, Tunisia, Libya, Egypt, Jordan, the Palestinian Authority, Israel, and Lebanon) and the western CIS countries (Russia, Belarus, Ukraine, and Moldova). It was an attempt to structure and standardize the EU approach to friendly neighbors, offering them more market access and interaction but also making clear that they were not welcome to become members. In October 2003 the highest EU body, the European Council, endorsed the ENP and asked the European Commission to formalize initial action plans with the individual countries.

7. This discussion of the ENP is based on Milcher, Slay, and Collins (2007). See also De Souza et al. (2005), CEPS (2006), and Sushko (2006). The ENP strategy is developed in Commission of the European Communities (2004).

The initial reaction from Ukraine (and Moldova) was highly negative. According to the EU founding treaty, the 1957 Treaty of Rome, all European countries are entitled to apply for membership of the European Union, and by any definition Ukraine is European. Thus Ukrainian diplomats interpreted the ENP primarily as an alternative to membership designed to keep Ukraine out of the European Union. They were insulted to be treated the same as North African and Middle Eastern countries, which were certainly not European. However, as Russia and Belarus excluded themselves from the ENP, Ukraine and Moldova forged ahead as the frontrunners within the CIS, which appeared more palatable to Ukraine.[8]

The European Union had opened a door, but the political relationship between the European Union and Ukraine was bad because of EU protestations against Ukraine's democratic flaws. Little progress could be made until Ukraine took a determined step toward democracy, but that was just about to happen.

8. Russia refused to be called a neighbor and excluded itself. The European Union kept Belarus outside because of its frozen relations with the European Union. Armenia, Azerbaijan, and Georgia, by contrast, were upset to have been left out. They asked to be included in the ENP, which the European Union accepted.

7

The Orange Revolution, 2004

> The fifteenth day of Ukraine's orange revolution, I arrived in Kiev. My car got stuck in a traffic jam caused by a demonstration at the parliament. I abandoned the car and joined the rally. The demonstrators' determination was stunning. The sea of people was perfectly orderly and calm. Two slogans predominated: "Yushchenko is our President" and "Do not stop our Freedom!" A third line ran "East and West together!"
>
> This was a call for law and order, freedom, and national unity. Some groups marched under Ukrainian flags, some under the orange flags of opposition candidate Viktor Yushchenko emblazoned with the name of their town or village. The demonstration didn't seem to have any class identity at all. Hardly any names of businesses, parties, or organizations were to be seen. No one talked about social or economic issues. This was pure politics. Ukraine's orange revolution is a classical liberal revolution, like 1848, or the Velvet Revolution in Prague in 1989. This rising against lawlessness and repression, for democracy and freedom, is a true bourgeois revolution.
>
> Half in jest, people call it a revolt of the millionaires against the billionaires. (Åslund 2004).

The Orange Revolution was Ukraine's epic moment. For one month from November 22 until December 26, Ukraine dominated world news. People learned that Ukraine was a brave, well-organized, peaceful, and democratic nation of high ideals. The three political leaders—Viktor Yushchenko, Yuliya Tymoshenko, and Viktor Yanukovych—became known globally in spite of their difficult names. Everything worked out peacefully and democratically. It was a moment of national euphoria and pride.[1]

1. Overall sources of this chapter are Åslund and McFaul (2006), Wilson (2005), Karatnycky (2005), and Krushelnycky (2006). Stanislawski (2005) offers a useful summary of facts.

Seldom has the coming of a major political event been so evident. For years the presidential election had been scheduled for the end of October 2004, when President Kuchma's second term would end, and the 1996 constitution did not allow a president more than two consecutive terms. Moreover, Kuchma's popularity was in the single-digit doldrums, making his reelection impossible. The old regime was tired, divided, and increasingly authoritarian.

Ukrainian citizens were facing a clear-cut choice. For the foreseeable future, the presidential elections represented their only chance for greater freedom and more rule of law. Russia clarified the alternative with its just-held managed "elections." The choice was democracy or Putin-style authoritarianism. As Askold Krushelnycky (2006, 1) noted: "Ukrainians recognized they were at a historic crossroads: these were the most important elections ever held in their country and the vote would determine whether Ukraine chartered a path westwards towards democracy, or whether it would be subsumed in a putative new authoritarian Russian empire."

When I visited Kyiv in late July 2004, the all-dominant topic was whether Ukraine would have a "chestnut" revolution. The tentative name derived from Kyiv's chestnut-lined streets. Yanukovych's campaign leader Serhiy Tyhypko even had a press conference on that theme in August. The two leading presidential nominees were Yanukovych and Yushchenko. People said three things would happen. First, Yushchenko would win the real election. Second, Yanukovych would steal it through fraud. Third, protesters would take to the streets and repeat the Georgian Rose Revolution of November 2003. The question was whether sufficiently many people would take to the streets fast enough to mount a popular revolution or whether protests would dissipate once again. This scenario played out exactly as predicted, so both sides were well prepared.

The center-right opposition had been making all possible mistakes since 1991. They were tired of their own irrelevance and determined to bring about change. The old regime was also preoccupied with the elections, but even more with its internal struggles. The fast economic growth had bred greater economic diversity and divisions in the government camp. After a long rule, the old regime was complacent and overconfident in its own skills, while contemptuous of the opposition.

The outside world paid new attention to Ukraine. Russia's President Vladimir Putin intervened personally with great vigor, but his endeavors failed miserably. The United States stayed on the sidelines, letting nongovernmental organizations act. The new members of the European Union, especially Poland and Lithuania, activated their foreign policies, and the European Union became the international winner of the Orange Revolution.

Options of the Old Regime

Since the March 2002 parliamentary elections, Ukraine's politicians had been thinking of little but the upcoming presidential elections. The main policymakers of the old regime were Leonid Kuchma, his chief of staff Viktor Medvedchuk, and Rada Speaker Volodymyr Lytvyn. They were seasoned political foxes, representing Machiavellian politics at its technical best. Democracy was not necessarily their second thought. Facing a problem, they played with several alternative solutions.

As the October 2004 presidential elections approached, the rulers realized they were between a rock and a hard place. Yushchenko looked like the inevitable victor. Three alternative means of stopping him were considered: constitutional reform depriving the president of most of his power, prolonging Kuchma's presidency, and a vigorous popular campaign combined with election fraud.

Constitutional reform has been a persistent theme since Ukraine's independence, and it dominated the Rada's work in the spring of 2004. Until then, Kuchma had wanted to strengthen presidential power, but fearing that Yushchenko would become his successor, he opted for stronger parliamentary powers. Medvedchuk drafted such a constitution, and the oligarchic center joined hands with the communists and socialists, who always favored a parliamentary system. On April 8 the draft constitution received only 294 votes, six votes short of the required two-thirds majority for constitutional change (Wilson 2005, 81). The option of constitutional change was closed.

The constitution stated that "one and the same person shall not be the president for more than two consecutive terms," but it had been adopted in June 1996, two years into Kuchma's first term. The presidential administration argued that his second term was his first term after the adoption of the new constitution, and in December 2003 the obedient constitutional court affirmed this interpretation, allowing Kuchma to run again. But after "Kuchmagate," his popularity stayed in the single digits, and his reelection was not a realistic option. He could stay on only if the presidential elections failed or by declaring a state of emergency (Wilson 2005, 79–80).

The only option left was to select a reasonably popular presidential candidate who could be elected with fraud. However, given the mood in the country, and the remaining freedom, this was difficult. To its credit, the regime was reluctant to pursue more serious repression.

Mobilization of the Opposition and Civil Society

In February 2004 Borys Tarasiuk, former foreign minister and one of seven deputy chairmen of Our Ukraine, organized a big international conference Ukraine in Europe and the World, which I attended. It made a strong impression, showing how the opposition had set the stage for the Orange Revolution. The opposition was fully mobilized, feeling that it was now or never.

The organizers intended to break through the domestic media blockade and reach out to the international community, and they did. Two hundred people from 24 countries participated. The top foreign speakers were former US Secretary of State Madeleine Albright and former Swedish Prime Minister Carl Bildt, while Czech President Vaclav Havel addressed the conference via video.

This opposition conference was allowed, but official intervention was extensive. The Ukrainian Ministry for Foreign Affairs dissuaded serving foreign ministers from attending. The day before the conference, the organizers were told they could not use City Hall as planned, so they resorted to Hotel Rus, a Soviet-era relic. The State Tax Administration had just investigated two leading businessmen and Our Ukraine parliamentarians, Petro Poroshenko and Yevhen Chervonenko. Three radio stations had been forced to stop broadcasting Radio Liberty: One was taken over by a friend of Medvedchuk, another's license was revoked, and the owner of a third died in a road accident. Yet our visas were issued in due order, and the conference took place without disturbance. After having failed to avert the conference, the government tried to coopt it. Prime Minister Viktor Yanukovych and several ministers attended.[2]

The conference had gathered over 100 Ukrainian journalists. Most were very young, enthusiastic, and worked for regional newspapers. *Ukrainska pravda*, the internet newspaper of the hapless Heorhiy Gongadze, spearheaded the free media, through which Ukrainians could follow daily events minute by minute both in Ukrainian and Russian. Poroshenko was allowed to develop his cable television Channel 5. The government dominated the big media, but the truth could be found with some effort.

International nongovernmental organizations, mainly from the United States were there in force. Characteristically, Freedom House, the German Marshall Fund, the National Democratic Institute, and the International Republican Institute cosponsored the conference.

Yushchenko was the self-evident center-right candidate, and no other candidate with similar views challenged him. Tymoshenko had indicated that she would not stand against him, and she attended the Our Ukraine conference, displaying her good relationship with Yushchenko.

He had a keen understanding of the real powers in Ukraine. He knew the importance of support from big businessmen and substantial business financing, and his campaign would suffer no shortage of funds. David

2. I had the honor of appearing on a panel with Yushchenko and Yanukovych, and the discussion was perfectly polite.

Zhvania, his chief fundraiser, stated that Yushchenko's presidential campaign and the protests cost more than $150 million, financed by Ukrainian businessmen. Big and small businessmen were happy to support him against the oligarchs.[3]

Yushchenko reached out to recent defectors from the old regime and integrated them. Before the 2002 elections, Roman Bezsmertnyi, who had been Kuchma's spokesman, joined him as his campaign manager. In July 2004 he replaced Bezsmertnyi with an even later defector from Medvedchuk, Oleksandr Zinchenko. He was a partner of Medvedchuk in television companies as well as deputy speaker of the Rada for the social democrats. When Zinchenko fell ill with cancer, however, Medvedchuk excluded him from their common corporations, which naturally upset him.[4]

In Ukrainian society with its deep sense of symbols, the choice of campaign color was crucial. Blue and yellow, symbolizing the sky and corn fields, were the traditional colors of Ukrainian nationalists, dating back to the Springtime of Nations in 1848. Yushchenko knew that such colors would alienate most Ukrainians. His campaign wisely chose orange instead. Orange had no traditional meaning, though it was conspicuous and the color of chestnut trees in the fall (Wilson 2005, 72–73).

A final weapon in the Yushchenko armory was the student organization *Pora* formed in April 2004. A model student organization, *Otpor*, had developed in Serbia in opposition to President Slobodan Milosevic in 2000, and a similar organization, *Kmara*, emerged in Georgia before the Rose Revolution. Next, the Belarusian *Zubr* evolved, but no revolution took place in Belarus. Pora took two forms, black and yellow, which were both independent organizations. They were highly decentralized to impede infiltration. Pora means "it is time," and its symbol was a watch, signifying that it was time for the old regime to go. Pora was systematically built with Western technical assistance but little financial assistance. It might have engaged 30,000 activists. When the Orange Revolution began, Pora functioned as intended as the revolutionary avant-garde (Demes and Forbrig 2006).

Yushchenko was at his peak. He knew it all, building on his success from the parliamentary elections in 2002. He was not running as a Ukrainian nationalist but as a defender of all good values, from family and Orthodox Christianity to good governance, private property, and European integration. Although he spoke Ukrainian on all occasions, he did not emphasize ethno-nationalism. His campaign focused on universal values, notably freedom and legal justice, directed against oligarchs, repression, and corruption. His key slogans were "I believe in Ukraine!" and "I believe, I know, we can."

---

3. "Business Bankrolled Orange Revolution," Agence France Presse, Kyiv, February 17, 2005.

4. Interview with Zinchenko in April 2004.

Our Ukraine represented the essential values of successful liberal-conservative European parties: liberal economics, moderate nationalism, and Christianity. Under Ukrainian conditions, Yushchenko could top it up with freedom and democracy. Considering his track record as a successful prime minister and chairman of the National Bank of Ukraine, this was too good an offer to be refused. At long last, the liberal and democratic center-right had matured into a plausible alternative to the eternal government of the oligarchic center.

The Regime: Mobilized but Divided

In 2004, just before its demise, Ukraine's oligarchic regime appeared stronger than ever.[5] It dominated the parliament, controlled the government, including law enforcement, and ruled the media, but the oligarchs were too strong to be united. They spent more effort on fighting one another than the opposition. They frantically seized as many assets as possible, and the economy boomed with improved enterprise management after privatization.

After Medvedchuk had become Kuchma's chief of staff in June 2002, the regime had become more ruthless in its use of repression, so-called administrative resources. Medvedchuk took control over the Central Election Commission (CEC). Authorities were instructed to prohibit opposition meetings in public premises. Government inspectors, especially the tax administration, harassed businessmen who supported the opposition.

The media control tightened further. Medvedchuk ruled over Ukraine's three most popular channels (1+1, Inter, and UT-1), and other oligarchs owned the rest. As before, the authorities used television for their propaganda, but this media manipulation backfired because it was too crude to be believed.

The regime also mobilized huge campaign funding. According to the Yushchenko campaign, as early as July 2004 the Yanukovych campaign planned to spend $600 million, half of which was to come from Russian enterprises, mainly Gazprom, and half from Ukrainian oligarchs, primarily Rinat Akhmetov.[6] This was more than 1 percent of Ukraine's GDP in 2004. Even larger amounts have been alleged. This was by far the most expensive election campaign in Ukraine's history.

5. This section draws on Åslund (2006).

6. I obtained this information from Yushchenko's chief of staff Oleh Rybachuk in September 2004, which he had received from his sources at the Security Services of Ukraine.

As the center-right assembled around Yushchenko, all the oligarchic factions agreed on Yanukovych as their single presidential candidate as early as April 14, 2004.[7] Many have disputed the wisdom of their choice of Yanukovych, an ex-convict who spoke both Russian and Ukrainian poorly. However, he had delivered more votes than anybody else for the ruling elite in the 2002 elections, and he proved to be an able popular politician with a splendid rags-to-riches story (Kuzio 2006, 32). Nobody was more at ease with the Donbas miners than Yanukovych, and he captured the eastern working class from the communists. He was Akhmetov's candidate, and he could run on a record as successful prime minister.

The regime also attempted to transform the election from a struggle between Yushchenko standing up as a David against a Goliath of corrupt government to a regional competition between east and west. Its propaganda presented Yushchenko as a western nationalist and more crudely as an American agent, although Kuchma had sent Ukrainian troops to Iraq while Yushchenko campaigned for their withdrawal.

But the oligarchs had little in common. Only three of the biggest businessmen supported Yanukovych officially, Akhmetov, Medvedchuk, and Victor Pinchuk. Most big businessmen were afraid that Yanukovych and Akhmetov would wipe them out. In fact, only Akhmetov was truly committed to Yanukovych. In the fall of 2004, Pinchuk's three television channels turned objective. Privat Group stayed out of the campaign, and the Industrial Union of Donbas tacitly supported the Orange Revolution because of its rivalry with Akhmetov.

Nor was Kuchma enamored with Yanukovych, seeming more interested in his own future than the election outcome. Throughout the election campaign, Kuchma was suspected of wanting the elections to fail to be able to stay in power.

Strangely, the Yanukovych campaign had not one but three competing campaign headquarters. Serhiy Tyhypko led the official campaign headquarters. Serhiy Kliuev, a prominent businessman from Donetsk and the brother of Deputy Prime Minister Andriy Kliuev, commanded an unofficial headquarters for dirty tricks beyond the control of Tyhypko. The newly established Russian Club functioned as a third campaign headquarters for the Russian political advisers. With such a lack of top-level coordination, no campaign could succeed.

The Yanukovych campaign was heavy-handed and inept. Its television propaganda was too crude and its messages were mixed. Government interference was too obnoxious, while repression was too limited to make people obey.

7. "Yanukovicha vysunuli yedynym kandydatom?" ["They Presented Yanukovych as the Single Candidate?"], *Ukrainska pravda*, April 14, 2007.

Russia's Role

Rarely has a country played such a prominent role in the election campaign of another country as Russia did in the Ukrainian elections. Nor was Russia ever so engaged in Ukraine. President Putin handled the campaign personally, and his failure was spectacular.[8] Two independent Russian scholars, Nikolai Petrov and Andrei Ryabov (2006, 145), concluded:

> Russia's involvement in the Ukrainian presidential election in October and November 2004 is widely viewed as the Kremlin's greatest foreign relations blunder since 1991. The problem is not that the Kremlin gambled on a candidate who lost, but that the Kremlin's involvement was so conspicuous and crude. . . . As the election progressed, the Kremlin's clumsy intrusion drove Russia ever further into a dead end, while raising the stakes. The result was not simply a defeat, but a scandalous humiliation.

In 2003 and 2004 Putin and his chief of staff Aleksandr Voloshin were preoccupied with Ukraine's elections. Putin and Kuchma met almost every month. During his two terms, Putin met Kuchma more than any other head of state. Shrewdly, Kuchma acted as the senior partner. Conversely, Kuchma's chief of staff, Medvedchuk, had a close relationship with Voloshin and his first deputy Dmitri Medvedev. As early as the summer of 2003, the Kremlin decided to support whichever candidate Kuchma proposed. At a meeting with Kuchma in Crimea on July 26, 2004, Putin expressed his public support for Yanukovych. Yushchenko's repeated appeals to Moscow for friendly cooperation fell on deaf ears (Petrov and Ryabov 2006, 146–47).

The Kremlin tried to influence the Ukrainian elections through economic benefits and campaign support. However, Russia's Common Economic Space initiative, launched in February 2003, was more controversial than helpful. On September 15, 2004, at a Common Economic Space summit of the four heads of state, Putin accepted a long-standing Ukrainian demand to change the value-added tax system, transferring an annual revenue stream of $800 million from the Russian to the Ukrainian treasury. This decision was criticized in Russia as excessively generous (Petrov and Ryabov 2006, 150). The Kremlin also resolved the many bilateral trade disputes in September 2003 by lifting many unilateral Russian protectionist measures against Ukrainian exports to Russia.

The Security Services of Ukraine (SBU) taped the key July 2004 meeting in Crimea between the two chiefs of staff, Voloshin and Medvedchuk and reported to Yushchenko's chief of staff Oleh Rybachuk[9] that the two

---

8. This section draws primarily on the outstanding article Petrov and Ryabov (2006). See also Wilson (2005, 86–95).

9. Rybachuk told me this in September 2004.

agreed to mobilize $600 million for the election campaign. They would share the responsibility 50-50, with the Russian side extracting money for the Yanukovych campaign from Russian businessmen active in Ukraine.

Russia's propaganda in the Ukrainian election was a crude broadside employing Russian television, political campaign advice, and Putin's personal appearances. In the summer of 2004, dozens of Moscow's loudmouthed, well-paid political technologists descended upon Ukraine. Prominent names were the Kremlin spin doctors Gleb Pavlovsky, Marat Gelman, Vyacheslav Nikonov, and Sergei Markov.

On August 31 Pavlovsky opened a Russian Club in Kyiv as the Russian center for the Yanukovych campaign. These advisers had proven useful in the 1999 presidential elections but failed miserably in the 2002 parliamentary elections, which they blamed on excessive restrictions on their actions. This time they showed no inhibitions, but they disagreed on policy. Gelman wanted to run a positive campaign for Yanukovych; Pavlovsky favored a populist campaign with higher pensions and possible use of violence; while Nikonov preferred criticism of Yushchenko.

The Russian political advisers appeared all the time on Ukrainian and Russian television slandering Yushchenko and praising Yanukovych, as if no Ukrainian wanted to do so. Sergei Markov declared in the *Financial Times* that the Kremlin had hired him "to defend Russia's interests" in Ukraine. He claimed that Yushchenko "is regarded as extremely anti-Russian . . . not as an independent politician but a puppet. I think he is very weak."[10]

According to opinion polls, Putin was the most popular politician among Ukrainians. He tried to exploit his popularity by campaigning twice for Yanukovych in Ukraine. Spectacularly, he visited Kyiv for three days just before the elections. On October 26 Putin made a speech praising the successes of the Yanykovych government, which was broadcast on most Ukrainian television channels. He also participated in a long phone-in broadcast. Three days before the elections, Kyiv held an unusual military parade with 8,000 soldiers and veterans to celebrate Ukraine's liberation from Nazi occupation (Stanislawski 2005, 11–13).

Moscow also tried to mobilize the Ukrainian diaspora in Russia for Yanukovych. On October 8 a big congress of its representatives was held in Moscow, adopting an appeal to all Ukrainians to support Yanukovych. The Kremlin adorned Moscow streets with banners ambiguously proclaiming "Yanukovych Is Our President."

The Kremlin demanded that over 400 polling stations be set up in Russia for its alleged 1.5 million Ukrainian nationals, whose voting would no doubt be controlled by the Kremlin. However, because of Yushchenko's

10. Andrew Jack and Tom Warner, "Putin's Move on Ukraine Poll Risks Failure," *Financial Times*, October 20, 2004.

resolute resistance and Kuchma's hesitancy, the Ukrainian Central Election Commission (CEC) decided to open only 41 additional polling stations in Russia, and the Ukrainian Supreme Court reduced the number to four (Petrov and Ryabov 2006, 156–57). The Kremlin also rolled out the Russian Orthodox Church with Patriarch Alexei II endorsing Yanukovych.

The massive Russian intervention could do nothing but undermine Yanukovych, who was patronized by Putin and the rude Russian political advisers. Nor would a Yanukovych victory necessarily have benefited Russia. After having defeated his own oligarchs, Putin supported the most oligarchic party in Ukraine. As governor and prime minister Yanukovych had kept Russian companies out of Donbas, while then—prime minister Yushchenko had allowed Russian corporations to purchase big Ukrainian companies and settled large arrears to Russia for gas imports, while Yanukovych only demanded gifts. Former Russian Prime Minister Viktor Chernomyrdin, who was ambassador to Ukraine, commented sensibly after the first round of the election that "anybody who becomes Ukrainian president will be compelled to develop good-neighborly relations with Russia."

The Election Campaign: Yushchenko versus Yanukovych

Never had Ukraine experienced such an election campaign. Officially, the candidates were many, but Yushchenko and Yanukovych were all-dominant. On the left, Petro Symonenko, Oleksandr Moroz, and Natalia Vitrenko were of some significance. So was Anatoliy Kinakh in the center.

The election season started ominously. In April 2004 Mukachevo, a town in Transcarpathia, which was Medvedchuk's territory, held mayoral elections. Viktor Baloha, a local business competitor of Medvedchuk who had made a political alliance with Yushchenko, won the election with a solid 57 percent, but Medvedchuk stole the election through blatant falsification, disqualifying more than one-third of the winner's votes (Wilson 2005, 82). Seeing the importance of this vote-rigging, Yushchenko made it the starting point for his campaign.

On July 2 Tymoshenko and Yushchenko signed an agreement to unite and coordinate their campaign, which they named Power of the People. Their understanding was that Yushchenko would make Tymoshenko prime minister if he won. On July 4 Yushchenko formally launched his candidacy and started an election campaign superior to anything Ukraine had seen. He campaigned as a whirlwind, making one major speech and a few local appearances every day in American fashion. He drew enormous crowds wherever he appeared, not least because he could not be seen on national television. In Kyiv and Lviv, he gathered masses of 100,000 people, but even in eastern Kharkiv 20,000 came to listen to him and 15,000 in the Donbas steel town of Kryvyi Rig. Tymoshenko, who is an outstanding orator, attracted crowds in many parts of the country of 10,000 to 20,000 people.[11]

Yanukovych had a near monopoly in the official media, so people had seen enough of him. He could not attract a crowd in western and central Ukraine, and even in Kyiv he could barely gather 500 people. He had to make do with official meetings and traditional factory visits, which made him look old-fashioned.

The West was seriously concerned about election fraud. A steady stream of official statements called on the Ukrainian authorities to safeguard free and fair elections. In his congratulatory note to Kuchma on Ukraine's Independence Day on August 24, US President George W. Bush stated: "Ukraine has made great strides in the thirteen years since independence. Nothing can secure that legacy more than the holding of free, fair, and transparent election this fall and turning your high office over to a successor who embodies the democratic choice of the Ukrainian people."[12] The West mobilized multiple election monitoring organizations, notably the Council of Europe and the Organization for Security and Cooperation in Europe (OSCE). The Ukrainian government did not object, and long in advance the largest international election monitoring ever was organized.

The authorities played dirty, disturbing events every day. Airplanes in which Yushchenko was travelling were refused landing rights. More than 350 Pora student activists were temporarily arrested on implausible grounds in September and October. Governors, heads of government agencies, the military, and universities were asked to deliver their subordinates' votes. Often such statements were filmed on mobile phones, and Pora exposed many official transgressions via the internet.

More serious incidents also occurred. On August 12 a big truck (KamAz) mysteriously forced Yushchenko's car off the road and almost hit him near Kherson in southern Ukraine. On August 20 a bomb detonated at a market in Kyiv, killing one person and injuring 11, and a smaller bomb went off a couple of weeks later. Pora and Our Ukraine activists were repeatedly arrested for alleged possession of bombs (Stanislawski 2005, Wilson 2005).

On the night of September 5, Yushchenko was poisoned at a late dinner with three men, the chairman and deputy chairman of the SBU, Ihor Smeshko and Volodymyr Stasiuk, and his financier, David Zhvania. He got terribly sick, but his Ukrainian doctors could not diagnose the cause.

---

11. Personal report from trip to Kyiv, October 11–16, 2004.

12. "Letter to President of Ukraine Leonid Kuchma on the Occasion of the 13th Anniversary of Ukraine's Independence," White House, Washington, August 20, 2004. www.whitehouse.gov (accessed on August 24, 2004).

Fortunately, five days later he flew to a specialized hospital in Vienna, where doctors found that he had suffered from a rare dioxin poisoning. His previously handsome face was inflamed and disfigured, but the official media scorned him.

From the outset, Stasiuk—a Medvedchuk politician with strong Russian connections—was the prime suspect. After the Orange Revolution he fled to Russia, where he stays. The culprits have never been established by court. The dioxin appears to have come from a Russian laboratory, which the Kremlin has never admitted.

Yushchenko was badly sick, but he survived. On September 18 he held his first speech after the poisoning, and it was his greatest speech ever. He spoke on the European Square in Kyiv to a crowd of about 100,000. The speech was broadcast live to squares in almost all regional centers, where half a million people watched him, thus bypassing official television (Diuk 2006, 79; Prytula 2006, 119). The poisoning had radicalized him, and he spoke with new anger on his pock-marked face. This speech was his clearest program declaration, worth quoting at length. It provided few details but plenty of morals and good rhetoric:

> I would like to pay a special 'compliment' to the government: You won't poison us! You will lack bullets and KamAZes! Not one or thousands but tens of thousands of new Hiya Gongadzes, Vyacheslav Chornovils, Vadym Hetmans and many other good people will always turn up in Ukraine. . . .[13]
>
> We pledge: there are millions of us and you won't stop us! We will win. . . . Yes! We are eager for changes! We, Ukrainian citizens are craving for decent living. We, the people of Ukraine, demand what belongs to us by right. . . . People want to discharge a criminal regime that is planting cynicism and lawlessness over our land. The gangster government is striving for only one thing—to preserve its power by all means. . . .
>
> We are one Ukrainian nation either in the West or the East, the North or South; all of us are suffering form poverty and lawlessness. . . . We are of Cossack family. We will get over the difficulties and become free like our glorious forefathers!
>
> I have traveled all over the country and seen. The government is in death agony. Still you cannot watch it on television. They cut off channels and close down newspapers for a single true word. A TV screen has turned into a distorting mirror. We don't recognize ourselves and our country in it. We are fed up with the lie.
>
> Nevertheless they won't deceive us. It is our government that is afraid of facing the truth. They are not without reason to be afraid of us. The gangsters in power realize the upcoming elections will be a sentence upon this government passed by the people themselves. The bandits will be imprisoned!
>
> . . . I will do my best to provide a peaceful power transfer, without any upheavals and violence.
>
> . . . We will make the shadow economy transparent. . . . I am not going to revise the results of privatization, but to cease the plundering of our state. . . .

---

13. Referring to their political murders in 2000, 1999, and 1998, respectively. Hiya is a nickname for Heorhiy.

> We will do away with the corruption that spoils our lives. . . . Honest professionals are to replace corrupted officials. Law enforcers are to protect people against criminals. Courts will judge justly but not for the money. . . .
>
> I am running for the Presidency of Ukraine because I believe in Ukraine. . . . Glory to God and glory to Ukraine! (Yushchenko 2004)

Yushchenko demanded "bandits to prison," but he also promised a peaceful transfer of power and no revision of privatization. He said virtually nothing about foreign policy, but he had pledged to withdraw the Ukrainian troops from Iraq.[14] Populist or economic slogans were absent. The entire appeal amounted to a call for Ukraine whole and free, although he did not use those terms.

Yushchenko supporters started wearing something orange, a scarf, a tie, or just a little ribbon. In the beginning the display of orange appeared dangerous, an act of defiance. But the number of orange ribbons mushroomed, and by October Kyiv was draped in orange. Political consciousness grew, engaging everybody. A revolutionary fervor had arisen in western and central Ukraine.

Yanukovych competed with a popular groundswell, but his resources were immense. His greatest election appeal was a doubling of public pensions. As a consequence, Ukraine's already high pension costs skyrocketed to a projected 16 percent of GDP for 2005. This was fiscally irresponsible, causing a sudden budget deficit of 4.5 percent of GDP in 2004 (figure 7.1). This populism contradicted Yanukovych's claim to economic achievements, displaying the desperation of the old regime.

On September 24, as if to show that Yanukovych also suffered from dirty tricks, the regime alleged that several large objects were thrown at him while campaigning in Ivano-Frankivsk in western Ukraine. However, Poroshenko's Channel 5 had filmed the incident, which showed Yanukovych falling after being hit by a single egg, thus ridiculing this big, strong man (Wilson 2005, 99).

On September 27 Yanukovych played his Russian card with the slogan "Ukraine-Russia: Stronger Together." He committed himself to making Russian an official language, allowing dual citizenship for Russians and Ukrainians and abandoning all attempts at closer cooperation with the North Atlantic Treaty Organization (NATO). Russia reciprocated with a radical liberalization of travel regulations, allowing Ukrainians to stay in Russia for 90 days without visa or registration and to enter Russia with domestic Ukrainian identity cards (Wilson 2005, 89–90, 93).

On October 23 Yushchenko held a last big preelection rally in Kyiv, gathering once again 100,000 people. The theme was to stop election fraud, and the demonstration marched on the CEC, demanding an honest

14. "Yushchenko Will Withdraw Troops from Iraq," Our Ukraine website, August 10, 2004, www.razom.org.ua (accessed on August 11, 2004).

Figure 7.1 Ukraine's budget balance, 2000–2007

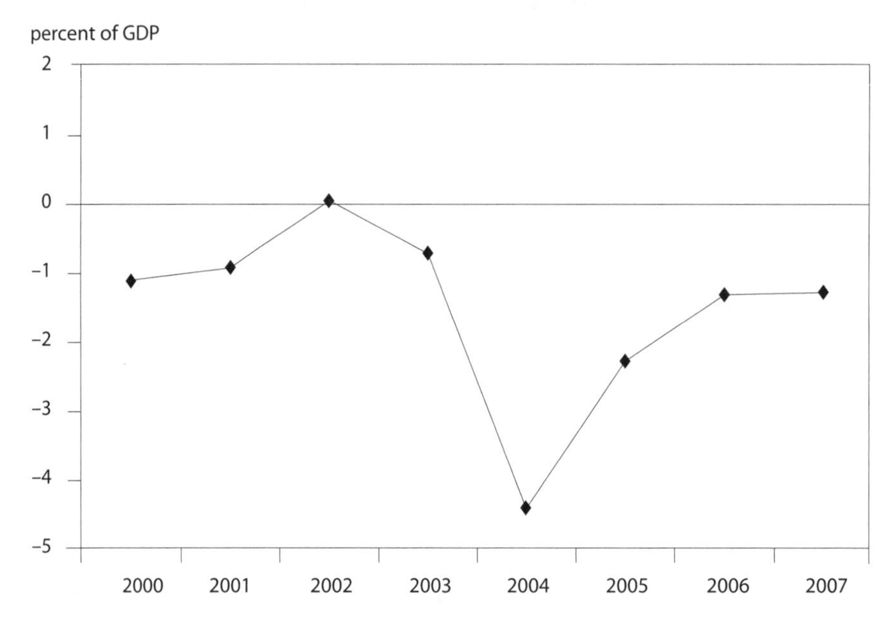

Source: European Bank for Reconstruction and Development online database, www.ebrd.com (accessed on July 1, 2008).

election. The CEC was already guarded by armored personnel carriers (Stanislawski 2005, 10).

In mid-October I spent a week in Kyiv. The mood was tense. Everybody understood the importance of the elections and feared the worst. Ukrainian civil society was fully mobilized, but people did not believe that Yushchenko would be allowed to win. They were shocked by his poisoning and thought that his victory would be stolen or that he would be killed. Members of the regime were afraid that Yanukovych and Akhmetov would purge them after victory. All were waiting for Damocles' sword to fall.

The Presidential Elections

After the first round of the presidential election on October 31, the authorities seemed at a loss. They delayed the publication of the official returns for 10 days, rendering fraud evident. Even so, Yushchenko won 39.9 percent of the votes, narrowly beating Yanukovych, who received 39.3 percent (table 7.1). Independent exit polls gave Yushchenko 44 to 45 percent and Yanukovych 37 to 38 percent (Wilson 2005, 111). As expected, the two leading candidates crowded out the others. Socialist Moroz received only

Table 7.1 Results of presidential election, 2004 (percent of votes)

Candidate	First round, October 31, 2004	Second round, November 21, 2004	Rerun of second round, December 26, 2004
Viktor Yushchenko	39.9	46.6	52.0
Viktor Yanukovych	39.3	49.5	44.2
Oleksandr Moroz	5.8		
Petro Symonenko	5.0		
Natalia Vitrenko	1.5		
Anatoliy Kinakh	0.9		
Others or against all	4.9	2.3	2.3
Total[a]	100	100	100
Voter turnout (percent)	74.6	80.4	77.2

a. Total includes invalid ballots, not counted as votes.

Source: Central Election Commission of Ukraine, www.cvk.gov.ua (accessed on July 18, 2008).

5.8 percent, communist Symonenko 5 percent, progressive socialist Vitrenko 1.5 percent, and centrist Kinakh 0.9 percent.

In spite of the slender margin, the result was an outstanding victory for Yushchenko and the democrats, since the incumbent regime had used all means to bring him down. International observers agreed that fraud was rampant. Undoubtedly, some of the votes cast for Yushchenko and Symonenko had been illicitly reallocated to Yanukovych. The Ukrainians understood the stakes and stood up for their democratic choice with a participation of 75 percent.

Still, most of all, the election was a fight between east and west. The division of the country was nearly total. Yanukovych won with an average of 71 percent in 10 eastern and southern regions, while Yushchenko obtained an average of 78 percent in 17 western and central regions. The Yanukovych campaign had succeeded in dividing the country, but Yushchenko had avoided being caught in the western Ukrainian linguistic box, being victorious in the largely Russian-speaking central Ukraine, including the capital.

Yushchenko stood for Western democracy and a European choice. Yanukovych represented the ruling oligarchic system and the Russian speakers, while opposing NATO. Ideological differences were limited, and economic issues were largely irrelevant. Both candidates favored a free market economy, private enterprise, financial stability, and high growth.

The greatest ideological development was that Yanukovych had obliterated the communist vote. It had fallen precipitously from 20 percent in the 2002 parliamentary elections to 5 percent in these presidential elections, never to recover. Although the communists suffered from fraud, Yanukovych appeared more desirable to pro-Russian forces in Ukraine, and his populism appealed to the eastern working class and pensioners.

Notwithstanding rampant election fraud, Yushchenko did not call for protest actions. After all, he had won, but he had no absolute majority, so a second round was required. Some students demonstrated between the two election rounds, but the main developments were the losing candidates distributing their sympathies, the journalists' revolt, a surprise televised debate between Yushchenko and Yanukovych, and a change in Russian strategy.

Moroz and Kinakh declared their support for Yushchenko in the runoff on November 21. Both made a coalition agreement with Yushchenko and Tymoshenko, and their four parties negotiated a government program. Yushchenko made significant concessions, notably accepting the socialist demand for a moratorium on private sales of agricultural land until 2008.

Yanukovych found few new sympathizers. Symonenko was so upset over gross falsification in the east that he refused to support Yanukovych and called upon communists to vote against all in the second round. Only Vitrenko, who was considered a fake left-winger paid by oligarchs, expressed her support for Yanukovych.

Journalists on the official television channels had started revolting before the elections, and on October 28, 40 journalists representing five television channels declared that they would no longer obey *temnyky*. Soon, almost all journalists on the official television channels defected to the opposition, and television coverage became normal (Prytula 2006, 118).

Now the candidates could as well debate on television. On November 15 the first televised debate between the two candidates took place. The whole country watched. Yanukovych was mild and cautious, while Yushchenko came out swinging. Speaking to his voters, he repeated his campaign theme: "You are not cattle but citizens who have the right to vote." He claimed 3 million citizens had been blocked from voting because of incorrect voter lists. Once again, he made a moral appeal: "This is not a conflict between two Victors. This is a conflict between two world views, two moralities. Our choice is very simple. Either we live according to the code of ethics of the criminal underworld or we live like free and affluent people." He attacked the privatization of Kryvorizhstal, which he called "theft." Curiously, Yanukovych criticized Yushchenko for having sold off four Ukrainian oil refineries to foreigners, carefully avoiding mentioning that they had been sold to Russian companies. The consensus view was that Yushchenko won this debate overwhelmingly.[15]

The Russian strategy changed after the first round. On November 12–13 Putin went to Crimea to meet Kuchma and Yanukovych with limited publicity. He reportedly told Yanukovych to rely more on administrative resources and repression, and he showed that Kuchma had lost

15. "Debaty Yushchenka ta Yanukovycha. Stenograma" ["Debate between Yushchenko and Yanukovych. Stenogram"], *Ukrainska pravda*, November 16, 2004. The four refineries were sold to Lukoil, TNK, Tatneft, and Alliance.

his trust because of his attempt to negotiate with the opposition (Petrov and Ryabov 2006, 157).

The Orange Revolution

After the polling stations closed on November 21, mass falsification was evident. The independent nongovernmental organization Committee of Voters of Ukraine claimed that no less than 85,000 officials were involved in election fraud. They had received most of the election financing (Wilson 2005, 119–20).

The means of deception were many. Voter lists were tampered with, excluding some living people while including many "dead souls," in the words of classical Ukrainian author Nikolai Gogol. Multiple voting through so called carousels was common. Voters willing to vote several times were transported by bus and train between different polling stations. Home visits with ballot boxes were frequent. Some ballot boxes were stuffed, and results were revised afterwards. Election monitors from the Council of Europe, the OSCE, and the European parliament concluded that the elections were neither free nor fair, while the speaker of the Russian Duma, Boris Gryzlov, and observers from the Commonwealth of Independent States stated that the elections had been correct (Stanislawski 2005, 35).

As the opposition foresaw fraud, they had planned their protests. Yushchenko called for protests on Kyiv's Independence Square, commonly called Maidan, immediately after the polling stations closed at 8 p.m. on Sunday, November 21. Some 30,000 protesters came, and the first tents were set up on Khreshchatyk, Kyiv's main street that goes through Maidan. The Orange Revolution had erupted.

This time the regime-controlled CEC did not hesitate but delivered well-cooked, though preliminary, numbers by Monday noon, the day after the election. Officially, Yanukovych won by 2.85 percentage points in the second round with 49.5 percent of the votes against 46.6 percent for Yushchenko (table 7.1). By contrast, an independent exit poll based on 28,000 interviews indicated that Yushchenko had won with 53 percent against 44 percent for Yanukovych (Wilson 2005, 2).

Turnout in the second round increased by 5.8 percent, but only by 0.6 percent in the 17 regions where Yushchenko prevailed against a whopping 9.1 percent surge in the 10 regions carried by Yanukovych. In the Donetsk region, turnout increased 18.6 percent to a remarkable 96.7 percent, with 96.2 percent of the voters allegedly supporting Yanukovych.[16] Mass fraud was evident, and Yushchenko emerged the clear winner.

16. See the website of the Central Election Commission of Ukraine, www.cvk.gov.ua (accessed on November 23, 2004).

The regime was in disarray. Early on election night, Yanukovych's campaign manager Tyhypko stated that it was possible that Yushchenko had won.[17] His declaration sounded like a protest against his own campaign, and he resigned one week later. Kuchma was uncharacteristically passive, indicating his limited sympathy for Yanukovych. In his book *After Maidan*, Kuchma presented himself as even-handed, clearly thinking of his own standing after the elections (Kuchma 2007).

The opposition mobilized on November 22, Monday morning. Yushchenko called all to Maidan, and his message was spread by mobile phones and the internet but also through the newly liberated media. No less than 200,000 people turned up. The protesters had gathered a critical mass. The following day, November 23, Yushchenko took the presidential oath on Maidan.

The crowds on Maidan expanded daily until they exceeded one million in a photogenic sea of orange in the midst of the freezing winter. Demonstrators occupied the streets and squares in central Kyiv. Tens of thousands of people flooded in from the provinces, mainly from the west. The revolutionary fervor caught on, but so did order. The spontaneous discipline was striking. No drinking or rowdy behavior was allowed, as the revolutionaries were afraid of provocations, as had happened on March 9, 2001. People organized themselves. Almost all wore something orange, an armband, a lapel, a scarf, a hat, or a vest. The slogans were few and simple: "Yushchenko is our president," "Freedom," and "East and West together." Thousands of businessmen donated food and warm clothes because the winter was freezing.

The demonstrators blocked ministries and major public buildings. Kuchma and his staff were thus not able to go to their offices, and the administration was disrupted. On the heights opposite the cabinet of ministers building, a score of people persistently beat on steel barrels, creating an enormous noise so that the government could not work. Police were absent, only guarding major public buildings. Outside the presidential administration, special forces in riot gear stood in double rows night and day, facing serious-looking older, orange guards. Their calm professionalism suggested they were retired special forces. They looked far more fearsome than the nervous young government troops.

The big stage on Maidan was the focal point of the Orange Revolution. The four main revolutionary agitators were Tymoshenko, Zinchenko, the young socialist Yuriy Lutsenko, and Mykola Tomenko (a liberal from Rukh). Yushchenko did not work the crowds but made a daily statement. Tymoshenko, with her hair in plaits, mimicking the national hero Lesia Ukrainka, was the radical leader. She was no longer called the Gas

17. "Tigipko gotov idti v oppozitsiyu" ["Tyhypko Is Ready to Go into Opposition"], *Ukrainskaya pravda*, November 21, 2004.

Princess but the Orange Princess or simply Our Yulka. One of the revolutionaries was the liberal former Russian first deputy prime minister Boris Nemtsov, who appeared on Maidan on Ukrainian television wearing an orange scarf.

Ukrainians disproved all the negative stereotypes: They were well organized rather than ambivalent and disorderly; sober rather than drunk; intellectual rather than indifferent. I had heard similar reflections in Poland after Pope John Paul II's first visit in the summer of 1979 and later during the Solidarity period. Someone said: "Ukraine received independence in 1991; now it has earned it."

Putin did not give up. On November 22 he congratulated Yanukovych on his victory. On November 25 he repeated his congratulations with an official letter. The Central Asian presidents followed suit (Stanislawski 2005, 48–49). On November 24 a Russian State Duma resolution expressed "deep concern over the extremist actions by the radical opposition forces in Ukraine, which could lead to tragic consequences."[18] Not very graciously, Pavlovsky turned on his Ukrainian hosts, claiming that "very many Ukrainian politicians and officials have exhibited serious political incompetence which created the pause, the power vacuum, of which the opposition took advantage."[19] His message was that the Ukrainian authorities had not been sufficiently ruthless. Numerous official Russian spokespersons complained colorfully about American interference in Ukraine and disrespect for Ukrainian law.

On November 23 the White House declared that the "United States is deeply disturbed by extensive and credible indications of fraud committed in the Ukrainian presidential election. We strongly support efforts to review the conduct of the election. . . ."[20] US Secretary of State Colin L. Powell made a strong statement on November 24:

> [T]oday the United States stand with the people of Ukraine and their effort to ensure their democratic choice. Indeed, this is a critical moment. It is time for Ukrainian leaders to decide whether they are on the side of democracy or not. . . . We cannot accept this result as legitimate because it does not meet international standards and because there has not been an investigation of the numerous and credible reports of fraud and abuse. . . . We call for a full review of the conduct of the election and the tallying of the election results.[21]

---

18. "Rossiiskaya duma nazvala Yushchenko 'ekstremistom'" ["The Russian Duma Called Yushchenko 'Extremist'"], *Ukrainskaya pravda*, November 24, 2004.

19. Federal News Service, NTV, 22:00, November 23, 2004.

20. "Statement on Ukrainian Elections," Office of the Press Secretary, White House, Washington, November 23, 2004, www.whitehouse.gov (accessed on November 23, 2004).

21. "Briefing by Secretary of State Colin L. Powell," US Department of State, Washington, www.state.gov (accessed on November 24, 2004).

Numerous European politicians and newspapers complained about the evident vote fraud in Ukraine. Within Ukraine, one force after the other abandoned the authorities. One early group of official defectors was Ukrainian diplomats. The armed forces split. Two former SBU generals spoke on Maidan on November 25, and the SBU leadership seemed to follow. The same day, the commander of Ukraine's Western Military Command declared that his troops would not be used against the nation, indicating that the military was regionally divided, as were the civilian police. The regime could deploy only select special forces of the Ministry of Interior for a crackdown.

The Settlement

The regime made some threatening maneuvers, but evidently Kuchma would not accept serious use of violence, and he was still in charge.[22] On the orange side, Tymoshenko advocated the storming of some official buildings to force a settlement, but Yushchenko overruled her.

The enigma was how to find a peaceful settlement. What would it be and how could it be reached? The orange camp and a united West wanted the falsified results from the runoff disqualified. Kuchma suggested that the elections start all over again with a first round, but the dominant view was that only the runoff between Yushchenko and Yanukovych should be repeated. Three parallel processes evolved. Yushchenko filed complaints at the Supreme Court about the falsifications. Kuchma convened a roundtable, and the Rada confirmed major decisions through legislation.

On November 23 Kuchma appealed to all political forces to start negotiations to prevent a split of the country, and parliamentary speaker Lytvyn summoned the authorities and the opposition to a roundtable discussion. Two days later, Kuchma invited Polish President Alexander Kwasniewski and Lithuanian President Valdas Adamkus to participate in the roundtable as mediators. Kwasniewski engaged the reluctant Javier Solana, the EU high representative for common foreign and security policy, and Yanukovych included Russian State Duma Speaker Boris Gryzlov. The United States—fearing that any US representation would provoke the Russians to match them—was not represented, happily leaving the mediation to the European Union and Kwasniewski. The Polish president played the leading role because he knew the Ukrainian leaders well, and the Orange Revolution reminded Poles of their own Solidarity movement (though Kwasniewski had been on the communist side). Yushchenko and Yanukovych both participated. Three sessions of the

22. This section draws its facts from Wilson (2005) and Stanislawski (2005) and on my own observations in Kyiv and Donetsk on December 7–14, 2004, documented in my trip report.

roundtable convened in a villa south of Kyiv on November 26, December 1, and 6.

After the first roundtable, the Rada met on November 27. Speaker Lytvyn had started playing an independent role, and with more than 100 centrist deputies, he had become the critical powerbroker. The Rada declared the elections had violated the law and did not reflect the will of the citizens. It censured the CEC and asked Yanukovych and Yushchenko to negotiate a solution. At this stage, Pinchuk and his Labor Ukraine also defected from the regime, leaving Yanukovych's Regions and Medvedchuk's social democrats alone. The first big step toward a solution had been taken.

On November 28, Sunday night, over 10,000 Ministry of Interior special forces were brought to Kyiv from the south, but fortunately nothing happened. SBU Chairman Smeshko claimed to have averted violence, but Kuchma would hardly have allowed military action, which would have become very bloody.

The same day Yanukovych's people organized a big conference in the Donbas mining town of Sevorodonetsk. The conference demanded a referendum on the federalization of Ukraine, an old eastern demand, which aroused new worries about the breakup of Ukraine, but it led nowhere. Yanukovych's main sponsor, Akhmetov, who owned enterprises all over Ukraine, opposed any federalization.[23]

Tens of thousands of Yanukovych supporters in his blue-and-white colors were bussed from Donbas to Kyiv. They set up their own tent city in the park outside parliament, but they seemed timid, not quite knowing what to do. The feared confrontation with the orange protesters never occurred.

On December 1 the new Rada majority dismissed Yanukovych as prime minister, but he stayed as caretaker, resigning only on December 31.

For good reasons, Ukraine's courts suffered a poor reputation. The president controlled the constitutional court, but the parallel Supreme Court was more independent. Strangely, both sides let the Supreme Court pronounce on the fairness of the elections. On December 3 it passed a clear verdict: The authorities had carried out massive fraud. It invalidated the election results and dictated its own political decision: The second round of the election would be repeated on December 26. Yanukovych accepted its judgment.

The parliament adopted the final settlement on December 8, when it promulgated constitutional reform, a new election law, and local government reform, as well as approved a new chairman of the CEC. While the decisions on the rerun of the second round of the election suited Yushchenko and Tymoshenko, the constitutional changes did not. The

23. Interview with Akhmetov in Donetsk on December 8, 2004.

main authors were Medvedchuk and Lytvyn, who revived their failed April 2004 attempt to reduce presidential powers through a constitutional change.

Tymoshenko and Yushchenko objected to the reduced presidential powers and the sheer inconsistency of the new constitutional order. Tymoshenko argued it was a halfway house that could not work.[24] She did not vote on the package in protest against the constitution, and her faction voted against it. Nor did Yushchenko vote, and one-fifth of his Our Ukraine faction abstained.

The constitutional changes increased the powers of the parliament and the prime minister at the expense of the president. The parliamentarians were supposed to form a coalition and nominate a prime minister, who would appoint all ministers but those of defense and foreign affairs. The president would propose those two ministers and appoint the chairman of the SBU and the prosecutor general. His power to dissolve the parliament would be restricted. The regional governors were to be appointed by the president but carry out the orders of the government. The constitutional amendments were to come into force on January 1, 2006, but this inconsistent constitutional order has not worked well.

The new election law was much better. It introduced fully proportional elections from March 2006, but the threshold for representation would be lowered from 4 to 3 percent of the votes cast. The parliament would serve for five rather than four years. The obsolete parliament would stay on until March 2006. Logically, new parliamentary elections should have been held, but only Tymoshenko and some in Our Ukraine pursued that argument.

In effect, the compromise meant that the orange camp won on the presidential election, but it lost both on the constitutional change and the parliamentary election date, while the transition to proportional elections was approved by consensus. Thus, it was less of a victory for the orange side than it appeared at the time.

The constitutional decisions by parliament on December 8 marked the end of the Orange Revolution, which had lasted for 17 days since November 22. That evening, Lutsenko spoke on Maidan and told the victors they could go home and drink 50 grams of vodka. Euphoria prevailed and people danced on Khreshchatyk. I stopped by one orchestra that was playing national tunes. All of a sudden, the whole street was singing and dancing in lines and circles. I thought of Milan Kundera's line in his *Book of Laughter and Forgetting*, "Also I have danced in ring." Suddenly, three old ladies dragged me off my feet, and off we flew in an extended ring. The revolution had bred its own songs. Everyone was happy. The leading refrain went: "Together we are many. We cannot be

24. Interview with Tymoshenko in March 2005.

defeated!"[25] Another was: "We have fun in Ukraine." Ever so often, the tune switched to the militant chant "Yu-shchen-ko!" as clinched fists rose into the air. The 1,500 tents and their inhabitants stayed until December 26, but the masses dwindled.

On December 20, before the final round of the presidential elections, another televised debate was held between the two candidates. Incredibly, 63 percent of the population watched, but they found the debate rather boring, knowing all the arguments. Once again Yushchenko was perceived as the winner.

On December 26 the Ukrainians voted for the third time in two months, and no less than 77 percent participated. The election took place in good order under the most extensive monitoring possible, which judged it free and fair. Yushchenko won with 52 percent of the votes and Yanukovych obtained 44 percent, reflecting what the exit polls had indicated after the second round (table 7.1). Neither candidate gained nor lost votes, indicating very loyal electorates with as sharp regional division as before. Donbas voters really supported Yanukovych, even if they did not show the same passion as their western compatriots.

Democracy had arrived. With this election, Ukraine had passed the test of a free society and a democracy. For the first time, authoritative Freedom House (2008) raised Ukraine's ranking to "free." For Ukrainians, the Orange Revolution was their catharsis. They had finally proven themselves both to themselves and the world.

Assessment of the Orange Revolution

Looking back, the Orange Revolution seemed quite predictable. For years, it had been discussed in detail. Both the opposition and the regime possessed all relevant information. In the end, the regime committed a number of serious mistakes, while the opposition got it right.

The Orange Revolution was not a singular event. In November 2003 the Rose Revolution had overthrown President Eduard Shevardnadze in Georgia, and the Orange Revolution was followed by the Tulip Revolution, which toppled President Askar Akaev in Kyrgyzstan in March 2005. These three post-Soviet "colored" revolutions had seven conditions in common for democratic breakthrough, and the Ukrainians examined the Georgian precedent.[26]

First, the incumbent regime was neither strong nor united. It was semidemocratic or mildly authoritarian, with a skillful old president dividing and ruling between oligarchic clans. In Ukraine only one oligarchic clan

25. *Razom nas bahato! Nas ne podolaty!*

26. This section draws on McFaul (2006a).

fully supported the old regime's presidential candidate (Yanukovych), while the others were lukewarm or opposed.

Second, a similar fissure ran through law enforcement. Especially the Ministry of Interior and the SBU were rivals. Substantial parts of the SBU sided with Yushchenko early on and fed his campaign with vital intelligence. As the troops were not reliable, the old regime did not know whether it could use them against demonstrators.

Third, the old regime had an unpopular leader, and Kuchma tried to appoint a successor. The old leaders had originally been popular, but corruption or nepotism had eroded their popularity.

Fourth, a strong, well-organized, and legal opposition existed. The opposition was structured in a few major parties, which acted together. It had a popular leader who had substantial executive experience and parliamentary representation. In the Orange Revolution, the billionaires supported the regime, while the multimillionaires opposed it, generously funding the revolution.

Fifth, the opposition had access to independent media. The Orange Revolution marked the breakthrough of the internet era, as *Ukrainskaya pravda* became the foremost news medium. Mobile phones that could take photos transmitted revolutionary news. Strangely, both the Georgian and Ukrainian old regimes permitted the opposition access to a minor TV channel, which proved vital. These countries were sufficiently free so that foreign broadcasting could not keep up with events and lost local attention (Prytula 2006).

A sixth condition was timely, independent, national election monitoring and the instant spreading of the actual election results. This required strong domestic nongovernmental organizations as well as international election monitors. Initially, exit polls were taken, then alternative vote counts, and in the end the actual fraud was revealed.

Finally, the opposition could mobilize the population through strong nongovernmental organizations, especially the student organization Pora, which initiated street demonstrations. The number of people in the streets was vital for the success of the protest, and people were caught by the sense that it was now or never: The election had evidently been stolen and it was unclear whether people would be allowed to protest again.

In all the regime changes, foreign actors were conspicuous. Western nongovernmental organizations assisted with the training of activists, election monitors, and independent journalists. The Orange Revolution was top news throughout the world for one month, and prominent international politicians participated in the roundtable with the Ukrainian leaders on how to end the revolution. The Kremlin and other incumbent dictators labeled the colored revolutions Western conspiracies. That was an exaggeration, but the opposition did enjoy strong Western sympathy (McFaul 2006b). The minimal return on the heavy-handed Russian involvement showed the limited impact of money, media propaganda, and "political technologists."

The colored revolutions showed that the "captured" regimes were not all that entrenched but harbored seeds of democracy. According to more stringent political science definitions of revolution, the colored revolutions did not quite qualify. They were peaceful, and constitutions were obeyed. The critical decisions were made through compromises around a roundtable, by the Supreme Court, and through legislation in parliament. No major redistribution of property occurred. It might be more appropriate to call them democratic breakthroughs (McFaul 2006a).

The colored revolutions bred counterrevolution in the remaining, more authoritarian, oligarchic regimes. In May 2005 an armed uprising in the Uzbek city of Andijan was quashed, costing hundreds of lives. In Russia the Kremlin decided to become more autocratic, tightening authoritarian controls over all factors that may have contributed to the colored revolutions. Effective one-party rule was imposed. All media of significance were brought under Kremlin control. A new restrictive law on nongovernmental organizations gave the Kremlin arbitrary control over their registration and funding. Independent election monitoring was prohibited by law, as was criticism of public officials. Judicial reform was halted to the benefit of the secret police.

8

Aftermath of the Orange Revolution, 2005–08

The hangover was as heavy as the Orange Revolution had been gorgeous. Viktor Yanukovych had learned the trick. After the rerun on December 26, he did not concede but filed hundreds of suits about electoral fraud. Although he had no apparent cause, his complaints prolonged uncertainty for almost a month. Viktor Yushchenko's inauguration was in limbo. He could make no appointments, which greatly irritated the orange victors, who feared that the old regime would steal the government bare, while President Leonid Kuchma continued making appointments.

Within the old regime, recrimination was awful. The day after the rerun, Minister of Railways Heorhiy Kirpa, a strongman vital for election fraud and financing, allegedly committed suicide, but with two bullets. Soon afterward, Yuriy Lyakh, a leading banker close to Viktor Medvedchuk, was stabbed to death. In March 2005, just before he was supposed to give evidence as the key witness in the Heorhiy Gongadze murder, former Minister of Interior Yuriy Kravchenko committed suicide (Wilson 2005, 5–6, 156). The old gas oligarch Ihor Bakai emigrated to Russia, while Oleksandr Volkov joined Yuliya Tymoshenko. Leonid Kuchma quietly retired to his dacha outside of Kyiv without suffering any legal consequences. Most oligarchs enjoyed parliamentary immunity.

The Orange Revolution had changed everything, including the composition of the parliament. In the orange bloc, Our Ukraine had 100 deputies, Tymoshenko's bloc 19, and the socialists 20, adding up to only 139 deputies out of 450. The opposition of 144 consisted of 56 deputies of the Donetsk party the Regions (down from 66), 29 social democratic deputies (the Medvedchuk-Surkis group, down from over 40), and 59 communists. The remaining third of the deputies had drifted away into loose, opportunistic centrist factions. In 2005 the Our Ukraine faction cracked up as well. The parliament was no longer representative, and Ukraine badly needed new parliamentary elections. Alas, for constitutional reasons, new elections were not deemed possible. Ukraine had to survive with a deficient parliament until March 2006, but the cost would prove considerable.

All politicians focused on the March 2006 parliamentary elections, and Ukraine never enjoyed its moment of "extraordinary politics," as Leszek Balcerowicz (1994) has called the brief period of political suspension after a democratic breakthrough when greater reforms than usual are possible.

Ukraine recorded two great achievements: democratization and closer relations with the West and the European Union. Freedom was suddenly taken for granted. Everybody freely spoke their mind. The media were unrestricted and voiced diverse opinions. Street demonstrations and minor popular protests became everyday events. The problem was rather how to make and implement democratic decisions.

The political situation proved exceedingly unstable. In the ensuing four years, Ukraine had no less than four governments, led in turn by Tymoshenko, Yuriy Yekhanurov, Yanukovych, and Tymoshenko again. Parliamentary elections were held in March 2006 and again in September 2007. Ukraine joined the World Trade Organization (WTO) on May 16, 2008, and the economy continued growing at a high rate, but no political modus vivendi was found. The three dominant political leaders could not form a lasting or operative compromise because of the dysfunctional constitutional order. The greatest bone of contention was Ukraine's relation to the North Atlantic Treaty Organization (NATO), and Russia's president, Vladimir Putin, did what he could to aggravate the situation.

Formation of an Orange Coalition

The orange leaders were all lobbying for high posts in the new administration, and the delayed election results aggravated their infighting. For ten days, Yushchenko took a well-deserved holiday in the Carpathian mountains together with Georgian President Mikheil Saakashvili, but he made the elementary management mistake of appointing a working group of eight leaders to agree on the composition of the new government. As they all wanted to become prime minister, the working group failed miserably.

The two strongest contenders were Yuliya Tymoshenko and Petro Poroshenko. Both were striking personalities, highly intelligent and capable. Tymoshenko was both the most liked and disliked politician, perceived as highly partisan. She claimed that Yushchenko had promised her the job when she supported his candidacy last July. Her short-term goal was to maximize her eponymous bloc's votes in the March 2006 parliamentary elections, and she thought populist policies would serve her best.

Poroshenko's problem was his substantial business interests. He complained that he had lost two-thirds of his assets because of his opposition to the old regime. People feared that he would use power to claw back his lost fortune. Poroshenko was supported by the other big orange businessmen, David Zhvania, Mykola Martynenko, and Yevhen Chervonenko. Their reputations were worse than Poroshenko's.

On January 23 Yushchenko was finally inaugurated, and the next day he appointed Tymoshenko acting prime minister. On February 4 the Rada approved her candidacy with an overwhelming majority of 373 votes.

Yushchenko formed the government. Tymoshenko received no ministerial portfolios, though her right-hand man, Oleksandr Turchinov, became chairman of the Security Services of Ukraine (SBU).[1] Yushchenko's old liberal ally, Viktor Pynzenyk, returned to the government as minister of finance. Yushchenko's men controlled foreign policy. His loyal chief of staff Oleh Rybachuk was named deputy prime minister for European integration; Borys Tarasiuk returned to his old job as minister for foreign affairs; and Anatoliy Hrytsenko became minister of defense. The Poroshenko group was also richly rewarded, with Poroshenko becoming secretary of the National Security and Defense Council and receiving two ministerial posts.

Somewhat surprisingly, the small Socialist Party received four ministerial posts, including the popular Yuriy Lutsenko as minister of interior and the dogmatic socialist Valentyna Semeniuk as chairman of the State Property Fund. Thus socialists, who opposed privatization, were given this key ideological portfolio. The fourth coalition partner, Anatoliy Kinakh, became first deputy prime minister.

The presidential administration was badly divided from the outset. As his first assistant, Yushchenko took Oleksandr Tretyakov, a gas trader, who had invited the Yushchenko family to stay with him in his fortified residence after the poisoning. Oleksandr Zinchenko, the late arrival from the Medvedchuk camp, became Yushchenko's chief of staff.

Both the government and the presidential administration harbored too many ambitions and opposing interests. They were set for an all-consuming internecine struggle.

Ukraine Turns to Europe

After the government was formed, Yushchenko disappeared from the domestic scene into foreign affairs. He toured the world, celebrating his victory in the Orange Revolution, and recovered from the poisoning.

---

1. This section draws extensively on interviews recorded in my personal trip reports from January 11–14, March 6–18, and April 24–27, 2005.

On January 24, 2005, the day after his inauguration, Yushchenko met Putin in the Kremlin, anxious to put Ukrainian-Russian relations on a normal footing, and on March 19 he received Putin in Kyiv. But most substance had disappeared from Ukrainian-Russian relations, and ministerial exchanges almost ceased.

On March 1 Ukraine declared that it would withdraw its troops from Iraq. The United States had long accepted Yushchenko's position. His greatest feat was his trip to Washington, where he was given the rare honor of addressing a joint session of the US Congress on April 6.

The Orange Revolution greatly improved Ukraine's political relations with the European Union, which became the priority of the new government. It wanted Ukraine to become an EU member. Deputy Prime Minister for European Integration Oleh Rybachuk, a revolutionary hero, promoted EU integration with great fervor. With his enthusiastic rhetoric, excellent command of English from Georgetown University in Washington, and whirlwind diplomacy, Rybachuk transformed the European face of Ukraine.

As the European Union turned more positive about Ukraine, the nature of its European Neighborhood Policy (ENP) for Ukraine changed. The Yanukovych government had prepared an initial action plan for the ENP but never concluded it with the European Union. It had complained that the European Union imposed many demands on Ukraine while offering little itself. Many EU demands, however, were badly needed Ukrainian reforms. The European Union emphasized that ENP action plans would not be standardized as the preceding partnership and cooperation agreements had been but designed individually for each country, with more cooperation with countries closer to the European Union. On February 21 Ukraine concluded a substantial initial action plan with the European Union.

The action plan laid out the strategic objectives for EU-Ukraine cooperation for the ensuing three years. It envisioned a free trade agreement between Ukraine and the European Union to be concluded as soon as Ukraine became a member of the WTO. It also included substantial Ukrainian cooptation of useful EU institutions, and the European Union offered Ukraine some scientific and education exchanges.

The new government was also determined to pursue Ukraine's accession to the WTO, which remained a top national priority regardless of government, and it became a major focus of legislation.

The Tymoshenko Government: Reprivatization

The Tymoshenko government came to power promising earth-shattering reforms. Corruption would be purged and the state administration would start functioning. Several organizations had formulated concrete reform proposals and a broad consensus existed.[2] The new government adopted a program, but it was of no consequence. Alas, no broad, comprehensive reforms were launched, and the orange coalition plunged into internecine strife.

Tymoshenko dominated the cabinet and deprived the deputy prime ministers of their staff and powers, centralizing their power to herself. She kept the cabinet of ministers in long meetings two days a week. The poorly prepared discussions were long and often indecisive. Then the prime minister decided on her own, in what Ukrainians called *ruchnoe upravlenie* (manual management). She attacked ministers in public with great vitriol. Yushchenko's secretariat was a similar wonder of disorganization. The Ukrainian government had not seen such chaos since Leonid Kravchuk's days.

The new government focused on cleansing taxation and customs, Ukraine's WTO membership, and closer relations with the European Union, but also on populist policies of reprivatization, price regulation, arresting culprits of the old regime, and increased public expenditures to boost the prime minister's popularity before the parliamentary elections.

Pynzenyk pursued fiscal reform. Since Tymoshenko considered it politically impossible to scale back Yanukovych's pension hikes, tax revenues had to be boosted. Pynzenyk did so by abolishing loopholes and improving tax collection. He eliminated tax exemptions for specific industries and all the free economic zones, which had mainly benefited Donbas and Transcarpathia, leveling the playing field. As part of its accession to the WTO, the government lowered customs tariffs to liberalize legitimate trade, while tightening controls. As a result, customs revenues rose sharply. Total state revenues rose impressively by 4.9 percent of GDP from 2004 to 2005, halving the budget deficit to 2.3 percent of GDP after Yanukovych's excesses.[3] The notorious demands for 20 to 30 percent commission for the reimbursement of value-added taxes (VAT) for exporters abated.

The all-consuming issue for the Tymoshenko government, however, was reprivatization. Yushchenko had campaigned for one repeat privatization, Kryvorizhstal, but now he went further. On February 10, 2005, he stated: "We will revoke every privatization case that was conducted in breach of law. Nothing will stop me."[4] Yet Tymoshenko took the lead. On February 16 she raised the legal reconsideration of 3,000

---

2. For example, Blue Ribbon Commission for Ukraine (2005), EBA (2004), and OECD (2004).

3. European Bank for Reconstruction and Development online database, www.ebrd.com (accessed on August 16, 2007).

4. Dragon Capital, *The Dragon Daily*, February 11, 2005.

privatizations in the last five years, while Yushchenko tried to limit the number to 20 to 30 specific reprivatizations. The government elaborated several draft laws, with criteria and procedures for privatizations, and the top politicians spent much of their time discussing the flaws of various privatizations.

The reprivatization discussion became highly personal. Tymoshenko took pleasure in pinpointing enterprises belonging to Victor Pinchuk and Rinat Akhmetov. The two competing oligarchic groups, Privat Group and the Industrial Union of Donbas, welcomed reprivatization, although some of their factories were also questioned because they hoped to seize assets from Pinchuk and Akhmetov. The businessmen who had suffered large losses to the Kuchma oligarchs but paid millions to the Yushchenko campaign reckoned it was payback time.

Virtually everybody argued for the swift expropriation and resale of Kryvorizhstal from Pinchuk and Akhmetov. This sale of June 2004 for $800 million could result in revenues of $3 billion, and the courts decided the reprivatization of Kryvorizhstal. Pinchuk and Akhmetov complained to the highest courts but lost.

The most aggressive battle took place between Pinchuk and Ihor Kolomoiskiy of Privat Group over the Nikopol Ferroalloy Plant. Pinchuk had gained it in the spring of 2003 in competition with Privat because Privat had only offshore funds, while a condition imposed by the International Monetary Fund (IMF) was that only onshore funds could be used. Kolomoiskiy demanded this valuable factory. He persuaded Tymoshenko to order 2,000 interior troops to seize the factory, while Pinchuk asked thousands of his workers to defend their place of work. Fortunately, no violence erupted. The case was eventually settled amicably out of court between Pinchuk and Kolomoiskiy.

Reprivatization became reminiscent of corporate raiding, which was the scourge of Ukrainian capitalism. Typically, a raider acquired a minority share in a company with several owners already divided. He used his ownership to demand information about the company. Since no firm could act legally in Ukraine's inconsistent legal framework, the raider sued or blackmailed the main owner, and a corrupt court could decide anything. Usually, a raider was paid off, but often he seized the firm, especially if the main owner was short of cash. Tens of thousands of such illicit corporate raidings occurred after 2000.

By March 2 the prosecutor general announced that criminal cases of violations of the law during privatization had been initiated against about 2,000 people.[5] One opinion poll showed that 71 percent of Ukrainians

5. "Genprokuratura obvinyaet 2 tysyach chelovek v nezakonnoi privatizatsii" ["The General Prosecutor Accuses 2,000 People of Illegal Privatization"], *Ukrainskaya pravda*, March 2, 2005.

supported a revision of privatization of the biggest state enterprises, and only 11 percent preferred to leave everything as it was.[6]

Another hallmark of the new government was huge social transfers. Yanukovych had doubled pensions from September 1, 2004, but the new government hiked the wages of all public employees by 60 percent.

Tymoshenko largely adopted Yanukovych's policies of populist public expenditures and price controls, appealing to his poor and uneducated electorate. Her policy was almost exactly the opposite of the liberal Yushchenko's. She effectively favored state capitalism, aspiring to government control over the commanding heights of the economy to establish vertically integrated state monopolies: "Those big enterprises, at which it is very easy to organize effective management, and which generate excellent profit to the state as owner, must not be privatized."[7] She launched a campaign to reinforce state monopolies, raise their tariffs, and boost their profits as well as their payments to the state.

She started regulating prices. As domestic oil prices rose in line with global prices, Tymoshenko blamed Russian oil companies for the rising Ukrainian prices: "You know, certain countries were not very satisfied with the elections in Ukraine. During the last months, Russia has increased the prices of oil by 30 percent. . . . Russia's oil traders wanted to obtain excessive profits at the expense of Ukraine and set their prices considerably higher, because they are monopolists and think that they momentarily can turn Ukraine's hands around."[8] Although Ukraine's oil market was competitive with numerous private companies, Tymoshenko capped gas prices, and refineries and gas stations started closing. When the Russian oil companies protested, Tymoshenko abused them with delight.

Similarly, she tried to regulate meat prices, demanding that producers and shopkeepers sell at low prices. At a televised cabinet meeting in early April, she announced: "Meat prices will be under my personal control." In an eerily Leninist vein, she stated: "We must do what it takes to combat the speculators (middlemen)."[9] She commanded the governors to draw up plans for meat production in their regions: "This is an imperative directive. You have half a year to draft projects on meat production, engage enter-

6. "Bolshinstvo ukraintsev podderzhivaet ideyu peresmotra itogov privatizatsii" ["A Majority of Ukrainians Supports the Idea of a Revision of the Results of Privatization"], *Ukrainskaya pravda*, May 14, 2005.

7. "'Posevnaya': Do, Posle i Vmesto" ["'Sowing:' Before, After and Instead of"], *Zerkalo nedeli*, April 16–22, 2005.

8. "Timoshenko obvinyaet rossiyan v benzinnovom shantazhe iz-za pobedy Yushchenko" ["Tymoshenko Accuses Russians of Gas Extortion because of Yushchenko's Victory"], *Ukrainskaya pravda*, May 15, 2005.

9. "Prime Minister Timoshenko Tackles Meat Prices," *New Europe* (Athens), May 9, 2005.

prises and draw investments."[10] This sounded like the old-style Soviet command economy, and meat started disappearing from the market.

The Orange Revolution had aimed at introducing the rule of law, but the government appeared to penalize some oligarchs and favor others. In April Ukraine's richest man, Akhmetov, fled to Moscow after his partner Borys Kolesnikov was arrested for alleged racketeering and returned to Ukraine only after Tymoshenko's ouster.

The protracted public debate over reprivatization undermined property rights and business confidence, and the increased tax pressure aggravated the burden. As a consequence, GDP growth fell by about one percentage point each month until it had become negative in August. Tymoshenko's economic policy was a disaster.

Ukrainian society woke up only slowly from its euphoria of the Orange Revolution. In late March, the intellectual weekly *Zerkalo nedeli* started complaining about "revolutionary populism."[11] Yushchenko was the only possible counterweight, but since 1999 he had refrained from public criticism of Tymoshenko. Yet in mid-May he started scolding her, first criticizing her relentless campaign for reprivatization: "From the first day, I said that neither I nor my team aim at the nationalization or reprivatization of any object of property."[12] He also criticized the price controls: "I shall guarantee that the government uses exclusively market methods to respond to questions on the markets of meat, petroleum products and crude oil."[13]

On May 19 a political bomb detonated. At a large meeting with businessmen on oil price controls, Tymoshenko argued against Yushchenko. Finally, Yushchenko asked her to submit her resignation.[14] She did not do so, but in effect the orange coalition was over. The government and presidential administration were so antagonistic and divided that neither could work.

On September 3 Zinchenko resigned as head of the presidential administration, and two days later he held a scandalous press conference. He accused Secretary of the National Security and Defense Council Porosh-

---

10. "PM Tymoshenko Orders Governors to Draft Projects to Supply Regions with Meat by December," Ukrainian News Agency, May 16, 2005.

11. Nataliya Yatsenko, "Revolyutsionnaya byudzhetnaya tselesoobraznost" ["Revolutionary Budgetary Expediency"], *Zerkalo nedeli*, March 26, 2005.

12. "Yushchenko ne otdast Krivorozhstal gosudarstvu, no eshche dolzhen podumat'" ["Yushchenko Does Not Give Kryvorizhstal to the State, But He Needs to Think More"], *Ukrainskaya pravda*, May 13, 2005.

13. "Yushchenko govorit, chto 'Zerkalo nedeli' pishet bashni" ["Yushchenko Says that 'Zerkalo nedeli' Writes Tales"], *Ukrainskaya pravda*, May 25, 2005.

14. Yuliya Mostovaya, "Igra so spichkama vokrug benzyna" ["Play with Matches around Gas"], *Zerkalo nedeli*, May 21, 2005.

enko, First Presidential Assistant Tretyakov, and their partners of using the government for their personal corrupt aims. However, he did not specify actual corruption.[15]

Yushchenko did the inevitable on September 8, sacking both sides, Tymoshenko as well as Poroshenko and Tretyakov. He nominated his close loyalists Yuriy Yekhanurov as prime minister and Rybachuk as state secretary, head of the president's secretariat. Yushchenko had made Yekhanurov governor of Dnipropetrovsk oblast, as if he had kept him as a reserve outside of the Kyiv squabbles.

The orange revolutionaries had fallen apart in scandals and disputes. Yushchenko was accused of being ineffective, disorganized, and naïve. Tymoshenko's popularity had fallen in parallel with Yushchenko's, as businessmen were upset by her populist economic policy. Under her watch, economic growth fell month by month from 12 percent in 2004 to −1.6 percent in August 2005. Few laws were enacted because of the government chaos. Her defenders praised the adoption of several WTO laws and the elimination of 3,600 unnecessary regulations. Nobody called her our Yulka any longer.

The orange coalition government was the victim of revolutionary hubris and the absence of new parliamentary elections. The victors felt invincible and infallible, with power being their privilege. Everybody focused on the March 2006 elections, and Tymoshenko was convinced that populism would win. Moreover, the very construction of the government was divisive, leaving the prime minister without any minister of her own.

The Yekhanurov Government: Return to Order

After the fall of the Tymoshenko government, disappointment and disillusion spread to the orange voters at large.[16] Yet a new sense of democratic normalcy and order had taken hold, as democracy and freedom persevered. The many scandals reflected transparency and freedom of the media. As Yushchenko and Tymoshenko floundered, Yanukovych recovered in a quick metamorphosis. After all, he had managed the Ukrainian economy well and possessed a devoted eastern electorate.

In this situation, Yekhanurov appeared the natural choice for prime minister. He was unassuming and usually described as a technocrat, but he had carried out Ukraine's mass privatization from 1994 to 1997 without any stains on his reputation, which was political mastery. He knew the apparat inside out, being perfectly organized and hardworking. Amazingly,

15. "Skandal'naya press-konferentsiya Zinchenko" ["Zinchenko's Scandalous Press Conference"], *Ukrainskaya pravda*, September 5, 2005.

16. This section draws on my personal trip report from a visit to Kyiv, October 11–16, 2005.

for such a prominent politician, he had few enemies. His weakness was that he was less of a popular politician. Given that parliamentary elections were due in March 2006, his was a caretaker government.

The parliament had to confirm Yekhanurov. The initial attempt on September 20 failed by three votes as 223 deputies from seven party factions voted for him, while the Bloc of Yuliya Tymoshenko (BYuT), the Communist Party of Ukraine, and three oligarchic parties, including the Regions and Medvedchuk's social democrats, opposed him.[17] Yushchenko could have mobilized three additional votes for Yekhanurov in a repeat vote, but he preferred to play it safe, making an agreement with Yanukovych. On September 22 the Rada approved Yekhanurov with 289 votes thanks to the Regions' 50 votes.[18]

Yekhanurov quickly appointed a new government that was a coalition among Our Ukraine, the socialists, and Kinakh's industrialists. It was reasonably cohesive, apart from two socialist ministers blocking privatization. Eleven of the 25 ministers were exchanged as BYuT and the big businessmen from Our Ukraine departed. The new ministers were largely young professionals from Yushchenko's Our Ukraine. The rising star Arseniy Yatseniuk became minister of economy. Kinakh replaced Poroshenko as secretary of the National Security and Defense Council. This cabinet kept a lower public profile than Tymoshenko's, but it worked.

Yushchenko outlined the task, "to restore economic, political and social stability,"[19] which suited Yekhanurov. To reassure the businessmen he organized the first meeting ever between the president and the 20 biggest Ukrainian businessmen, following the example of Boris Yeltsin in Russia in the mid-1990s (Hoffman 2002). Yushchenko's message was that the businessmen had nothing to fear and the government demanded nothing from them, and they dared to stay and work in their country again.

Yekhanurov's overwhelming priority was to stop reprivatization and secure existing property rights. He accepted reselling one company, Kryvorizhstal, fulfilling Yushchenko's campaign commitment. On October 24, Kryvorizhstal was resold in a televised auction, with the two biggest steel companies in the world, Arcelor and Mittal Steel, bidding against one another. Mittal won with a cash bid of $4.8 billion, six times the price paid by Akhmetov and Pinchuk in June 2004 (steel prices had risen sharply in the interim). This sale was a great success and boosted

17. "Parlament ne podderzhal kandidatury Yekhanurova" ["Parliament Did Not Support Yekhanurov's Candidacy"], *Ukrainskaya pravda*, September 20, 2005.

18. "Rada Approves Yekhanurov as Prime Minister," Ukrainian News Agency, September 22, 2005.

19. "President Interviewed by Four Ukrainian National TV Channels," BBC Monitoring Service, October 4, 2005.

both state revenues and foreign direct investment, which took off in 2005. Politically, however, it benefited Tymoshenko, who attended the auction.

Yekhanurov had little time before the parliamentary elections scheduled for March 26, 2006, but by stopping reprivatization he managed to revive business confidence and thus economic growth, because Ukraine's businessmen had been so frightened by Tymoshenko's reprivatization drive that some had held back production. He and Yushchenko had no visible conflicts.

Russia Disrupts Gas Deliveries: Higher Prices

The biggest drama during Yekhanurov's term as prime minister was that on January 1, 2006. In the midst of the winter, Russia's Gazprom turned off gas to Ukraine because the two countries had not agreed on a price for 2006.[20] Since 80 percent of Russia's gas exports to Europe went through Ukraine, gas supplies to eight European countries, Austria, France, Germany, Hungary, Italy, Poland, Romania, and Slovakia, were reduced. Moscow had not warned them, so this supply disruption provoked strong international protests.

As a reaction, Russia ended its gas embargo after two days, and a Ukrainian delegation hastened to Moscow to reach an agreement. Ukraine had a five-year agreement from 2004 on gas deliveries from Russia, which Tymoshenko and the Ukrainian steel barons insisted was valid, but Gazprom objected that Ukraine had not fulfilled that agreement so it no longer applied. Three key issues were:

- Would Ukraine buy Turkmen or Russian gas?
- Would RosUkrEnergo (RUE) be allowed to continue as an intermediary?
- What would the price be? Gazprom demanded $230 per 1,000 cubic meters, while Ukraine had paid $50 in 2005.

Public discussion focused on the price. World energy prices had risen sharply in 2004. After the Orange Revolution, Ukraine had advocated market prices out of principle. Yushchenko stated: "If Ukraine really wants to become economically independent, sooner or later we have to move to market relations in the energy sector and organize our energy consumption rationally."[21] Gazprom appreciated such statements,

20. Sources of this section are Global Witness (2006), Stern (2006), Teylan and Gustafson (2006), Dubien (2007), and Milov and Nemtsov (2008).

21. "Yushchenko obeshchaet ne ustraivat' shokovoi terapii" ["Yushchenko Promises Not to Organize Shock Therapy"], *Ukrainskaya pravda*, December 17, 2005.

as it desired swift transition to European prices that were four to five times higher.

In the wee hours of January 4 the Ukrainian state energy company Naftohaz Ukrainy and Russia's state-dominated gas company Gazprom came to an agreement with the enigmatic trading company RUE about deliveries of Russian and Central Asian gas to Ukraine. The agreement was greeted with relief, but it was hastily concocted and left much unclear. The gas price was set at only $95 per 1,000 cubic meters, less than what any other country apart from Belarus paid, but just for the first half of 2006. Almost all the gas would come from Turkmenistan. A clear improvement was that barter would be abandoned and all payments made in cash.

The new gas agreement was controversial from the beginning for several reasons. RUE was given a major role in trade in and around Ukraine. It became the sole legal importer of gas in Ukraine. Together with Naftohaz Ukrainy it set up a joint venture, Ukrgaz-Energo, which became the dominant seller of gas to factories in the country, which was the most profitable part of the domestic gas market. RUE also exported substantial volumes of natural gas further to the West into Europe.[22]

Yekhanurov underlined that Gazprom insisted on RUE transiting Ukraine's gas purchased from Turkmenistan and that Ukraine had no choice, since Gazprom controlled the supply route. RUE's official explanation was that an intermediary was needed to trade natural gas from the four producing countries, Russia, Turkmenistan, Kazakhstan, and Uzbekistan, and transit it to Ukraine, but the Ukrainian public never accepted that argument.[23] BYuT and the Regions exploited this outcome for a vote of no confidence in Prime Minister Yekhanurov and his cabinet on January 10, 2006, assembling 250 votes.[24] However, this vote was ruled unconstitutional, having no legal effect, and Yekhanurov's government stayed on.

Ultimately, the issue was possible Russian control over the Ukrainian gas sector, Russian-Ukrainian relations, and large-scale corruption. As details became known, criticism amplified. RUE was a joint venture between Gazprombank and Centragas, a private trust with hitherto un-

22. "The Text of the Agreement between Naftohaz Ukrainy, Gazprom and RosUkrEnergo," Ukrainian Independent Information Agency, January 5, 2006; "Gazovoe SP sozdano. 5 let po $95" ["Gas Joint Venture Created. Five Years at $95"], *Korrespondent*, February 2, 2006; Vladimir Soccor, "UkrGazEnergo: New Russian Joint Venture to Dominate in Ukraine," *Eurasian Daily Monitor* (Jamestown Foundation), February 16, 2006; Roman Kupchinsky, "A Profile of RosUkrEnergo," Radio Free Europe/Radio Liberty, January 18, 2006.

23. Interview with RosUkrEnergo official Robert Shetler-Jones in Kyiv, January 2006.

24. "Rezultaty golosovaniya za otstavku Yekhanurova" ["Results of the Voting for Yekhanurov's Demise"], *Ukrainskaya pravda*, January 10, 2006.

known beneficiaries. On April 26, 2006, the Kremlin-controlled Moscow newspaper *Izvestiya* revealed the names of RUE's owners: Dmytro Firtash held 90 percent of Centragas and Ivan Fursin, an Odesa banker, 10 percent.[25]

Parliamentary Elections, March 2006

On March 26, 2006, Ukraine held its first ordinary parliamentary elections after the Orange Revolution. They were free and fair with a high participation of 67 percent, showcasing Ukraine's maturity as a democracy. These first purely proportional elections led to the desired consolidation of the party system. The number of party factions was reduced from 12 to 5 parties. Only 22 percent of the votes were wasted on parties not crossing the 3 percent hurdle compared with 24 percent in 2002.

The Regions came roaring back, receiving 32 percent of the votes against 22 percent for BYuT and a mere 14 percent for Our Ukraine. These three center-right parties obtained no less than 90 percent of the seats. The socialists entered parliament with 5.7 percent and the communists with a tiny 3.7 percent, as the marginalization of the hard left continued (table 8.1).

This vote reflected an amazing constancy between the orange and blue camps. In December 2004 Yushchenko defeated Yanukovych with a margin of eight percentage points, while the balance between the orange and blue coalitions shrunk to six percentage points this time. The geographic dividing line remained the same as in 2004 (Clem and Craumer 2008).

Within the orange coalition, however, Tymoshenko's bloc won overwhelmingly over Yushchenko's Our Ukraine. Tymoshenko was an outstanding campaigner, and she railed against the old regime in moralistic rhetoric. Her main slogan was justice, reminding the voters of Yushchenko's unfulfilled promise from 2004: "Bandits to prison!" She attacked the Russian-Ukrainian gas deal of January 4 but no longer mentioned reprivatization and played down social promises, as her populism faded. Our Ukraine's campaign was inept and featured its least popular representatives, such as the discredited Poroshenko, while the president and Yekhanurov kept low profiles.

These elections marked Ukraine's transition to a presidential-parliamentary democracy with reduced presidential powers. A prime minister had to assemble a coalition in parliament of at least 226 deputies.

Ukrainian elections remained extremely expensive. Before these elections, Speaker Volodymyr Lytvyn stated that seats on party lists would

25. Tom Warner, "Dmytro Firtash, Ukrainian Billionaire Nobody Knows," *Financial Times*, April 27, 2006.

Table 8.1 Results of election to the Supreme Rada, March 26, 2006[a]

Party	Votes (percent)	Seats
Left	13.1	54
Communist	3.7	21
Socialist	5.7	33
Center-Right	82.9	396
Party of Regions	32.1	186
Yuliya Tymoshenko Bloc	22.3	129
Our Ukraine	14.0	81
Against all or not valid	4.0	0
Total	100	450
Voter turnout (percent)	67.1	

a. Pure proportional election.

Source: Central Election Commission of Ukraine, www.cvk.gov.ua (accessed on September 31, 2007).

cost up to $5 million. Yanukovych retained the support of Akhmetov, who for the first time decided to become a member of parliament, taking no less than 60 of his senior employees to the Rada and forming his own company party within the Regions. The Industrial Union of Donbas supported Yushchenko, and Privat Group was closest to BYuT, while Pinchuk kept a new distance from politics and left parliament. Other large business groups were also engaged, rendering all parties, including the communists, oligarchic.

After the parliamentary elections, seemingly endless coalition negotiations ensued. As two or three of the five parties in parliament were needed for a coalition government, this game was almost unsolvable. An incredible circus of intrigue started. Five coalitions were seriously discussed until a government was formed in August, more than four months after the elections. Meanwhile, Yekhanurov ran his caretaker government.

Initially, a renewed orange coalition looked obvious. BYuT, Our Ukraine, and the socialists discussed the formation of a new government program. But Oleksandr Moroz demanded the speakership of the Rada, no NATO accession, and no land privatization,[26] and Yushchenko did not want Tymoshenko as prime minister again. Finally, the big businessmen in Our Ukraine, who hated Tymoshenko, persuaded Yushchenko to drop her for an alliance with the Regions.[27]

26. Oleg Varfolomeyev, "End of Orange Coalition Looming?" *Eurasian Daily Monitor* (Jamestown Foundation), June 14, 2006; Yuliya Mostovaya, "Koalivshchina" ["Coalition Games"], *Zerkalo nedeli*, May 13, 2006.

27. "'Liubi druzi' ybedili Yushchenko ob'edinit'sya s Yanukovichem?" ["The 'Dear Friends' Convinced Yushchenko to Unite with Yanukovych?"], *Ukrainskaya pravda*, April 18, 2006.

In early June, Akhmetov and Yekhanurov successfully negotiated a coalition government between the Regions and Our Ukraine. The Regions accepted virtually all Our Ukraine's demands. Yekhanurov would stay as prime minister, and each party would receive half the portfolios. A full agreement was ready for Yushchenko's approval on June 18.

But on June 20 Tymoshenko stormed into Yushchenko's office and convinced him to form a new orange coalition, alleging socialist support. Without consultation, Yushchenko dropped an alliance between Our Ukraine and the Regions.[28]

Moroz, however, who was supposed to yield the speakership to Poroshenko, defected. On July 6 he was unexpectedly elected speaker of the Rada with the support of the Regions, the socialists, and the communists. The following day these three parties signed an agreement on a majority coalition with 241 seats. Both Yushchenko and Tymoshenko had lost out. Tymoshenko claimed that Moroz had received $300 million to change sides, for which he sued her. The socialists insisted that the Regions gave them both the policy and posts they wanted.[29]

Yushchenko seemed to have outintrigued himself. He had ended up with the coalition that suited him the least. On July 25, two months had passed since the cabinet's resignation, entitling Yushchenko to call new elections. He used this leverage to convene a roundtable with all parties and propose a draft declaration (*universal*) of national unity. This declaration roughly coincided with the government program agreed between the Regions and Our Ukraine in June. His main demand was support for Ukraine's Euro-Atlantic integration.[30]

On August 3 the Regions, Our Ukraine, and the socialists signed the *universal*, while the communists did so with a reservation. Tymoshenko refused and went into opposition. Yushchenko's coalition of national unity formed the government, and Yushchenko accepted Yanukovych as prime minister. Yanukovych graciously praised the positive influence on Ukraine of the Orange Revolution: "However hard it was, this period has been of benefit to the state. . . . We have started to free ourselves from dirt that had accumulated for years."[31]

The Rada confirmed Yanukovych by 271 votes, with support from the Regions, the socialists, the communists, and 30 of Our Ukraine's

---

28. Oleg Varfolomeyev, "Orange Coalition Parties Re-Establish Government Coalition" *Eurasian Daily Monitor* (Jamestown Foundation), June 28, 2006.

29. Yuliya Mostovaya, "Na stsene maidana—Zanaves" ["The Curtain Drops on the Maidan Stage"], *Zerkalo nedeli*, July 18, 2006.

30. Oleg Varfolomeyev, "Yushchenko Lays Out His Conditions for Accepting Yanukovych," *Eurasian Daily Monitor* (Jamestown Foundation), July 28, 2006.

31. "Yanukovich budet prazdnovat' po-muzhski" ["Yanukovych Will Celebrate Like a Man"], *Ukrainskaya pravda*, August 4, 2006.

80 deputies.[32] The new government was supposed to incorporate checks and balances. The Regions received the whole economic bloc in the government with Mykola Azarov as first deputy prime minister and minister of finance again, Andriy Kliuev as deputy prime minister, and Yuriy Boiko as minister of fuel and energy. The heavies from Donetsk were back. Moroz stayed as speaker, and Semeniuk, the sworn enemy of privatization, remained chair of the State Property Fund.

The president's men, Borys Tarasiuk and Anatoliy Hrytsenko, returned as foreign minister and defense minister, respectively. Our Ukraine received law enforcement and the humanitarian bloc in the government with the portfolios for interior, justice, culture, family, health care, and education.[33]

The declaration of national unity represented a historical compromise and was supposed to be the government program.[34] Ukraine was to be a unitary state. Ukrainian would remain the official state language, but "every Ukrainian citizen is guaranteed the right to use Russian or any other native language in all walks of life." Private sales of agricultural land would be introduced no later than January 1, 2008. Ukraine was to "take all necessary legislative steps to join the WTO before the end of 2006." All wanted European integration, leading to membership in the European Union, and to negotiate a free trade zone with the European Union. Ukraine accepted the Russian-sponsored Common Economic Space but only as a free trade area. It favored "mutually beneficial cooperation with NATO," but a referendum on accession had to be held.

Our Ukraine and the Regions differed most on foreign policy, which Yushchenko dominated, while both parties professed similar free-market policies. Both favored liberal tax reform, judicial reform, and anticorruption measures. National tensions were resolved, and the Regions accepted a Western-oriented foreign policy, while Tymoshenko offered pragmatic but challenging opposition. The four months of governmental crisis suddenly seemed productive, generating a potentially constructive administration.

The Second Yanukovych Government: Oligarchy Restored

Unfortunately, the second Yanukovych cabinet did not work out because of devastating disputes over foreign policy and the constitution. Yanu-

32. "Yanukovich—prem'er. Moroz pokazal emu ego mesto" ["Yanukovych Is Prime Minister. Moroz Showed Him His Place"], *Ukrainskaya pravda*, August 4, 2006.

33. "Novoe pravitel'stvo utverzdeno" ["The New Government Is Confirmed"], *Ukrainskaya pravda*, August 4, 2006.

34. "Universal natsional'nogo edintstvo" ["Declaration of National Unity"], *Ukrainskaya pravda*, August 3, 2006.

kovych steamrolled through his decisions, while Our Ukraine indulged in infighting. Meanwhile, corruption gained new momentum.

Yanukovych immediately intruded in foreign affairs. His first foreign trip as prime minister took him to Putin's summer residence in Sochi. Before his trip, Yanukovych speculated that Russia would symbolically reduce its gas prices, but Putin made clear that Yanukovych should pay back, so he returned empty-handed.[35] Ukrainian-Russian relations remained insubstantial and cool.

On September 14, 2006, Yanukovych visited NATO headquarters in Brussels. Contrary to the Declaration of National Unity, he desired no closer cooperation with NATO, infuriating Yushchenko, Tarasiuk, and Hrytsenko. Although the president appointed the minister for foreign affairs, Yanukovych forced Tarasiuk out on January 30 by cutting financing for his ministry.

In September 2006 Yushchenko changed his liberal and pleasant chief of staff Oleh Rybachuk for a tough manager, Viktor Baloha, a businessman from Transcarpathia. Baloha was a crisis manager and fighter with no apparent ideology.[36] He took firm command over Yushchenko's secretariat and cleansed it of all liberals and orange revolutionaries. Soon he established his reputation as Ukraine's Rasputin.

For a couple of months, Our Ukraine continued quarrelling about whether to join the coalition with the Regions, although it already had 10 ministers in the government. Eventually, a majority of Our Ukraine deputies voted against the coalition, and most propresidential ministers resigned on October 19. Our Ukraine seemed to be pursuing slow hara-kiri.

In an ultimate insult to Yushchenko, Yanukovych and Tymoshenko settled constitutional matters without him. On December 21, 2006, the Regions persuaded BYuT to vote with them, the socialists, and the communists for a Law on the Cabinet of Ministers. This law would reinforce the powers of the parliament and the prime minister at the expense of the president. Although Tymoshenko favored strong presidential powers, she supported it in exchange for an "imperative mandate," which meant that a deputy could not change party faction after being elected to parliament for one party because the mandate belonged to the party. Yushchenko vetoed this law, but the four other parties overruled his veto. In reality, little changed.

The Yekhanurov and Yanukovych governments restored economic growth to the prior growth path with 7.3 percent in 2006 and 2007.

35. Vladimir Soccor, "Yanukovych Cold-Shouldered on First Visit to Russia," *Eurasian Daily Monitor* (Jamestown Foundation), August 17, 2006.

36. Viktor Chyvkunya, "Baloha: Yushchenko's New Favorite," *Ukrainskaya pravda*, September 19, 2006.

However, apart from the laws needed for WTO accession, Ukraine hardly legislated, and no structural reforms occurred.

Old corrupt practices gained new momentum. The Tymoshenko and Yekhanurov governments had successfully reduced the corruption in VAT refunds for exporters, but with the return of Yanukovych and Azarov, demand for commissions of 20 to 30 percent to obtain VAT refunds reemerged.

The three main Ukrainian officials involved in RUE were, once again, Yuriy Boiko, chairman of Naftohaz Ukrainy in 2002–05 and now minister of energy; Ihor Voronin, long-time deputy chairman of Naftohaz Ukrainy but also president of Ukrgaz-Energo; and Serhiy Levochkin, formerly Kuchma's first assistant and now Yanukovych's chief of staff (Global Witness 2006, Dubien 2007). In a complete conflict of interests, Boiko and Voronin were Ukraine's top gas officials but also represented RUE.

The gas sector posed persistent problems. Domestic consumer prices were fixed at a low level, which meant that the Ukrainian state subsidized the importation of natural gas. Domestic producers were paid less for their gas by Naftohaz than Ukraine paid for its imported gas, as domestic production was theoretically earmarked for residential customers. In spite of many attempts, no significant foreign energy producers managed to work in Ukraine. Naftohaz comprised a nontransparent and poorly managed maze of state enterprises and partially private companies. About once a year, the Ukrainian government was forced to bail it out with a couple of billions of dollars because of its chronic losses. Meanwhile, Ukraine continued to be one of the most energy inefficient countries in the world.[37]

The casus belli for Yushchenko was that the Regions gradually purchased deputies from Our Ukraine and BYuT. Its leaders spoke aggressively about increasing their majority, together with the socialists and communists, to 300 to reach a constitutional majority to be able to override presidential vetoes and amend the constitution. At the end of March 2007 Kinakh, now one of the leaders of Our Ukraine, joined the government as minister of economy together with 10 other deputies from Our Ukraine and BYuT. Such transactions always cost big money. Yushchenko decided to act before he lost his constitutional powers.

Ironically, the informal owner of the Regions, Akhmetov, was also unhappy with Yanukovych and his government. Akhmetov had declared that he joined parliament to improve legislation, especially to reinforce private property rights, so that he never had to flee his country again as in the summer of 2005. But he had little influence on legislation, and none of Akhmetov's people became ministers. Instead, the Regions was splitting

37. Edward Chow and Jonathan Elkind, Where East meets West: European Gas and Ukrainian Reality. *Washington Quarterly*, January 2009.

into two factions of similar size, a powerless Akhmetov party and a ruling Yanukovych party, including the heavyweights Azarov, Kliuev, and Boiko.

Dissolution of Parliament and New Parliamentary Elections, September 2007

The president was pressed against the wall with few options left. Contrary to the 2004 constitutional changes, Yanukovych had not allowed the president to appoint his own chairman of the SBU and minister for foreign affairs. The amended constitution did not allow deputies to change factions in parliament, but the Regions unabashedly bought deputies. Yet Yushchenko's constitutional ground to call for new elections was questionable, but Tymoshenko, who had been campaigning for the dissolution of parliament since August 2006, supported him.

On April 2, 2007, Yushchenko dissolved the parliament with three motivations: Party factions had been formed illegally, the parliament had been ineffective, and it had adopted nonconstitutional decisions (referring to the Law on the Cabinet of Ministers) (Åslund 2007c). A huge demonstration of some 100,000 people laid the groundwork for his action. Yushchenko acted fast, securing his control over law enforcement and most regional governors.

Yanukovych had gone too far. Corporate raiding was thriving as never before, and the government did nothing to stop it. Gas trade corruption was rampant, as was tax corruption. A constitutional court judge was caught red-handed accepting a bribe of $12 million. Yushchenko sacked her, but Yanukovych's side reinstated her.[38]

Yanukovych did not accept the dissolution of parliament, and in late May, his and the president's special forces entered into a televised fistfight outside the general prosecutor's office. Hardly ever had Ukraine been so close to civil violence, but once again Yushchenko and Yanukovych reached a compromise: Yanukovych accepted the holding of new parliamentary elections on September 30, 2007.

Free and fair democratic elections had become a routine, but the electorate was tired. Participation fell to 62 from 67 percent in 2006, still far higher than in neighboring Poland. As in 2006, five parties passed the 3 percent hurdle. The main winner was BYuT, which increased its votes from 22 percent in 2006 to 31 percent. The Regions expanded slightly—from 32 to 34 percent. Our Ukraine maintained its share of 14 percent, partly because of Yushchenko's recent resolute behavior and partly because popular Yuriy Lutsenko had joined Our Ukraine (table 8.2).

38. Pavel Korduban, "Can Ukraine's Constitutional Court Be Unbiased?" *Eurasian Daily Monitor* (Jamestown Foundation), April 17, 2007.

Table 8.2 Results of election to the Supreme Rada, September 30, 2007

Party	Votes (percent)	Seats
Left	10.0	27
Communist	5.4	27
Socialist	2.9	0
Center-Right	87.1	423
Party of Regions	34.4	423
Bloc of Yuliya Tymoshenko	30.7	156
Our Ukraine—People's Self-Defense	14.2	72
Lytvyn Bloc	4.0	20
Against all, or not valid	2.9	0
Total	100	450
Voter turnout (percent)	62.0	

Source: Central Election Commission of Ukraine, www.cvk.gov.ua (accessed on October 16, 2007).

In addition, the communists and the newly formed Lytvyn Bloc entered parliament. The latter was a centrist party sponsored by three big businessmen. The left continued to be marginalized, receiving only 10 percent of the votes and 6 percent of the seats. The socialists fell out of parliament because they were seen as traitors and blatantly corrupt. Party consolidation proceeded, as the share of votes wasted halved to 11 percent from 22 percent in 2006.

As in all democratic Central and Eastern European countries, corruption was the dominant election theme, and it was naturally blamed on the incumbent government. The eminent Bulgarian political scientist Ivan Krastev has observed that nearly all incumbent Central and Eastern European governments have lost elections. Accordingly, Tymoshenko won as the most effective critic of corruption. One effect of Ukraine's democracy was that a party could gain votes by going into opposition.

The political appeal of the three big parties had changed considerably. Their economic programs had converged, and by European standards, they all belonged to the democratic center-right. They wanted deregulation, more privatization, stable macroeconomic policy, lower taxes, accession to the WTO, and membership in the European Union. Such a broad consensus about economic policy is rare for any country. Gone were radical demands for higher social transfers and reprivatization. BYuT changed the most. In 2005 it had applied for membership to the Socialist International. Now, it joined the European People's Party, of which Our Ukraine already was a member. The Regions, however, only cooperated with Putin's United Russia party. The biggest policy difference remained in foreign policy, as only Our Ukraine insisted on an early membership action plan for NATO, while the Regions opposed closer cooperation with NATO, and BYuT took no clear stand.

The overall rather stable results hid huge voter streams, as people voted less than previously with region and more with class. Although the parties' regional concentration remained strong, all parties lost votes in their strongholds and gained votes in enemy land. As a result, all parties became more national, as an urban-rural class divide had been superimposed over the east-west division (Clem and Craumer 2008). Our Ukraine emerged as a rural party for its fight for private sales of agricultural land. The Regions, as the most credible advocate of low taxes, attracted the urban upper middle class. BYuT appealed to the populist lower middle class.

The big Ukrainian businessmen stood behind this convergence of economic policy. They poured a fortune to the tune of $500 million into these extraordinary elections, paying a record $10 million for a safe party list seat. The big business groups reportedly paid about $100 million each to their parties.[39] Akhmetov continued to support the Regions and extended his personal parliamentary group from 60 to 90 deputies, but Yanukovych enjoyed other business support as well. Amazingly, Privat Group and the Industrial Union of Donbas undertook a short castling between the 2006 and 2007 elections, as Privat switched its support from BYuT to Yushchenko, while the Industrial Union of Donbas went from Yushchenko to BYuT. Tymoshenko also benefited from support from Konstantin Zhevago of Ferrexpo, now the fifth wealthiest business group with a large iron ore mine in Poltava. One prominent businessman reportedly paid $30 million for 10 deputies, hoping to trade them for $70 million.[40]

To form a government this time, two of the three big parties had to conclude a coalition. That might have seemed easy given their similar policies, but since any two parties could form a coalition, the game had no natural conclusion. They all talked to one another but with profound distrust in this game of cheating and chicken. The big businessmen further complicated the game because of their proven habit of ditching politicians and their sharp mutual competition. They put the politicians in an impossible dilemma. The politicians had to betray either their business sponsors, who expected corrupt returns, or their voters, who abhorred corruption. The voters could nothing but be disappointed. The persistent war over the constitutional powers added to the complication.

This political system failed to deliver what the country needed: a government that worked and a parliament that legislated. Instead it generated dysfunctional corruption. Ukrainians were increasingly tired of politicians doing nothing for them.

---

39. Information from conversations with insiders in Kyiv before and after the elections.

40. Tymoshenko alluded to him in her televised speech: "Moreover, those people who paid $30 million for treason will no longer have those shadow millions" (Ukrainian Independent Information Agency, December 20, 2007).

The Second Tymoshenko Government: Stalemate

BYuT and Our Ukraine had a majority of only two seats, which quickly shrank to one. Even so, because of a firm preelection agreement, Yushchenko and Tymoshenko concluded a substantial coalition agreement after only two weeks. Tymoshenko would become prime minister. BYuT and Our Ukraine would each receive 12 cabinet posts. An orderly balance of power between the president and the prime minister was prescribed. Tymoshenko would control all economic posts and Our Ukraine foreign policy, security, and humanitarian affairs. The agreement also included a package of a dozen draft bills.[41]

The formation of the government was delayed, however, because of Our Ukraine's minimal party discipline. Some deputies insisted on a broader coalition including the Lytvyn Bloc or the Regions. Finally, on November 29 a new orange coalition was formed, and on December 18 the parliament confirmed Tymoshenko as prime minister with a bare minimum of 226 votes. She appointed her new government immediately. Big businessmen were absent from the new cabinet as a consequence of prior scandals.[42]

Tymoshenko and Yushchenko had drawn the opposite conclusions from her first cabinet. Tymoshenko emphasized that she had learned her lesson from 2005: She sought cooperation, stuck to a normal market economy, and did not raise reprivatization. Although food and energy prices rose sharply, she liberalized foreign trade and limited her efforts to control prices. She delegated within the cabinet. It helped that she had a trustworthy inner cabinet, consisting of Turchinov as her first deputy, Hryhoriy Nemyria as deputy prime minister for European integration, and heavyweight Minister of Finance Viktor Pynzenyk. She was also conciliatory toward the Our Ukraine ministers, among whom the most prominent were First Deputy Prime Minister Ivan Vasyunyk and Minister of Defense Yekhanurov. The young political star Yatseniuk became speaker of the parliament.

Yushchenko had drawn the opposite lesson. He had lost out to Prime Ministers Tymoshenko and Yanukovych because he had been too conciliatory. His apparent insight was to never be reasonable again. Together with his militant chief of staff Baloha, he tried to maximize presidential powers. He never gave Tymoshenko a chance to govern, and he achieved a complete government stalemate. From April, he vetoed nearly all legis-

41. Viktor Chyvokunya, "Tymoshenko and Yushchenko Share Power," *Ukrainskaya pravda*, October 16, 2006; Pavel Korduban, "Differences within Ukrainian Coalition Escalate," *Eurasian Daily Monitor* (Jamestown Foundation), October 31, 2007.

42. "Ukraine Has New Government," Interfax Ukraine, December 24, 2007.

lation and decisions emanating from Tymoshenko. According to the constitution, the regional governors were subordinate to the president. Baloha drew this oddity to its logical extreme, prohibiting them from seeing the prime minister.

Tymoshenko adopted an extensive government program in line with the coalition agreement. To begin with, the budget inherited from Yanukovych was tightened. She carried out the few steps remaining for Ukraine to enter the WTO and initiated negotiations on a free trade agreement with the European Union.

She focused on privatization, quickly composing a substantial program with 19 big state-owned companies slated for privatization in 2008. Sensibly, the new government offered majority stakes, appealing to strategic investors. In February the government extended the list to 406 companies to be sold in open auctions, the most transparent form of privatization. To render privatization popular, Tymoshenko wanted to spend the privatization revenues on compensation for savings that had been inflated away in the old Soviet Savings Bank by the hyperinflation in the early 1990s. As the moratorium on private sales of agricultural land ran out, two laws were drafted to legalize sales.

In April, however, Yushchenko prohibited all these privatizations in a series of decrees. Having always favored privatization, he complained that the privatizations reminded him "of a seasonal sale in a Kyiv department store." State assets had declined to 21 percent of all national assets, which he called a "critical volume of state assets." No privatization should be undertaken until the government had approved a national privatization program. The privatization of electricity companies threatened the country's national security.[43] Yushchenko spoke like an old-style socialist, even vetoing Tymoshenko's decree allowing private sales of land as contrary to the constitution.[44] When Tymoshenko attempted to sack socialist Semeniuk, as chair of the State Property Fund, Yushchenko blocked her decision.

In gas trade, Tymoshenko minimized the role of Ukrgaz-Energo, the domestic gas trade joint venture between RUE and Naftohaz Ukrainy. Next she persuaded Gazprom and Naftohaz to exclude RUE and trade gas without any intermediary from 2009. On October 2 Tymoshenko visited Prime Minister Putin in Moscow with suspect mutual friendliness, and they tentatively agreed on a three-year transition to European prices for Ukraine.

---

43. "Yushchenko sovetuet Timoshenko krasit' kryl'ya i menyat' bamper" ["Yushchenko Advises Tymoshenko to Paint the Wings And Change Bumper"], *Ukrainskaya pravda*, April 24, 2008.

44. "Yushchenko zablokiroval Timoshenko v zemel'nom voprose" ["Yushchenko Blocked Tymoshenko in the Land Question"], *Ukrainskaya pravda*, April 25, 2008.

Customs, which Tymoshenko had cleaned up in 2005, had again become a focal point of corruption, so she appointed a strong head, Valeriy Khoroshkovskiy, who repeated her prior success. Restoring VAT refunds for exporters was another priority, but she recorded no success there.

WTO Accession, May 2008

On February 6, 2008, after completing negotiations, the WTO General Council invited Ukraine to join the organization. Subsequently, the Ukrainian parliament ratified the accession, and on May 16, 2008, Ukraine became the 152nd member of the WTO, marking the greatest achievement of the four governments after the Orange Revolution.

Ukraine had applied for membership in November 1993, but it did little in the 1990s.[45] From 1998 to 2003, four small countries in the Commonwealth of Independent States (CIS) became members of the WTO: the Kyrgyz Republic, Georgia, Moldova, and Armenia. Ukraine and Russia were negotiating their accessions in parallel, carefully watching one another. Russia repeatedly asked Ukraine for coordination of their WTO accessions, but Ukraine had no interest in such a demand, which would only cause delays.

Ukraine needed the WTO more than Russia did because of its export structure. About two-thirds of Ukraine's exports consisted of so-called sensitive products, goods often exposed to protectionist measures such as antidumping, namely steel, agricultural goods, chemicals, and textiles. International studies suggested that Ukraine could gain one to two percentage points in economic growth from WTO accession in the next half decade (Copenhagen Economics et al. 2005a, 2005b, 2005c). These numbers are uncommonly high because Ukraine is an open economy with many institutional barriers that WTO rules could mitigate.

From the Yushchenko government in 2000, Ukraine started paying more attention to the WTO, adopting several major laws required for accession, such as the customs code of July 2002. Our Ukraine and BYuT made WTO accession their priority, and the first Tymoshenko government adopted a substantial package of WTO laws in the summer of 2005. At that time, the Regions still opposed liberalizing agriculture and steel, but in early 2006 it turned positive on the WTO. In exceptional unity, all three big parties worked for WTO membership. The WTO negotiations were carried out by a steady team of civil servants led by

45. Overall sources of this section are Williamson (1995); Åslund (2003a); and Burakovsky, Handrich, and Hoffmann (2003).

Deputy Economy Minister Valeriy Pyatnyskiy regardless of government changes.

In parallel, the European Union acknowledged Ukraine as a market economy in December 2005, and the United States did so in February 2006. These were unilateral assessments of market conditions in Ukraine, which were important for its defense against antidumping complaints. A nonmarket economy always loses antidumping cases, while a country classified as a market economy can defend itself.

A US peculiarity was the so-called Jackson-Vanik amendment to the US Trade Act of 1974. It required the Soviet Union to allow free emigration of Jews as a condition for most favored nation status in trade, which was subject to annual review. After the collapse of the Soviet Union, the Jackson-Vanik amendment was applied to all the CIS countries, although the Soviet Union was gone and emigration of Jews was free. In March 2006 the US Congress finally "graduated" Ukraine from the Jackson-Vanik amendment and granted it permanent normal trading relations after the United States had concluded its bilateral protocol with Ukraine for its entry into the WTO, one of 50 bilateral protocols Ukraine had to conclude.

Ukraine's accession was not particularly complicated. Its tariffs were low and caused little concern, though its institutions had to be improved. Agriculture posed the greatest problems as in most countries (Von Cramon-Taubadel and Zorya 2000). The burgeoning Ukrainian chicken industry called for protection through exceedingly strict inspections of imported poultry. The oversized and overprotected sugarbeet industry desired the maintenance of import quotas, but partner countries were satisfied with Ukraine raising bilateral import quotas. Ukrainian governments repeatedly imposed temporary prohibitions of grain exports, which had to go. Its agricultural subsidies were small, but the agrarian lobby wanted to keep the option of higher future subsidies open. Intellectual property rights were largely a new field for Ukraine requiring new legislation, and the government had to defeat piracy in audiovisual production. The last concern was to eliminate export tariffs, notably on scrap iron, an important input for the steel industry, which was settled in early 2008.

As a member of the WTO, Ukraine can demand bilateral negotiations on market access to Russia, which is still trying to become a member. This is Ukraine's best opportunity to solve its many trade problems with Russia.

NATO Controversies and Russia's War in Georgia

Until 2004, President Kuchma and his various governments had worked in consensus for closer relations with NATO. During the presidential campaign in 2004, however, Yanukovych made NATO the most contentious foreign policy issue.[46]

Immediately after independence, Ukraine had started developing its contacts with NATO, and it did so in parallel with Russia in the 1990s. In 1994 Ukraine was the first former Soviet state to join NATO's Partnership for Peace. In 1997, when Poland, the Czech Republic, and Hungary became members of NATO, it formed a NATO-Ukraine Commission.

NATO suffered only one serious backlash in Ukrainian public opinion, when it bombed Yugoslavia in 1999. Ukrainians reacted like Russians in solidarity with the orthodox Serbs. They had seen NATO as a defense alliance, but it attacked Serbia. Yet Ukraine contributed troops to all peacekeeping operations in the former Yugoslavia.

In May 2002 President Kuchma announced that Ukraine's ultimate goal was to join NATO, for the first time proceeding much further than Russia. However, since Ukraine did not fulfill NATO's democratic requirements, Kuchma's statement attracted little attention and no controversy. The Ukrainian public was largely indifferent to NATO. In early 2003 Ukraine contributed 1,700 troops to the US-led invasion of Iraq, as Kuchma attempted to improve his poor relations with the United States.

The presidential election campaign in the fall of 2004 changed the situation. Yanukovych campaigned against NATO, which the communists, the socialists, and the Russian government also opposed. Yushchenko had all along favored NATO, but he sensibly focused his campaign on more vote-winning issues. Thus Ukrainians heard many criticize NATO, while hardly anybody defended it, which turned the public attitude lastingly negative.

After the Orange Revolution, President Yushchenko ran foreign policy together with Foreign Minister Tarasiuk and Defense Minister Hrytsenko, who all aspired to Ukraine's full integration into the Euro-Atlantic community, including NATO. In April 2005 the NATO foreign ministers agreed to intensify their dialogue with Ukraine, which appeared to be a precursor to a membership action plan (MAP).

Yushchenko designed the August 2006 Declaration of National Unity as a step toward a MAP for Ukraine to be given by NATO at its summit in Riga in November 2006. However, as newly appointed prime minister, Yanukovych went to the North Atlantic Council in Brussels in September 2006, stating that he favored close cooperation with NATO but not a MAP.

In January 2008 Yushchenko started anew, sending a letter to NATO Secretary General Jaap de Hoop Scheffer, asking for a MAP to be granted to Ukraine at the NATO summit in Bucharest in April 2008. He persuaded newly appointed Prime Minister Tymoshenko and Speaker Yatseniuk to sign it in line with the coalition agreement. This request unleashed vicious

46. This section draws on Pifer (2004, 2008).

tirades from Russia, as Ukraine's relationship with NATO had become a focus of Russian foreign policy.

US President George W. Bush supported Ukraine's MAP, and so did the new eastern NATO members, but most old European members opposed it because of limited domestic Ukrainian support for NATO and staunch Russian opposition. The summit in Bucharest did not offer a MAP to Ukraine, but its communiqué stated boldly: "NATO welcomes Ukraine's and Georgia's Euro-Atlantic aspirations for membership in NATO. We agreed today that these countries will become members of NATO. . . . MAP is the next step for Ukraine and Georgia on their direct way to membership. Today we make clear that we support these countries' applications for MAP."[47]

President Putin also attended this summit, where he, on April 4, intimidated Ukraine sharply and at length, effectively threatening to end its existence:

- "As for Ukraine, one third of the population are ethnic Russians. According to official census statistics, there are 17 million ethnic Russians there, out of a population of 45 million. . . . Southern Ukraine is entirely populated with ethnic Russians."
- "Ukraine, in its current form, came to be in Soviet-era days. . . . From Russia the country obtained vast territories in what is now eastern and southern Ukraine."
- "Crimea was simply given to Ukraine by a CPSU Politburo's decision, which was not even supported with appropriate government procedures that are normally applicable to territory transfers."
- "If the NATO issue is added there, along with other problems, this may bring Ukraine to the verge of existence as a sovereign state."[48]

Thus Putin disqualified Ukraine's claim to sovereign statehood and territorial integrity, in a sharp reversal of Boris Yeltsin's policy and in contradiction with the 1997 Russian-Ukrainian Treaty on Friendship, Cooperation and Partnership. He suggested that its composition was artificial, its borders arbitrary, and the transfer of Crimea to Ukraine illegal. More nationalist Russian politicians, notably Moscow Mayor Yury Luzhkov, hammered away on their theme that Sevastopol and Crimea belonged to Russia. In June 2008 Luzhkov stated: "Sevastopol was never

47. Bucharest Summit Declaration, issued by the Heads of State and Government participating in the meeting of the North Atlantic Council, Bucharest, April 3, 2008, available at www.nato.int.

48. "What Precisely Vladimir Putin Said at Bucharest," *Zerkalo nedeli*, April 19, 2008.

given to Ukraine. I have studied all basic documents carefully, and I can make such a declaration."[49]

From April, Russian aggression against Georgia intensified. In early August 2008 military action escalated in the secessionist Georgian territory of South Ossetia. On August 7 Georgian troops went into South Ossetia but were immediately rebuffed by well-prepared and overwhelming Russian troops. Russia secured South Ossetia and Abkhazia, both Russia-friendly secessionist Georgian territories. Russian troops also occupied some other parts of Georgia. Several Russian planes were shot down with missiles bought from Ukraine, while the United States refused to deliver arms to Georgia for defense against Russia. Soon afterward, Russia recognized Abkhazia and South Ossetia as independent states, justifying their action with the Western recognition of Kosovo and the large number of Russian citizens there, but they resulted from Russian distribution of passports there.

These Russian acts scared even its closest allies, Belarus and Kazakhstan. Yushchenko took an immediate and strong stand for Georgia and his friend Saakashvili. Yanukovych, by contrast, praised Russia's recognition of Abkhazia and South Ossetia, while Tymoshenko said as little as possible. Although she eventually defended Georgia's territorial integrity in the same terms as the European Union, Yushchenko accused her of high treason and of being a Russian agent, opening a criminal case against her.

Suddenly Ukraine faced a new threat from Russia. Although Russia's attack on Georgia had been successful, it revealed Russia's military weakness: Its military power was limited to remnants of the now obsolete Soviet military. Russia could not plausibly attack Ukraine with conventional forces. Instead, Russia's threat to Ukraine lay in destabilization, against which NATO was no obvious defense. Moreover, the United States had already provided substantial security guarantees to Ukraine in connection with its denuclearization. In the trilateral statement by the presidents of the United States, Russia, and Ukraine in Moscow on January 14, 1994, "Presidents Clinton and Yeltsin informed President Kravchuk that the United States and Russia are prepared to provide security assurances to Ukraine."[50]

Renewed Financial Crisis and IMF Agreement

In 2008 Ukraine was hit by renewed financial crisis. The Ukrainian economy was overheating after eight years of unprecedented boom, and as

49. "Luzhkov izuchil vopros Sevastopolya i reshil, chto ego ne peredali" ["Luzhkov Studied the Sevastopol Question and Decided That They Had Not Transferred It"], *Ukrainskaya pravda*, June 24, 2008.

50. US Department of State Dispatch, Trilateral Statement by the Presidents of the United States, Russia, and Ukraine in Moscow, January 14, 1994.

elsewhere in the region, inflation became the biggest economic concern in early 2008. In May 2008 inflation peaked at 31 percent over May 2007 (figure 8.1, Dragon Capital 2008). In spite of persistent government crisis, Ukraine maintained a tight budget policy with a budget deficit of around 1 percent of GDP.

Rising inflation, mainly food and energy prices, was a global phenomenon, but Ukraine's inflation was the third highest in the world. In a region dominated by the euro, Ukraine kept its exchange rate pegged to the US dollar. Given that the dollar had fallen by 15 percent in relation to the euro in a year, Ukraine imported substantial inflation through its peg. The high inflation allowed commercial banks to charge over 50 percent a year in hryvnia for consumer loans, which they could finance at about 6 percent a year in Europe. The National Bank of Ukraine (NBU) bought hard currency to maintain the exchange rate, boosting the money supply and inflation. With a refinance rate of only 16 percent a year, Ukraine had a negative real interest rate of 15 percent a year. Large consumer expenditures went to imports, which rose sharply. As a consequence, trade and current account deficits expanded fast, as did private foreign debt.[51]

Commercial bankers were reaping brisk speculative profits, and few understood how dangerous this policy was, but this Ponzi scheme could not continue. Ukraine would become uncompetitive and overindebted. An untenable financial disequilibrium was mounting which would naturally erupt in a financial crisis. The key problem was the exchange rate policy, for which the national bank was responsible. The dollar peg needed to give way to a floating exchange rate, and the NBU needed to focus on keeping inflation low through inflation targeting (Truman 2003). Yet, any change of the exchange rate was unpopular, as savings in either dollars or hryvnia would be devalued. Fortunately, the NBU loosened its peg in late April, which moderated the inflow of speculative money, and inflation moderated month by month.

Reminiscent of the Asian and Russian crises in 1997–98, in late September the international financial crisis that had originated in the United States hit Ukraine, which was effectively frozen out from international finance. Nobody wanted to refinance any credit to Ukraine, so when one fell due, the debtor was bankrupted. The domestic banking system froze, and with it large construction projects working on credit. The stock market fell precipitously, and by late October, it had fallen as much as 82 percent from the beginning of the year.[52]

Ukraine was one of the first countries to be hit, although its financial indicators were reasonable. The state budget was close to balance, and

51. Åslund (2008). The statistics are from Dragon Capital, *The Dragon Daily*, various dates.

52. Dragon Capital, *The Dragon Daily*, various dates.

Figure 8.1 Ukraine's inflation rate (consumer price index), 2000–2007

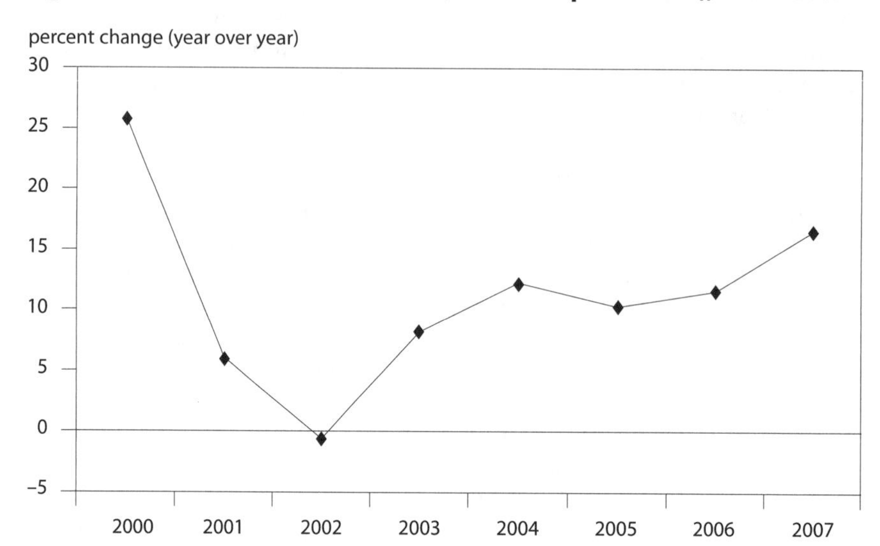

Source: European Bank for Reconstruction and Development online database, www.ebrd.com (accessed on July 1, 2008).

public debt was tiny, at 10 percent of GDP. The international currency reserves peaked at a respectable $38 billion in August 2008. About 40 percent of the banking system was owned by respectable foreign banks, facilitating access to international finance. The most worrisome indicator was the current account deficit, but it had been moderate at 4.2 percent of GDP in 2007, and it was more than financed by foreign direct investment. Yet it rose to 7.2 percent of GDP in 2008 because of the excessive short-term capital inflows and falling export prices for steel.

In 2007 steel accounted for nearly half of Ukraine's exports, but in the fall of 2008 prices and demand for steel plummeted. Global steel prices peaked in July but had fallen by half in October. Ukraine's steel producers responded by cutting production of crude steel output by 49 percent in October 2008 over October 2007.[53] Ukraine had too many steel producers, and most were not sufficiently efficient. Neglect during the good years became harmful. The whole steel industry fell in sudden, rampant crisis and called for consolidation.

Yet Ukraine's messy politics singled out the country as one of the first victims of the international financial crisis. International investors did not believe its policymakers were able to undertake the necessary belt-tightening to handle the deteriorating balance of payments.

53. Ibid.

The Ukrainian government sensibly called on the IMF again and asked for a large emergency credit line to open up international finance again, unfreeze the domestic credit market, and salvage the exchange rate from a sharp dip. On October 26 Ukraine concluded a two-year IMF Stand-By Arrangement with financing of no less than $16.5 billion. The conditions were many and arduous, anticipating a fall in GDP of 3 percent in 2009 and a slump in imports of 20 percent, but the orange parties voted it through in parliament on October 31. Yet Ukraine was set for a severe recession with the devastation of its steel and construction sectors.

Yushchenko Insists on New Elections

In the midst of this severe crisis, Yushchenko insisted once again on new elections. From April 2008 Yushchenko and Baloha devoted all their efforts to three related endeavors: to break up the coalition between Our Ukraine and BYuT, oust the Tymoshenko government, and provoke early parliamentary elections. In the summer of 2008, opinion polls indicated that Yushchenko enjoyed the support of only 5 percent of the population, Yanukovych 20 percent, and Tymoshenko 25 percent in a presidential election, and their parties had a similar standing.

It made no apparent sense for Yushchenko to provoke early parliamentary elections. He, his divided party, and his nation would be devastated. New elections would not solve any problem but leave Ukrainian politics in shambles until the presidential elections scheduled for January 2010. But Yushchenko seemed obsessed with Tymoshenko, speaking and acting as if his only endeavor was to destroy her. Strangely, Yushchenko apparently hoped to be reelected despite blocking all legislation and enjoying minimal popularity.

In early September Tymoshenko turned Yushchenko's sword against him. Tired of political stalemate, she got together with Yanukovych, and they passed two important laws with massive majorities. The first act was a renewed Law on the Cabinet of Ministers, which deprived Yushchenko of most of his powers, transforming Ukraine into a parliamentary state. The temporary Tymoshenko-Yanukovych alliance also adopted the long-desired Law on Joint Stock Companies, which Yushchenko had advocated for years to constrain illicit corporate raiding, but Our Ukraine voted against this keystone law, claiming that it was not perfect, while the communists voted for it. Eventually, Yushchenko signed it into law.

An intensified political circus with Yushchenko and Tymoshenko as the main actors ensued. Yushchenko put maximum pressure on the Our Ukraine faction in parliament, which finally voted to break the orange coalition with a minimal majority on September 2 and officially left the coalition.[54] On October 7 and 9 Yushchenko issued decrees dissolving the parliament, calling for extraordinary parliamentary elections.[55] Tymoshenko complained to a court, which dismissed the president's decision. Yushchenko responded by sacking the judge, but the council of judges reinstated the judge, leaving the dissolution of parliament in legal limbo.[56] Human Rights Watch protested against both Yushchenko and Tymoshenko interfering in the judiciary.[57] For days, Yushchenko blocked the vital IMF anticrisis legislation, demanding that the parliament first allocate financing for new elections.

Ukraine is dominated by three political personalities, Tymoshenko, Yanukovych, and Yushchenko. The general expectation is that they will be the dominant candidates again in the presidential elections scheduled for January 2010. Yushchenko seems to have burned the last of his capital of trust in 2008. Tymoshenko is likely to suffer from the financial crash, as she was prime minister when it took place, though she might save her skin by the decisive anti-crisis measures. Yanukovych is lucky to have been out of power at this time of hardship.

Yushchenko's behavior in 2008 was perplexing. Although he formed a coalition with Tymoshenko, he never gave her government a chance to work. His whole presidency has been marked by legislative stalemate. The only legislation worth mentioning during his tenure was the WTO accession and annual budgets. His own popularity was at an all-time low, and his old party, Our Ukraine, risked being wiped out in the next elections. Ukraine faced both an evident security threat from Russia and an acute menace of financial collapse primarily because of domestic political instability, but Yushchenko insisted on new elections.

Approaching the end of the Yushchenko presidency, disappointment prevails. His two achievements have been to maintain democracy and to bring Ukraine closer to the European Union. Yet his term has restored the gridlock of the Kravchuk presidency, and the danger is evident that this inability of government discredits democracy in Ukraine.

---

54. "Our Ukraine Voted to Leave Coalition," *Ukrayinska Pravda*, September 2, 2008, available at www.pravda.com.ua (accessed on October 21, 2008).

55. "Votes of Verkhovna Rada and Tymoshenko Did Not Prolong Parliament's Life," *Ukrayinska Pravda*, October 21, 2008, available at www.pravda.com.ua (accessed on October 21, 2008).

56. US Agency for International Development (USAID) Parliamentary Development Project, "Council of Judges reinstates head of court dismissed by President," October 20, 2008, available at www.iupdp.org (accessed on October 21, 2008).

57. "BYuT Will Defend Court that Has Revoked Election," *Ukrayinska Pravda*, October 14, 2008, available at www.pravda.com.ua (accessed on October 21, 2008).

Limited Social Achievements

So far I have not mentioned social reforms in this book because almost none have been accomplished.[58] The main exceptions were trimming Nomenklatura benefits and the adoption of a new labor code and a law on pension reform, but that was never implemented. The Ministries of Health Care and Education have been consistently inert. They have been manned by Soviet-era bureaucrats and have resisted any structural reforms, just calling for more resources to be wasted on the old overcentralized Soviet systems.

Kuchma (2003, 179) recognized this failure:

> Our first steps toward market economy were based on a formula: reforms come first, social issues later. This formula resulted in reforms at the expense of social issues. . . . Income inequality was as large as in Western Europe in the last third of 19th century, in conditions preceding a social revolution.

The most devastating social statistic in Ukraine is male life expectancy (figure 8.2). It increased for a couple of years after Gorbachev's ferocious antialcohol campaign that started in 1985, reaching a high of 66 years in 1989, which was not very impressive. With post-Soviet transition, male life expectancy fell to 62 years, the level of a rather poor developing country. Worse, male life expectancy has not recovered significantly but stayed at about 62.5 years.

Ukraine shares this problem with Russia, where the situation is even worse. For years, Russia's life expectancy for men has been about 59 years. The overwhelming explanation is that East Slavic and Baltic men often drink themselves to death. Drinking was always heavy, and in the transition the government could no longer collect the previously exorbitant excise taxes on alcohol (Brainerd 1998). More profoundly, these men were company men who were lost in transition and did not know how to adjust to changed circumstances. While women adapted and lived long, men suffered so badly from the stress that they drank too much and died from violence or heart attack, as Judith Shapiro (1995) so perceptively noticed in the early transition in Russia and as has been well documented in later research (Shkolnikov, Andreev, and Maleva 2000). No Ukrainian government has undertaken a badly needed antidrinking campaign.

A better measurement of the efficacy of the health care system than life expectancy is infant mortality. It increased from 13 infants per 1,000 births in 1989 to 15 in 1993 during the collapse of communism. Since 1993, infant mortality has fallen by one-third to 9.5 in 2007 (figure 8.3). Although this is a significant improvement, it is not impressive. In Poland and the Czech Republic, infant mortality has fallen by two-thirds since the

58. Major sources of this section are Góralska (2000) and Malysh (2000).

Figure 8.2 Male life expectancy at birth, 1989–2006

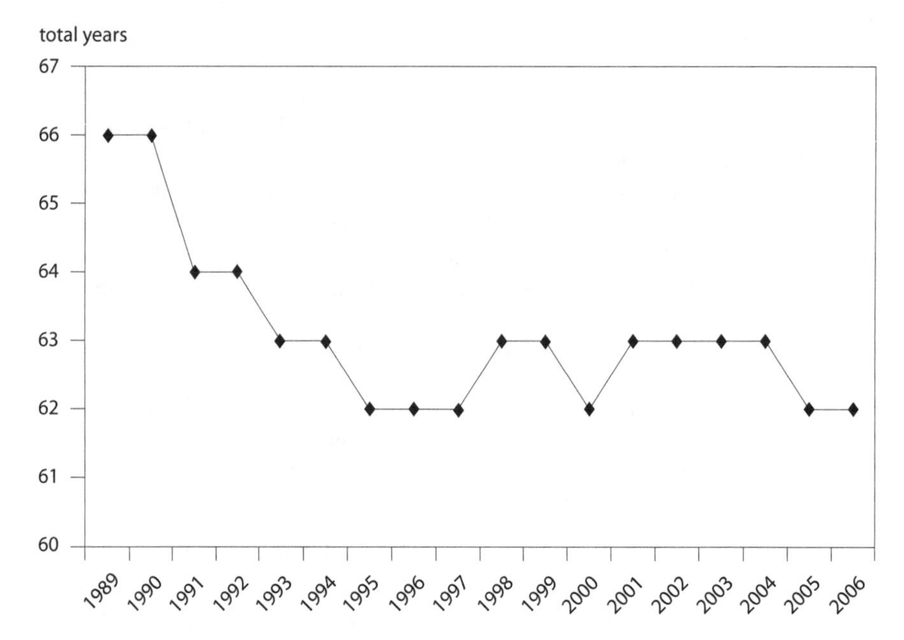

Source: World Bank, *World Development Indicators* database, http://devdata.worldbank.org/dataonline (accessed on July 1, 2008).

Figure 8.3 Infant mortality, 1989–2007

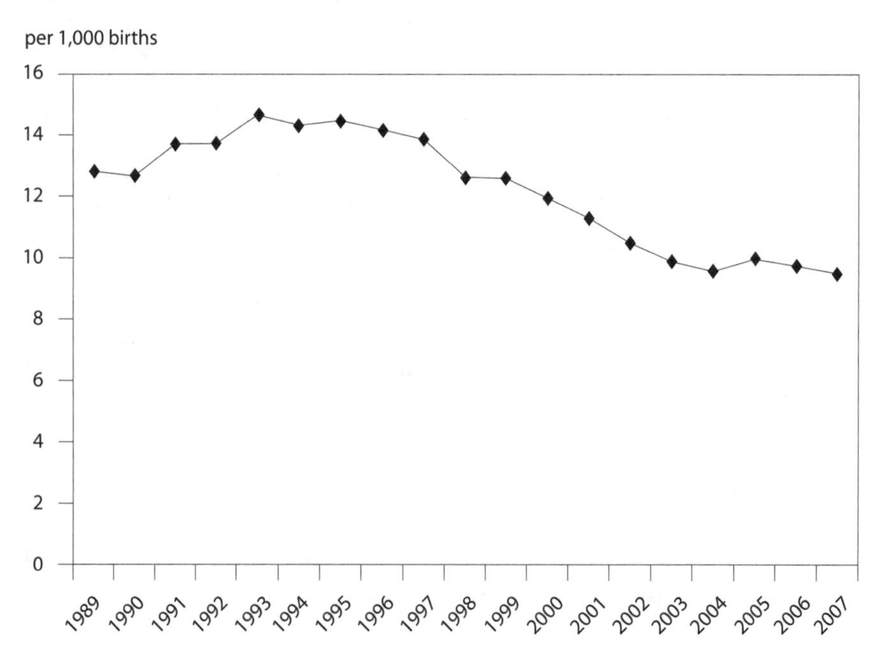

Source: US Census Bureau international database, www.census.gov/ipc (accessed on July 30, 2008).

Figure 8.4 Ukraine's population, 1990–2008

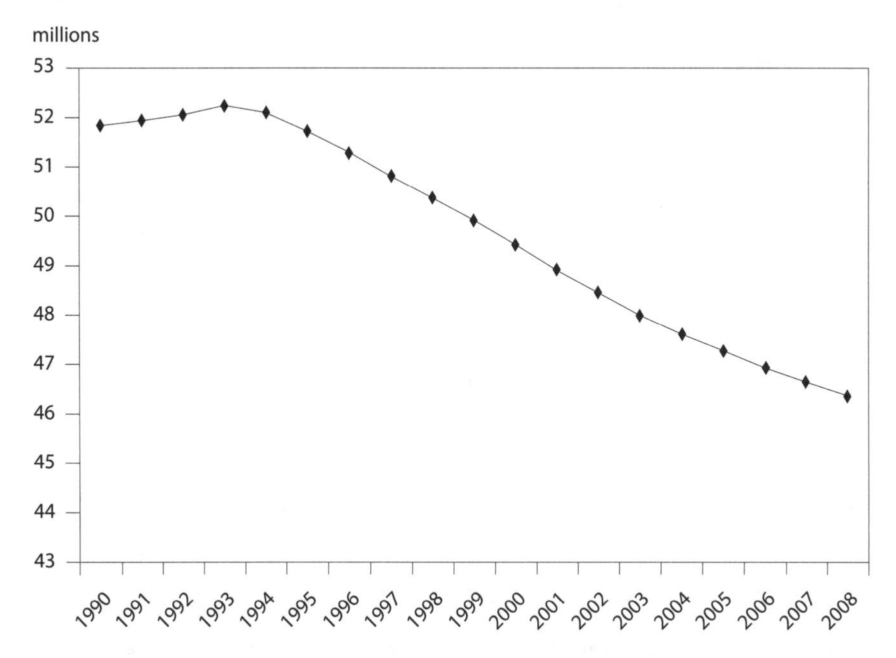

Sources: Statistics Committee of Ukraine, www.ukrstat.gov.ua (accessed on November 4, 2008).

end of communism. The main reason for this decline is probably greater access to drugs rather than any improvement within the public health care system.

Another shocking statistic is the decline in Ukraine's population. Officially, it has shrunk from 52 million in 1992 to 46 million in 2008 (figure 8.4). But even this figure is embellished because an additional 5 million to 7 million Ukrainians are abroad, largely working illegally in Europe, typically in construction, agriculture, and households. The population actually living in Ukraine has thus shrunk from 52 million to about 40 million to 42 million, or by some 20 percent in 15 years, which is a great blow to the nation, even though the population has plummeted even more in Georgia, Armenia, and Moldova.

The most positive social statistic is the investment Ukrainian youth make in their own and the country's human capital. By the narrow UNICEF definition, the share of Ukrainian youth pursuing higher education has increased two and a half times from 19 percent in 1993 to 48 percent in 2005 (figure 8.5). According to UNESCO (2008), which uses a broader definition, no less than 73 percent of young Ukrainians went on to tertiary studies in 2006. These numbers show the ambitions of young Ukrainians, and most of them pay substantial official or unofficial tuition fees, but much of the education on offer is unfortunately of poor quality.

Figure 8.5 Share of college-age youth pursuing higher education, 1989–2005

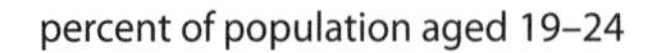

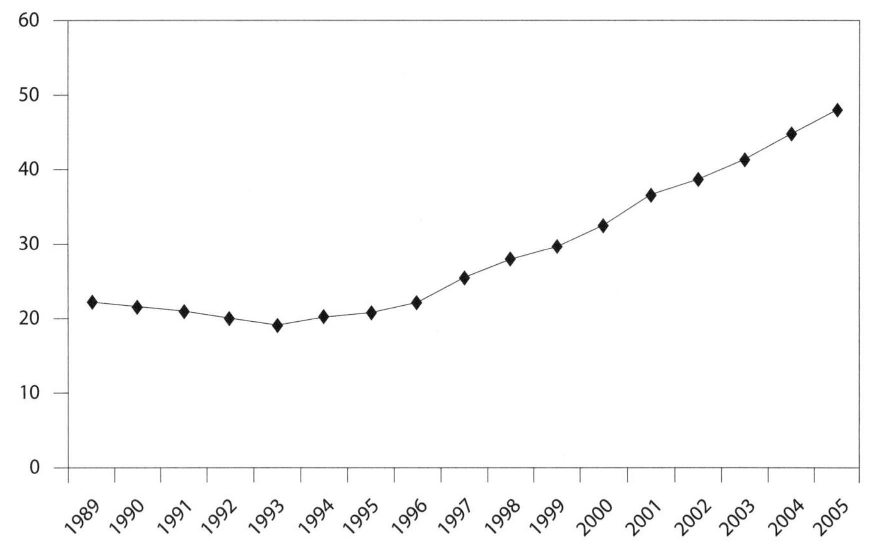

Source: UNICEF, TransMONEE Database, 2007, www.unicef-irc.org/databases/transmonee (accessed on August 16, 2007).

One of the most important reform efforts in education was the introduction in 2008 of national tests for all high school graduates so as to reduce the notorious corruption in the admission process in higher education institutions.

Ukraine needs social reforms in health care and education to make them more efficient and raise their quality. The pension system also needs to be reformed. Public social expenditures, however, have persistently been quite high and larger than characteristic for a country at Ukraine's level of economic development (Tanzi and Tsibouris 2000). Lack of efficiency, not resources, is Ukraine's constraint.

9

Lessons from Ukraine's Transformation

We know we are a European nation and that we are going to join the European Union.
—Deputy Prime Minister Hryhoriy Nemyria[1]

Ukraine has gone through 17 turbulent years of independence. During this time, it has recorded many achievements. The greatest triumph is that hardly any Ukrainian questions the sovereignty of the state. Another feat is that Ukraine has become a democracy, and a third accomplishment is that the country has a market economy with predominant private ownership.

At the same time, many tasks remain incomplete. The European Union has not yet recognized Ukraine's long-expressed desire to become a member. The most blatant shortcoming is the malfunctioning constitutional order, which gives the president the power to block government decisions and legislation but no incentive to be constructive. A transition to a parliamentary order would be most helpful. The electoral system for parliament, however, has undergone a successful evolution.

Among postcommunist countries, Ukraine is an exception because it delayed reforms for three years and even so built a market economy and democracy. The delayed reforms greatly aggravated the social cost of reforms. Their eventual success was probably brought about by the Ukrainians' strong sense of nationalism. The International Monetary Fund (IMF) played an important and useful role in deregulation and financial stabilization.

1. Speech at the Yalta European Strategy conference, July 12, 2008.

In few countries are oligarchs as strong as in Ukraine, and they are a double-edged sword. They take advantage of their privileged access to state services, but they also offer a kernel of competition in politics as well as business, which should be encouraged. Ukraine's democracy has much going for it, but the critical test is whether it can deliver sufficient results to the population.

With its European location and open market economy, Ukraine is bound to catch up with the developed West with sensible economic policies. In foreign policy, Ukraine has little choice but to turn to the West because Russia does not offer anything. An important Ukrainian achievement is its membership of the World Trade Organization (WTO). The next step is an Association Agreement with the European Union. An outstanding controversial issue is Ukraine's relationship with the North Atlantic Treaty Organization (NATO).

Constitutional Evolution and Shortcomings

Ukrainian politics came alive with the election of the republican parliament in March 1990, and it has remained an exciting political laboratory. The country's gradual political and economic evolution is peculiar. Most Central and Eastern European postcommunist countries were radical reformers and quickly became democracies, while most countries in the Commonwealth of Independent States (CIS) moved slowly on reform and fell into an authoritarian trap (Åslund 2007a, Havrylyshyn 2006). Today Ukraine is the only country within the CIS that the authoritative Freedom House (2008) classifies as "free" or democratic.

In its political evolution, Ukraine is more reminiscent of nonrevolutionary democracies, such as England and Sweden, than other postcommunist countries that had a quick democratic breakthrough or became authoritarian. True, it experienced the Orange Revolution, but most political scientists classify it as a democratic breakthrough rather than a revolution (McFaul 2006a). Three fundamental constitutional issues have been the choice between presidential and parliamentary rule, the electoral system for parliament, and central-regional relations. A fourth, judicial reform, has barely entered the political agenda.

Because of problems in reaching a substantive compromise, the constitution of June 1996 left many things to be determined by laws, most of which have not been adopted. Ukraine has ended up with a dysfunctional hybrid between a presidential and parliamentary system. Leonid Kuchma tried to resolve the problem by becoming moderately authoritarian. The constitutional compromise of December 2004 transferred substantial power from the president to the government and parliament, but it barely hangs together. The Rada has adopted some laws of constitutional significance, notably the Law on the Cabinet of Ministers twice, but since it is only a law and not a part of the constitution, it has been contested and not stuck as a constitutional rule. Therefore, most constitutional issues remain open and need to be settled.

Presidential or Parliamentary Rule

Ukraine's crucial problem is that it has been caught in the gray zone between a presidential and parliamentary system. The president has substantial power and could oust the prime minister, but he can do little constructive beyond foreign policy and appointments, since detailed executive power rests with the cabinet of ministers. As a consequence, all the three presidents of independent Ukraine have suffered from an interminable temptation to dismiss their prime minister, who has regularly been sacked once a year regardless of performance.

Ukraine's dilemma has two logical solutions. Either the president obtains more power—though all postcommunist presidential systems but Georgia have become authoritarian—or a parliamentary system is adopted. All postcommunist countries with such a system are democracies. Therefore, Ukraine needs a parliamentary system.

The persistent strife over whether Ukraine should have a presidential or parliamentary system has been aggravated by the absence of the clear division of powers that Montesquieu [1748] recommended. Admittedly, Article 6 of the constitution provides for such a separation of state power among the legislative, executive, and judicial powers, but the organization of state power has not allowed that commitment to be substantiated (Futey 1997). The parliament has engaged in executive decision making, especially on budget allocation and privatization, while President Kuchma insisted on using his quasi-legislative powers to issue presidential decrees on major economic issues. Intermittently, the prime minister assumed substantial power, playing parliament and president against one another.

In comparison with other postcommunist countries, Ukraine has promulgated a minimum of legislation. A comparative World Bank study of 2005 singled out Ukraine and Georgia as reformist transition countries displaying a disconcerting lacuna of legislation (Anderson, Bernstein, and Gray 2005, 24). The president, and sometimes the prime minister, has complained about the parliament legislating too little, but the parliament has responded that the president aspired to authoritarian power without sufficient checks and balances. Both are right.

The stalemate developed into a caricature in 2008, when Prime Minister Tymoshenko could make no decision without President Viktor Yushchenko vetoing it. The parliamentary minority has also continued a long-held tradition of blocking work in parliament by walking out to eliminate a quorum or by physically occupying parliament. In the otherwise peaceful Ukrainian society, rowdy parliamentarians disregard elementary order.

Law does not apply to them because parliamentary immunity goes too far, and sabotage has worked.

Paul D'Anieri (2006, 55) has offered a plausible explanation for the dearth of legislation. The parliamentary majority had so little power over the executive that it had little incentive to form or maintain a majority and thus to legislate. By this reasoning, "the very existence of a strong presidency reduces the chances of maintaining a parliamentary majority." People interested in legislation did not try to enter parliament. Instead, businessmen intent on solving their personal business concerns paid big money for a seat. D'Anieri (2006, 56) concludes: "Ukraine's strong presidency is inherently problematic for the construction of liberal democracy."

A substantial political science literature has analyzed the comparative advantages of presidential and parliamentary systems, and the dominant view is that parliamentary systems are preferable from a democratic point of view (Linz 1990), as reflected in the postcommunist world. Moreover, in Central and Eastern Europe mixed presidential-parliamentary systems have evolved in a parliamentary direction with democracy. In the CIS, the most democratic countries—Ukraine, Kyrgyzstan, Moldova, and Armenia—have recently been moving in a parliamentary direction, while the authoritarian countries have reinforced presidential rule. The correlation between democracy and parliamentary system is strong (Åslund 2007a, Freedom House 2008).

Analytically, it is easy to understand why parliamentary systems breed stronger democracies in the postcommunist world. Parliamentary systems offer more transparency and accountability than a presidential system does. A parliament can supervise a government relatively closely, while presidents and their administrations tend to be nontransparent and unaccountable. In the former Soviet countries in particular, presidential administrations recreate the central committee of the communist party, and the gubernatorial administrations the regional party committees, with their "telephone law" of secretive, arbitrary, lawless, and unaccountable intervention. Characteristically, the Ukrainian presidential administration is housed in the old central committee building. Under these conditions, parliamentary rule is preferable.

An additional explanation is that the Central and Eastern European countries are members of the European Union. Although the European Union does not require parliamentary rule, peer pressure makes candidates conform to most political institutions of the older EU members.

Until his last year in power, President Kuchma called for more presidential power to carry out economic reform. Russian Presidents Boris Yeltsin and Vladimir Putin and President Nursultan Nazarbayev in Kazakhstan pursued the same argument. The postcommunist record, however, is the opposite: The stronger the parliamentary powers (and democracy), the more far-reaching and comprehensive the market economic reforms (Bunce 1999, Åslund 2007a).

In reality, however, presidential decrees have turned out to be far less effective than laws promulgated through parliament. Suddenly written and adopted presidential decrees lack both credibility and following, while laws that are scrutinized and amended in parliamentary committees are usually of superior quality and generate an influential support group. Thus, laws are preferable to presidential decrees for substantial reforms (Protsyk 2004; Remington, Smith, and Haspel 1998).

Kuchma's presidency had two reform periods, fall of 1994 and 2000. Pavlo Lazarenko easily reversed many of the 1994 reforms, most of which were carried out through decrees and could be easily changed, while none of the 2000 reforms was reversed, as they were properly legislated by parliament.

A strong state is legal, transparent, and accountable. Naturally, a vital complement is a far-reaching law on public information, which offers maximum transparency. Characteristically, the most far-reaching laws on public information exist in Scandinavian countries, which are parliamentary stalwarts.

Electoral System for Parliament

The evolution of the electoral system has been the most productive. In 1990 Ukraine started off with a one-chamber parliament elected entirely through majority vote in single-mandate constituencies, without parties but with repetitive elections because of high turnout requirements. This cumbersome system did not reveal the population's political preferences and multiple reruns were demoralizing, leading to weak party factions. On the positive side, Ukraine has stuck to a one-chamber parliament, which has facilitated the maintenance of democracy.

The 1994 elections brought no real change. Political parties were allowed but suffered from discrimination. Repeat elections were even worse than in 1990 because of higher voter turnout requirements, and the parliament was never completely filled. But these tedious reruns prompted electoral reform.

The 1998 parliamentary elections introduced two significant improvements. First, the turnout requirement was relinquished, ending the annoying repeat elections and allowing the parliament to be filled on election night. Second, the elections became semiproportional, with half the seats being elected through party lists, while the other half were still filled through majority vote in single-mandate constituencies. In the proportional elections, a threshold of 4 percent was introduced. This system rendered the party factions more cohesive, but at 14 they were still too many, because the internal parliamentary rules promoted splits in many party factions to achieve more committee representation and resources from the parliament.

In 2002 the same electoral rules applied as in 1998, and the results were overtly similar with 13 party factions, but these elections discredited the single-mandate constituencies, because the distribution of seats varied greatly from the proportional vote, exposing the outcome as grotesquely unjust. The opposition won no less than 70 percent of the votes in the proportional elections, but the incumbent government maintained power by buying or bullying "independent" deputies.

The 2006 elections introduced purely proportional elections, which profoundly changed the party system. At long last, the number of parties represented in parliament declined to five, with three big center-right parties and two small left-wing parties. The threshold for representation had been reduced to 3 percent. The Ukrainian parliament seemed to have found its structure. The extraordinary elections in 2007 produced a very similar result, with five parties being represented in parliament.

Thus, by 2006, Ukraine seemed to have found a suitable form of parliamentary representation. The electoral system had moved from individual to party-based, from a majority election in single-mandate constituencies to proportional party list elections with a threshold of 3 percent. The party system had consolidated into three major parties and two small parties. The only remaining discussion about the electoral system is the means to impose party discipline and whether the threshold for representation should be raised.

Unfortunately, much of the political activity aims at breaking up other parties rather than finding compromises with them. A solution, which Yuliya Tymoshenko has championed, is a so-called imperative mandate, making a party rather than the individual deputy owner of a seat in parliament. If a deputy abandons a party, he or she would have to give up the seat to the next person on the party list.

A major concern is political financing. The two recent parliamentary elections have cost about half a billion dollars each in private campaign financing, approximately as much as an election to the US House of Representatives, but the United States is nearly 100 times richer than Ukraine. This money is given by big Ukrainian businessmen who want to defend their assets and promote their commercial interests. Some businessmen have made politics their business. In the 2007 elections, some businessmen reportedly paid up to $10 million for safe seats on party lists compared with $5 million in the 2006 elections.

The best means of avoiding the purchasing of seats on party lists would be to introduce personal choice of any person within a party list, abandoning fixed party lists. The German and Finnish systems of proportional elections with personal choice have found such a solution. To return to single-mandate constituencies is no cure because the 2002 elections showed that businessmen preferred to buy such seats as they were cheaper than party list seats. Transparency in political funding would be desirable but appears utopian.

Finally, much less should be up for sale in parliament. If a parliament attracts this kind of financing, it should have no say in privatization, which needs to be completed, and less of a say in the distribution of public funding, which should be standardized, simplified, and made more transparent. Parliamentary and budget rules should minimize horse-trading in parliament. The corruption in parliament is a strong argument for a very small public sector in ownership and redistribution in Ukraine.

Central-Regional Relations

Ukraine maintains the communist overcentralization of state administration, and a rational division of power between the central state and regional and local governments is still to be found. The number of regional governments, 27, seems about right. The central government has feared losing control over the regional executives, but the outcome has been excessive centralization, leaving regional governments disfranchised and dysfunctional. At the same time, disputes have prevailed between appointed regional executives and elected regional assemblies, resulting in poor regional governance. Substantial state powers need to be decentralized to regions and municipalities. Ukraine must not try to reestablish the old communist or Putin's "strong vertical," which has caused such damage to Russia through policy paralysis and aggravated corruption.

Ukraine has inherited extreme financial centralization from the Soviet Union. As in the old Soviet system, virtually all taxes go to the central treasury, and the Ministry of Finance determines the expenditures of regional authorities, but formal power and actual control do not coincide. The situation is untenable. A first attempt at solution came through the 1996 constitution, which centralized power to the president, who received the right to appoint the regional governors. In parallel, the central government centralized financial flows.

However, the extreme financial and political centralization paralyzed the whole Ukrainian state because regional authorities had few legal rights to do anything on their own. Only a few percent of their financial resources originated in their own taxes. The central government's allocations were often haphazard because of poor budgeting and arbitrary sequestration. Barter and offsets evolved as a means for regional governments to divert tax revenues from the central state to the regions. Regional and local taxes started proliferating.

Each regional government invented taxes to cover its own needs. These taxes were usually licensing fees or penalties, extracted through arduous inspections, often designed for individual, profitable enterprises (Kravchuk 1999). As a consequence, profit-making enterprises without political protection were overgrazed, often fatally. In 1997 I met a devastated director of the Kyiv brewery Obolon, who told me that her cash-strapped city district had introduced a hefty licensing tax on mineral water. This brewery was the only producer of mineral water in that district, so this was an individual tax, which was actually legal.

Regional governments had flawed incentives, with no rewards for collecting more official revenues or delivering them to the center. Kravchuk (1999) found that the marginal tax effect on Ukrainian regional governments was over 100 percent. Thus, if they collected more revenue, they retained less income.

The incentives of regional and local governments need to be aligned so that they stop behaving like predators, raiding enterprises in the hunt for penalty fees. Shleifer and Treisman (2000) investigated the same problem in Russia. They argued that local authorities would respect enterprises if they were dependent on taxes from them. Similarly, if local governments were given charge of regional services, they would be more responsible. The logical conclusion was that taxes and expenditures should be clearly divided between the center, the regions, and the municipalities, while tax transfers should be minimized. Each level of government should be fully responsible for certain taxes with separate tax bases. Value-added taxes and foreign trade taxes are typical central state taxes, while land and small enterprise taxes are usually local taxes. Defense and foreign affairs are characteristic central expenditures, while schools, roads, and local infrastructure belong in the local sphere.

The necessary political complement to regional self-government is the full democratization of regional and municipal governments. Both regional and municipal executives and legislative assemblies should be elected, as is currently the case, but the regional governors should also be elected rather than appointed by the president. The central government should give real powers to regional and municipal governments.

Need for Judicial Order

One of Ukraine's greatest failures has been reform of its judiciary, which is corrupt and in a state of disarray. A profound and comprehensive judicial reform is needed. Elementary order must be established in the judicial system. Four criteria need to be fulfilled: a clear hierarchy of justice, independence and qualifications, sufficient financing, and transparency. In order to accomplish such a judicial reform, Ukraine would need to adopt a large number of laws (Blue Ribbon Commission for Ukraine 2005).

The 1996 constitution outlined the judicial system in too rudimentary a fashion. Judge Bohdan Futey (1997) identified its fundamental flaw: "[T]he Constitution, in fact, prevents the establishment of a truly unified judiciary, because divisions between the courts of general jurisdiction and the Constitutional Court are not clear." Often parties to a conflict are entitled to take one case to different courts at the same level, and the courts fight it out. A clear distribution of jurisdiction and hierarchy is needed. In particular, Soviet superiority of the prosecutors over the judges must end.

At present, judges depend on the executive for financing and appointments. Instead, the judicial system should be rendered independent of the executive but also be made accountable. Judges need a fair amount of freedom, but it should be possible to sack corrupt judges. Therefore, independent associations of judges should evaluate and appoint judges to reinforce the integrity of the judicial system. The qualification demanded of judges should be specified, and the appointment of judges should be transparent.

Corruption in Ukrainian courts is pervasive (EBRD and World Bank 2002, 2005). Bribes are paid at every step from entry into law school to the appointment of judges. Corruption has to be fought by many means. Transparent examination and evaluation of judges would be a start. Judges have to be decently remunerated, and courts need to be properly financed and equipped. Financing should be transparent and firmly regulated, free of administrative pressure.

Transparency is the best means of exposing corruption and incompetence, and the internet offers unique new opportunities. Not only all laws and decrees but also all verdicts should be published on the internet, exposing inconsistencies in judgments. Finally, if legal verdicts are to be respected, they have to be executed effectively and expediently within a reasonable time through an effective bailiff service.

To a considerable extent, Ukraine is evolving without a judicial system. Decent parties avoid going to Ukrainian courts, which are often coconspirators in corporate raiding. Instead, serious Ukrainian companies apply international law to settle their conflicts. As a consequence, Ukrainian lawyers are thriving on double work, having to avoid Ukrainian law as well as applying foreign law.

To date, Ukraine has been remarkably successful without a judiciary, but this good fortune is unlikely to continue. Functioning legislative and judiciary branches are necessary to guarantee property rights because foreign legislation and courts may be used to reinforce contracts but not domestic property rights (Acemoglu and Johnson 2005).

Ukrainians increasingly turn to the European Court of Human Rights at the Council of Europe in Strasbourg when they are dissatisfied with the judicial proceedings in their own country, and fortunately Ukraine recognizes the verdicts by this international court, which serves as an important corrective.

Why Ukraine's Capitalist Transformation Succeeded

Ukraine is a market economy, according to the definition presented in the introduction. Among the most important milestones are: Prices and trade have been sufficiently free since November 1994. In 1996 Ukraine's inflation had abated, and by 2000 its financial stabilization was secure. Since 2000, more than 60 percent of Ukraine's GDP has originated in its private sector (figure 3.3).

The most relevant measure of a country's degree of market economy is the composite transition index of the European Bank for Reconstruction and Development (EBRD), which ranks countries from no market economy (0) to normal Western market economy (1). By 2000 Ukraine had just about reached 0.7, the level of a full-fledged market economy (figure 5.2).[2]

The key feature of a market economy is that free individuals and independent firms predominantly make economic decisions. Ukraine's distribution is completely private and independent. No State Planning Committee tells enterprises what to produce. Nor does the state allocate goods. Prices and trade are mostly free, and Ukraine's subsidies are small. Transactions are overwhelmingly monetized, and financial markets have evolved.

The most damaging features of the Ukrainian economy are the degree of lawlessness and bureaucratic interference. On the annual Doing Business index of the World Bank and International Finance Corporation (2008), Ukraine ranks 145th among 181 countries, while Poland ranks 76th and Russia 120th (figure 9.1). Curiously, Ukraine's only good rankings are for getting credit (28) and enforcing contracts (49), which is clearly not done through Ukrainian courts (figure 9.2). Ukraine is rated as one of the worst countries in the world when it comes to dealing with construction permits and paying taxes. All activities that involve the state are exceedingly difficult for enterprises in Ukraine, including closing a business, protecting investors, registering property, trading across borders, and starting a business. The Ukrainian business and investment environment is very poor.

Ukraine's transition to capitalism has arrived, and it appears irreversible. The remarkable thing about this transition is that it succeeded despite the three-year initial delay, during which Ukrainians had to endure hyperinflation and miserable economic failure. Hyperinflation usually leads to regime change, and in other semidemocratic former Soviet republics it augured authoritarianism, but in Ukraine its political effects were surprisingly limited.

---

2. This definition does not include any criterion for rule of law, which does not seem to be a necessary prerequisite.

Figure 9.1 Ease of doing business rankings, 2008

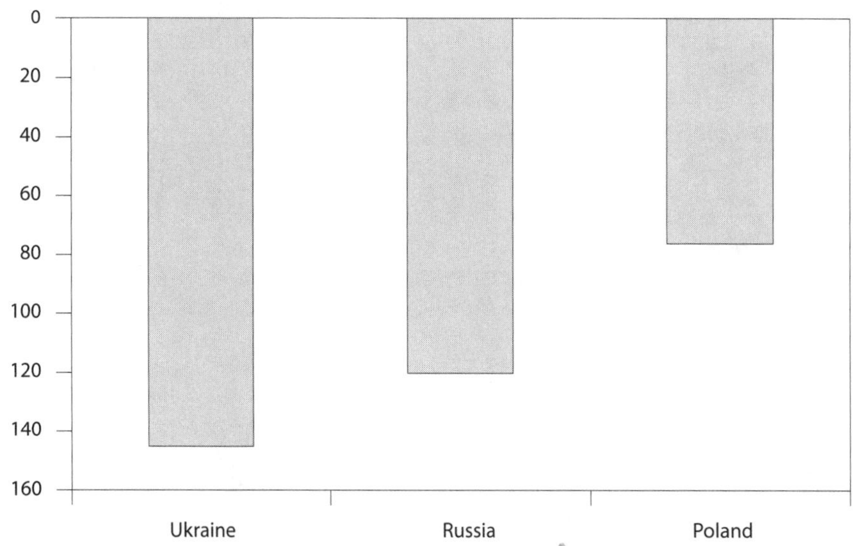

Source: World Bank, *Doing Business Report 2009*, www.doingbusiness.org (accessed on September 16, 2008).

In economic terms, Ukraine verifies the danger of delayed transition to a market economy, which did not benefit the nation in any regard. It aggravated inflation, output collapse, social suffering, and corruption.[3] Nor did the agony contribute to any great intellectual insights. Those who complained about Russia's rash reforms (notably Stiglitz 1999, 2002) had better pair it with the far greater misery in Ukraine.

Yet, Ukraine displayed impressive moral strength, enabling its population to stoically endure. Nobody thought transition would be easy, but nobody showed more patience than Ukrainians. A major mitigating factor was Ukrainian nationalism. Ukrainians knew they were suffering in order to attain independence for their state, and they thought that was worth their endurance. Ukrainians say derogatively of themselves, *moia khata z kraju*, which means "my cottage is to the side," indicating their desire to stay out of world affairs. This indifference lasted until the Orange Revolution, when Ukrainians engaged in society and posed new demands.

After three years of no policy, 1991–94, Ukraine carried out a classical, orthodox macroeconomic stabilization. Public expenditures were cut by

3. De Melo and Gelb (1997), De Melo, Denizer, and Gelb (1997), Berg et al. (1999), Fischer and Sahay (2000), Havrylyshyn (2000), Havrylyshyn and Wolf (2001), Campos and Coricelli (2002), Fischer (2005), and Havrylyshyn (2006).

Figure 9.2 Ease of doing business in Ukraine, by category, 2008

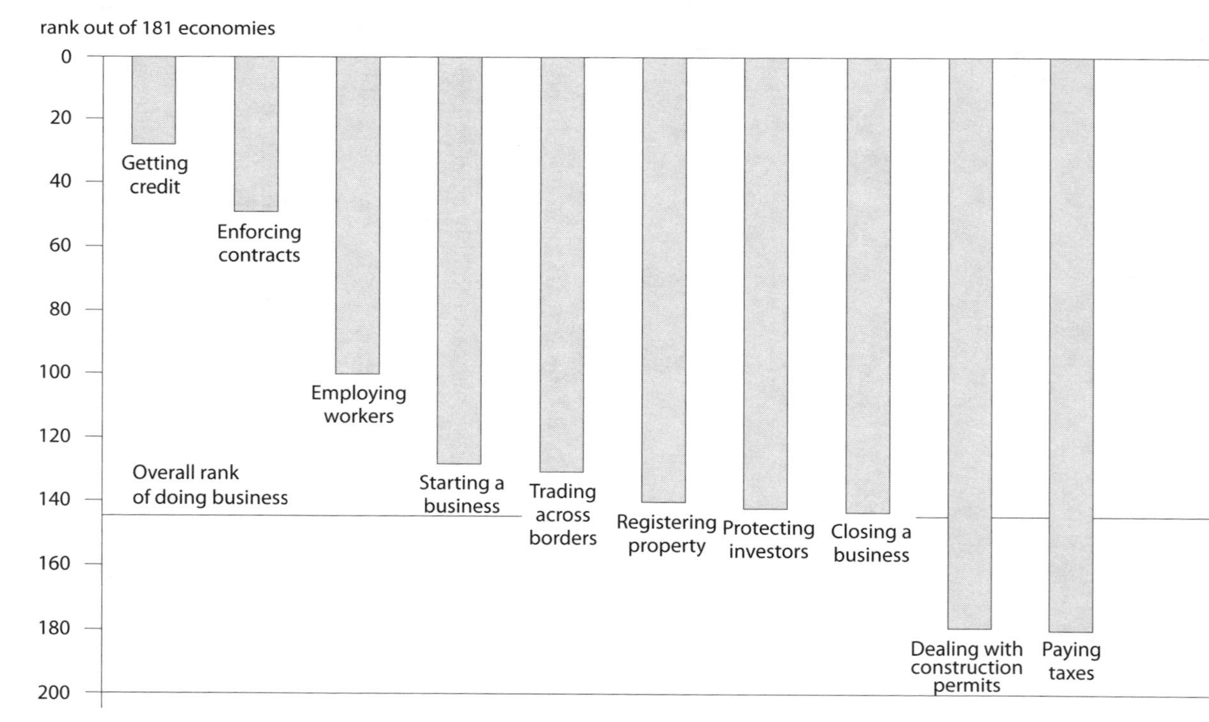

Source: World Bank, *Doing Business Report 2009*, www.doingbusiness.org (accessed on September 16, 2008).

11 percent of GDP from 1994 to 1996, shrinking the budget deficit from 8.7 to 3.2 percent of GDP (figure 3.1). The stabilization was severely complicated by the delay. Because of no international creditworthiness, even such a limited budget deficit was difficult to finance. As a consequence, Ukraine's real interest rates were extremely high for years. The tax system had become confiscatory and driven a large part of the economy underground. An extensive system of rent seeking had developed, involving numerous tax loopholes, subsidies, and dishonest practices. An early stabilization could have halted these malpractices before they became entrenched (Boycko 1991; Murphy, Shleifer, and Vishny 1993).

The political origin of the financial stabilization was Kuchma's election as president in July 1994. The crowning of the stabilization was the symbolically important introduction of the hryvnia in September 1996, which was managed by the chairman of the National Bank of Ukraine, Viktor Yushchenko. As prime minister in 2000, Yushchenko completed the stabilization by cleaning out the worst remaining rent-seeking practices.

Also, with regard to privatization, Ukraine wasted its first years of independence. The breakthrough year was 1994, when a certain legal and administrative base was laid, and Yuriy Yekhanurov became chairman of the State Property Fund. Like Anatoly Chubais in Russia, he was determined to carry out Ukraine's privatization however possible. He chose a three-pronged approach: First, he accepted substantial insider privatization; second, he promoted mass privatization through vouchers; and third, he encouraged some outside purchases.

In the end, most stocks went to insiders because privatization had been delayed and the powers of the incumbents had grown too strong to be overruled. As elsewhere, privatization to outsiders was most controversial, and the more transparent such sales were, the more upset the public became, as the Kryvorizhstal auction showed. With some delay, privatization led to restructuring, and as in other postcommunist countries little positive happened before privatization (Estrin and Rosevear 1999; Akimova and Schwödiauer 2000, 2002, 2004).

Role of the IMF

From 1994 to 2000, the IMF was the dominant international organization in Ukraine. It played a major and very helpful role in the country's macroeconomic stabilization.

From early 1992 until August 1994, IMF missions visited Ukraine, but they failed to win the ear of the government and could thus not help in composing any reform or stabilization program. Still, the very presence of the IMF and iterative conversations helped the few progressive forces in the Ukrainian government to evolve and structure their economic thinking.

The finest deed of the IMF was the Systemic Transformation Facility that it agreed with the Ukrainian government in the fall of 1994. It started with a visit by IMF Managing Director Michel Camdessus, and throughout the 1990s both he and his first deputy Stanley Fischer kept a keen eye on Ukrainian developments. The IMF and the Ukrainian government acted with speed and agility. This agreement marked Ukraine's transition to a market economy, deregulating prices and trade as well as leading to financial stabilization.

The IMF was highly active in Ukraine during the period 1994–2000. It provided many services. Perhaps most important, it forced the Ukrainian government to focus on its financial problems and suggested solutions. The IMF had only a few technical resident experts in Kyiv, but they made major contributions. By and large, IMF policy advice was sound. The worst piece of advice was probably the adoption of a currency corridor from 1996 until 1998, as in Russia, which led to an abrupt devaluation in the fall of 1998 after a severe loss of international currency reserves.

The Ukrainian leaders listened carefully to IMF officials because the IMF was Ukraine's main source of international funding in these years of crisis. From 1994 until 1999, it gave Ukraine credits of a total of 2.5 billion special drawing rights (about $3.5 billion) in stabilization funding (Åslund 2002, table 10.5). This funding boosted Ukraine's meager international reserves, which tended to hover around $1 billion. The IMF also assisted Ukraine with its complex debt negotiations, primarily on gas arrears owed to Russia and Turkmenistan.

Ukraine and the IMF concluded approximately annual Stand-By Arrangements, and the IMF gave Ukraine a few hundreds of millions of dollars each year in credits. Importantly, the IMF carried out detailed reviews every quarter, and the money was disbursed in tranches. About every second time, the IMF held up its disbursements because Ukraine had not fulfilled some of the conditions. By frequently refusing to pay, the IMF imposed more authority and was listened to. At the time, the IMF was in the center of the public discussion about Ukraine, with some arguing that the IMF was too tough, while others claimed it was too lenient.

The irony is that when Prime Minister Yushchenko carried out Ukraine's second big reform in 2000, he had to do so without IMF support because the IMF had cut off Ukraine from credits after the revealed manipulation of central bank reserves in 1996–98, which had made the IMF pay three more tranches than it otherwise would have done (IMF 2000b). Yet the IMF persisted in the background and made an intellectual contribution by setting a standard for procedure and policy.

On the whole, the IMF as an organization can pride itself in having achieved its goals in Ukraine at limited cost and with limited resources. Ukraine has long paid back all the IMF credits with interest. Apart from the Soros Foundation, no other organization could measure itself in importance with the IMF. The World Bank also played an important role, but structural reforms, which are its bailiwick, are still lagging behind. Together with the US Agency for International Development, the World Bank can claim Ukraine's privatization as its greatest success.

When Ukraine unexpectedly entered a new financial crisis in October 2008, the IMF easily and effectively returned to Ukraine and quickly concluded a substantial Stand-By Arrangement both in terms of conditionality and financing ($16.4 billion).

Impact of the Oligarchs

Two critical intertwined questions for Ukraine's future are how its oligarchy will develop and whether its democracy will survive. Few societies are as oligarchic and still formally democratic. Oligarchies as well as democracies have certain characteristics that drive them in specific directions.

Daron Acemoglu (2003) investigated the problems of property rights in an oligarchic versus democratic society. He defined an oligarchic society as a "society where political power is in the hands of the economic elite," comparing its distortions with those of a democracy, in which political power is more equally distributed.

The disadvantage of democracies is that they tend to drive up taxes and redistribute income from entrepreneurs to workers, discouraging entrepreneurial investment. Ukraine faces this challenge. It has as high a tax burden on its official sector as the democratic Central Europe (figure 5.4, Tanzi and Schuknecht 2000). It rose with the Orange Revolution, and the tax revenues go predominantly to social transfers.

The problem with an oligarchic society, in Acemoglu's view, is that it offers a less level playing field. It restricts the entry of new enterprises, distorts the allocation of resources, and redistributes income toward entrepreneurs by reducing wages. One may say that oligarchs have less interest in law because laws and rule of law tend to defend the small against the big (Sonin 2003), which Ukraine confirms.

Growth depends on which distortion has the greatest economic impact. Acemoglu (2003) suggested that typically an oligarchy first grows faster but later is less dynamic than a democratic society. Postcommunist transition initially produced the opposite pattern. Until 1998, democracy drove market reforms and economic growth because the main problem was extraordinary rent seeking, which benefited the oligarchs. From 1999, however, the opposite pattern has emerged. The negative effects of high taxation, high social transfers, and overregulated labor markets kept growth down in Central Europe, while the CIS oligarchies took off in 1999 and delivered about 9 percent annual growth until 2007. Low taxes and free labor markets drove their growth (Åslund 2007a).

Yet the liberal argument for leveling the playing field, reducing corruption, and facilitating entry of new entrepreneurs remains strong and sound. Corruption in Ukraine is severe and benefits the wealthy, endowing them with more rights than other people have. Eventually, the wealthiest will have an interest in reinforcing their property rights. The scare of reprivatization in 2005 showed that not even the richest were safe. Currently, the Ukrainian oligarchs spend inordinate amounts of money on politics to reinsure their property rights in each election. But these expenditures warrant them great privilege unattainable to ordinary businessmen. Legally, political financing is strictly limited, which has only rendered it clandestine.

Oligarchy and democracy are often discussed in static terms, but dynamics are key. Ideally, competition among big oligarchic groups should be so intense that they check each other's power and elaborate standardized rules, and that many competing business groups emerge. This happened from 2000 until 2004, laying the foundation for the Orange Revolution, in line with Robert B. Ekelund and Robert D. Tollison's (1981) interpretation of the evolution of competition between the crown and the parliament in Britain, which led to both economic and political competition—that is, a competitive market economy and democracy.

The situation after the Orange Revolution, however, is more reminiscent of a suboptimal equilibrium or a game without a stable solution. Three major oligarchic groups back three different oligarchic parties, and they balance one another so effectively that hardly any decisions are made. Neither progress nor regression occurs, which is characteristic of a conservative society in equilibrium. However, this equilibrium is probably only temporary because all the four leading oligarchic groups are primarily in steel, and they have benefited from an extreme boom in international steel, which ended in 2008 and is not likely to be repeated. The financial crisis and steel recession will probably lead to profound political and economic change.

The worst threat to democracy would be that one oligarch buys Ukrainian politics lock, stock, and barrel and runs it as his private enterprise, as Kazakhstan's President Nursultan Nazarbayev or Azerbaijan's President Ilham Aliyev have done. After the elections, such an oligarch could recoup his investment through a couple of friendly privatizations. The current concentration of wealth combined with the absence of law and ethical standards make it all too tempting to buy politics. However, the risk of such an oligarchic purchase is not all too likely in Ukraine because its civil society and freedom are too great.

Ukraine is still run by its steel barons, who have rationalized and streamlined their corporate structures (Frishberg 2006), but several of them will probably not be able to survive or move to other industries. The weakest companies will lose out, and some owners will choose to sell their assets. It is easy to predict that the steel groups that are not shielded from price vagaries through vertical integration or diversification will go under. Businessmen in other industries will rise and overtake the steel barons in wealth. Structural change is likely to result in increased economic and political pluralism.

When asked how to normalize their society, Ukrainian oligarchs' usual answer is complete privatization. Big businessmen invest so much in unreliable politicians because the government has many valuable companies left to sell. If privatization were completed, the incentives for extreme corruption would dwindle. Even if privatization has been standing almost still since the Orange Revolution, it appears irreversible and is making some progress. One huge privatization within reach is that of agricultural land, which will occur when private sales of agricultural land are permitted.

Ukraine is strongly influenced from abroad by both East and West. Strong, positive Western influences are apparent, from foreign trade and investment, from Ukrainian investment activities abroad, and from EU peer pressure.

Foreign direct investment in Ukraine is a powerful influence. Often, foreign companies buy big enterprises that Ukrainian businessmen have restructured. In recent years the Ukrainian banking system has been cleaned up because the country's big bankers realized they could sell their banks to foreigners for splendid profits if they cleaned up their corporate structures and accounts before selling them. About 40 percent of Ukraine's banking assets belong to foreign banks, twice as much as in Russia. The Ukrainian banking system is almost entirely private and, as a consequence, stronger and cleaner than Russia's banking system, which is half owned by the state. Russia, however, has better commercial legislation and a functioning judiciary.

In recent years, big Ukrainian businessmen have been selling shares of their companies through initial public offerings, usually on the London Stock Exchange. Because of such prospects, Ukraine's biggest businessmen, Rinat Akhmetov and Victor Pinchuk, streamlined their corporate structures and maintained internationally audited accounts for years before selling shares of their companies. Meanwhile, the publicly assessed value of their assets multiplied.

The European Union's enlargement process puts multiple peer pressures on burgeoning new members. Ukraine aims to become a member of the European Union, so the prospect of this peer pressure exists, but it has not become effective as yet. Ukraine has already committed itself to dozens of institutional improvements in the initial action plan that it concluded with the European Union in February 2005 as part of the EU European Neighborhood Policy. Ukraine is currently negotiating a European Association Agreement, which will contain many more institutional demands. The European Union is offering direct institutional interaction through its twinning of state agencies. The European Union also directly influences Ukrainian subjects. The big Ukrainian business corporations, notably the Industrial Union of Donbas, System Capital Management, and EastOne, are all interested in investing in the West and are aware that they can do so only if they keep up their reputation.

However, these positive trends are counterbalanced by bad habits such as corporate raiding. Some businessmen know that old-style business is their comparative advantage, and they do not want to move on. Corporate raiding thrives in Ukraine, and it is sustained by the rudimentary corporate legislation. An expanding businessman can buy any court. According to Ukrainian corporate law, a general shareholders' meeting must gather 60 percent of the votes to achieve quorum, which has made it possible for Privat Group to control Ukrnafta for years with only 42 percent of the shares, although the state owns the majority (EBA 2004, OECD 2004). Thus strong vested interests long opposed the adoption of an ordinary law on joint stock companies.

To a considerable extent, Ukrainian companies have escaped these problems when enforcing contracts by applying international law and utilizing private arbitration courts abroad, but they always risk a Ukrainian court declaring such practices illegal. The combination of rudimentary legislation, arbitrary courts, and contested state power is hazardous and uncertain because the state interferes in the most surprising fashion.

A big question is whether Ukraine can impose the rule of law on its oligarchs. The introduction of guaranteed property rights would mark the crossing of the threshold to mature capitalism, and the Ukrainian oligarchy would gradually reduce its corruption and be transformed into a democracy. Then a normal legal system, which can discipline the oligarchs, could evolve. This usually happens when developing semiauthoritarian countries become democracies, and the Orange Revolution seemed to complete that process. Yet no political solution is likely to hold if it is not supported by a strong and broad ideological commitment to the sanctity of private property. If people are not convinced that they need capitalism for their own good, they are not likely to accept the permanence of the super-rich.

Will Ukraine's Democracy Survive?

The postcommunist countries have chosen either full democracy or authoritarianism. Ukraine is unique, in that it is the only CIS country Freedom House (2008) ranks as free. Figure 9.3 contrasts Ukraine with Russia and Poland. Poland, like the rest of Central Europe and the Baltic states, became free with the end of communism and has stayed democratic.

Ukraine and Russia, however, were semidemocratic in the 1990s. Substantial political and civil freedom was granted as communism collapsed, but they were not properly legislated or implemented. Still, Boris Yeltsin

Figure 9.3 Civil and political rights, 1991–2007

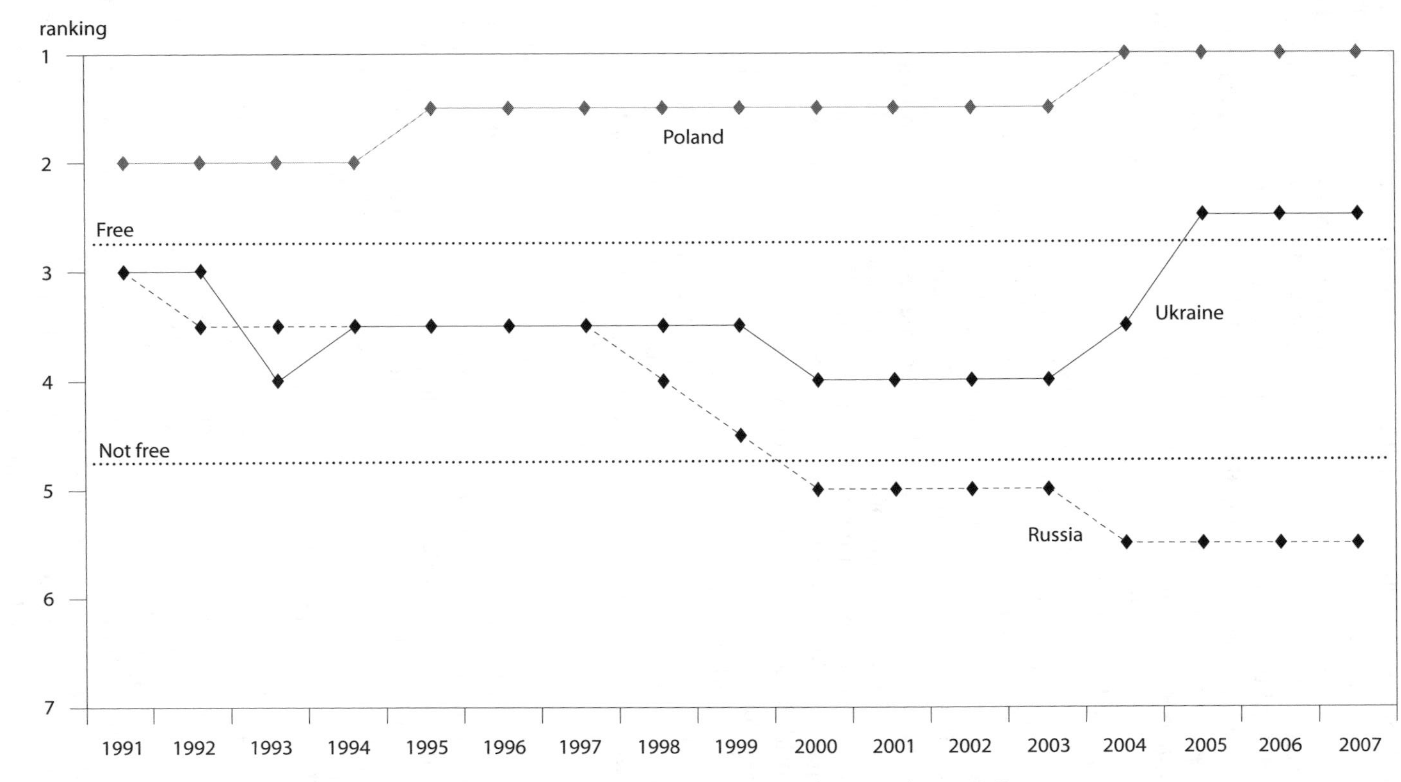

Source: Freedom House, *Freedom in the World Historical Rankings*, http://freedomhouse.org (accessed on September 16, 2008).

and Leonid Kuchma did not try to concentrate all power in their hands. They played everybody against each other, being the ultimate arbitrators. As a consequence, pluralism prevailed. In the late 1990s freedom in Russia started declining and the country became successively more authoritarian under Vladimir Putin, who concentrated power in his own hands with the help of the old KGB structures (Åslund 2007b).

Ukraine never endured the same decline in civil and political rights as Russia under Putin, thanks to Kuchma's continued divide and rule. The Orange Revolution enhanced freedom, rendering Ukraine a democracy. The freedoms of media, expression, assembly, and belief have been fully respected, and Ukraine has held three free and fair elections. Its main shortcomings are poor rule of law and a high level of corruption.

Again, a comparison with Russia is helpful. Both Ukraine and Russia are profoundly corrupt by international standards. Transparency International's (2008) corruption perceptions index offers an annual comparison (figure 9.4). From 2000 until 2004 Ukraine was more corrupt than Russia, but since 2005 Ukraine has become less corrupt and Russia more so. The Orange Revolution exposed corruption, while Russia's increased authoritarianism facilitated corruption. The Business Environment and Enterprise Performance Survey (BEEPS) carried out by the EBRD and the World Bank in 2002 and 2005 offer the same conclusion (Anderson and Gray 2006). Yet anecdotal evidence adds another dimension. Businessmen are often exasperated with Ukraine because it is impossible to get decisions made due to disorderly corruption. They do not know whom to pay, or the official they have paid does not deliver (Shleifer and Vishny 1993). In Russia, by contrast, it is usually easier, but the ultimate problem is when a top official decides to take over an enterprise because then no rescue exists.

Will Ukraine lead the CIS countries toward democracy, or will it succumb to the authoritarianism characteristic of this region? As discussed in the introduction, Ukraine easily fulfills the criteria for a democracy that Juan Linz (1978, 5) offers: freedom to formulate and advocate political alternatives, rights to free association and free speech and other basic freedoms, free and nonviolent competition among leaders with periodic validation of their claim to rule (elections), inclusion of all effective political offices in the democratic process, and freedom to participate in the political process regardless of political preferences.

The critical issue is whether the nation, its political institutions, and socioeconomic system may be considered legitimate. Linz's (1978, 18) minimal definition of "a legitimate government is one considered to be the least evil of the forms of government."

The legitimacy of the nation falls into two issues: the security of the borders and the cohesion of the nation. Dankwart Rustow (1970) emphasized the importance of securing the borders of a state before any democracy could be built. A state without secure borders cannot be stable (McFaul

Figure 9.4 Corruption perceptions index, 2000–2007

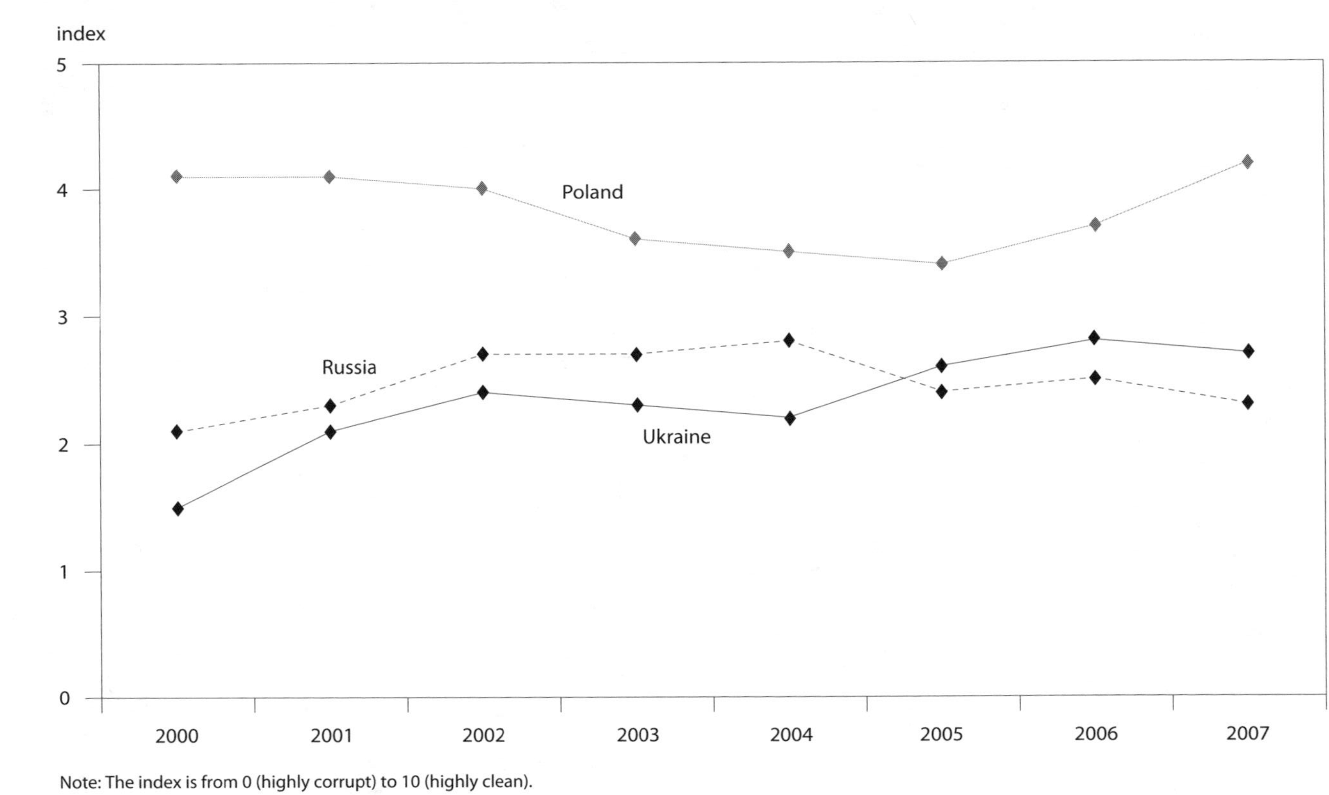

Note: The index is from 0 (highly corrupt) to 10 (highly clean).

Source: Transparency International, www.transparency.org (accessed on July 1, 2008).

2001, 9). Thanks to Yeltsin guaranteeing the security of the borders of the former Soviet republics early on and peacefully dissolving the Soviet Union in December 1991, Ukraine's borders were quite secure, even if various Russian politicians grumbled about Crimea from time to time. The Russian-Ukrainian Treaty of 1997 seemed to settle the integrity of the Ukrainian nation for good.

The Ukrainian elections might have appeared to divide the country on occasion, notably the presidential elections in 1994 and 2004, but these divisions were fortunately quite superficial, and no serious separatism erupted. However intangible, Ukraine appears to have bred a national identity.

After the Orange Revolution, Ukraine developed a remarkable ideological consensus. In 2007 all the three dominant parties embraced confusingly similar liberal-democratic ideas, and the left was marginalized. Common values were democracy, freedom, private ownership of the means of production, market economy, international openness, and European integration. Three free and fair elections in the course of four years were held. Ukraine's political institutions as well as the socioeconomic system were considered highly legitimate.

Nor do the armed forces or the security police pose any danger, while they were major forces in Russia's reversal to autocracy. Also Ukraine's economic performance has contributed to the legitimacy of the regime, with a steady average growth rate of 7.5 percent a year from 2000 to 2008.

In comparison with Russia, Ukraine is blessed with the absence of several Russian curses. First, with small oil and gas revenues, it does not suffer from the curse of energy rents that a small elite can easily extract (Fish 2005, Diamond 2008). Second, Ukraine does not have Russia's strong authoritarian tradition, which Richard Pipes (2005) has emphasized. Third, Russia suffers from imperial nostalgia, while Ukrainians see their newly won independence as a blessing.

The frailty of Ukraine's democracy, however, is captured in Alfred Hirschman's (1965) phrase that democratic leadership must prove its ability. Ukraine suffers from three related weaknesses. First, legislation securing property rights is missing and it is too limited to satisfy society's need for law and order. Second, the government lacks efficacy. Third, corruption remains extensive and disruptive.

The risk of outrageous mismanagement of the state is evident, and by most measures the efficacy of the state seems to have declined after the Orange Revolution, while public demands have increased. Rising popular demands and patent state failure provide a potentially explosive cocktail. Yet in a free society, people find many means of solving their problems without the state. Ukraine's democracy underperforms, but its demise is neither evident nor necessary. The financial crisis that erupted in October 2008 will offer Ukraine's democracy a severe test.

European Economic Convergence

A dominant idea in economic growth theory is that with the same economic system, similar preconditions, and similar economic policies, economies should converge at a similar economic level (Barro and Sala-i-Martin 2004).

Central and Eastern Europe have provided beautiful examples of such convergence. In 2007 their GDP per capita in purchasing power parity (PPP) averaged half of the level of the old EU-15 countries (IMF 2008). In current exchange rates their GDP per capita was just under one-third of the old EU-15 level. Russia has already undergone a similar convergence, having reached one-quarter of the EU-15 level in 2007 (IMF 2008).

Ukraine has jumped on this bandwagon. From 1992 to 2000, its GDP in current dollars vacillated at a low level, but from 2000 to 2007 it grew steadily by an average of 24 percent a year, surging from $31 billion in 2000 to $140 billion in 2007 (figure 9.5). This meant that Ukraine's GDP per capita at current exchange rates nearly tripled from 2.8 to 7.4 percent of the level of the eurozone (IMF 2008). Ukraine is lagging so far behind the other Central and Eastern European countries that its growth rate may continue at a high rate until Ukraine reaches one-third of the EU-15 level.

In the next decade, Ukraine should have superior nominal growth. The market economy has come to stay and enjoys solid political support. Two-thirds of the GDP comes from the private sector, and the share is set to increase. Ukraine is a very open economy, and it will become even more so with its WTO accession. After the financial crisis, growth should return with a vengeance. Corruption is a serious problem, but that is true of many fast-growing economies.

So far the European Union has adopted a rather passive approach to Ukraine, but EU engagement is increasing. The European Union will put pressure on and engage with Ukraine to undertake multiple institutional reforms, most of which will be growth-enhancing. It has a sound habit of putting the most liberal reforms, such as market access and cutting of red tape, first. It will set a peer standard that is likely to dominate Ukrainian institutional thinking and debate, as has been the case in Central and Eastern Europe.

In spite of the ravages of the current financial crisis, the material reasons why Ukraine's long-term economic growth should stay high are many. Remonetization has boosted the volume of money (M3) as a ratio to GDP from 16 percent in 2000 to 47 percent in 2007 (figure 9.6). The increasing demand for money is reflected in a long credit cycle, leading to greater investment. Thus, investment as a share of GDP has increased in parallel, from barely 20 percent in 2000 to 27 percent in 2007, and it should rise further after a temporary lull in the business cycle (figure 6.3).

Figure 9.5 Ukraine's GDP in US dollars, 1992–2007

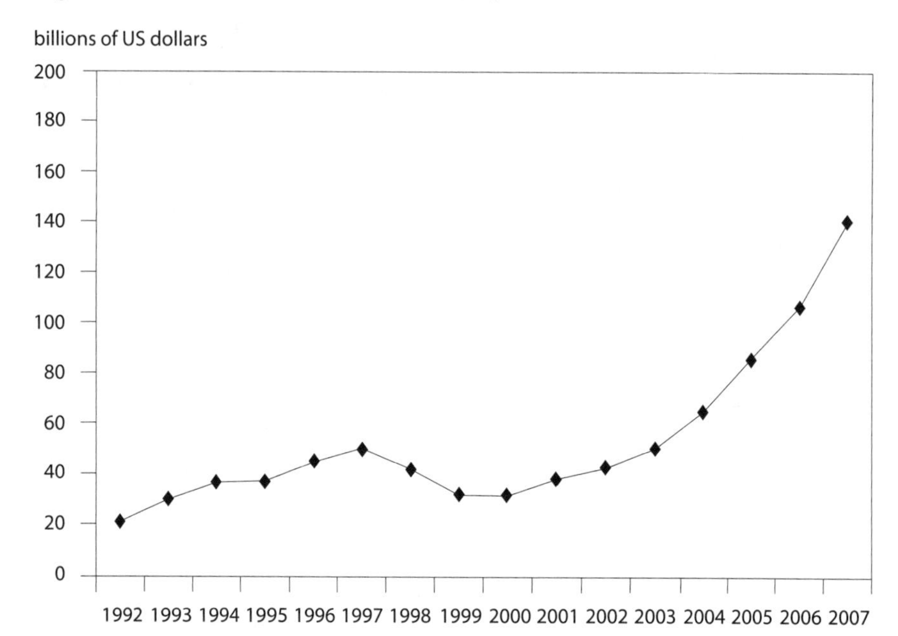

Source: IMF (2008).

Part of the rising investment is foreign direct investment (FDI), which is increasing relentlessly and reached 6.5 percent of GDP in 2007 (figure 9.7). With little notice, Ukraine has caught up with Central European countries such as Poland in FDI as a share of GDP, and it is far above Russia. Apart from temporary disturbances, FDI is likely to stay high for a long time judging by the Central European experience. Also, structural normalization proceeds as underperforming Soviet enterprises close down, while other industries evolve.

The most important growth potential lies in the 73 percent of Ukrainian youth who opt for some form of higher education, making a huge investment in their own and the country's human capital.

Ukraine is an open market economy centrally located in Europe, and it is quite integrated. The European Union is its model and institutional standard, and even if Ukraine has so far imitated the European Union relatively slowly, it endeavors to do so. After 2000, it gained better market access to the European single market, which is now its largest export market. Ukraine's proximity to the European Union is no guarantee of convergence, but its politicians would have to make many mistakes to fail to achieve European convergence.

Figure 9.6 Ukraine's volume of money (M3) as a ratio of GDP, 2000–2007

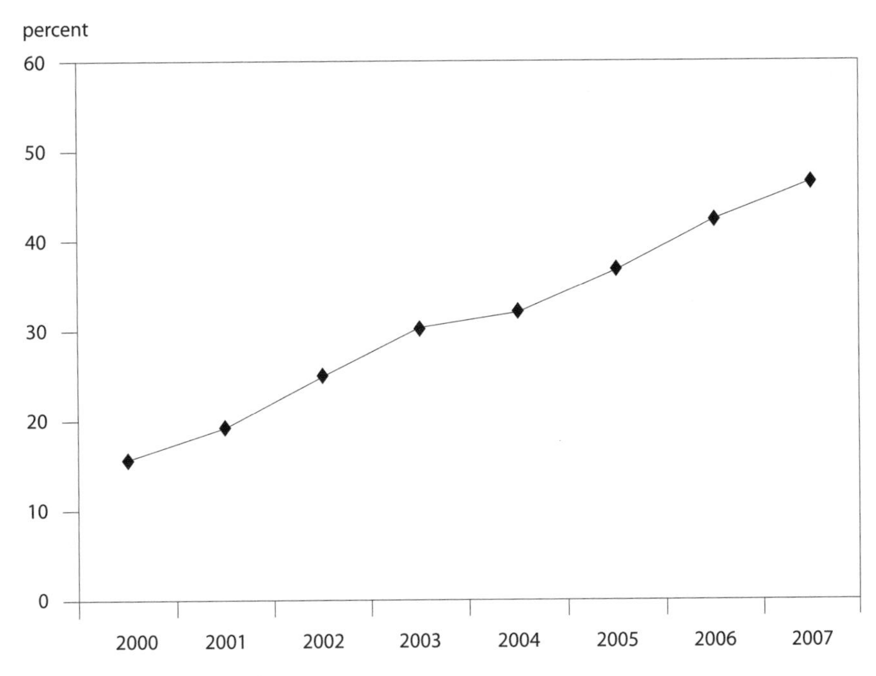

Source: Concorde Capital, March 2008.

Putin's Alienation: Ukraine Turning to the West

Ukraine's foreign policy has gradually become ever more Western-oriented since independence. Leonid Kravchuk's term may be characterized as isolationist. Ukraine was too preoccupied with itself to deal with the outside world, and its only important asset was nuclear arms.

Kuchma wanted to improve Ukraine's relations with both Russia and the West. His policy was pragmatic, using opportunities as they opened up. In 1994–96 two international forces dominated Ukraine: the IMF and the United States. The IMF helped Ukraine to undertake its financial stabilization, and the United States instigated Ukraine's denuclearization and provided substantial technical assistance. President Bill Clinton's visit to Kyiv in May 1995 stands out as the high point in US enchantment with Ukraine. In the ensuing years, human rights and arms trade caused rising concerns in the United States. After Ukraine's economy turned around in 2000, the role of the IMF was naturally reduced.

In 2001–04 the West turned its back on Ukraine after the Heorhiy Gongadze murder, giving Kuchma little choice but to turn to Russia. The

Figure 9.7 Foreign direct investment as a share of GDP, 2000–2007

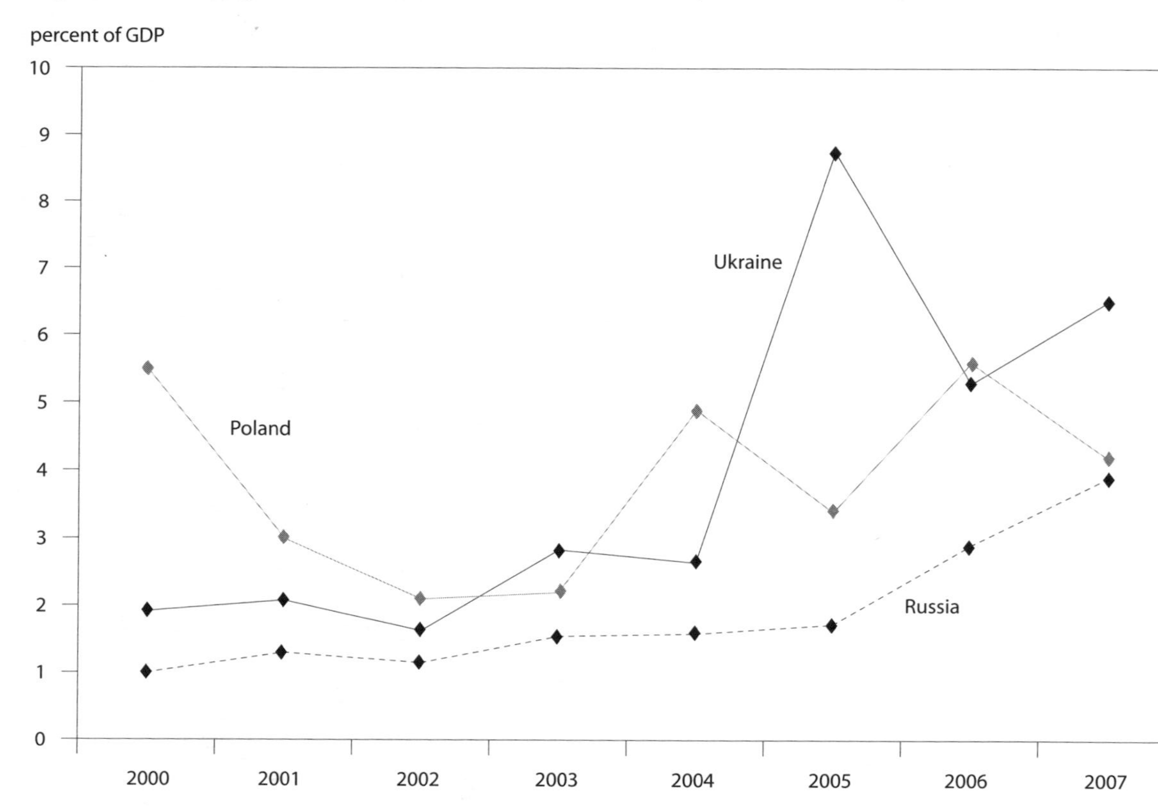

Sources: Dragon Capital, July 2008; JPMorgan, July 2008; Eurostat, April 2008.

Ukrainian population had reacted against the 1999 NATO bombing of Yugoslavia as the Russians in solidarity with orthodox Serbs. In 2003–04, President Vladimir Putin undertook Russia's greatest charm offensive toward Ukraine, offering the Common Economic Space, substantial tax and trade concessions, plentiful campaign financing, and more bilateral meetings than ever. However, the Russian initiative to form a Common Economic Space in 2003, the Tuzla border conflict with Russia in October 2003, and the massive Russian intervention in the Ukrainian presidential election in the fall of 2004 aroused sharp Ukrainian reactions.

After the Orange Revolution, Russia offered nothing. Having had 12 meetings with President Kuchma in 2004, President Putin minimized his contacts with Ukraine. He visited Yushchenko in Kyiv once in 2005 as well as 2006, but on the whole Russia ignored Ukraine. Hardly any Russian ministers visited the country. Russia's policies toward Ukraine boiled down to four hostile activities: threatening Ukraine with higher gas prices, declaring an embargo on one Ukrainian export product after the other, making populist noises about Crimea and the Black Sea Fleet, and complaining about Ukraine's desire to join NATO. In short, Russia's Ukraine policy consisted of four sticks and no carrots. As if to add insult to injury, Russian television, which was watched in half of Ukraine, indulged in stark anti-Ukrainian propaganda.

Putin had transformed Russia's policy toward Ukraine to one of outcries and embargoes. Ukraine could do nothing but be repelled. The unspoken rationale of Putin's policy was that democratic and Western-oriented Ukraine offered an alternative to the Russian public. If Ukraine's democracy succeeded, it would be a devastating threat to Putin's authoritarian system. Therefore, Putin had every interest in seeing Ukraine fail through destabilization. Then he could tell credulous Russians that democracy unfortunately did not work in East Slavic countries.

Russia left Ukraine with only one choice, namely to turn to the West, which meant the WTO, the European Union, and NATO. Ukraine had applied for membership of the WTO in December 1993, and in May 2008, it was accepted. An effect was that Ukraine's access to EU markets became much safer, but as Russia remained outside the WTO, its market was as inaccessible as it had been.

With Ukraine's European location, one would assume that the European Union would have a great impact on its postcommunist transition. Sadly, that was not the case. President Kuchma pleaded for Ukraine's membership in the European Union starting in 1996, but the European Union barely responded. Throughout the 1990s the greatest EU demand was that Ukraine close down the Chornobyl nuclear power station without offering financing for this expensive undertaking. Yet, however passive the European Union was, it was the Ukrainians' ideal model.

The Orange Revolution became a breakthrough for Ukraine's relations with the European Union. Europeans supported human rights in

Ukraine, and European politicians acted as mediators between the two presidential candidates. The European Union had already offered its European Neighborhood Policy to Ukraine, and after the Orange Revolution the ensuing action plan became more substantial than had been expected and was agreed in February 2005. On September 9, 2008, the European Union decided to offer Ukraine a European Association Agreement, which contains a free trade agreement and more. It aims at deep free trade with far-reaching integration. As a consequence, the European Union is likely to become Ukraine's all-dominant export market.

The third leg of Ukraine's Western orientation is NATO. In the 1990s Russia and Ukraine stepped up cooperation with NATO in parallel. Under Putin, however, Russia started treating NATO as an enemy, while Ukraine continued to cooperate ever more closely with it. In January 2008 Ukraine applied for a membership action plan with NATO, which was the natural next step in their ever closer relationship. However, the NATO summit in Bucharest in April 2008 turned down this application because Ukrainian popular support for NATO membership was minimal, and Russia strongly opposed it. The Russian opposition is a two-edged sword. The stiffer Russia's opposition is toward Ukraine's membership of NATO, the more endangered Ukraine's national security seems (Pifer 2008).

Ukraine's concrete need today is security, not NATO. The United States has amply guaranteed Ukraine's security through the trilateral US-Russian-Ukrainian declaration of January 14, 1994, and the Strategic Arms Reduction Treaty (START). It would be more appropriate for the United States to refer to these commitments already made rather than pursuing a course that facilitates the Kremlin's intention to destabilize Ukraine.

* * * * * * * * *

As this book goes to press in March 2009, three big clouds darken Ukraine's path forward: domestic political instability; a renewed, explicit Russian threat to Ukraine's sovereignty; and a severe financial crisis.

The answer to these challenges lies in the quotation that opens this chapter, Deputy Prime Minister Hryhoriy Nemyria's assurance: "We know we are a European nation and that we are going to join the European Union." Immediately after the end of communism, the Central European countries declared their "return to Europe." Ukraine did not do so because of its preoccupation with building the shattered Ukrainian nation. That great task has been accomplished, and Ukrainians have set their eyes on Europe as a model, civilization, community, and market. The European Union needs to respond by offering a substantial European Association Agreement. It should include not only deep free trade but also considerable support for cooperation in higher education to help Ukraine build the necessary capacity for its development.

The next assignment is to improve Ukrainian constitutional order. As I have argued in this book, Ukraine needs full Western European parliamentarianism, for which the European Union offers the best models. The European Union should also assist Ukraine in building its state agencies and civil service.

As long as Russia offers no other policy than destabilization, Ukrainian leaders have to manage that relationship at arm's length, which they know how to do.

The current financial crisis will severely test Ukraine's democracy, and hopefully it will improve it. Many of the existing big corporations will undoubtedly go under. Old businesses will be streamlined or go bankrupt. Bad business practices, such as corruption, will be exposed and questioned. Then much of the current political financing will disappear. Ukraine can come out with a more level playing field economically and a better democracy. This is a time for Ukrainians to demand more and better laws and deal a decisive blow against corruption. It will not be easy, but it may be productive.

The United States has played an important and positive role in the life of independent Ukraine, and it needs to continue doing so. Uniquely, only the United States can guarantee Ukraine's security, and it has committed itself to doing so in multiple agreements on Ukraine's denuclearization. The United States should also catch up with the European Union and offer Ukraine a bilateral free trade agreement to favor economic integration between the two countries. Ukraine needs to develop a new elite, and the United States can help by offering a large number of student scholarships at American universities. Finally, the United States should facilitate visa regulations for Ukrainians, all the more so as Ukraine allows all American citizens to enter Ukraine without a visa.

Bibliography

Acemoglu, Daron. 2003. *The Form of Property Rights: Oligarchic vs. Democratic Societies.* NBER Working Paper 10037. Cambridge, MA: National Bureau of Economic Research.

Acemoglu, Daron, and Simon Johnson. 2005. Unbundling Institutions. *Journal of Political Economy* 113 (October): 949–95.

Akimova, Iryna. 2002. Performance of Small and Medium Sized Manufacturing Firms in Ukraine: Does the Quality of Governance Matter? In *Fostering Sustainable Grows in Ukraine,* eds. Stephan von Cramon-Taubadel and Iryna Akimova. Heidelberg: Physica-Verlag.

Akimova, Iryna, and Gerhard Schwödiauer. 2000. Restructuring Ukrainian Enterprises after Privatization: Does Ownership Matter? *Atlantic Economic Journal* 28, no. 1: 48–59.

Akimova, Iryna, and Gerhard Schwödiauer. 2002. *Determinants of Enterprise Restructuring in Ukraine: the Role of Managerial Ownership and Human Capital.* Working Paper 13. Kyiv: Institute for Economic Research and Policy Consulting.

Akimova, Iryna, and Gerhard Schwödiauer. 2004. Ownership Structure, Corporate Governance, and Enterprise Performance: Empirical Results for Ukraine. *International Advances in Economic Research* 10, no. 1: 28–42.

Anderson, James H., David S. Bernstein, and Cheryl W. Gray. 2005. *Judicial Systems in Transition Economies: Assessing the Past, Looking to the Future.* Washington: World Bank.

Anderson, James H., and Cheryl W. Gray. 2006. *Anticorruption in Transition 3: Who Is Succeeding . . . and Why?* Washington: World Bank.

Åslund, Anders. 1985. *Private Enterprise in Eastern Europe: The Non-Agricultural Sector in Poland and the GDR.* New York: St. Martin's Press.

Åslund, Anders. 1995. *How Russia Became a Market Economy.* Washington: Brookings Institution.

Åslund, Anders. 1996. Reform vs. "Rent-Seeking" in Russia's Economic Transformation. *Transitions (OMRI)* no. 26 (January): 12–16.

Åslund, Anders. 1997. Economic Causes of Crime in Russia. In *The Rule of Law and Economic Reform in Russia,* eds. Jeffrey D. Sachs and Katharina Pistor. Boulder, CO: Westview Press.

Åslund, Anders. 1999. Why Has Russia's Economic Transformation Been So Arduous? Paper presented at the Annual World Bank Conference on Development Economics, Washington, April 28–30.

Åslund, Anders. 2000. Why Has Ukraine Failed to Achieve Economic Growth? In *Economic Reform in Ukraine: The Unfinished Agenda,* eds. Anders Åslund and Georges de Ménil. Armonk, NY: M. E. Sharpe.

Åslund, Anders. 2001. Ukraine's Return to Economic Growth. *Post-Soviet Geography and Economics* 42, no. 5: 313–28.

Åslund, Anders. 2002. *Building Capitalism: The Transformation of the Former Soviet Bloc.* New York: Cambridge University Press.

Åslund, Anders. 2003a. *A Foreign Trade Policy Strategy for Ukraine.* UNDP Report (March 31). Kyiv: United Nations Development Programme.

Åslund, Anders. 2003b. Left Behind. *The National Interest* (Fall): 107–16.

Åslund, Anders. 2004. Ukraine Whole and Free: What I Saw at the Orange Revolution. *The Weekly Standard* (December 27): 11–12.

Åslund, Anders. 2005. The Economic Policy after the Orange Revolution. *Eurasian Geography and Economics* 46, no. 5: 327–53.

Åslund, Anders. 2006. The Ancien Régime: Kuchma and the Oligarchs. In *Revolution in Orange,* eds. Anders Åslund and Michael McFaul. Washington: Carnegie Endowment for International Peace.

Åslund, Anders. 2007a. *How Capitalism Was Built: The Transformation of Central and Eastern Europe, Russia, and Central Asia.* New York: Cambridge University Press.

Åslund, Anders. 2007b. *Russia's Capitalist Revolution: Why Market Reform Succeeded and Democracy Failed.* Washington: Peterson Institute for International Economics.

Åslund, Anders. 2007c. On the Dissolution of Ukraine's Parliament. *National Interest Online* (April 4).

Åslund, Anders. 2008. Reflections on Ukraine's Current Economic Dilemma. *Eurasian Geography and Economics* 49, no. 2: 152–59.

Åslund, Anders, and Georges de Ménil, eds. 2000. *Economic Reform in Ukraine: The Unfinished Agenda,* Armonk, NY: M. E. Sharpe.

Åslund, Anders, and Andrew Warner. 2004. The EU Enlargement: Consequences for the CIS Countries. In *Beyond Transition: Development Perspectives and Dilemmas,* eds. Marek Dabrowski, Ben Slay, and Jaroslaw Neneman. Aldershot: Ashgate.

Åslund, Anders, and Michael McFaul, eds. 2006. *Revolution in Orange: The Origins of Ukraine's Democratic Breakthrough.* Washington: Carnegie Endowment for International Peace.

Åslund, Anders, and Marek Dąbrowski, eds. 2007. *Europe after Enlargement.* New York: Cambridge University Press.

Åslund, Anders, Peter Boone, and Simon Johnson. 1996. How to Stabilize: Lessons from Post Communist Countries. *Brookings Papers on Economic Activity* 26, no. 1: 217–313.

Åslund, Anders, Peter Boone, and Simon Johnson. 2001. *Escaping the Under-Reform Trap.* IMF Staff Papers, Special Issue 48, no.4: 88–108. Washington: International Monetary Fund.

Balcerowicz, Leszek. 1994. Understanding Postcommunist Transitions. *Journal of Democracy* 5, no. 4: 75–89.

Balmaceda, Margarita Mercedes. 1998. Gas, Oil and the Linkages between Domestic and Foreign Policies: The Case of Ukraine. *Europe-Asia Studies* 50, no. 2: 257–86.

Banaian, King. 1999. *The Ukrainian Economy Since Independence.* Cheltenham, UK: Edward Elgar Publishing.

Barro, Robert J., and Xavier Sala-i-Martin. 2004. *Economic Growth.* Cambridge, MA: MIT Press.

Berg, Andrew, Eduardo Borensztein, Ratna Sahay, and Jeronim Zettelmeyer. 1999. *The Evolution of Output in Transition Economies: Explaining the Differences.* IMF Working Paper 73. Washington: International Monetary Fund.

Birch, Sarah. 2000a. *Elections and Democratization in Ukraine.* Basingstoke: Palgrave Macmillan.

Birch, Sarah. 2000b. Interpreting the Regional Effect in Ukrainian Politics. *Europe-Asia Studies* 52, no. 6: 1017–41.

Blue Ribbon Commission for Ukraine. 2005. *Proposals for the President: A New Wave of Reform.* Kyiv: United Nations Development Programme.

BOFIT (Bank of Finland). 2008. Russia Statistics Online. Available at www.bof.fi (accessed on various dates).

Boycko, Maxim. 1991. Price Decontrol: The Microeconomic Case for the "Big Bang" Approach. *Oxford Review of Economic Policy* 7, no. 4: 35–45.

Boycko, Maxim, Andrei Shleifer, and Robert Vishny. 1995. *Privatizing Russia.* Cambridge, MA: MIT Press.

Brainerd, Elizabeth. 1998. Market Reform and Mortality in Transition Economies. *World Development* 26, no. 11: 2013–27.

Brzezinski, Zbigniew. 1994. The Premature Partnership? *Foreign Affairs* 73, no. 2: 67–82.

Bukkvoll, Tor. 2004. Private Interests, Public Policy: Ukraine and the Common Economic Space Agreement. *Problems of Post-Communism* 51, no. 5: 11–22.

Bunce, Valerie. 1999. The Political Economy of Postsocialism. *Slavic Review* 58, no. 4: 756–93.

Burakovsky, Ihor, Lars Handrich, and Lutz Hoffmann. 2003. *Ukraine's WTO Accession: Challenge for Domestic Economic Reforms.* Heidelberg: Physica-Verlag.

Bush, George H. W. 1991. Remarks to the Supreme Soviet of the Ukrainian Soviet Socialist Republic, Kiev, Ukraine, USSR. *US Department of State Dispatch* 2, no. 32 (August 12). Washington: US Department of State

Cagan, Philippe. 1956. The Monetary Dynamics of Hyperinflation. In *Studies in the Quantity Theory of Money*, ed. Milton Friedman. Chicago: University of Chicago Press.

Campos, Nauro F., and Fabrizio Coricelli. 2002. Growth in Transition: What We Know, What We Don't, and What We Should. *Journal of Economic Literature* 40, no. 3: 793–836.

CEPS (Centre for European Policy Studies). 2006. *The Prospect of Deep Free Trade between the European Union and Ukraine.* Report prepared for European Commission's Directorate-General for Trade. Brussels: Centre for European Policy Studies.

Christoffersen, Peter, and Peter Doyle. 2000. From Inflation to Growth: Eight Years of Transition. *Economics of Transition* 8, no. 2: 421–51.

Clem, Ralph S., and Peter R. Craumer. 2005. Shades of Orange: The Electoral Geography of Ukraine's 2004 Presidential Elections. *Eurasian Geography and Economics* 46, no. 5: 364–85.

Clem, Ralph S., and Peter R. Craumer. 2008. Orange, Blue and White, and Blonde: The Electoral Geography of Ukraine's 2006 and 2007 Rada Elections. *Eurasian Geography and Economics* 49, no. 2: 127–51.

Commission of the European Communities. 2003. *Wider Europe—Neighbourhood: A New Framework for Relations with our Eastern and Southern Neighbours.* Communication from the Commission to the Council and the European Parliament, Com (2003) 104, March 11. Brussels: Commission of the European Communities.

Commission of the European Communities. 2004. *European Neighbourhood Policy Strategy Paper.* Communication from the Commission, Com (2004) 373, May 12. Brussels: Commission of the European Communities.

Conquest, Robert. 1986. *Harvest of Sorrow: Soviet Collectivization and the Terror-Famine.* Oxford, UK: Oxford University Press.

Copenhagen Economics, IER (Institute for Economic Research and Policy Consulting), and Institute for East European Studies Munich. 2005a. *Analysis of Economic Impact of Ukraine's Accession to the WTO.* Study on Service Sectors in Ukraine. Copenhagen, Kyiv, and Munich.

Copenhagen Economics, IER (Institute for Economic Research and Policy Consulting), and Institute for East European Studies Munich. 2005b. *Analysis of Economic Impact of Ukraine's Accession to the WTO.* Overall Impact Assessment. Copenhagen, Kyiv, and Munich.

Copenhagen Economics, IER (Institute for Economic Research and Policy Consulting), and Institute for East European Studies Munich. 2005c. *Analysis of Economic Impact of Ukraine's Accession to the WTO.* Study on Industry and Agriculture in Ukraine. Copenhagen, Kyiv, and Munich.

Cornelius, Peter K., and Patrick Lenain, eds. 1997. *Ukraine: Accelerating the Transition to Market*. Washington: International Monetary Fund.

D'Anieri, Paul. 2006. *Understanding Ukrainian Politics: Power, Politics, and Institutional Design*. Armonk, NY: M. E. Sharpe.

Dabrowski, Marek. 1994. The Ukrainian Way to Hyperinflation. *Communist Economies & Economic Transformation* 6, no. 2: 115–37.

Dabrowski, Marek. 1995. The Reasons for the Collapse of the Rouble Zone. *Studies and Analyses* 58. Warsaw: Center for Social and Economic Research (CASE).

Dabrowski, Marek, Marcin Luczyński, and Malgorzata Markiewicz. 2000. The Phases of Budgetary Reform. In *Economic Reform in Ukraine: The Unfinished Agenda,* eds. Anders Åslund and Georges de Ménil. Armonk, NY: M. E. Sharpe.

Dalia, Marin, and Monika Schnitzer. 2002. *Contracts in Trade and Transition: the Resurgence of Barter*. Cambridge, MA: MIT Press.

De Long, Bradford. 2002. Robber Barons. In *Ocherki o mirovoi ekonomiki: Vydayushchiesya ekonomisty mira v Moskovskom Tsentre Karnegie [Series of Lectures on Economics: Leading World Experts at the Carnegie Moscow Center]*, eds. Anders Åslund and Tatyana Maleva. Moscow: Carnegie Endowment for International Peace.

Demes, Pavol, and Joerg Forbrig. 2006. Pora—"It's Time" for Democracy in Ukraine. In *Revolution in Orange: The Origins of Ukraine's Democratic Breakthrough*, eds. Anders Åslund and Michael McFaul. Washington: Carnegie Endowment for International Peace.

Demyanenko, Serhiy, and Serhiy Zorya. 2002. *Taxation and Ukrainian Agriculture after 2004*. Working Paper 18. Kyiv: Institute for Economic Research and Policy Consulting.

De Melo, Martha, and Alan Gelb. 1997. Transitions to Date: A Comparative Overview. In *Lessons from the Economic Transition: Central and Eastern Europe in the 1990s*, ed. Salvatore Zecchini. Norwell, MA: Kluwer.

De Melo, Martha, Cevdet Denizer, and Alan Gelb. 1997. From Plan to Market: Patterns of Transition. In *Macroeconomic Stabilization in Transition Economies,* eds. Mario I. Blejer and Marko Skreb. Cambridge: Cambridge University Press.

De Ménil, Georges. 1997. The Volatile Relationship between Deficits and Inflation in Ukraine, 1992–1996. *Economics of Transition* 5, no. 2: 485–97.

De Ménil, Georges. 2000. From Hyperinflation to Stagnation. In *Economic Reform in Ukraine: The Unfinished Agenda,* eds. Anders Åslund and Georges de Ménil. Armonk, NY: M. E. Sharpe.

De Souza, Lúcio Vinhas, Rainer Schweickert, Veronika Movchan, Olena Bilan, and Igor Burakovsky. 2005. *Now So Near, and Yet Still so Far: Economic Relations between Ukraine, and the European Union*. Kiel Discussion Paper 419. Kiel: Institute für Weltwirtschaft.

De Tocqueville, Alexis. 1955 [1856]. *The Old Regime and the French Revolution*. New York: Doubleday.

Deutsche Beratergruppe Wirtschaft bei der Ukrainischen Regierung. 2001. *Die Ersten 365 Tage: Ein Konstruktiver Ruckblick auf die Wirtschaftsreformen in der Ukraine in Jahr 2000 [The First 365 Days: A Constructive Reflection on the Economic Reforms in 2000]*. Kyiv.

Diamond, Larry. 2008. *The Spirit of Democracy: The Struggle to Build Free Societies throughout the World*. New York: Times Books.

Diuk, Nadia. 2006. The Triumph of Civil Society. In *Revolution in Orange*, eds. Anders Åslund and Michael McFaul. Washington: Carnegie Endowment for International Peace.

Dornbusch, Rudiger. 1992. Monetary Problems of Post Communism: Lessons from the End of the Austro-Hungarian Empire. *Weltwirtschaftliches Archiv* 128, no. 3: 391–424.

Drazen, Allen, and Vittorio Grilli. 1993. The Benefit of Crises for Economic Reforms. *American Economic Review* 83, no. 3: 598–607.

Dragon Capital. Various years. *Ukraine: Macroeconomic Update*. Kyiv.

Dubien, Arnaud. 2007. Russie-Ukraine: Opacité des réseaux énergétiques [Russia-Ukraine: the Opacity of Energy Networks]. *Russie.Nei.Visions*, no. 19 (May). Available at www.ifri.org.

Dunlop, John. 1993. *The Rise of Russia and the Fall of the Soviet Empire*. Princeton, NJ: Princeton University Press.

Dunn, Jonathan, and Patrick Lenain. 1997. The Role of Monetary Policy in Ukraine's Medium-Term Adjustment Strategy. In *Ukraine: Accelerating the Transition to Market*, eds. Peter K. Cornelius and Patrick Lenain. Washington: International Monetary Fund.

Ekelund, Robert B., and Robert D. Tollison. 1981. *Mercantilism as a Rent-Seeking Society*. College Station: Texas A&M University Press.

Estrin, Saul, and Adam Rosevear. 1999. Enterprise Performance and Corporate Governance in Ukraine. *Journal of Comparative Economics* 27: 442–58.

EBA (European Business Association). 2004. *Barriers to Investment in Ukraine*. Kyiv.

EBRD (European Bank for Reconstruction and Development). 1994. *Transition Report 1994*. London.

EBRD (European Bank for Reconstruction and Development). 2000. *Transition Report 2000*. London.

EBRD (European Bank for Reconstruction and Development). 2007. *Transition Report 2007*. London.

EBRD (European Bank for Reconstruction and Development). 2008. Online Database. London.

EBRD (European Bank for Reconstruction and Development) and World Bank. 2002. *Business Environment and Enterprise Performance Survey (BEEPS)*. Available at www.worldbank.org (accessed on August 31, 2007).

EBRD (European Bank for Reconstruction and Development) and World Bank. 2005. *Business Environment and Enterprise Performance Survey (BEEPS)*. Available at www.worldbank.org (accessed on August 31, 2007).

European Commission. 2008. Eurostat Online Database. Available at http://epp.eurostat.ec.europa.eu (accessed on various dates).

Fischer, Stanley. 2005. *IMF Essays from a Time of Crisis: The International Financial System, Stabilization and Development*. Cambridge, MA: MIT Press.

Fischer, Stanley, and Ratna Sahay. 2000. *The Transition Economies after Ten Years*. IMF Working Paper 30. Washington: International Monetary Fund.

Fish, Steven. 2005. *Democracy Derailed in Russia: The Failure of Open Politics*. New York: Cambridge University Press.

Freedom House. 2008. *Freedom in the World 2008: Selected Data from Freedom House's Annual Global Survey on Political Rights and Civil Liberties*. Available at www.freedomhouse.org (accessed on October 10, 2008).

Freeland, Chrystia. 2000. *Sale of the Century: Russia's Wild Ride from Communism to Capitalism*. New York: Crown Business.

Frishberg, Alex. 2006. *The Steel Barons*. Kiev.

Frydman, Roman, Andrzej Rapaczynski, John S. Earle, et al. 1993. *The Privatization Process in Russia, Ukraine, and the Baltic States*. Budapest: Central European University Press.

Futey, Bohdan A. 1997. Comments on the Law on the Constitutional Court of Ukraine. *East European Constitutional Review* 6, no. 2–3.

Gaddy, Clifford G., and Barry W. Ickes. 1998. Russia's Virtual Economy. *Foreign Affairs* 77, no. 5: 53–67.

Gaidar, Yegor T. 1993. Inflationary Pressures and Economic Reform in the Soviet Union. In *Economic Transition in Eastern Europe*, ed. P. H. Admiraal. Oxford: Blackwell.

Gaidar, Yegor T. 1999. *Days of Defeat and Victory*. Seattle, WA: University of Washington Press.

Gaidar, Yegor T. 2007. *The Collapse of the Empire: Lessons for Modern Russia*. Washington: Brookings Institution.

Gambetta, Diego. 1993. *The Sicilian Mafia*. Cambridge, MA: Harvard University Press.

Garnett, Sherman. 1997. *The Keystone in the Arch*. Washington: Carnegie Endowment for International Peace.

German Advisory Group on Economic Reforms with the Ukrainian Government. 1999. *The Next 1,000 Days: An Economic Reform Agenda for Ukraine*. Kyiv.

Global Witness. 2006. *It's a Gas—Funny Business in the Turkmen-Ukraine Gas Trade*. Washington: Global Witness Publishing.

Goldgeier, James M., and Michael McFaul. 2003. *Power and Purpose: U.S. Policy toward Russia after the Cold War*. Washington: Brookings Institution.

Gongadze, Heorhiy. 2000. Everything about Aleksandr Volkov. *Ukrainska Pravda*, September 5. Available at www.pravda.com.ua.

Góralska, Helena. 2000. Funding of Social Benefits and the Social Service System in Ukraine. In *Economic Reform in Ukraine: The Unfinished Agenda*, eds. Anders Áslund and Georges de Ménil. Armonk, NY: M. E. Sharpe.

Gorbachev, Mikhail S. 1987a. *Izbrannye rechi i stati* [*Selected Speeches and Articles*], vol. 3. Moscow: Politizdat.

Gorbachev, Mikhail S. 1987b. *Perestroika: New Thinking for Our Country and the World*. New York: Harper & Row.

Goskomstat SSSR (State Committee of Statistics of the USSR). 1991. *Narodnoe Khoziaystvo SSSR v 1990g* [*USSR Economy in 1990*]. Moscow: Finansy i Statistika.

Goskomstat. 2006. *Rossiisky statistichesky yezhegodnik 2006* [*Russian Statistical Yearbook 2006*]. Moscow.

Granville, Brigitte. 1995. So Farewell then Rouble Zone. In *Russian Economic Reform at Risk*, ed. Anders Åslund. New York: St. Martin's Press.

Granville, Brigitte. 2002. The IMF and the Ruble Zone: Response to Odling-Smee and Pastor. *Comparative Economic Studies* 44, no. 4: 3–29.

Grygorenko, Yegor, Yuriy Gorodnichenko, and Dmytro Ostanin. 2006. *Relative Property Rights in Transition Economies: Can the Oligarchs Be Productive?* Working Paper no. 4. Moscow: Economics Education and Research Consortium.

Havrylyshyn, Oleh. 2000. The Political Economy of Delayed Reform in Ukraine. In *Ukraine: The Search for National Identity*, eds. Sharon Wolchik and V. Zvigliyanich. Lanham, MD: Rowman & Littlefield.

Havrylyshyn, Oleh. 2003. What Makes Ukraine Not Grow? Political Economic and Historical Factors that Hamper Economic Growth. In *Society in Transition. Social Change in Ukraine in Western Perspectives*, ed. Wsevolod W. Isajiw. Toronto: Canadian Scholars Press.

Havrylyshyn, Oleh. 2006. *Diverging Paths in Post-Communist Transformation: Capitalism for All or Capitalism for the Few?* Basingstoke, UK, and New York: Palgrave Macmillan.

Havrylyshyn, Oleh, and Thomas Wolf. 2001. Growth in Transition Countries, 1990–1998: The Main Lessons. In *A Decade of Transition: Achievements and Challenges*, eds. Oleh Havrylyshyn and Saleh M. Nsouli. Washington: International Monetary Fund.

Hellman, Joel S. 1998. Winners Take All: The Politics of Partial Reform in Postcommunist Transitions. *World Politics* 50, no. 2: 203–34.

Hellman, Joel S., Geraint Jones, Daniel Kaufmann, and Mark Schankermann. 2000. Measuring Governance and State Capture: The Role of Bureaucrats and Firms in Shaping the Business Environment. European Bank for Reconstruction and Development and World Bank, Washington. Photocopy.

Herron, Erik S. 2002. Causes and Consequences of Fluid Faction Membership in Ukraine. *Europe-Asia Studies* 54, no. 4: 625–39.

Hinich, Melvin J., Valeri Khmelko, and Peter C. Ordershook. 1999. Ukraine's 1998 Parliamentary Elections: A Spatial Analysis. *Post-Soviet Affairs* 15, no. 2: 149–85.

Hirschman, Alfred. 1965. *Journeys toward Progress: Studies of Economic Policy-Making in Latin America*. Garden City, NY: Doubleday.

Hoffman, David. 2002. *The Oligarchs*. New York: Public Affairs.

ICPS (International Center for Policy Studies). 1999a. *Business Opinion Review* 5 (July). Kyiv.

ICPS (International Center for Policy Studies). 1999b. New Economic Legislation, 1998–1999. *Policy Studies* (July-August). Kyiv.

IMF (International Monetary Fund). 1992. The Coordination of Monetary Policy in the Ruble Area. Washington. Photocopy (April 29).

IMF (International Monetary Fund). 1993. *Economic Review: Ukraine 1993*. Washington.

IMF (International Monetary Fund). 1994. *Economic Review: Trade Policy Reform in Countries of the Former Soviet Union*. Washington.

IMF (International Monetary Fund). 1995. *Economic Review: Ukraine 1994*. Washington.

IMF (International Monetary Fund). 2000a. Allegations about the Use of Ukraine's International Reserves. News Brief no. 00/15 (March 14). Washington.

IMF (International Monetary Fund). 2000b. Release of PriceWaterhouseCoopers Report on the National Bank of Ukraine. News Brief no. 00/26 (May 4). Washington.

IMF (International Monetary Fund). 2008. *World Economic Outlook* (April). Washington.

Johnson, Simon, Daniel Kaufmann, and Andrei Shleifer. 1997. The Unofficial Economy in Transition. *Brookings Papers on Economic Activity* 27, no. 2: 159–239. Washington: Brookings Institution.

Johnson, Simon, John McMillan, and Christopher Woodruff. 2000. Entrepreneurs and the Ordering of Institutional Reform: Poland, Slovakia, Romania, Russia and Ukraine Compared. *Economics of Transition* 8, no. 1: 1–36.

Karatnycky, Adrian. 2005. Ukraine's Orange Revolution. *Foreign Affairs* 84, no. 2: 35–52.

Karatnycky, Adrian. 2006. The Fall and Rise of Ukraine's Political Opposition: From Kuchmagate to the Orange Revolution. In *Revolution in Orange: The Origins of Ukraine's Democratic Breakthrough*, eds. Anders Åslund and Michael McFaul. Washington: Carnegie Endowment for International Peace.

Kaufmann, Daniel. 1995. Diminishing Returns to Administrative Controls and the Emergence of the Unofficial Economy: A Framework of Analysis and Applications to Ukraine. *Economic Policy* 19 (supplement): 52–69.

Kaufmann, Daniel. 1997. Corruption: Some Myths and Facts. *Foreign Policy* 107: 114–31.

Kaufmann, Daniel, and Aleksander Kaliberda. 1996. Integrating the Unofficial Economy into the Dynamics of Post-Socialist Economies: A Framework of Analysis and Evidence. In *Economic Transition in Russia and the New States of Eurasia*, ed. Bartlomiej Kaminski. Armonk, NY: M. E. Sharpe.

Kornai, János. 1992. *The Socialist System. The Political Economy of Communism.* Princeton, NJ: Princeton University Press.

Krasnov, Gregory, and Josef Brada. 1997. Implicit Subsidies in Russia-Ukrainian Energy Trade. *Europe-Asia Studies* 49, no. 5: 825–43.

Kravchuk, Leonid. 2001. Pokhorony Imperii [Funeral of Empire]. *Zerkalo nedeli*, no. 32 (August 23–September 1).

Kravchuk, Robert S. 1999. The Quest for Balance: Regional Self-Government and Subnational Fiscal Policy in Ukraine. In *State and Institution-Building in Ukraine*, eds. Taras Kuzio, Robert S. Kravchuk, and Paul D'Anieri. New York: St. Martin's Press.

Kravchuk, Robert S. 2002. *Ukrainian Political Economy: The First Ten Years*. New York: Palgrave Macmillan.

Krushelnycky, Askold. 2006. *An Orange Revolution: A Personal Journey through Ukrainian History*. London: Harvill Secker.

Kuchma, Leonid D. 1994a. Ukraine's Blueprint. *Financial Times*, September 30.

Kuchma, Leonid D. 1994b. Zvernennia Prezydenta Ukrayiny do Verkhovnoyi Rady. [Address of the President of Ukraine to Verkhovna Rada]. *Uryadovyi kur'er*, October 11.

Kuchma, Leonid D. 2003. *Ukraina- ne Rossiia* [*Ukraine is not Russia*]. Moscow: Vremia.

Kuchma, Leonid D. 2007. *Posle Maydana* [*After Maydan*]. Moscow: Vremia.

Kuzio, Taras. 1997. *Ukraine under Kuchma*. New York: St. Martin's Press.

Kuzio, Taras. 2004. Oligarch's Privatize Ukraine before Elections. *Jamestown Eurasia Daily Monitor* (June 17).

Kuzio, Taras. 2006. Oligarchs into Businessmen: Ukraine's Transition to the Post-Kuchma Era. Contemporary Change in Ukraine. *Baltic and East European Studies* 5: 10–34.

Kuzio, Taras, [and Andrew Wilson]. 2000 [1994]. *Ukraine: Perestroika to Independence.* New York: St. Martin's Press.

Larrabee, Stephen F. 1996. Ukraine's Balancing Act. *Survival* 38, no. 2: 143–65.

Lerman, Zvi. 1999. Land Reform and Farm Restructuring in Ukraine. *Problems of Post-Communism* 46, no. 3 (May/June): 42–55.

Lieven, Dominic. 2000. *Empire: The Russian Empire and Its Rivals*. New Haven, CT: Yale University Press.

Linz, Juan. 1978. *The Breakdown of Democratic Regimes: Crisis, Breakdown, and Reequilibrium*. Baltimore, MD: Johns Hopkins University Press.

Linz, Juan. 1990. The Perils of Presidentialism. *Journal of Democracy* 1 (Winter): 51–71.

Lipset, Seymour Martin. 1959. Some Social Requisites of Democracy: Economic Development and Political Legitimacy. *American Political Science Review* 53, no. 1: 69–105.

Lovei, Laszlo. 1998a. Gas Reform in Ukraine: Monopolies, Markets, and Corruption. *Viewpoint*, no. 169. Washington: World Bank.

Lovei, Laszlo. 1998b. Electricity Reform in Ukraine: The Impact of Weak Governance and Budget Crises. *Viewpoint*, no. 168. Washington: World Bank.

Lovei, Laszlo and Konstantin Skonik. 1997. Commercializing of Ukraine's Energy Sector. In *Ukraine. Accelerating the Transition to Market*, eds. Peter K Cornelius and Patrick Lenain. Washington: International Monetary Fund.

Malysh, Nadia. 2000. Ukraine Needs a Fundamental Pension Reform. In *Economic Reform in Ukraine: The Unfinished Agenda*, eds. Anders Åslund and George de Ménil. Armonk, NY: M. E. Sharpe.

McFaul, Michael. 2001. *Russia's Unfinished Revolution: Political Change from Gorbachev to Putin*. Ithaca, NY: Cornell University Press.

McFaul, Michael. 2006a. Conclusion: The Orange Revolution in a Comparative Perspective. In *Revolution in Orange*, eds. Anders Åslund and Michael McFaul. Washington: Carnegie Endowment for International Peace.

McFaul, Michael. 2006b. *The 2004 Presidential Elections in Ukraine and the Orange Revolution: The Role of U.S. Assistance*. Washington: US Agency for International Development.

Mel'ota, Iryna, and Paul Gregory. 2001. *New Insights into Ukraine's Shadow Economy: Has it Already Been Counted?* Working Paper 11. Kyiv: Institute for Economic Research and Policy Consulting.

Michalopoulos, Constantine, and David G. Tarr. 1996. *Trade Performance and Policy in the New Independent States*. Washington: World Bank.

Milanovic, Branko. 1998. *Income, Inequality, and Poverty during the Transition from Planned to Market Economy*. Washington: World Bank.

Milcher, Susanne, Ben Slay, and Mark Collins. 2007. The Economic Rationale of the "European Neighborhood Policy." In *Europe after Enlargement*, eds. Anders Åslund and Marek Dabrowski. New York: Cambridge University Press.

Milov, Vladimir, and Boris Nemtsov. 2008. *Putin i Gazprom* [*Putin and Gazprom*]. Moscow.

Ministry of Statistics of Ukraine. Various years. *Economy of Ukraine*. Statistics Yearbook. Kyiv.

Montesquieu, Charles de Secondat. 1977 [1748]. *The Spirit of Laws*. Berkeley: University of California Press.

Morck, Randall, Daniel Wolfenzon, and Bernard Yeung. 2005. Corporate Governance, Economic Entrenchment, and Growth. *Journal of Economic Literature* 43, no. 3: 655–720.

Motyl, Alexander J. 1980. *The Turn to the Right: The Ideological Origins and Development of Ukrainian Nationalism, 1919–1929*. New York: Columbia University Press.

Motyl, Alexander J. 2003. Making Ukraine, and Remaking It. The Petryshyn Memorial Lecture, Harvard University, April 14. In *Harvard Papers in Ukrainian Studies*.

Murphy, Kevin A., Andrei Shleifer, and Robert W. Vishny. 1992. The Transition to a Market Economy: Pitfalls of Partial Reform. *Quarterly Journal of Economics* 57, no. 3: 889–903.

Murphy, Kevin A., Andrei Shleifer, and Robert W. Vishny. 1993. Why Is Rent-Seeking So Costly to Growth? *American Economic Review* 83, no. 2: 409–14.

OECD (Organization for Economic Cooperation and Development). 2004. Improving the Conditions for Enterprise Development and the Investment Climate for Domestic and International Investors in Ukraine: Legal Issues with Regard to Business Operations and Investment. Washington and Kiev. Photocopy.

Odling-Smee, John, and Gonzalo Pastor. 2002. The IMF and the Ruble Area, 1991–1993. *Comparative Economic Studies* 44, no. 4: 3–29.

Olcott, Martha Brill, Anders Åslund, and Sherman Garnett. 1999. *Getting It Wrong*. Washington: Carnegie Endowment for International Peace.

O'Loughlin, John, and James E. Bell. 1999. The Political Geography of Civic Engagement in Ukraine. *Post-Soviet Geography and Economics* 40, no. 4: 233–66.

Orlowski, Lucjan. 1993. Indirect Transfers in Trade among Former Soviet Union Republics: Sources, Patterns and Policy Responses in the Post-Soviet Period. *Europe-Asia Studies* 45, no. 6: 1001–24.

Paskhaver, Alexander. 1999. Bureaucratic Capitalism Is Being Created in Ukraine. *ICPS Newsletter*, no. 10 (March 22).

Paskhaver, Alexander, and Lidiya Verkhovodova. 2006. *Privatizaciya do i posle oranzhevoy revolucii* [*Privatization before and after the Orange Revolution*]. Kyiv: CASE Ukraine.

Pasvolsky, Leo. 1928. *Economic Nationalism of the Danubian States*. London: George Allen & Unwin.

Perotti, Enrico C., and Stanislav Gelfer. 2001. Red Barons or Robber Barons? Governance and Investment in Russian Financial-Industrial Groups. *European Economic Review* 45: 1601–17.

Petrov, Nikolai, and Andrei Ryabov. 2006. Russia's Role in the Orange Revolution. In *Revolution in Orange*, eds. Anders Åslund and Michael McFaul. Washington: Carnegie Endowment for International Peace.

Pifer, Steven. 2004. Ukraine's Future and U.S. Interests. Testimony before the House International Relations Committee, Subcommittee on Europe. US Department of State, Washington. Available at www.state.gov (accessed on July 10, 2008).

Pifer, Steven. 2008. Ukraine and NATO at the Bucharest Summit. Testimony before the United States Commission on Security and Cooperation in Europe. Available at www.csce.gov (accessed on July 29, 2008).

Pinto, Brian, Vladimir Drebentsov, and Alexander Morozov. 1999. *Dismantling Russia's Nonpayments System: Creating Conditions for Growth*. Report by the World Bank, Moscow (September).

Pipes, Richard. 2005. *Russian Conservatism and Its Critics: A Study in Political Culture*. New Haven, CT: Yale University Press.

Prizel, Ilya. 1997. Ukraine between Proto-Democracy and "Soft" Authoritarianism. In *Democratic Changes and Authoritarian Reactions in Russia, Ukraine, Belarus and Moldova*, eds. Karen Dawisha, and Bruce Parrott. Cambridge: Cambridge University Press.

Protsyk, Oleh. 2004. Ruling with Decrees: Presidential Decree Making in Russia and Ukraine. *Europe-Asia Studies* 56, no. 5: 637–60.

Prytula, Olena. 2006. The Ukrainian Media Rebellion. In *Revolution in Orange*, eds. Anders Åslund and Michael McFaul. Washington: Carnegie Endowment for International Peace.

Puglisi, Rosaria. 2003. The Rise of the Ukrainian Oligarchs. *Democratization* 10, no. 3: 99–123.

Pynzenyk, Viktor. 1999. *Koni ne vinovaty: Reformy ili ikh imitatsiya* [*Horses Are Not Guilty: Reforms or Their Imitation*]. Kyiv: Akademia.

Pynzenyk, Viktor. 2000. How to Find a Path for Ukrainian Reforms. In *Economic Reform in Ukraine: The Unfinished Agenda*, eds. Anders Åslund and Georges de Ménil. Armonk, NY: M. E. Sharpe.

Remington, Thomas F., Steven S. Smith, and Moshe Haspel. 1998. Decrees, Laws, and Inter-Branch Relations in the Russian Federation. *Post-Soviet Affairs* 14, no. 4: 287–322.

Roeder, Phil G. 1994. Varieties of Post-Soviet Authoritarian Regimes. *Post-Soviet Affairs* 10, no. 1: 61–101.

Rostowski, Jacek. 1993. The Inter-Enterprise Debt Explosion in the Former Soviet Union: Causes, Consequences, Cures. *Communist Economies and Economic Transformation* 5, no. 2: 131–59.

Rostowski, Jacek. 1994. *Interenterprise Arrears in Post Communist Economies*. IMF Working Paper (April). Washington: International Monetary Fund.

Rossiiskaya Federatsiya. 1999. Federalny Zakon o Ratifikatsii Dogovora o Dryzhbe, Sotrudnichestve i Partnerstve mezhdu Rossiiskoi Federatsiei i Ukrainoi [Federal Law on the

Ratification of the Treaty on Friendship, Cooperation and Partnership between the Russian Federation and Ukraine], March 2. Available at www.akdi.ru (accessed at August 28, 2008).

Rustow, Dankwart. 1970. Transitions to Democracy: Toward a Dynamic Model. *Comparative Politics* 2, no. 3: 337–64.

Sachs, Jeffrey D., and David A. Lipton. 1993. Remaining Steps to a Market-Based Monetary System. In *Changing the Economic System in Russia*, eds. Anders Åslund and Richard Layard. New York: St. Martin's Press.

Sargent, Thomas J. 1986. The Ends of Four Big Inflations. In *Rational Expectations and Inflation*, ed. Thomas J. Sargent. New York: Harper and Row.

Shapiro, Judith. 1995. The Rising Mortality Crisis and its Causes. In *Russian Economic Reform at Risk*, ed. Anders Åslund. New York: St. Martin's Press.

Sherr, James. 1997. Russia-Ukraine Rapprochement? The Black Sea Fleet Accords. *Survival* 39, no. 3: 33–50.

Shkolnikov, V. M., E. M. Andreev, and T. M. Maleva. 2000. *Neravenstvo pered litsom smerti v Rossii* [*Inequality Facing Death in Russia*]. Moscow: Carnegie Moscow Center.

Shleifer, Andrei. 2005. *A Normal Country: Russia after Communism*. Cambridge, MA: Harvard University Press.

Shleifer, Andrei, and Daniel Treisman. 2000. *Without a Map: Political Tactics and Economic Reform in Russia*. Cambridge, MA: MIT Press.

Shleifer, Andrei, and Robert W. Vishny. 1993. Corruption. *Quarterly Journal of Economics* 108, no. 3: 599–617.

Shleifer, Andrei, and Robert W. Vishny. 1998. *The Grabbing Hand: Government Pathologies and Their Cures*. Cambridge, MA: Harvard University Press.

Shpek, Roman. 2000. Priorities of Reform. *Russian and East European Finance and Trade* 36, no. 1: 7–27.

Siedenberg, Axel, and Lutz Hoffmann, eds. 1999. *Ukraine at the Crossroads—Economic Reforms in International Perspective*. Frankfurt: Physica-Verlag.

Solchanyk, Roman. 2001. *Ukraine and Russia: the Post-Soviet Transition*. Lanham, MD, and Oxford: Rowman & Littlefield Publishers.

Sonin, Konstantin. 2003. Why the Rich May Favor Poor Protection of Property Rights. *Journal of Comparative Economics* 31: 715–31.

Soros, George. 1991. *Underwriting Democracy*. New York: Free Press.

Stanislawski, Wojciech. 2005. *The Orange Ribbon. A Calendar of the Political Crisis in Ukraine (Autumn 2004)*. Warsaw: Centre for Eastern Studies.

State Property Fund of Ukraine. 1996. *Mass Privatization in Ukraine: Results and Projections*. Kyiv.

State Statistics Committee of Ukraine. Various years. *Statistical Yearbook of Ukraine*. Kyiv.

Steele, Gordon John. 2004. *An Empire of Wealth: The Epic History of American Economic Power*. New York: HarperCollins.

Stern, Jonathan P. 2005. *The Future of Russian Gas and Gazprom*. Oxford: Oxford University Press.

Stern, Jonathan. 2006. *The Russian-Ukrainian Gas Crisis of January 2006*. Oxford: Oxford Institute for Energy Studies.

Stiglitz, Joseph E. 1999. Whither Reform? Ten Years of Transition. Paper presented at the Annual World Bank Conference on Development Economics, Washington, April 28–30.

Stiglitz, Joseph E. 2002. *Globalization and Its Discontents*. New York: Norton.

Subtelny, Orest. 2005 [1988]. *Ukraine: A History*. Toronto, Buffalo, and London: University of Toronto Press.

Sushko, Oleksandr. 2006. *Ukraine-EU Relations after the Parliamentary Elections—2006*. Kyiv: Center for Peace, Conversation, and Foreign Policy of Ukraine.

Szporluk, Roman. 1994. Reflections on Ukraine after 1994: The Dilemmas of Nationhood. *The Harriman Review* 7, no. 7–9: 1–10

Tanzi, Vito, and Hamid Davoodi. 1997. *Corruption, Public Investment, and Growth*. IMF Working Paper 139. Washington: International Monetary Fund.

Tanzi, Vito, and Ludger Schuknecht. 2000. *Public Spending in the 20th Century*. Cambridge: Cambridge University Press.

Tanzi, Vito, and George Tsibouris. 2000. *Fiscal Reform over Ten Years of Transition*. IMF Working Paper 113. Washington: International Monetary Fund.

Tarr, David G. 1994. The Terms-of-Trade Effects of Moving to World Prices on Countries of the Former Soviet Union. *Journal of Comparative Economics* 18, no. 1: 1–24.

Teriokhin, Serhyi. 2000. Tax Policy. In *Economic Reform in Ukraine: the Unfinished Agenda*, eds. Anders Åslund and Georges de Ménil. Armonk, NY: M. E. Sharpe.

Teylan, Christine, and Thane Gustafson. 2006. Russia and Ukraine's New Gas Agreement: What Does it Mean and How Long Will It Last? *CERA Decision Brief* (January). Cambridge Energy Research Associates, Inc.

Thiessen, Ulrich. 2001. *Presumptive Taxation for Small Enterprises in Ukraine*. Working Paper 6. Kyiv: Institute for Economic Research and Policy Consulting.

Timoshenko, Viktor. 1998. Vse bogatye lyudi Ukrainy zarabotali svoy kapital na rossiyskom gaze [All Rich People in Ukraine Made Their Capital on Russian Gas]. *Nezavisimaya gazeta*, October 16.

Transparency International. 2008. Corruption Perceptions Index. Available at http://transparency.org (accessed on October 13, 2008).

Truman, Edwin M. 2003. *Inflation Targeting in the World Economy*. Washington: Institution for International Economics.

UNECE (UN Economic Commission for Europe). 1993. *Economic Survey of Europe, 1992–1993*. New York: United Nations.

UNECE (UN Economic Commission for Europe). 2004. *Economic Survey of Europe*, no. 2. New York: United Nations.

UNECE (UN Economic Commission for Europe). 2007. Statistical Database. Available at www.unece.org (accessed on various dates).

UNESCO Institute for Statistics. 2008. *Public Report on Education*. Available http://stats.uis.unesco.org (accessed on July 30, 2008).

UNICEF. 2008. TransMONEE Database. Florence: UNICEF Innocenti Research Center. Available at www.unicef-icdc.org/resources/transmonee.html (accessed on September 28, 2008).

Volkov, Vadim. 2002. *Violent Entrepreneurs: The Use of Force in the Making of Russian Capitalism*, Ithaca, NY: Cornell University Press.

Von Cramon-Taubadel, Stephan, and Iryna Akimova, eds. 2002. *Fostering Sustainable Growth in Ukraine*. Heidelberg: Physica-Verlag.

Von Cramon-Taubadel, Stephan, and Sergiy Zorya. 2000. *Agricultural Aspects of Ukrainian Membership in the WTO*. Kyiv: Institute for Economic Research and Policy Consulting.

Von Hirschhausen, Christian. 1999. Gas Sector Restructuring in Ukraine: Import Dependence, Price Formation, and Socio-Economic Effects. In *Ukraine at the Crossroads—Economic Reform in International Perspective*, eds. Axel Siedenberg and Lutz Hoffmann. Heidelberg, Germany, and New York: Springer-Physica.

Von Hirschhausen, Christian, and Volkhart Vincentz. 2000. Energy Policy and Structural Reform. In *Economic Reform in Ukraine: The Unfinished Agenda*, eds. Anders Åslund and Georges de Ménil. Armonk, NY: M. E. Sharpe.

Wagstyl, Stefan, and Tom Warner. 2006. How the British Connection Helped the Rise of Dmytro Firtash ROSUKRENERGO. *Financial Times*, April 29.

Whitmore, Sarah. 2004. *State Building in Ukraine: The Ukrainian Parliament, 1990–2003*. New York: Routledge.

Williamson, John. 1995. Ukraine's Application for Membership of WTO. Remarks at a conference on Evolution of Ukraine's GATT/WTO Membership and Alternatives," IIASA, Laxenburg, Austria, July 2–4.

Williamson, Oliver E. 1975. *Markets and Hierarchies*, New York: Free Press.

Wilson, Andrew. 2002 [2000]. *The Ukrainians. Unexpected Nation*. New Haven, CT: Yale University Press.

Wilson, Andrew. 2005. *Ukraine's Orange Revolution*. New Haven, CT: Yale University Press.

Wolczuk, Roman. 2002. *Ukraine's Foreign and Security Policy 1991-2000*. Basees/Curzon Series on Russian and East European Studies. New York: RoutledgeCurzon.

World Bank. 1994. *Averting the Old Age Crisis: Policies to Protect the Old and Promote Growth*. Oxford: Oxford University Press.

World Bank. 2005. *Growth, Poverty, and Inequality: Eastern Europe and the Former Soviet Union*. Washington.

World Bank. 2008. *World Development Indicators*. Washington. Available at http://devdata.worldbank.org (accessed on various dates).

World Bank and International Finance Corporation. 2008. *Doing Business in 2009: Creating Jobs*. Washington: World Bank. Available at www.doingbusiness.org (accessed on October 20, 2008).

Yekhanurov, Yuri I. 2000. The Progress of Privatization. In *Economic Reform in Ukraine: The Unfinished Agenda*, eds. Anders Åslund and Georges de Ménil. Armonk, NY: M. E. Sharpe.

Yeltsin, Boris. 1994. *The Struggle for Russia*. New York: Crown.

Yushchenko, Viktor. 2000. Monetary Policy in the Transition to a Market Economy. *Russian and East European Finance and Trade* 36, no. 1: 94–110.

Yushchenko, Viktor. 2004. Speech at the European Square, Kyiv, September 18. In *Ukrainska Pravda*. Available at www.pravda.com.ua.

Zimmer, Kerstin. 2003. The Captured Region, Actors and Institutions in the Ukrainian Donbass. In *Making Regions in Post-Socialist Europe: The Impact of History, Economic Structure and Institutions*, ed. Melanie Tatur. Opladen, Germany: Leske & Budrich.

Brief Biographies of Leading Politicians and Businessmen

Akhmetov, Rinat L. Born in 1966. Graduated as an economist from Donetsk State University (2001). Major owner of System Capital Management (founded in 2000). Owner of Shakhtyar Donetsk soccer club.

Azarov, Mykola Y. Born in 1947. Graduated as a geologist from Moscow State University (1971) and earned a doctorate in geology (1986). Deputy director of research institute for mining geology (1984–95), head of the State Tax Administration (1996–2000), first deputy prime minister (2002–05), and minister of finance (2006–07).

Bakai, Ihor M. Born in 1963. Russian citizen since 2005. In international search since 2005. Graduated as a forestry technician from Bereznivskiy College of Forestry (1982). Worked as a manager at a soccer club (early 1980s) and at a sawmill in Yakutia (1989–91). Head of Naftohaz Ukrainy (1998–2000) and of the presidential administration's property management (2003–04).

Baloha, Viktor I. Born in 1963. Gradated as a manager of merchandise from Lviv Trade and Industry Institute (1984). Senior merchandise manager (1984–92). Minister of extraordinary situations (2005–06) and head of the secretariat of the president (since 2006).

Boiko, Yuriy A. Born in 1958. Gradated as an engineer from Moscow Institute of Chemistry and Technology (1981) and as an economist from East-Ukrainian University (2001). Chairman of Lysychansk Oil Refinery (1999–2001), of UkrTatNafta (2001–02), and of Naftohaz Ukrainy (2002–05).

Deputy minister of fuel and energy (2003–05) and minister of fuel and energy (2006–07).

Derkach, Leonid V. Born in 1939. Graduated as an engineer from Dnipropetrovsk State University. Attended KGB Program in Minsk (1973). Member of KGB administration (1972–92), head of the Customs Service (1996–98), and chairman of the Security Services of Ukraine (1998–2001).

Fokin, Vitold P. Born in 1932. Graduated from Donetsk Mining Institute (1954) and earned a doctorate in technical sciences. Held top management positions at mines in Luhansk oblast (1954–63). Head of the Council of Ministers of the Ukrainian Soviet Socialist Republic (1990–91) and Ukraine's prime minister (1991–92).

Haiduk, Vitaliy A. Born in 1957. Graduated as an engineer-economist from Donetsk Polytechnic Institute (1980). Senior economist at Donetsk auto service company (1981–87). One of the founders and co-owner of Industrial Union of Donbas (founded in 1995). Minister of fuel and energy (2000–02), deputy prime minister for fuel and energy affairs (2002–03), and secretary of the State Council of Security and Defense (2006–07).

Holovatyi, Serhiy P. Born in 1954. Graduated with a degree in international law from Kyiv State University (1977) and earned a doctorate in law (1980). Senior fellow at the Institute of Social and Economic Issues of Foreign Countries (1986–90) and president of Ukrainian Legal Foundation (since 1992). Ukraine's minister of justice (1995–97 and 2005–06).

Kinakh, Anatoliy K. Born in 1954. Graduated from Leningrad Institute of Shipbuilding (1978). Worked as a shipyard worker and later promoted to shipyard manager (1978–90). Minister of industrial policy (1995–96), deputy prime minister for industrial affairs (1995–96), first deputy prime minister (1999 and 2005), prime minister (2001–02), presidential candidate (2004), secretary of the State Council of Security and Defense (2005–06), and minister of economy (2007).

Kolomoiskiy, Ihor V. Born in 1964. Graduated as an engineer from Dnipropetrovsk Institute of Metallurgy (1985). Major owner and managing partner of Privat Group (PrivatBank founded in 1992) and owner of Dnepr and KrivBass soccer clubs.

Kravchenko, Yuriy F. (1951–2005). Graduated from School of Ministry of Interior Affairs USSR (1978). Minister of interior affairs (1995–2001) and head of the State Tax Administration (2002–04).

Kravchuk, Leonid M. Born in 1934. Graduated as an economist from Kyiv State University (1958) and earned a doctorate in economics. Worked as a teacher at Chernivtsi Financial College (1958–60) and held various positions in the Ideological Department of the Central Committee of the Communist Party of Ukraine (1960–88). Chairman of the Supreme Rada (1990–91) and president of Ukraine (1991–94).

Kuchma, Leonid D. Born in 1938. Graduated as an engineer from Dnipropetrovsk State University (1960) and earned a doctorate in technical sciences. Was a professor, an engineer at Baikonur space center (1960–82), and a manager of Pivdenmash company (1986–92). Prime minister (1992–93) and president of Ukraine (1994–2004).

Lanovyi, Volodymyr T. Born in 1952. Graduated as an economist from Kyiv Institute of Economics (1973) and earned a doctorate in economics. Minister of property and entrepreneurship (1991–92), deputy prime minister and minister of economy (1992), presidential candidate (1994), and head of the State Property Fund (1997–98).

Lazarenko, Pavlo I. Born in 1953. Graduated from Dnipropetrovsk Institute of Agriculture (1978) and earned a doctorate in economics (1996). Worked as driver and senior agronomist at a *kolkhoz* (1970–85). Representative of the president in Dnipropetrovsk (1992–95). First deputy prime minister (1995–96) and prime minister (1996–97).

Lutsenko, Yuriy V. Born in 1964. Graduated as an engineer from Lviv Polytechnic Institute (1989). Worked as an engineer and constructor at Rivne GazTron plant (1989–96). Leader of the popular movement Ukraine without Kuchma (2001). Minister of interior affairs (2005–06 and since 2007).

Lytvyn, Volodymyr M. Born in 1956. Graduated as a historian from Kyiv State University (1978) and earned a doctorate in history (1995). Professor of history at Kyiv State University (1978–90 and since 2006). Head of the presidential administration of the (1999–2002) and speaker of the Supreme Rada (2002–06).

Marchuk, Yevhen K. Born in 1941. Graduated as a teacher from Kirovograd Pedagogical Institute (1963) and earned a doctorate of law. KGB officer (1963–91); minister of defense, national security, and extraordinary situations (1991); chairman of the Security Services of Ukraine (1991–94); first deputy prime minister (1994–95); prime minister (1995–96); presidential candidate (1999); secretary of the National Security and Defense Council (1999–2003); and minister of defense (2003–04).

Masol, Vitaliy A. Born in 1928. Graduated as an engineer from Kyiv Polytechnic Institute (1951) and earned a doctorate in technical sciences (1972). Senior manager at Kramatorsk machine-building factory (1951–71). Prime minister of Ukraine (1987–90 and 1994–95).

Medvedchuk, Viktor V. Born in 1954. Graduated with a law degree from Kyiv State University (1978) and earned a doctorate of jurisprudence. Was a lawyer (1978–91) and chairman of the Association of Lawyers of Ukraine (1990–97). Deputy speaker (1998–2000), first deputy speaker of the Supreme Rada (2000–01), head of the administration of the president (2002–05), and a leading oligarch.

Mitiukov, Ihor O. Born in 1952. Graduated as a mathematician-economist from Kyiv State University (1978) and earned a doctorate in economics. Held various academic positions at the Institute of Economics (1975–90). Deputy prime minister for banking and finance (1994–95), representative of the Ukrainian government in the European Union with special powers of deputy prime minister (1995–97), minister of finance (1997–2001), and ambassador of Ukraine in the United Kingdom (2002–05).

Moroz, Oleksandr O. Born in 1944. Graduated as an engineer from the Academy of Agriculture (1965) and as a political scientist from the Highest Party School of Communist Party of Ukraine (1983). Worked as an engineer at the agricultural union of Taraschansk region and Kyiv oblast (1974–76). Head of the Socialist Party of Ukraine (since 1991), presidential candidate (1999 and 2004), and speaker of the Supreme Rada (1994–98 and 2006–07).

Pinchuk, Victor M. Born in 1960. Graduated as an engineer from Dnipropetrovsk Institute of Metallurgy (1983) and earned a doctorate in engineering (1987). Worked as an engineer at various pipe plants (1981–83). Founder and major owner of the Interpipe Group (founded in 1990; renamed EastOne in 2007).

Poroshenko, Petro O. Born in 1965. Graduated as international economist from Kyiv State University (1989) and earned a doctorate of law (2002). Held top management positions at various industrial companies (since 1990). Major owner of UkrPromInvest Group (founded in 1993). Secretary of the National Security and Defense Council (2005) and chairman of the Council of the National Bank of Ukraine (since 2007).

Pustovoitenko, Valeriy P. Born in 1947. Graduated as an engineer from Dnipropetrovsk Institute of Construction and Engineering (1975) and earned a doctorate in technical sciences. Worked as a turner at Odessa factory in the 1960s. Mayor of Dnipropetrovsk (1989–93), minister of the cabinet of ministers (1993, 1994), prime minister (1997–99), and minister of transport (2001–02).

Pynzenyk, Viktor M. Born in 1954. Graduated as an economist from Lviv State University (1975) and earned a doctorate in economics (1989). Held academic positions at Lviv State University (1975–92). Minister of economy, deputy prime minister for economy (1992–93), first deputy prime minister, deputy prime minister for economic reform (1994–96), deputy prime minister (1996–97), and minister of finance (2005–06 and since 2007).

Rybachuk, Oleh B. Born in 1958. Graduated as a translator from Kyiv State University (1980) and as an economist from Kyiv Institute of Economics (1996). Translator at the Indian branch of ZakordonNaftoBud (1986–91). Head of the foreign affairs department of the National Bank of Ukraine (1992–99). Head of the office of Prime Minister Viktor Yushchenko (1999–2001). Deputy prime minister for European integration (2005) and head of the secretariat of the president (2005–06).

Shpek, Roman V. Born in 1954. Graduated as an engineer from Lviv Institute of Forestry (1976) and earned an MBA degree from the International Institute of Management. Worked on various positions in forestry industry (1976–92). Minister of privatization and demonopolization of production (1992) and minister of economy (1993–95).

Stelmakh, Volodymyr S. Born in 1939. Graduated from the Kyiv Institute of Economics (1967) and earned a doctorate in economics. Adviser to president-minister of the National Bank of Cuba (1981–86). Chairman of the National Bank of Ukraine (2000–02 and since 2004).

Symonenko, Petro M. Born in 1952. Graduated as an engineer from Donetsk Polytechnic Institute (1974) and with a degree in political science from Kyiv Institute of Political Science (1991). Head of the Communist Party of Ukraine (since 1993), runner-up in presidential election (1999), and presidential candidate (2004).

Tarasiuk, Borys I. Born in 1949. Graduated as an engineer from Kyiv College of Communication (1968) and with a degree in international relations from Kyiv State University (1975). Ambassador to Belgium, Netherlands, and Luxemburg (1995–98), head of Ukrainian mission to the North Atlantic Treaty Organization (1997), and minister of foreign affairs (1998–2000 and 2005–06).

Taruta, Serhiy O. Born in 1955. Graduated as an engineer from Zhdanov Institute of Metallurgy (1979) and as a manager of foreign trade from the Donetsk Academy of Administration (1999). Held various positions, including top management, at AzovStal factory (1979–95). Co-owner of Industrial Union of Donbas (founded in 1995) and owner of Donetsk Metallurg soccer club.

Tyhypko, Serhiy L. Born in 1960. Graduated as an engineer from Dnipropetrovsk Institute of Metallurgy (1982) and earned a doctorate in economics (1996). Chairman of PrivatBank (1992–97). Deputy prime minister for economic reform (1997), deputy prime minister for economy (1997–99), minister of economy (1999–2000), chairman of the National Bank of Ukraine (2002–04), and head of Viktor Yanukovych's presidential campaign (2004).

Tymoshenko, Yuliya V. Born in 1960. Graduated as an economist from Dnipropetrovsk State University (1984) and earned a doctorate in economics (1999). Worked as an engineer at Dnipropetrovsk machine-building plant (1984–88). Owner of a small business of video rentals (1988–91). Head and co-owner of Yedyni Energetychni Systemy Ukrayiny (United Energy Systems of Ukraine) (1995–97). Deputy prime minister for fuel and energy (1999–2001) and prime minister (2005 and since 2007).

Vitrenko, Natalia M. Born in 1951. Graduated as an economist from Kyiv Institute of Economics (1973) and earned a doctorate in economics (1994). Founder and head of the Progressive Socialist Party of Ukraine (since 1996) and presidential candidate (1999 and 2004).

Volkov, Oleksandr M. Born in 1948. Graduated as an engineer from the Kyiv Institute of Trade and Economics (1972) and with a law degree from the Academy of the State Tax Administration and earned a doctorate in political science (1998). Was in charge of Leonid Kuchma's presidential campaign (1999).

Yanukovych, Viktor F. Born in 1950. Graduated as an engineer from Donetsk Polytechnic Institute (1980) and as a master of international law from the Ukrainian Academy of Foreign Trade (2001) and earned a doctorate in economics. Worked as an electrician (1972) and held various top management positions in transportation companies of Yenakiieve and Donetsk (1976–96). Governor of Donetsk oblast (1997–2002), prime minister (2002–05 and 2006–07), and runner-up in presidential elections (2004).

Yatseniuk, Arseniy P. Born in 1974. Graduated with a law degree from Chernivtsi State University (1996) and a degree in accounting from Chernivtsi Institute of Trade and Economics (2001) and earned a doctorate in economics. Senior partner in a law firm (1992–97). Minister of economy of Crimea (2001–03), first deputy chairman of the National Bank of Ukraine (2005), minister of economy (2005–06), minister of foreign affairs (2007), and speaker of the Supreme Rada (since 2007).

Yekhanurov, Yuriy I. Born in 1948. Graduated as an economist from Kyiv Institute of Economics (1973) and earned a doctorate in economics. Held various positions in the construction industry (1967–91). Head of the State Property Fund (1994–97), minister of economy (1997), first deputy prime minister (1999–2001), prime minister (2005–06), and minister of defense (since 2007).

Yushchenko, Viktor A. Born in 1954. Graduated as an accountant from Ternopil Institute of Economics and Finance (1975) and earned a doctorate in economics. Was an accounting associate at a *kolkhoz* (1975) and held top management positions in various banks (1976–93). Chairman of the National Bank of Ukraine (1993–99), prime minister (1999–2001), and president of Ukraine (since 2004).

Zinchenko, Olexandr O. Born in 1957. Graduated as a teacher from Chernivtsi State University (1975) and a political scientist from Moscow Academy of Social Science (1992) and earned a doctorate in physics (1982). CEO (1995–98) and president (1998–2002) of Inter TV channel. Deputy speaker of the Supreme Rada (2002–05) and head of the secretariat of the president (2005).

Zviahilskiy, Yukhym L. Born in 1933. Graduated as an engineer from Donetsk Industrial Institute (1956) and earned a doctorate in technical sciences. Director of Zasiadko mine (1979–92). First deputy prime minister (1993) and acting prime minister (1993–94).

Sources: Open media sources (see www.file.liga.net for details) and official websites of Ukraine's government, www.kmu.gov.ua (accessed on August 15, 2008), and parliament, www.rada.gov.ua (accessed on August 15, 2008).

Chronology

Date	Event
1990	
March 4	Parliamentary elections; communists retain power
July 16	Parliament adopts Declaration of State Sovereignty
October	Prime Minister Vitaliy Masol resigns because of hunger-striking students; Vitold Fokin becomes prime minister
November 19	Boris Yeltsin and Leonid Kravchuk sign the Treaty on the Basic Principles of Relations between Russia and Ukraine
1991	
March 17	Referendum on the future of the USSR
August 1	US President George H. W. Bush makes "Chicken Kiev" speech in the Ukrainian parliament
August 19–21	Abortive Moscow coup
August 24	Ukraine declares independence
August 30	Communist Party of Ukraine is prohibited

(chronology continues next page)

Date	Event
December 1	National referendum supports Ukrainian independence; Leonid Kravchuk elected Ukraine's first president
December 8	Treaty between Belarus, Russia, and Ukraine dissolves the USSR
December 21	Eleven Soviet republics form the Commonwealth of Independent States in Alma-Ata
1992	
January 2	Russia liberalizes prices, forcing Ukraine to do the same
March 24	Parliament adopts Kravchuk and Oleksandr Yemelianov's economic reform program
March	Minister of Economy Volodymyr Lanovyi presents first market reform program
September 3	Ukraine joins the International Monetary Fund (IMF)
September 30	Kravchuk dismisses Prime Minister Fokin
October 13	Leonid Kuchma is confirmed as prime minister
November 18	Kuchma receives special powers on economic policy for six months
1993	
January 26	Viktor Yushchenko is appointed chairman of the National Bank of Ukraine (NBU)
February 7	Parliament ratifies Kuchma's economic reform program
June 16	Kravchuk issues presidential decree asserting control over government
June	Ten-day strike by coal miners in Donbas
June 23	Parliament rejects Kuchma's improved economic reform program
June 24	Russia and Ukraine conclude bilateral free trade agreement

Date	Event
August 31	Kuchma resigns
September	Ruble zone finally ends
September 22	Yukhym Zviahilskiy is appointed acting prime minister
September 24	Kravchuk and parliament agree to hold early parliamentary and presidential elections
October	Kravchuk attempts to return to command economy
1994	
January 14	Presidents Boris Yeltsin, Bill Clinton, and Leonid Kravchuk sign Trilateral Accord on Ukraine's denuclearization
February 3	The Rada ratifies START I
March 27	First round of parliamentary elections
April 10	Second round of parliamentary elections
June 16	Kravchuk appoints Vitaliy Masol prime minister
June 26	First round of presidential election
July 10	Second round of presidential election; Kuchma defeats Kravchuk
October 11	Kuchma's presidential address on radical market economic reform
October 26	First IMF credit is approved
October	Unified exchange rate is to be set by the Ukrainian Interbank Currency Exchange (UICE)
November	Parliament approves freeing of the exchange rate and liberalizing prices
November 22	The Rada ratifies the Nuclear Non-Proliferation Treaty (NPT)
November 20–23	Kuchma goes on official visit to Washington

(chronology continues next page)

Date	Event
1995	
March 1	Masol resigns and First Deputy Prime Minister Yevhen Marchuk is appointed acting prime minister
April 4	Kuchma holds his second annual address on "correction" of reforms
May 12	US President Bill Clinton visits Kyiv
June 8	Kuchma and Oleksandr Moroz sign constitutional agreement; Kuchma appoints Yevhen Marchuk prime minister
October 11	Parliament approves Marchuk's economic program of "corrected reforms"
1996	
April 19–20	G-7 meeting in Moscow on closure of Chornobyl nuclear power plant
May 27	Kuchma fires Marchuk and appoints Pavlo Lazarenko prime minister
June 28	New constitution is adopted
June	Ukraine frees itself of nuclear weapons
July 10	Parliament confirms Lazarenko as prime minister
July 16	Lazarenko escapes assassination attempt in Kyiv
August 24	Currency reform is announced with great fanfare
September 2–16	New Ukrainian currency hryvnia replaces *karbovanets*
October 15	Lazarenko presents Deputy Prime Minister Viktor Pynzenyk's three-year economic program to the Ukrainian parliament, which approves it
1997	
April 2	Parliament rejects tax reforms; Pynzenyk resigns as deputy prime minister
May 28	Ukraine and Russia sign agreement on the division of the former Soviet Black Sea Fleet
May 31	Kuchma and Yeltsin sign a friendship treaty between Russia and Ukraine

Date	Event
June 19	Kuchma dismisses Lazarenko
July 9	Kuchma signs NATO-Ukraine special partnership charter at Madrid summit
July 16	Valeriy Pustovoitenko is confirmed as prime minister
August 25	IMF approves one-year stand-by credit for Ukraine
October 10	Georgia, Ukraine, Azerbaijan, and Moldova establish GUAM in Strasbourg
1998	
March 1	Treaty on partnership and cooperation between Ukraine and the European Union comes into effect
March 29	Parliamentary elections
April 22	Former NBU Chairman Vadym Hetman is assassinated
August 17	Russian financial crisis leads to sharp hryvnia devaluation
September 4	IMF approves a three-year credit for Ukraine under the Extended Fund Facility
November	Kuchma rejects IMF advice to combat financial crisis, calling for currency controls, monetary expansion, and limits NBU independence
1999	
February 17	Parliament strips Lazarenko's immunity, and he is arrested in the United States three days later
March 25	Rukh leader Vyacheslav Chornovil dies in a car crash
July	Parliament agrees to deploy 800 soldiers for peace-keeping in Kosovo
October 31	First round of presidential election
November 14	Second round of presidential election; Kuchma is reelected

(chronology continues next page)

Date	Event
December	Kuchma abolishes collective farms; land to be divided among farm workers with the right to rent the land but not to sell it
December 14	Parliament fails to confirm Pustovoitenko as prime minister
December 22	Viktor Yushchenko is confirmed as prime minister
2000	
March	IMF accuses Ukraine of manipulating its currency reserves
April 6	Parliament adopts big economic reform package
June 5	Clinton meets Kuchma in Kyiv; Ukraine announces the closure of the Chornobyl nuclear power plant
September 16	Journalist Heorhiy Gongadze is murdered
November 28	Oleksandr Moroz publicizes a tape recording from Kuchma's office of illegal actions against Gongadze
December 15	Chornobyl nuclear power plant is shut down
2001	
January 19	Kuchma dismisses Deputy Prime Minister Yuliya Tymoshenko
February	Large demonstrations call for Kuchma's impeachment
February 13	Tymoshenko is arrested on charges of tax evasion
March 26	Kuchma dismisses Interior Minister Yuriy Kravchenko
March 27	Tymoshenko is released from detention
April 26	Parliament sacks Yushchenko's government through no-confidence vote
May 29	Anatoliy Kinakh is confirmed as prime minister

Date	Event
2002	
March 31	Parliamentary elections
April 15	Evidence is made public that Kuchma authorized the sale of Kolchuga radar to Iraq in violation of UN sanctions
September 16	Large demonstration in Kyiv demands Kuchma's resignation
November 16	Kuchma dismisses Kinakh's government
November 21	Viktor Yanukovych becomes prime minister
December 17	Serhiy Tyhypko is appointed chairman of NBU
2003	
May	Ukraine reforms tax code, introducing 13 percent flat income tax
October	Border dispute with Russia erupts on the island of Tuzla
December 30	Ukraine's Constitutional Court rules that Kuchma can run for a third five-year term
2004	
June	Victor Pinchuk and Rinat Akhmetov buy steelworks Kryvorizhstal
July 26	Russian President Vladimir Putin meets Kuchma and Yanukovych in Yalta
September 5	Yushchenko is poisoned
October 26–29	Putin meets Kuchma in Kyiv and campaigns for Yanukovych
October 31	First round of presidential election; Yushchenko wins with slight margin
November 12–13	Putin meets Kuchma
November 21	Second round of presidential election; Yanukovych wins; Yushchenko claims election rigged
November 22	Mass demonstration in Kyiv against rigged election starts Orange Revolution

(chronology continues next page)

Date	Event
November 28	Regional leaders in eastern Ukraine call for a referendum on federation in Severodonetsk
December 1	Parliament votes no confidence in Yanukovych's government; Yanukovych refuses to step down
December 2	Kuchma meets Putin in a Moscow airport (12th meeting in 2004)
December 3	Ukraine's Supreme Court recognizes massive electoral fraud and orders a rerun of the second round
December 8	Parliament passes constitutional amendments and other legislative measures to resolve the presidential election crisis
December 26	Rerun of the second round of presidential election; Yushchenko wins
December 31	Yanukovych resigns as prime minister
2005	
January 20	Ukraine's Supreme Court rejects final appeal from Yanukovych
January 23	Yushchenko is sworn in as Ukraine's new president
January 24	Yushchenko nominates Yuliya Tymoshenko as prime minister; he makes first trip abroad to Moscow
February 4	Parliament confirms Tymoshenko as prime minister
February 21	The European Union and Ukraine sign action plan as part of the European Neighborhood Policy
February 23	Yushchenko addresses European parliament in Brussels
March 1	Ukraine announces the withdrawal of its troops from Iraq
March 4	Former minister of interior Yuriy Kravchenko is found dead

Date	Event
March 19	Putin meets Yushchenko in Kyiv
April 6	Yushchenko speaks to Joint Session of the US Congress in Washington
September 3	Yushchenko's chief of staff Oleksandr Zinchenko resigns
September 8	Yushchenko sacks both Tymoshenko's government and Secretary of National Security Petro Poroshenko
September 22	Yuriy Yekhanurov is approved as prime minister on second vote
October 24	Kryvorizhstal is reauctioned
December 1	The European Union grants Ukraine market economy status
2006	
January 1	New constitution comes into force transforming Ukraine into parliamentary-presidential republic; Russia cuts gas supply to Ukraine
January 4	Ukraine signs agreement on gas supply with Gazprom and RosUkrEnergo
January 10	Parliament votes no confidence in Yekhanurov's government, but the vote is declared unconstitutional
February 17	The United States recognizes Ukraine's market economy status
March 26	Parliamentary elections
June 22	Three Orange Revolution's parties agree to form a coalition government
July 6	Socialist Party switches to coalition with the Party of Regions, and Moroz is elected speaker of the parliament
August 3	Four parties sign Declaration of National Unity

(chronology continues next page)

Date	Event
August 4	Parliament confirms Yanukovych as prime minister
October 19	Four propresidential ministers resign after Our Ukraine votes against the ruling coalition
December 1	Parliament dismisses Interior Minister Yuriy Lutsenko and Foreign Minister Borys Tarasiuk for advocating strong ties with the European Union and NATO
2007	
January 30	Tarasiuk resigns
March 21	Parliament approves Yushchenko's choice for foreign minister Arseniy Yatseniuk
April 2	Yushchenko issues a decree to dismiss parliament and calls a snap election
May 27	Agreement is reached between Yushchenko, Yanukovych, and Moroz to hold early parliamentary election
September 30	Extraordinary parliamentary elections
December 18	Tymoshenko is appointed prime minister
2008	
January 15	Yushchenko, Tymoshenko, and Yatseniuk sign letter to NATO secretary general asking for membership action plan (MAP) for Ukraine
April 3–4	NATO summit in Bucharest does not offer MAP to Ukraine
April	Yushchenko blocks privatization by decree
May 16	Ukraine becomes 152nd member of the World Trade Organization
July 6	Two deputies leave coalition, which makes it one deputy shy of parliament majority
August 8–12	Russia-Georgia War in South Ossetia

Date	Event
September 2	Bloc of Yuliya Tymoshenko and the Party of Regions adopt the Law on the Cabinet of Ministers, weakening presidential authority
September 3	Our Ukraine faction withdraws from a coalition with Tymoshenko's Bloc
October 9	Yushchenko issues decree dissolving the parliament and calling for extraordinary parliamentary elections
October 26	Agreement between government and IMF on economic program supported by a US$16.5 billion loan
October 31	Parliament passes anticrisis legislation
November 5	IMF approves a two-year Stand-By Arrangement for US$16.5 billion to help Ukraine restore financial and economic stability

Abbreviations

BYuT	Bloc of Yuliya Tymoshenko
CEC	Central Election Commission
CES	Common Economic Space
CFE	Treaty on Conventional Armed Forces in Europe
CIS	Commonwealth of Independent States
CPI	consumer price index
CPSU	Communist Party of the Soviet Union
CPU	Communist Party of Ukraine
EBA	European Business Association
EBRD	European Bank for Reconstruction and Development
ENP	European Neighborhood Policy
EU	European Union
FDI	foreign direct investment
FSU	former Soviet Union
GDP	gross domestic product
GKChP	State Committee for the State of Emergency
GNP	gross national product
GUAM	regional organization of Georgia, Ukraine, Azerbaijan, and Moldova
ICBM	intercontinental ballistic missile
ICPS	International Center for Policy Studies
IMF	International Monetary Fund
IPO	initial public offering
ISD	Industrial Union of Donbas
KGB	Committee for State Security
MAP	membership action plan

NATO	North Atlantic Treaty Organization
NBU	National Bank of Ukraine
NKVD	People's Commissariat for Internal Affairs
NPT	Nuclear Non-Proliferation Treaty
OECD	Organization of Economic Cooperation and Development
OSCE	Organization of Security and Cooperation in Europe
OUN	Organization of Ukrainian Nationalists
PCA	partnership and cooperation agreements
PPP	purchasing power parity
RSFSR	Russian Soviet Federal Socialist Republic
RUE	RosUkrEnergo
SBU	Security Services of Ukraine
SCM	System Capital Management
START	Treaty on the Reduction and Limitation of Strategic Offensive Arms
UESU	United Energy Systems of Ukraine
UNA-UNSO	Ukrainian National Assembly and the Ukrainian National Self-Defense Force
UNECE	United Nations Economic Commission for Europe
UNICEF	United Nations Children's Fund
UPA	Ukrainian Insurgent Army
USAID	United States Agency for International Development
USSR	Union of Soviet Socialist Republics
VAT	value-added tax
WTO	World Trade Organization

Index

Andijan, massacre in, 104, 199
antidumping concerns, WTO accession and, 224–25
Anti-Monopoly Committee, 99
antitrust case, Microsoft, 110
apparatchiki caricature, 43
arbitrage
competitive oligarchy and growth, 6
Kuchma's reforms as president, 4, 74
oligarchs' rise and, 110, 112
Soviet economic reforms and crisis, 24–25
Zviahilskiy and rent seeking, 47
Arcelor, 163, 210
ArcelorMittal, 109*n*
armed forces. *See also specific entities*
crime and law enforcement, 115
democracy's survival as concern, 258
national independence and, 32, 35
Nikopol Ferroalloy Plant seizure, 206
parade celebrating liberation, 183
peacekeeping troops in Yugoslavia, 104, 172, 226
presidential election of 2004, 192, 194, 198
Russia's war in Georgia, 228
Tuzla incident, 171
Ukraine's liberation from Russia, 36–37, 39
Ukraine's turning to West, 9
Armenia
ENP and, 173*n*
hyperinflation and economic crisis, 49
population decline in, 235
presidential or parliamentary rule issue, 240
referendum on Soviet Union (1991), 22
Soviet Union dissolution, 31, 33*n*
WTO accession, 224
arms trade, 261
arrears. *See also* foreign debt; *specific aspects*
economic boom of 2004, 164
economic growth program and, 99
gas trade intricacies, 105
interenterprise arrears and payment system, 52
Kuchma's reforms as president, 61, 71, 90
lessons from Ukraine's transformation, 250
port facility leasing and, 102
presidential election of 2004, 184
Yushchenko's reforms, 126, 136, 138, 147
Asian financial crisis, 129, 229
audiovisual production, piracy in, 225
Austria
Putin's Ukrainian policy, 170
Russian gas embargo, 211
Autocephalous Orthodox Church, 14
Azarov, Mykola
CES launching and, 171
crime and law enforcement, 113, 115
parliamentary elections of 2006, 216
tax system and, 54
Yanukovych governments and, 161–62, 218–19
Yushchenko's ouster as prime minister, 146
Azerbaijan
ENP and, 173*n*
Kuchma's foreign policy, 105
oligarchs' impact, 252
Soviet Union dissolution, 31, 33*n*
Azov Sea, territorial dispute regarding, 101

Babakov, Aleksandr, 141
bailiffs, oligarchs' rise and, 111
Bakai, Ihor
bodyguards of, 113
gas trade intricacies, 106
Kuchma administration and, 87
oligarchs' rise, 107–08, 112
Orange Revolution aftermath, 201
parliamentary elections of 1998, 118
Yushchenko's ouster as prime minister, 145
Yushchenko's reforms, 138–39, 148–49
Baker, James, 36
Baloha, Viktor, 184, 217, 222–23, 231
Baltic states. *See also specific states*
awakening under Gorbachev, 16, 18
Baltic diaspora, 61
democracy's survival as concern, 254
history of Ukraine, 13
male life expectancy, 233
market reform in, 121
national independence and, 31–32
referendum on Soviet Union (1991), 22
Ukraine's liberation from Russia, 37
banking sector. *See also specific entities*
competitive oligarchy and growth, 6
currency reform, 76–77
hyperinflation and economic crisis, 54
Larenko's excesses, 96
oligarchs' impact, 253
oligarchs' rise, 109
renewed financial crisis, 229–30
rent seeking and early economic policy, 55
Soviet economic reforms and crisis, 24–27
Ukraine's liberation from Russia, 37

Yushchenko's reforms, 129, 131, 136, 139, 250
bank savings. *See* savings
barter and offsets
central-regional relations, 243
gas trade intricacies, 106
Kuchma's reforms as president, 69
Larenko's excesses, 94*n*
oligarchs' rise, 108
Russian gas embargo, 212–13
Yushchenko's reforms, 126, 135–36, 138
Batkivshchyna Party. *See* Fatherland Party
BBC World Service, demise of media, 116
Belarus
CES launching, 170
Chornobyl meltdown, 15
denuclearization concerns, 40
ENP and, 172, 173, 173*n*
gas trade intricacies, 105
Lukashenko compared with Kuchma, 75
privatization in, 81
Russia-Belarus currency union project, 62
Russian gas embargo, 212
Russia's war in Georgia, 228
Soviet Union dissolution, 33*n*
student organization in, 179
Ukraine's liberation from Russia, 37
Ukrainian independence and, 32–33
Belovezhskaya Pushcha accord, 33
Berezovsky, Boris, 120*n*
Bezsmertniy, Roman, 179
big business. *See also* large and medium-sized enterprises; oligarchs; *specific individuals and entities*
Kinakh government and, 153
Kryvorizhstal privatization, 163
Kuchmagate and, 145
lessons from Ukraine's transformation, 242, 253–54
media freedom and, 116
oligarchs' rise, 107, 109–12
opposition mobilization, 178–79
opposition organization, 154
parliamentary elections of 1998, 118
parliamentary elections of 2006, 214
parliamentary elections of 2007, 220–22
presidential election of 1999, 119–20
presidential election of 2004, 184
regime mobilization, 181
Soviet economic reforms and crisis, 24
underreform trap and, 121–22
Yekhanurov government and, 210
Yushchenko's reforms, 139–41, 149
bilateral trade. *See* foreign trade
Bildt, Carl, 178
billionaires. *See also* big business; oligarchs
competitive oligarchy, 154, 158
oligarchs' rise, 107, 108–09
Orange Revolution and, 175, 198
presidential election of 2004, 7
black-market exchange rates. *See* exchange rates
Black Sea Fleet, 36–37, 39, 57, 101–02, 263
Black Sea region, Kuchma's foreign policy, 104. *See also specific countries*
Bloc of Yuliya Tymoshenko (BYuT)
orange coalition formation, 202
origins of, 155
parliamentary elections of 2002, 156
parliamentary elections of 2006, 213–14
parliamentary elections of 2007, 219–21
Tymoshenko government, 222
WTO accession, 224
Yanukovych government, 217
Yekhanurov government, 210, 212
Yushchenko's call for new elections, 231
blue coalition. *See also specific individuals and entities*
blue and white as campaign colors, 195
parliamentary elections of 2006, 213
bodyguards, prevalence of, 113, 115
Bogoliubov, Gennadiy, 109
Boiko, Volodymyr, 109*n*
Boiko, Yuriy, 170, 216, 218–19
Bolsheviks, history of Ukraine, 13
bonds, Ukrainian, 105, 129
Bonet, Pilar, 31
Boone, Peter, 60*n*, 70
border concerns
Crimea secession threat, 57
democracy's survival as concern, 256, 258
denuclearization concerns and, 40
Kuchma's foreign policy, 101–02
national independence and, 34
NATO controversies, 227–28
peace as priority, 3
Putin's Ukrainian policy, 169, 171
Ukraine's liberation from Russia, 36
Ukraine's turning to West, 8
Boychyshyn, Mykhailo, 65
Bragin, Ahati, 113
"Brezhnev" Constitution, 84. *See also* Soviet Ukrainian Constitution of 1978
Brezhnev, Leonid, 15, 20*b*, 84
bribery. *See* corruption
Britain, competition between crown and parliament, 149, 252. *See also* United Kingdom

underreform trap and, 122
Yushchenko's reforms, 5, 128, 146–47
Centragas, 170, 212–13
Central Asia. *See also specific countries*
Putin's Ukrainian policy, 170
Russian gas embargo, 212
Ukrainian presidential election of 2004, 193
Central Bank of Russia, 37
central bank, Ukrainian. *See* National Bank of Ukraine (NBU)
Central Committee of Communist Party, 8, 240
Central Election Commission (CEC), 180, 184, 187–88, 191, 195
Central Europe. *See also specific countries*
challenges ahead, 264
democracy's survival as concern, 254
elections and corruption, 220
ENP and, 172
European economic convergence, 259–60
Kuchma's foreign policy, 103
market reform in, 121
oligarchs' impact, 251
oligarchs' rise, 110
presidential or parliamentary rule issue, 240
reform pace in, 238
taxation survey, 142
champagne factories, 99
Channel 5, 154, 178, 187
Charles XII, King of Sweden, 12
checks and balances. *See also* division of powers
constitution and, 84, 86
parliamentary elections of 2006, 216
presidential or parliamentary rule issue, 239
chemicals trade
economic reform delays and consequences, 4
Kuchma's foreign policy, 103
rent seeking and early economic policy, 55
WTO accession, 224
Chernivtsi, 19*b*
Chernomyrdin, Viktor, 169, 184
Chervonenko, Yevhen, 154, 178, 203
chestnut trees, 176, 179
chicken industry, 225
"Chicken Kiev" speech, 29–30
Children of the 20th Party Congress, 14
China, denuclearization concerns, 39
Chornobyl disaster
awakening under Gorbachev, 15–16
Chornobyl Fund, 136
denuclearization concerns, 39
Kuchma's foreign policy, 103
lessons from Ukraine's transformation, 263
peace as priority, 3
Chornovil, Vyacheslav
awakening under Gorbachev, 16–17, 20
death in traffic accident, 119
history of Ukraine, 14
Kravchuk characteristics as president, 35
presidential election of 1991, 32, 156
Yushchenko's European Square speech, 186
Chubais, Anatoly, 80, 249
CIS Agreement on the Creation of a Free Trade Zone, 38
civil code, adoption of, 79, 162. *See also* law and legislative activity
civil rights comparison, 254–56, 255*f*
Clean Hands program, 100
Clinton, Bill, 40, 91, 102, 228, 261
club of millionaires, parliament as, 158
coalition of the willing, 172
coal trade. *See also* miner's strikes; mines and mining
Kuchma's reforms as president, 70
oligarchs' rise, 107, 108
rent seeking and early economic policy, 56
Yushchenko's reforms, 138
collective farms. *See* agricultural sector
colored revolutions, 197–99. *See also* Orange Revolution; Rose Revolution
command-administrative system, 16
commercial banks. *See* banking sector; *specific entities*
Commission on Import Regulations, 74
Committee of Voters of Ukraine, 191
commodity sector. *See also* foreign trade; *specific commodities*
corruption issues and commodity trade, 87
Kuchma's reforms as president, 4
oligarchs' rise, 108, 110
rent seeking and early economic policy, 55
Yushchenko's reforms, 138, 140, 148–49
Common Economic Space (CES)
Putin's Ukrainian policy, 169, 170–71, 263
Ukraine's turning to West, 9
Ukrainian parliamentary elections of 2006, 216

Kinakh's reforms, 152
Kuchma's reforms, 86, 238
oligarchs' impact, 253, 254
oligarchs' rise, 110
Orange Revolution settlement, 7, 194, 195, 199
parliamentary elections of 2006, 216
parliamentary elections of 2007, 219
presidential election of 2004, 7, 184, 187, 194, 195, 199
presidential or parliamentary rule issue, 239
presidential term limits, 177
reform as urgent, 150
Tymoshenko's reforms, 206
Yanukovych's reforms, 162
Yushchenko's dissolution of parliament, 232
Yushchenko's ouster as prime minister, 146
Yushchenko's poisoning and, 186
Crimea
democracy's survival as concern, 258
NATO controversies, 227–28
Putin's Ukrainian policy, 263
regions of Ukraine, 19*b*
secession threat, 4, 56–57, 58, 63, 90–91
Sevastopol naval base, 9, 36–37, 57, 101–02, 227–28
vote on Ukrainian independence (1991), 32
winery destruction, 23
crime and criminal activity
author's trip through western Ukraine, 59–60
corporate law enactment, 79
criminal code adoption, 152
demise of media and, 115
gas trade intricacies, 106
Gongadze case convictions, 144
Kinakh's reforms, 152
Kuchma's policy stagnation, 100, 112–15
oligarchs' rise, 111
parliamentary elections of 1994, 65
presidential election of 1999, 119
presidential election of 2004, 186–87, 190
Putin's Ukrainian policy, 170
rent seeking and early economic policy, 55–56
Tymoshenko's reforms, 206, 208
Tymoshenko treason case, 228
Yanukovych and, 160, 162, 181
Yushchenko and oligarchs, 132
culture of Ukraine. *See* Ukrainian language and culture
currency. *See also* exchange rates; hryvnia; ruble and ruble zone
currency corridor adoption, 250
economic reform delays and consequences, 3
history of Ukraine, 12
Kuchma's reforms as president, 75–77, 131
national independence and, 32
nationalist economic policy, 43, 44
renewed financial crisis, 229–30
Russia-Belarus currency union project, 62
Soviet economic reforms and crisis, 23–27
Ukraine's liberation from Russia, 37
Yushchenko's reforms, 128–29
currency coefficients, Soviet economic reforms and crisis, 24
currency union, CES as, 170–71
current account deficit, 229–30
current account, hryvnia as convertable on, 77
current account surplus, 164, 166*f*
customs code, adoption of, 152, 224
Customs Committee, 162
customs reform, Tymoshenko and, 205, 224. *See also* foreign trade
customs union, CES as, 170
Czechoslovakia
Gongadze murder and, 144
partition of countries, 19*b*
Czech Republic
EU membership, 172
infant mortality in, 233
privatization vouchers, 79
Ukrainian economic policy and, 44

debt. *See* arrears; foreign debt; state debt
Declaration of Independence, Ukrainian, 32
declaration of national unity, Ukrainian, 215–16, 217, 226
Declaration of State Sovereignty, Ukrainian, 39
decrees. *See* governmental decrees; presidential decrees
democracy issues
amnesty for prisoners, 16
author's 1991 Ukraine trip, 30
awakening under Gorbachev, 9, 15, 17–18
central-regional relations, 244
challenges ahead, 265
constitutional evolution and shortcomings, 238, 241
democracy defined, 7, 251, 256
EU relations and, 173
founding elections and, 84

history of Ukraine, 12–13
Kravchuk as Father of Nation, 58
Kuchma regime's approach, 177
Kuchma's foreign policy, 103, 226
lessons from Ukraine's transformation, 237, 251, 254–58
oligarchs' impact and, 251–54
opposition organization, 153, 155
Orange Revolution aftermath, 6–7, 10, 202, 209, 213
Orange Revolution assessment, 197–99, 238
Orange Revolution events, 175–76
parliamentary elections of 2007, 219–20
political system overview, 8
presidential election of 2004, 193, 197
presidential or parliamentary rule, 239–40
Putin's Ukrainian policy, 263
regions of Ukraine, 20*b*
Ukraine's liberation from Russia, 36
underreform trap and, 123
Yushchenko's achievements as president, 232
Yushchenko's reforms, 128
Democratic Bloc, 18, 20
Democratic Council, 118
democrats, 189. *See also* national democrats; social democrats; *specific individuals and entities*
demonetization
hyperinflation and economic crisis, 52
rent seeking and early Ukrainian policy, 56
demonstrations and protests. *See also* miners' strikes; Orange Revolution
awakening under Gorbachev, 16, 18, 21
Masol and, 21, 66
Orange Revolution aftermath, 202
parliamentary elections of 2007, 219
presidential election of 2004, 175–76, 187–88, 190–95, 198
Ukraine without Kuchma movement, 144
denuclearization. *See also* nuclear arms
international assistance and, 89
Kravchuk and, 35, 39–41, 58, 228
lessons from Ukraine's transformation, 261
peace as priority, 3
Ukraine's liberation from Russia, 36
deregulation. *See specific areas of regulation*
Derkach, Leonid, 113, 145
de Tocqueville, Alexis, 164
diaspora, Ukrainian
history of Ukraine, 13
international assistance and, 89
Kuchma's reforms and, 60, 62
national independence and, 61
presidential election of 2004, 183
diplomatic corps of Ukraine, 34–35, 194
divide and rule approach
Kuchma and, 93, 112, 256
Yushchenko and, 149
division of powers, 84, 239. *See also* checks and balances
Dnipropetrovsk
economic growth and, 151
history of Ukraine, 15
Kuchma's reforms as president, 69
Larenko's excesses, 94, 96
new political forces, 43
oligarchs' rise, 108–10
opposition organization, 155
orange coalition end, 209
parliamentary elections of 1998, 118
presidential election of 1999, 120
presidential election of 2004, 159–60
Pustovoitenko as passive loyalist, 100
regions of Ukraine, 19–20*b*
Doing Business Index, 246, 247*f*, 248*f*
domestic prices. *See* prices
Donbas
awakening under Gorbachev, 18, 21
crime and law enforcement, 115
Kryvorizhstal privatization, 163
Kuchma's reforms as prime minister, 46
oligarchs' rise, 108
presidential election of 2004, 184, 185, 195, 197
Soviet economic reforms and crisis, 23
Tymoshenko's reforms, 205
Yanukovych background, 181
Donetsk
crime and law enforcement, 113, 115
economic growth, 151
Lazarenko and, 95
new political forces, 42
oligarchs' rise, 108–10
Orange Revolution aftermath, 201
parliamentary elections of 1998, 118
parliamentary elections of 2006, 216
presidential election of 2004, 159–60
regions of Ukraine, 19–20*b*
Yanukovych background, 160
Yanukovych's reforms, 161
Yushchenko's ouster as prime minister, 146
Yushchenko's reforms, 138

Zviahilskiy and rent seeking, 47, 48
Drach, Ivan, 16–17
Duma. *See* Russian State Duma
Dynamo soccer club, 107

earnings. *See* income
ease of doing business rankings, 246, 247*f*, 248*f*
eastern enlargement of European Union, Ukraine's turning to West, 9
Eastern Europe. *See also specific countries*
elections and corruption, 220
ENP and, 172
European economic convergence, 259
Kuchma's foreign policy, 102
NATO controversies and, 227
presidential or parliamentary rule issue, 240
reform pace in, 238
Eastern Orthodox Christianity, 11
EastOne, 109, 109*n*, 111, 254
East Slavic countries. *See also specific countries*
male life expectancy, 233
Putin's Ukrainian policy, 263
economic assistance, international. *See* international assistance
economic code, adoption of, 162
economic crises, Ukrainian. *See also* inflation
capitalist transformation and, 246
challenges ahead, 264–65
Crimea secession threat, 57
demise of media and, 115
democracy's survival as concern, 258
economic growth program and, 97
European economic convergence, 259
Kravchuk and, 10, 35, 44, 48–55, 58
Kuchma's policy stagnation, 10
Kuchma's reforms as president, 4, 71–73, 81
Kuchma's reforms as prime minister, 45–46
oligarchs' impact, 252
parliamentary elections of 1994, 64
presidential election of 1994, 66–68
presidential election of 2010, 231
reform delays and consequences, 3–4
renewed economic crisis, 228–31, 232, 251
Ukraine's liberation from Russia, 37
underreform trap and, 123
Yushchenko's reforms, 128–29, 132
economic growth
boom of 2004, 164–68, 165*f*, 166*f*
competitive oligarchy and growth, 6, 10, 151–73
democracy's survival as concern, 258
European economic convergence, 259–60
IMF role reduction, 261
Kuchma's reforms as president, 4–5, 86, 131
oligarchs' impact, 251
Orange Revolution and, 6, 164, 176, 202
presidential election of 2004, 180
Pynzenyk's program for, 93, 97–100
Tymoshenko's reforms and, 209
WTO accession and, 224
Yanukovych governments and, 162, 217
Yushchenko's reforms and, 5, 10, 125, 128–29, 135, 147
economic policy. *See also* economic reforms; *specific aspects*
as discussed in studies, 23
hyperinflation and economic crisis, 52
Kravchuk and nationalist policy, 43–44
Kravchuk as Father of Nation, 58
Kravchuk characteristics as president, 35
Larenko's excesses, 95–96
lessons from Ukraine's transformation, 238, 249–50
Moscow environment versus Ukraine, 60–61
new political forces and, 42
parliamentary elections of 2007, 220–21
presidential election of 1994, 66
presidential or parliamentary rule issue, 239
rent seeking and early policy rationale, 55–56
rent seeking and Zviahilskiy, 46–47
underreform trap and, 121–23
Economic Reform Committee, 30
economic reforms. *See also* Soviet economic reforms and crisis; *specific aspects*
author's 1991 Ukraine trip, 29
awakening under Gorbachev, 21–22
"evolutionary economic reform" program, 87
Kinakh and, 151, 152
Kravchuk and nationalist policy, 44
Kuchma's policy stagnation, 95, 128
Kuchma's reforms as president, 59–63, 68–73, 86–88, 131, 241
Kuchma's reforms as prime minister, 45–46
lessons from Ukraine's transformation, 237
national independence as goal, 2
nation-building as goal, 3
new political forces and, 42–43

presidential or parliamentary rule issue, 240
Pynzenyk's economic growth program, 93, 97–100
rent seeking and early policy, 55
Tymoshenko's reforms, 204–09
Yushchenko's ouster as prime minister, 5, 145–46
Yushchenko's reforms, 5, 10, 125–33, 151–53, 250
Economics Education and Research Consortium, International Advisory Board of, 89*n*
economics journal, Ukrainian, 30
economic statistics, issues with
credibility, 167
poor quality, 48
economies of scale
oligarchs' rise and, 110
underreform trap and, 121
education
challenges ahead, 264
education exchanges and EU, 204
higher education pursuit by youth, 235–36, 236*f*, 260
Kuchma's reforms and, 61, 75, 88, 89–90
national tests introduced, 236
efficacy of state, decline in, 258
elections (in general). *See also specific parliamentary and presidential elections by year, e.g,* presidential election of 1991
constitution and, 85, 184, 194–96
democracy's survival as concern, 256, 258
electoral system overview, 7, 8
"founding" elections and democratization, 84
Kravchuk as Father of Nation, 58
oligarchs' impact, 252
referendum on constitution, Kuchma's threats of (1995), 85
referendum on Crimea's status (1991), 57
referendum on federalization of Ukraine, demand for (2004), 195
referendum on Soviet Union (1991), 22
referendum on Ukrainian independence (1991), 2, 32–33, 57
regional divisions and, 18, 19*b*
Soviet Parliament (1989), 17, 18
electricity. *See also* energy sector
nuclear power as issue, 103
oligarchs' rise, 107
Tymoshenko government, 223
World Bank and reform, 89
Yushchenko's reforms, 138–39, 139*n*, 140–41
embargoes. *See* foreign trade; gas and oil trade
embassies, 38, 61
employment concerns. *See* labor and labor unions
energy-efficiency issues, 105, 105*n*, 218
energy sector. *See also* gas and oil trade
economic growth program, 99
energy-efficiency comparison, 105, 105*n*
hyperinflation and economic crisis, 54
Kuchma's foreign policy, 104
Kuchma's reforms as president, 4, 71, 74–75
Larenko's excesses, 94–95
renewed financial crisis, 229
rent seeking and early economic policy, 55–56
Tymoshenko government, 222
Ukraine's liberation from Russia, 36
Yanukovych's reforms, 162
Yushchenko's reforms, 5, 138–39, 139*n*, 146, 149
England, constitutional evolution, 238. *See also* Britain; United Kingdom
entrepreneurs, development of. *See* privatization
environmental issues. *See also* Chornobyl disaster
awakening under Gorbachev, 16
Larenko and, 94
Estonia
awakening under Gorbachev, 16
EU membership, 172
history of Ukraine, 13
referendum on Soviet Union (1991), 22
ethnic groups of Ukraine
national independence and, 31
regions of Ukraine and, 19*b*
EU-15 countries, European economic convergence, 259
Eural Trans Gaz, 169–70
euro bonds, Yushchenko's reforms, 129, 131
Europe. *See also specific countries and organizations*
challenges ahead, 264
consumer loan financing, 229
European economic convergence, 259–60
European Neighborhood Policy, 171–73
gas prices for, 105, 212, 224
Kryvorizhstal privatization and, 163
lessons from Ukraine's transformation, 263–64
NATO controversies and, 226, 227
oligarchs' rise and, 110
Orange Revolution aftermath, 202

Orange Revolution settlement, 7
Russian gas embargo, 211–12
Tymoshenko government, 223
Ukraine as strategic location in, 89, 263
Ukrainian parliamentary elections of 2006, 215, 216
Ukrainian workers in, 235
Yushchenko and European choice, 189
Yushchenko's foreign policy, 203–04
European Association Agreement, 9, 238, 253, 264
European Bank for Reconstruction and Development (EBRD)
Business Environment and Enterprise Performance Survey, 256
Chornobyl station closing and, 103
composite transition index, 126, 127*f*, 246
on Ukraine's GDP, 48, 81, 141
European Commission, 172
European Council, 172
European Court of Human Rights, 245
European Neighborhood Policy (ENP), 171–73, 173*n*, 204, 253, 264
European Parliament, 191
European People's Party, 220–21
European Square speech, 186–87
European Union (EU)
challenges ahead, 264–65
European economic convergence, 259
European Neighborhood Policy, 171–73, 173*n*, 204, 253, 264
food aid from, 69
Kuchma's foreign policy, 102–04
Kuchma's reforms as president, 131
lessons from Ukraine's transformation, 237, 238, 263–64
market economy definition, 5
oligarchs' impact, 253–54
Orange Revolution aftermath, 202
Orange Revolution settlement, 176, 194
presidential or parliamentary rule issue, 240
Russia's war in Georgia, 228
technical assistance from, 62, 90
Tymoshenko governments and, 205, 223
Ukraine acknowledged as market economy, 225
Ukraine's turning to West, 9
Ukrainian legislation and, 152
Ukrainian membership possibility, 93, 253–54, 263–64
Ukrainian parliamentary elections of 2006, 216
Ukrainian presidential election of 2004, 176, 194
Yushchenko's achievements as president, 232
Yushchenko's foreign policy, 204
euro, Ukrainian exchange rate peg and, 229
eurozone, European economic convergence, 259
Evraz group, 163
exchange rates
author's 1991 Ukraine trip, 29
energy-efficiency calculations and, 105*n*
European economic convergence, 259
Kuchma's reforms as president, 72–77
renewed financial crisis, 229, 231
Soviet economic reforms and crisis, 24–26
Yushchenko's reforms, 125–26, 129, 130*f*
executive powers. *See* presidential powers
expenditures, public. *See* budget issues
exports. *See* foreign trade; *specific commodities and sectors*
external default concerns. *See* foreign debt

farming. *See* agricultural sector
Fatherland Party, 97, 154–55
federalization of Ukraine, demand for referendum on, 195
female life expectancy, 233
Ferrexpo, 109*n*, 221
financial crises, Ukrainian. *See* economic crises, Ukrainian
financial stabilization. *See also* economic policy; economic reforms
capitalist transformation and, 246–49
Crimea secession threat, 57
hyperinflation and economic crisis, 52
Kuchma's characteristics as president, 91
Kuchma's economic policy reversal, 86–88
Kuchma's economic reforms, 4–5, 10, 62–63, 70–75
Kuchma's reforms as prime minister, 46
lessons from Ukraine's transformation, 237, 246–50, 261
rent seeking and early Ukrainian policy, 56
Yushchenko's reforms, 128
Financial Times
campaigns against Yushchenko, 146, 183
drafting of article for, 70, 70*n*
Finland
parliamentary elections, 242
parliamentary system, 8
fiscal issues. *See* budget issues
Fischer, Stanley, 250
Five-Hundred-Day Program, 21–22
flag of Ukraine, 12, 34

Fokin, Vitold, 21–22, 43–44
food and food supplies. *See also* agricultural sector
  donations to demonstrators, 192
  household plots and, 13, 125, 139
  Kuchma's reforms as president, 69, 71
  renewed financial crisis, 229
  Soviet economic crisis impacts, 24
  Tymoshenko governments, 207–08, 222
  WTO accession and, 225
For a United Ukraine bloc, 155–56
foreign assistance. *See* international assistance
foreign debt. *See also* arrears
  gas trade intricacies, 105
  Kuchma's reforms as president, 71, 74
  lessons from Ukraine's transformation, 250
  renewed financial crisis, 229–30
  Soviet economic reforms and crisis, 26
  Ukraine's liberation from Russia, 37–38
  Yushchenko's reforms, 5, 126, 128–32, 145, 147–49
foreign direct investment
  European economic convergence, 260, 262*f*
  Kryvorizhstal sale and, 211
  oligarchs' impact, 253
  renewed financial crisis, 230
foreign exchange. *See* exchange rates
foreign investment. *See also* stock ownership and privatization
  Asian financial crisis and, 129
  Kuchma's reforms, 45
  oligarchs' rise, 111
  privatization and, 139–40
foreign policy. *See also specific aspects and entities*
  capitalist transformation and, 247
  Kravchuk characteristics as president, 34–35
  Kuchma's policy, 8–9, 93, 101–04, 145, 172, 181
  lessons from Ukraine's transformation, 261, 263–64
  NATO controversies, 225–28
  parliamentary elections of 2006, 216
  parliamentary elections of 2007, 220
  Ukraine's liberation from Russia, 37
  Yanukovych government, 217–18
  Yushchenko's policy, 203–04
foreign trade. *See also* market economy; *specific sectors and entities*
  author's 1991 Ukraine trip, 30
  awakening under Gorbachev, 22
  CES launching and, 9, 170–71
  competitive oligarchy and growth, 6
  economic boom of 2004, 164, 165*f*, 166*f*, 167
  economic reform delays and consequences, 4
  exports and imports in billions of US dollars, 164, 165*f*
  gas trade intricacies, 104–06
  hyperinflation and economic crisis, 48, 54–55
  Kuchma and, 4, 69–71, 73–75, 88, 102–03
  Larenko's excesses, 95
  lessons from Ukraine's transformation, 246, 250, 260, 263, 264
  nationalist economic policy, 44
  presidential election of 2004, 182
  renewed financial crisis, 229–31
  rent seeking and early economic policy, 55–56
  rent seeking and Zviahilskiy, 47
  Soviet economic reforms and crisis, 24–26
  trade and current account balances, 164, 166*f*
  trade deficit expansion, 229
  trade taxes in Soviet system, 54
  Tymoshenko and, 205, 222, 224
  Ukraine acknowledged as market economy, 225
  Ukraine's liberation from Russia, 37–39
  Ukraine's turning to West, 9
  WTO accession, 9, 202, 224–25, 263
  Yanukovych and, 162–63, 218
  Yushchenko and, 128–29, 131, 136, 138–39, 141
former Soviet republics. *See also specific entities*
  democracy's survival as concern, 258
  hyperinflation and economic crisis, 54, 246
  lessons from Ukraine's transformation, 237
  presidential or parliamentary rule issue, 240
  Putin's Ukrainian policy, 168
  Ukraine's liberation from Russia, 37–39
Founding Act on Mutual Relations (NATO and Russia), 104
Fox, John, 60
France, Russian gas embargo and, 211
Franchuk, Elena, 109
Freedom House
  opposition conference, 178

Ukraine's ranking, 197, 238, 254, 255*f*
free economic zones
Tymoshenko's reforms, 205
Yanukovych's reforms, 162
free trade agreements. *See also* foreign trade
Kuchma's foreign policy, 102
lessons from Ukraine's transformation, 264
parliamentary elections of 2006, 216
Tymoshenko government, 223
Ukraine's turning to West, 9
Yushchenko's foreign policy, 204
French Revolution, 164
Fridman, Mikhail, 141
Front for National Salvation movement, 155
fruits and vegetables. *See also* agricultural sector; food and food supplies
sales income, 24
Soviet economic reforms and crisis, 23
WTO accession and, 225
Fursin, Ivan, 213
Futey, Bohdan, on constitution, 245

Gaidar, Yegor, 44, 72
gas and oil trade
competitive oligarchy and growth, 6
democracy's survival as concern, 258
economic boom of 2004, 164
economic reform delays and consequences, 4
intricacies of gas trade, 3, 94, 104–06
Kuchma's reforms as president, 61, 69–71, 74, 90
Larenko's excesses, 94–95
lessons from Ukraine's transformation, 250
oligarchs' rise, 107–09
parliamentary elections of 2006, 214
port facility leasing and gas arrears, 101
presidential election of 2004, 184, 190, 190*n*
Putin's Ukrainian policy, 169–70, 263
rent seeking and early economic policy, 55
Russian gas embargo, 211–13, 263
Soviet economic reforms and crisis, 25
Tymoshenko governments, 207, 208, 224
Ukraine's liberation from Russia, 36, 37
Ukraine's turning to West, 9
Yanukovych government, 217–18
Yushchenko's ouster as prime minister, 146
Yushchenko's reforms, 5, 126, 138–39, 140–41, 141*n*
Zviahilskiy and rent seeking, 47
Gazprom
gas embargo, 211–13
gas trade intricacies, 4, 105–06
Larenko's excesses, 94
presidential election of 2004, 180
Putin's Ukrainian policy, 169–70
rent seeking and early Ukrainian policy, 55
Tymoshenko government, 224
Gazprombank, 170, 212
Gelman, Marat, 183
genocide issues, *Holodomor* and, 13
Georgia
ENP and, 173*n*
gas trade intricacies, 105
Kuchma's foreign policy, 105
national independence and, 31, 33
NATO controversies and, 227–28
population decline in, 235
presidential or parliamentary rule issue, 239
referendum on Soviet Union (1991), 22
Rose Revolution, 176, 179, 197, 198
Russia's war in, 228
WTO accession, 224
German Advisory Group in Economic Reforms with the Ukrainian Government, 62, 133, 149
German Marshall Fund, 178
Germany
history of Crimea, 56
history of Ukraine, 13
parliamentary elections, 242
Russian gas embargo, 211
Gini coefficient of Ukraine, 56
glasnost, awakening under Gorbachev, 15–16
Gogol, Nikolai, 191
Gongadze, Heorhiy
murder of, 128, 143–45, 146, 201, 261
opposition conference, 178
Yushchenko's European Square speech, 186, 186*n*
Gorbachev, Mikhail
antialcohol campaign, 23–24, 233
author's 1991 Ukraine trip, 29, 31
awakening of society under, 9, 15–18, 20–22
history of Ukraine, 14
Soviet Union dissolution, 31, 33
Gore, Al, 89, 102
Gore-Chernomyrdin Commission, 89
Gore-Kuchma Commission, 89
governmental decrees
internet publishing of, 245

Kuchma's reforms as president, 72, 74
Kuchma's reforms as prime minister, 45
Yushchenko's reforms of 2000, 136
government inspections. *See* inspectors and inspections
government reforms. *See also* institution-building; *specific entities*
European economic convergence, 259
Yanukovych's reforms, 161
Yushchenko's reforms, 133–35
grain
exports, 71, 74, 95, 225
land reform and, 140
Yanukovych's reforms, 162–63
Grant, Ulysses, 158
Great Nordic War, 12
Greek Catholic Church, 14
Greens (political party), 118
Green World, 16
gross domestic product (GDP)
author's 1991 Ukraine trip, 30
budget deficit as percent of, 52, 53*f*, 54, 187, 188*f*
campaign finance as percent of, 180
capitalist transformation and, 246, 249
cumulative change, 125, 126*f*
debt as percent of, 129, 130*f*, 131, 147
economic boom of 2004, 167, 168
gas trade intricacies, 105, 106
growth, 97, 98*f*, 147, 148*f*, 259, 260*f*
hyperinflation and economic crisis, 48
investment as percent of, 48, 164, 167*f*, 259–60, 262*f*
Kuchma's reforms as president, 4, 70, 75
nationalist economic policy, 44
private enterprise as percent of, 48, 81, 82*f*, 246
public debt as percent of, 129, 130*f*, 147
renewed financial crisis, 229–31
rent seeking and early economic policy, 55–56
Soviet economic reforms and crisis, 23, 25–26
state revenues and expenditures as percent of, 52–54, 53*f*, 136, 137*f*
Tymoshenko's reforms, 205, 208
Ukraine's liberation from Russia, 37
underground economy as percent of, 48, 50*f*
volume of money as ratio of, 259, 261*f*
Yushchenko's government reforms, 136
Yushchenko's privatization reforms, 141
Yushchenko's trade reforms, 138
gross fixed investment, as percent of GDP, 164, 167*f*
gross national product (GNP), decline in, 48, 49*f*. *See also* output
Group of Seven (G-7), 40, 68, 70, 72, 103
Gryshchenko, Kostyatyn, 171
Gryzlov, Boris, 191, 194
GUAM, 104
Gusinsky, Vladimir, 115

Habsburg Empire, 14, 19*b*, 39
Haiduk, Vitaliy, 108, 148
Halchynskiy, Anatoliy, 69, 71
Havel, Vaclav, 178
Havrylyshyn, Oleh, 29, 30*n*, 61
Hawrylyshyn, Bohdan, 61
health care
cost issues, 75
medication issues, 136, 235
reform issues, 233–36
hetmans. *See* Cossacks
Hetman, Vadym, 119, 186
higher education pursuit by youth, 235–36, 236*f*, 260
high school graduates, national tests for, 236
history of Ukraine
nation-building as goal, 2
peace as priority, 3
proud but tragic legacy, 11–15
regions of Ukraine, 19*b*
Hitler, Adolf, 13
hoarding, Soviet economic reforms and crisis, 25
Holodomor, 13
Holovatiy, Serhiy, 71–72, 100, 153
homicide rate, 113, 114*f*
Hotel Rus, opposition conference, 178
household workers in Europe, 235
Hromada, 95–96, 118
Hrushevskiy, Mykhailo, 12
Hrytsenko, Anatoliy, 203, 216, 217, 226
hryvnia. *See also* currency
capitalist transformation and, 249
history of Ukraine, 12
Kuchma's reforms as president, 63, 69, 75–77, 91, 93
nationalist economic policy, 43
renewed financial crisis, 229
Yushchenko's reforms, 129, 131
Hugo, Victor, 12
humanitarian aid, food aid from European Union, 69
human rights concerns, lessons from Ukraine's transformation, 261, 263–64
Human Rights Watch, 232
Hungary
EU membership, 172

Russian gas embargo, 211
Hunger Death, 13
hunger strike, Masol ouster and, 21
Hurenko, Stanislav, 21
hyperinflation. *See also* inflation
capitalist transformation and, 246
compensation for savings loss, 223
defined, 47*n*
Kravchuk and, 10, 48–55, 58
Kuchma's reforms as president, 73
parliamentary elections of 1994, 64
Ukraine's liberation from Russia, 37, 39
Zviahilskiy and rent seeking, 47

ideology. *See also specific types of ideology and entities*
awakening under Gorbachev, 15, 21
constitutional concerns and, 84
democracy's survival as concern, 258
economic policy reversal and, 88
Moscow policy environment versus Ukraine, 60–61
national independence and, 32
orange coalition formation, 203
presidential election of 1994, 67–68
Ukrainian presidential election of 2004, 189
underreform trap and, 122
impeachment, constitution and, 85
imperative mandate, as Tymoshenko preference, 217, 242
imports. *See* foreign trade; *specific commodities and sectors*
income. *See also* taxes and taxation; wages and salaries
oligarchs' impact, 251
rent seeking and early economic policy, 56
Soviet economic reforms and crisis, 24–26
Yanukovych's reforms, 161
Yushchenko's reforms, 128
independence, national. *See* national independence
Independence Square (Maidan), Orange Revolution and, 191–94, 196
independents. *See also specific individuals and entities*
opposition organization, 154
parliamentary elections of 1998, 118
parliamentary elections of 2002, 157
Industrial Revolution, oligarchs' rise and, 110
Industrial Union of Donbas (ISD)
Kryvorizhstal privatization, 163
oligarchs' impact, 254
oligarchs' rise, 108–09, 109*n*
Orange Revolution and, 181
parliamentary elections of 2006, 214
parliamentary elections of 2007, 221
infant mortality, 233, 234*f*, 235
inflation
bank savings and, 83
capitalist transformation and, 246–47
compensation for savings loss, 223
currency union prematurity and, 171
economic reform delays and consequences, 3
inflation rate (consumer price index), 230*f*
Kravchuk and, 10, 35, 44, 48–55, 58
Kuchma and currency reform, 76, 77*f*
Kuchma and economic reforms, 4, 69, 72, 86
Kuchma and financial stabilization, 73
Kuchma's characteristics as president, 91
Kuchma's reforms as prime minister, 45–46
monthly inflation and monetary expansion, 49, 51*f*
renewed financial crisis, 229, 230*f*
rent seeking and early Ukrainian policy, 55–56
Soviet economic reforms and crisis, 24–25, 27
Ukraine's liberation from Russia, 37, 39
Yushchenko's reforms, 126
initial public offerings, 253
input, Soviet economic reforms and crisis, 26
insider privatization. *See also* privatization
capitalist transformation and, 249
Kuchma's reforms as president, 80, 81
oligarchs' rise, 108
Yushchenko's reforms, 140–41
inspectors and inspections
central-regional relations, 244
demise of media and, 116
Kuchma's policy stagnation, 95
presidential election of 2004, 180
Pynzenyk's economic growth program, 97, 99
Yushchenko's deregulation of small firms, 142–43
institution-building. *See also* state agencies; state-building; *specific entities*
nationalist economic policy and, 44
rent seeking and early economic policy, 55

Russian gas embargo, 212
Russia's war in Georgia, 228
Soviet Union dissolution, 33*n*
Ukraine's liberation from Russia, 37
Kerch Strait, territorial dispute regarding, 101, 169, 171
KGB, 113, 256
Kharkiv
presidential election of 2004, 184
regions of Ukraine, 20*b*
Khasbulatov, Ruslan, 84
Kherson
author's observations of enterprises in, 83
presidential election of 2004, 185
Khlib Ukrainy, 95
Khmelnytskiy, Bohdan, 12
Khoroshkovskiy, Valeriy, 162, 171
Khrushchev, Nikita, 14–15, 56
Kievskie vedomosti, demise of media, 115
Kinakh, Anatoliy
orange coalition formation, 203
presidential election of 2004, 184, 189–90
reform policies and, 151, 152–53
Yanukovych government, 218
Yekhanurov government, 210
Klaus, Vaclav, 44
Kliuev, Andriy, 216, 219
Kliuev, Serhiy, 181
Kmara, 179
Kolchuga radar sales, 145
Kolesnikov, Borys, 208
kolkhoz market prices, 24
Kolomoiskiy, Ihor, 109, 148, 206
Kornai, János, market economy definition, 5
Kosovo
Kuchma's foreign policy, 104
Western recognition of, 228
Kostenko, Yuriy, 153
Krastev, Ivan, 220
Kravchenko, Yuriy, 113, 115, 144–45, 201
Kravchuk, Leonid
author's 1991 Ukraine trip, 30
awakening under Gorbachev, 21
characteristics as president, 3, 34–35, 90, 91, 232
Crimea secession threat, 56–57
denuclearization and, 39–41, 58, 228
early economic policy rationale, 55–56
as Father of Nation, 58, 66
Gusinsky relationship with, 116
hyperinflation and economic crisis, 35, 44, 48–55, 58
Kuchma administration corruption and, 87
Kuchma as prime minister, 45–46
lessons from Ukraine's transformation, 261
liberation from Russia and, 35–39
national independence and, 2–3, 31–35
nationalist economic policy and, 43–44
new political forces and, 41–43
parliamentary elections of 1994, 63–65
parliamentary elections of 1998, 118
presidential election of 1991, 32
presidential election of 1994, 58, 59, 62, 66–68
Tymoshenko government comparison, 205
Ukrainian diaspora and, 61
US support for, 60
Zviahilskiy as prime minister, 46–48
Kryvorizhstal, privatization of, 109*n*, 152, 163–64, 190, 205–06, 210–11, 249
Kryvyi Rig, 185
Kuchmagate, 144, 177
Kuchma, Leonid
capitalist transformation and, 249
characteristics as president, 90–91
constitutional evolution and shortcomings, 238
constitutional reform legislation, 177
Crimea secession threat, 57
democracy's survival as concern, 256
ENP and, 171–72
Gongadze murder and, 128, 143–45, 146, 261
Kinakh's role and, 152–53
Kryvorizhstal privatization, 163
lessons from Ukraine's transformation, 261, 263
NATO controversies background, 225–26
new political forces and, 43
opposition organization, 153–55
Orange Revolution aftermath, 201
parliamentary elections of 1994, 63–66
parliamentary elections of 2002, 155, 158
policy stagnation under, 10, 93–123, 128
presidential addresses to parliament, 71–72, 86, 87, 133
presidential election of 1994, 59, 62, 66–68
presidential election of 1999, 94, 118–21
presidential election of 2004, 159–60, 176–77, 179–82, 184, 190–95, 198
presidential or parliamentary rule issue, 239–41
Putin's Ukrainian policy, 170–71, 263
radar sales to Iraq, 145
reforms as president, 4–5, 59–91, 226, 238, 241

reforms as prime minister, 45–46
regions of Ukraine, 20*b*
on social reform, 233
Tymoshenko's reforms, 206
Ukraine's turning to West, 8
Yushchenko's ouster as prime minister, 146, 153, 153*n*
Yushchenko's reforms, 131–33, 140, 142
Kundera, Milan, 196
Kwasniewski, Alexander, 145, 194
Kyiv
author's observations of, 1, 29–31, 151, 175–76, 196
awakening under Gorbachev, 16, 18, 21
"chestnut" revolution terminology, 176
crime and law enforcement, 113
demise of media, 115–16
economic growth and, 151–52
factory inspections in, 97, 99
Gongadze murder, 142–44
government reforms and, 161
history of Ukraine, 11–13, 14
Kuchma's reforms as president, 69
nation-building as goal, 2
oligarchs' rise, 107, 109–10
opposition organization, 151
presidential election of 2004, 159–60, 183–88, 191–95
regions of Ukraine, 19–20*b*
USAID mission establishment, 89
western organizations and embassies in, 61
Kyiv City Council, 17
Kyiv Orthodox Church, 14
Kyiv School of Economics, 62, 89*n*
Kyivstar, 141
Kyrgyzstan
presidential or parliamentary rule issue, 240
Soviet Union dissolution, 33*n*
Tulip Revolution, 197
WTO accession, 224
Kyrpa, Hryhoriy, 201

labor and labor unions
education issues and, 90
miners' union formation, 18
oligarchs' impact, 251
social reform achievements, 233
Soviet economic reforms and crisis, 24, 26
unemployment rate changes, 164, 168*f*
Labor Ukraine, 118, 159–60, 195
land code. *See also* law and legislative activity
Kinakh and, 152
Yushchenko and, 140
land privatization, 70, 139–40, 190, 216, 221, 223, 253. *See also* agricultural sector
language of Ukraine. *See* Ukrainian language and culture
Lanovyi, Volodymyr, 43–44, 52, 67, 122
large and medium-sized enterprises. *See also* big business; privatization; *specific entities*
awakening under Gorbachev, 24
competitive oligarchy and growth, 6, 163
Kuchma's reforms, 70, 72, 80–81
oligarchs' rise, 109–10
presidential election of 2004, 179
Yushchenko's reforms, 135, 140–43
Latin America, income disparity comparison, 56, 128
Latvia
awakening under Gorbachev, 16
EU membership, 172
history of Ukraine, 13
referendum on Soviet Union (1991), 22
Lavrynovych, Oleksandr, 162, 171
law and legislative activity. *See also* parliament, Ukrainian; *specific aspects and laws*
adaptation to EU legislation, 152
awakening under Gorbachev, 22
capitalist transformation and, 246, 249
central-regional relations, 243
challenges ahead, 265
constitutional evolution and shortcomings, 238
corporate laws first enacted, 79
crime and law enforcement, 112–15
democracy's survival as concern, 254, 256, 258
internet publishing of laws and decrees, 245
judicial reform needs, 244–45
Kinakh's reforms, 152
Kravchuk characteristics as president, 35, 232
Kuchma and economic reforms, 60, 62, 72, 131
Kuchma and international assistance, 88–90
Kuchma and new constitution, 84–86
Kuchma and privatization, 78–81
Larenko's excesses, 95
lessons from Ukraine's transformation, 237
national independence and, 32

Kuchma's reforms as prime minister, 46
mines and mining
new political forces and, 42
oligarchs' rise, 108–09, 112
Soviet economic reforms and crisis, 23
Yanukovych background and, 181
Zviahilskiy connections, 47
Ministry for Foreign Affairs, 34, 178, 217
Ministry of Defense, 32
Ministry of Economy, 52
Ministry of Education, 233
Ministry of External Economic Relations, 37, 74
Ministry of Finance, 52, 69, 75, 243
Ministry of Health Care, 233
Ministry of Interior, 113, 142, 144–45, 194–95, 198
Ministry of Security, 142
Ministry of Statistics, 48, 167
minority languages
Declaration of National Unity and, 216
national independence and, 31
nation-building as goal, 3
Mitiukov, Ihor, 69, 132–33, 153
Mittal Steel, 163, 210
Mkrtchan, Oleg, 108
MMK imeni Ilicha, 109*n*
mobile phones, Orange Revolution and, 185, 192, 198
moderates, awakening under Gorbachev, 20–21. *See also specific individuals and entities*
modernization theory, economic boom of 2004 and, 167
Moldova
ENP and, 172, 173
gas trade intricacies, 105
Kuchma's foreign policy, 105
population decline in, 235
presidential or parliamentary rule issue, 240
referendum on Soviet Union (1991), 22
Soviet Union dissolution, 31, 33*n*
underreform trap, 121
WTO accession, 224
Molotov-Ribbentrop Pact, 13
monetary expansion
hyperinflation and economic crisis, 49–50, 51*f*
Kuchma's reforms as president, 131
monetization, as market economy feature, 6, 246. *See also* demonetization; remonetization
money laundering, Larenko's excesses, 96
monopolies. *See also specific sectors and entities*
gas trade intricacies, 106
Pynzenyk's economic growth program, 99
Tymoshenko's reforms, 207
Yushchenko's reforms, 138, 142
Montesquieu, Charles de Secondat, 84, 239
Moroz, Oleksandr
constitutional agreement and, 85
economic policy reversal and, 88
Gongadze murder and, 143–44
on Larenko, 97
new political forces and, 41–42
parliamentary elections of 1994, 64
parliamentary elections of 2004, 158
parliamentary elections of 2006, 214–16
presidential election of 1994, 67
presidential election of 1999, 119–20
presidential election of 2004, 159, 184, 188–89
mortality, infant, 233, 234*f*, 235
Moscow Orthodox Church, 14
most favored nation status, US Trade Act and, 225
MTS, 141
Mukachevo mayoral elections, 184
multivector foreign policy, Kuchma and, 8, 101, 104, 145, 171. *See also* foreign policy; *specific entities*
municipal governments. *See* regional and local governments
murder rate, 113, 114*f*

Naftohaz Ukrainy
gas trade intricacies, 106
Putin's Ukrainian policy, 170
Russian gas embargo, 212
Tymoshenko government, 224
Yanukovych government, 218
Yushchenko's reforms of 2000, 138
national anthem of Ukraine, 12, 34
National Bank of Ukraine (NBU)
establishment of, 3, 44
German Advisory Group on Economic Reforms, 62
hyperinflation and economic crisis, 49, 52
Kuchma's reforms as president, 73, 75–77, 131
Kuchma's reforms as prime minister, 45, 46
lessons from Ukraine's transformation, 249, 250
renewed financial crisis, 229

oath of obedience for servicemen, 35
oblasts. *See also* regional and local governments; *specific locations*
Crimea secession threat, 57
Larenko's excesses, 95
regions of Ukraine, 19*b*
Obolon brewery, 244
Odesa, regions of Ukraine, 19–20*b*
offsets. *See* barter and offsets
oil trade. *See* gas and oil trade
oligarchs. *See also* big business; competitive oligarchy; *specific individuals and entities*
break in rent-seeking society, 147–50
characteristics of, 110
constitutional reform legislation, 177
crime and law enforcement, 113, 115
democracy's survival as concern, 258
economic boom of 2004, 164
gas trade intricacies, 106
Kryvorizhstal privatization, 163, 206
Kuchma's reforms as president, 5
lessons from Ukraine's transformation, 238, 251–54
oligarchic society defined, 251
opposition organization, 152, 154–55
Orange Revolution aftermath, 201
parliamentary elections of 1998, 117–18
parliamentary elections of 2002, 155, 157–59
parliamentary elections of 2006, 214
presidential election of 1999, 119–20
presidential election of 2004, 6–7, 159–60, 179–81, 184, 189–90, 197–99
regions of Ukraine, 20*b*
rise of, 94, 106–12
Soviet economic reforms and crisis, 27
Tymoshenko's reforms, 206, 208
underreform trap and, 121–22
use of term, 6, 107–08
Yanukovych governments and, 161, 216–19
Yekhanurov government and, 210–11
Yushchenko's government reforms, 128, 132–34, 136
Yushchenko's ouster as prime minister, 5, 145–46
Yushchenko's privatization reforms, 140–41
Yushchenko's reform successes, 5, 153
1+1 channel, 116, 180
open auctions, privatization and, 223
opposition parties. *See also specific factions and entities*
author's 1991 Ukraine trip, 30
awakening under Gorbachev, 16–18, 20
history of Ukraine, 13
organization of, 151, 153–55
parliamentary elections of 2002, 155–59
parliamentary elections of 2007, 220
presidential election of 2004, 7, 176–81, 190–93, 197–98
orange bloc. *See also* orange coalition; *specific individuals and entities*
campaign color selection and use, 175, 187, 192–93
Orange Revolution aftermath, 201
Orange Revolution assessment, 197–99
Orange Revolution settlement, 194–97
orange coalition. *See also specific individuals and entities*
first coalition begins, 202–03
first coalition ends, 208–09
new coalitions form, 215–16, 222
Our Ukraine's break with, 231–32
parliamentary elections of 2006, 213–15
renewed financial crisis, 231
Tymoshenko's reform goals, 205
Yanukovych government, 217
Orange Revolution
aftermath of, 7, 10, 201–36, 216
assessment of, 7, 197–99, 238
capitalist transformation and, 247
democracy's survival as concern, 256, 258
economic boom and, 6, 164, 176
end of, 196–97
events of, 7, 175, 191–92
global awareness of, 175
lessons from Ukraine's transformation, 238, 263–64
oligarchs' impact, 251–54
opposition mobilization, 177–80
presidential election and returns, 7, 188–91
presidential election campaign, 184–88
regime mobilization, 180–81
regime options, 177
rule of law and, 176, 208
Russia's role, 9, 176, 181–84, 190–91, 193–94, 198–99
settlement, 7, 194–97
Organization for Security and Cooperation in Europe (OSCE), 185, 191
Organization of Ukrainian Nationalists (OUN), 13, 17. *See also* Congress of Ukrainian Nationalists
organized crime. *See* crime and criminal activity
orthodox churches
history of Ukraine, 11, 12, 14

Perry, William J., 39
Peter I, Tsar, 12
petroleum products. *See* gas and oil trade
Petrov, Yuri, 101
pharmaceuticals. *See* health care
Pinchuk, Victor
  oligarchs' impact, 253
  oligarchs' rise, 109, 112
  opposition organization, 154
  parliamentary elections of 1998, 118
  parliamentary elections of 2006, 214
  presidential election of 2004, 159–60, 181, 195
  privatization and, 152, 163, 206, 210
  Yushchenko's reforms, 132, 148
pipeline systems. *See also* gas and oil trade
  gas trade intricacies, 105–06
  Yushchenko's reforms, 138
piracy in audiovisual production, 225
Pivdenmash, 45
pluralism
  competitive oligarchy and growth, 6
  democracy's survival as concern, 256
  new political forces and, 43
  Orange Revolution and, 6
plutocrats, oligarchs as, 107
poisoning of Yushchenko, 39, 185–86, 188, 203
Poland
  aristocratic constitutional order and, 84
  Balcerowicz policy, 43
  coal miners' unions and, 18
  composite transition index, 126, 127*f*
  Doing Business Index, 246
  economic growth in, 97
  EU membership, 172
  European economic convergence, 260
  Freedom House rankings, 254, 255*f*
  GDP changes, 125, 126*f*, 147, 148*f*
  history of Ukraine, 11–14
  hyperinflation and economic crisis, 49
  infant mortality in, 233
  Kuchma's curtailed travel and, 145
  privatization in, 81
  regions of Ukraine, 19*b*
  Russian gas embargo, 211
  taxation survey, 142
  Ukrainian economic policy and, 43, 72
  Ukrainian independence and, 193
  Ukrainian parliamentary elections of 2007, 219
  Ukrainian presidential election of 2004, 176, 194
  underground economy size, 48
  Yushchenko's deregulation of small firms, 142
police. *See* law enforcement; security police
Polish-Lithuanian Commonwealth, history of Ukraine, 11–12
political asylum, 96, 144
political consultants, Ukrainian elections and, 155–56. *See also* political technologists, Ukrainian elections and
political parties. *See also specific factions and entities*
  constitution and, 84, 86, 241–43
  democracy's survival as concern, 258
  oligarchs' impact, 252
  opposition organization, 151, 154
  parliamentary elections and, 20, 63–64, 116–18, 155–59, 213–21, 241–43
  political twins, 156–57
  presidential election of 2004, 190, 198
  underreform trap and, 121–22
political prisoners, awakening under Gorbachev, 16–17. *See also* prison camps; *specific individuals*
political rights comparison, 254–56, 255*f*
political structure, Ukrainian. *See also specific aspects and entities*
  awakening under Gorbachev, 20–21
  constitution and, 84–86
  Declaration of National Unity and, 215–16
  economic boom of 2004, 167
  Kravchuk characteristics as president, 35
  new political forces, 41–43
  Orange Revolution and, 7
  political system overview, 7–8
  underreform trap and, 121–23
  Yushchenko's reforms and, 147–48
political technologists, Ukrainian elections and, 120, 183–84, 199. *See also* political consultants, Ukrainian elections and
Poltava
  battle at, 12
  ore mine in, 221
Ponzi scheme, commercial bankers and, 229
Popular Democratic Party, 117–18, 152, 156
Popular Movement in Support of Perestroika. *See* Rukh
population decline, 235, 235*f*
populist nationalists, Ukraine's liberation from Russia, 37. *See also specific entities*
populist social policy
  parliamentary elections of 2006, 214
  Soviet economic reforms and crisis, 26

Tymoshenko's reforms, 207, 208–09
Pora, 179, 185, 198
Poroshenko, Petro
opposition organization, 154
orange coalition beginning, 202–03
orange coalition end, 208–09
parliamentary elections of 2006, 213, 215
presidential election of 2004, 187
State Tax Administration investigation, 178
Yekhanurov government, 210
poultry inspections, 225
Powell, Colin L., 193
"Power of the People" campaign, naming of, 184
presidential administration. *See also specific individuals and aspects*
attempt to merge cabinet of ministers with, 47
central-regional relations, 8, 244
judicial reform needs, 245
Kravchuk as Father of Nation, 58
orange coalition beginning, 203
orange coalition end, 208–09
Orange Revolution aftermath, 7
Orange Revolution demonstrations at, 192
political system overview, 8
presidential or parliamentary rule issue, 8, 240
State Property Fund chairmanship and, 78
term limits, 176–77
Yushchenko's government reforms, 134–35
presidential debates, 190, 197
presidential decrees
Kravchuk and, 35, 45
Kuchma and currency reform, 76
Kuchma and economic reforms, 72, 88, 131
Kuchma and financial stabilization, 74
Kuchma and new constitution, 85
Kuchma and privatization, 81, 83
Kuchma's reforms as prime minister, 45–46
presidential or parliamentary rule issue, 239, 241
Tymoshenko government, 223
Yushchenko's dissolution of parliament, 232
Yushchenko's reforms, 136, 150
presidential election of 1991
limit set by Chornovil, 156
nation-building as goal, 3
overview of, 32, 33*t*
presidential election of 1994
Kravchuk as Father of Nation, 58
Kuchma's aborted reforms, 46
lessons from Ukraine's transformation, 258
overview of, 4, 62, 66–68, 68*t*
presidential election of 1999
Kuchma's focus and, 100
Kuchma's policy stagnation, 93–94, 106
overview of, 118–21, 120*t*
Russia and, 183
presidential election of 2004
Kuchma's focus and, 154
lessons from Ukraine's transformation, 258, 263–64
opposition goals, 152
Orange Revolution aftermath, 7, 201–02, 213, 226
overview of, 176–98, 189*t*
parliamentary elections and, 158–60
Russia and, 9, 169–71
presidential election of 2010, parliamentary elections and, 231, 232
presidential-parliamentarian, constitution as, 85–86
presidential-parliamentary systems, evolution of, 240. *See also* parliament, Ukrainian
presidential powers
constitution adoption, 84–85
constitutional evolution and shortcomings, 7, 8, 237–41, 243
Kravchuk characteristics as president, 35
as Kuchma's goal, 94
Kuchma's reforms as president, 85–87, 91
Kuchma's reforms as prime minister, 45
parliamentary elections of 2006, 213
presidential election of 1994, 67
presidential election of 2004, 7, 177, 196
Tymoshenko government, 222–23
underreform trap and, 122–23
Yanukovych government, 217
Yushchenko's call for new elections, 231
presidential rule
parliamentary elections and, 63
presidential or parliamentary rule issue, 7, 8, 237–41
presidential vetoes. *See* vetoes by president
press. *See* media
prices
author's 1991 Ukraine trip, 29, 30
economic boom of 2004, 164

economic growth program and, 99–100
gas trade intricacies, 105
hyperinflation and economic crisis, 48, 52, 54
Kryvorizhstal privatization, 163–64
Kuchma's reforms as president, 4, 61, 70–73, 75
Larenko's excesses, 95
lessons from Ukraine's transformation, 246, 250
market economy definition, 5–6
nationalist economic policy, 44
oligarchs' impact, 253
oligarchs' rise, 112
Putin's Ukrainian policy, 170
renewed financial crisis, 229–30
rent seeking and early economic policy, 55–56
Russian gas embargo, 211–12
Soviet economic reforms and crisis, 23–25, 27
Tymoshenko governments, 205, 207–09, 222, 223
Yanukovych governments, 162–63, 218
Yushchenko's reforms, 135, 143
Zviahilskiy and rent seeking, 47
PricewaterhouseCoopers, 129
prikhvatizatsiya, 79
prime minister role. *See also specific individuals*
constitution and, 64, 84–85, 196
Kravchuk and, 35, 46
Kravchuk as Father of Nation, 58
Kuchma and, 93
Larenko's excesses, 95
Orange Revolution aftermath, 7, 209
parliamentary elections of 2006, 213
presidential or parliamentary rule issue, 8, 239
Tymoshenko government, 222
Yanukovych government, 217
Yushchenko's government reforms, 134
print media. *See* media
prison camps, 14, 16
Privatbank, 109
private enterprise. *See also specific sectors and entities*
author's 1991 Ukraine trip, 30
European economic convergence, 259
market economy definition, 6
as percent of GDP, 48, 81, 82*f*, 246
Soviet economic reforms and crisis, 24
underreform trap and, 122
private property rights. *See* property rights
Privat Group
oligarchs' impact, 254
oligarchs' rise, 109, 109*n*
parliamentary elections of 2006, 214
parliamentary elections of 2007, 221
presidential election of 2004, 181
Tyhypko and, 160
Tymoshenko's reforms, 206
privatization. *See also* Ukrainization of enterprises
agricultural land privatization, 70, 139–40, 190, 216, 221, 223, 253
awakening under Gorbachev, 21–22
capitalist transformation and, 237, 246, 249
competitive oligarchy and growth, 6, 152, 163–64
constitutional evolution and shortcomings, 243
exemptions from, 80
gas trade intricacies, 105
Kravchuk as Father of Nation, 58
Kryvorizhstal privatization, 109*n*, 152, 163–64, 190, 205–06, 210–11, 249
Kuchma and economic reforms, 4, 10, 62–63, 70, 72
Kuchma and international assistance, 89
Kuchma's characteristics as president, 91
Kuchma's reforms as president, 78–83, 93
Kuchma's reforms as prime minister, 45–46
Larenko and, 95
market economy definition, 6
oligarchs' impact, 252–53
oligarchs' rise, 108, 111
orange coalition formation, 203
parliamentary elections of 2006, 214, 216
presidential election of 2004, 186–87, 190
presidential or parliamentary rule issue, 239
Soviet economic reforms and crisis, 23, 27
Tymoshenko governments, 204–09, 221, 223–24
as World Bank success, 251
Yekhanurov government, 209–11
Yushchenko's reforms, 5, 139–41, 149–50
privatization vouchers
capitalist transformation and, 249
Kuchma's reforms as president, 79, 81, 83
oligarchs' rise, 108
production and productivity. *See also specific sectors*
competitive oligarchy and growth, 6
economic growth program and, 97

Kryvorizhstal privatization, 163
Kuchma's reforms as president, 78, 86
land acquisitions and taxation, 142
oligarchs' rise, 111
renewed financial crisis, 230
Soviet economic reforms and crisis, 25
Yushchenko's reforms, 149, 153
profits from enterprises. *See also* rent seeking; *specific entities*
central-regional relations, 244
Larenko's excesses, 95
Russian gas embargo, 212
Soviet economic reforms and crisis, 25
Tymoshenko's reforms, 207
Ukrainian Law on the Taxation of Enterprise Profit, 74
Yushchenko's government reforms, 136
Zviahilskiy and, 47
progressive socialists. *See also specific individuals and entities*
parliamentary elections of 1998, 117
parliamentary elections of 2002, 155
presidential election of 2004, 189
Progressive Social Party, 42, 120
property rights
competitive oligarchy and growth, 6
constitution and, 85
democracy's survival as concern, 258
intellectual property rights, 225
judicial reform needs, 245
Kuchma's reforms as president, 78
market economy definition, 6
oligarchs' impact, 251–52, 254
oligarchs' rise, 110
Tymoshenko's reforms, 208
Yanukovych government, 218
Yekhanurov government, 210
Yushchenko's reforms, 6
prosecution. *See* court system, Ukrainian
prosecutor general role
constitution and, 86, 196
crime and law enforcement, 113
protectionism
Kryvorizhstal privatization, 163
Kuchma's foreign policy, 103
presidential election of 2004, 182
WTO accession and, 224
Yushchenko's reforms, 153
protests. *See* demonstrations and protests
public debt. *See* arrears; foreign debt; state debt
"public education on market reform" slogan, 61
public expenditures. *See* budget issues
public opinion
democracy's survival as concern, 258
Gongadze murder and, 144
Kuchma's reforms as president, 73, 91
media and, 116
NATO bombing of Yugoslavia, 104, 226
NATO membership possibility, 264
nuclear power as issue, 3
Orange Revolution and, 164
on potential presidential candidates, 119, 231
on Putin, 183
reprivatization as issue, 206–07
underreform trap and, 122–23
Yushchenko's reforms, 149
Pushkin, Alexander, 12
Pustovoitenko, Valeriy
Kinakh and, 152
parliamentary elections of 1998, 117, 156
as passive loyalist, 93, 100–01
as weak prime minister, 131
Yushchenko's cabinet and, 153
Putin, Vladimir
central-regional relations and, 243
constitution and, 86
democracy's survival as concern, 256
Kuchma's curtailed travel and, 145
lessons from Ukraine's transformation, 9, 263–64
NATO controversies, 202, 227–28
oligarchs' rise and, 112
presidential or parliamentary rule issue, 240
Tymoshenko government, 223
Ukrainian presidential election of 2004, 9, 168–71, 176, 182–84, 190–91, 193
underreform trap and, 123
United Russia party and, 220
Yanukovych government, 217
Yushchenko's foreign policy, 204
Yushchenko's privatization reforms, 141
Pyatnyskiy, Valeriy, 225
Pylypchuk, Volodymyr, 22, 30
Pynzenyk, Viktor
economic growth program of, 93, 97–100
hyperinflation and economic crisis, 54
Kuchma's reforms as president, 69, 72, 75, 83
Kuchma's reforms as prime minister, 45–46
opposition organization, 153
orange coalition formation, 203
Tyhypko actions after replacing, 160
Tymoshenko governments, 205, 222

underreform trap and, 122
Yushchenko and oligarchs, 133

Rabinovich, Vadym, 87, 107, 115
racketeering. *See* crime and criminal activity
radar sales to Iraq, 145
Rada, Supreme. *See* parliament, Ukrainian
Radio Free Europe, demise of media, 116
Radio Liberty broadcasts, 178
radio stations. *See* media
Raiffeisen International Bank, 170
railways, rise of US oligarchs, 110
Rasputin, Baloha comparison, 217
rationing. *See also* food and food supplies; shortages of goods
awakening under Gorbachev, 22
Soviet economic reforms and crisis, 25
real estate sector. *See also* construction
economic growth and, 6, 152
oligarchs' rise, 107
recession, renewed financial crisis and, 231, 252
Red Army, 2, 13
red directors. *See* state enterprise managers
referendum on constitution, Kuchma's threats of (1995), 85
referendum on Crimea's status (1991), 57
referendum on federalization of Ukraine, demand for (2004), 195
referendum on Soviet Union (1991), 22
referendum on Ukrainian independence (1991), 2, 32–33, 57
regional and local elections. *See also* elections (in general)
central-regional relations, 244
local elections of 1990, 20
Mukachevo mayoral elections of 2004, 184
regional and local governments. *See also specific regions*
constitution and, 8, 85–86, 195–96, 223, 238, 243–44
dissolution of parliament, 219
Larenko's excesses, 94–95
oligarchs' rise and, 108–09, 111, 112
presidential or parliamentary rule issue, 8, 240
privatization and, 79–80
regions of Ukraine, 19–20*b*
Tymoshenko governments, 207–08, 223
Yanukovych's reforms, 163
Regional Revival, 145
Regions of Ukraine. *See* Party of Regions
Regions, Party of. *See* Party of Regions
religion and religious issues
amnesty for prisoners, 16
author's trip through western Ukraine, 60
changes in Kyiv, 1
history of Ukraine, 11, 12, 14
Kuchma's foreign policy, 104
remonetization
European economic convergence, 259
Yushchenko's government reforms, 135
rent seeking
capitalist transformation and, 249
competitive oligarchy and growth, 6
costs of reform delay, 3
democracy's survival as concern, 258
economic policy rationale and, 55–56
gas trade intricacies, 104–06
Kravchuk as Father of Nation, 58
Kuchma's reforms as president, 4, 74
Larenko's excesses, 95
new political forces and, 42
oligarchs' rise and, 110, 112
policy stagnation under Kuchma, 10
Soviet economic reforms and crisis, 25, 27
Ukraine's liberation from Russia, 37
underreform trap and, 121
Yushchenko's ouster as prime minister, 146
Yushchenko's reforms, 5, 128, 138–39, 139*n*, 142, 147–50, 153
Zviahilskiy and, 47–48
reprivatization. *See also* privatization
oligarchs' impact, 252
parliamentary elections of 2006, 213
parliamentary elections of 2007, 220
Tymoshenko governments, 204–09, 222
Yekhanurov government, 210–11
reserves, international. *See* international reserves
Respublika, 106
restaurants, price regulation and, 99
retail trade, competitive oligarchy and growth, 6
retirees. *See* pensions and pensioners
revenues. *See* budget issues; taxes and taxation
revolution, defined, 199
right-wing factions. *See also specific entities*
awakening under Gorbachev, 17
Gongadze murder and, 144
national independence and, 32
new political forces, 42–43
opposition organization, 154–55
parliamentary elections of 1994, 64

parliamentary elections of 1998, 116, 118
parliamentary elections of 2002, 156
presidential election of 1999, 119
Yanukovych's reforms, 161
Yushchenko and oligarchs, 132
Rivne, regions of Ukraine, 19*b*
robber barons (US), oligarchs' rise, 110
Romania
EU membership, 172
Russian gas embargo, 211
taxation survey, 142
underreform trap, 121, 123
Rome Treaty, 102
Roosevelt, Franklin, 102
Rose Revolution, 176, 179, 197, 198
RosUkrEnergo (RUE), 170, 211–13, 218, 224
ruble and ruble zone. *See also* currency
author's 1991 Ukraine trip, 29
CES launching, 170
economic reform delays and consequences, 3
hyperinflation and economic crisis, 49
Kuchma's currency reform, 76–77
Soviet economic reforms and crisis, 24–26
Ukraine's liberation from Russia, 36–37
Ukrainian nationalist economic policy, 43, 44
Rukh
author's 1991 Ukraine trip, 30
awakening under Gorbachev, 16–18, 20–21
Kravchuk characteristics as president, 35
nation-building as goal, 2
new political forces and, 41
opposition organization, 154
parliamentary elections of 1994, 63–65
parliamentary elections of 1998, 117–18
presidential election of 1994, 67
presidential election of 1999, 119
presidential election of 2004, 192
underreform trap and, 122
Yushchenko's ouster as prime minister, 146
rule of law. *See also* law and legislative activity
democracy's survival as concern, 256
market economy and, 246*n*
oligarchs' impact, 251, 254
Orange Revolution and, 176, 208
political system overview, 8
underreform trap and, 121–22
Rural Party, 118, 119
rural-urban class divide, 221
RUSAL, 141
Rus, history of Ukraine, 11–12
Russia. *See also* Soviet Union
author's 1991 Ukraine trip, 30
central-regional relations and, 243
challenges ahead, 264–65
composite transition index, 126, 127*f*
corruption perceptions index, 256
currency corridor adoption, 250
demise of media and, 115
democracy's survival as concern, 254, 256, 258
denuclearization concerns, 39–40, 58, 228
Doing Business Index, 246
economic growth, 97
energy-efficiency comparison, 105, 105*n*
ENP and, 172–73, 173*n*
European economic convergence, 259–60
Freedom House rankings, 254, 255*f*
gas embargo, 211–13
gas trade intricacies, 4, 93, 95, 105–06
GDP changes, 125, 126*f*, 147, 148*f*
Gorbachev reforms and Ukraine, 15–18, 20–22
Gore-Chernomyrdin Commission, 89
history of Crimea, 56–57
history of Ukraine, 11–12
homicide rate comparison, 113
income taxes, 161
Kuchma's curtailed travel, 145
Kuchma's foreign policy, 8–9, 93, 101–04, 172
Kuchma's reforms as president, 61, 69–75, 90, 91
Kuchma's reforms as prime minister, 45
lessons from Ukraine's transformation, 9, 250, 263–64
liberation from, 35–39
male life expectancy, 233
national independence and, 2, 33
nation-building and, 3
NATO controversies and, 202, 225–28, 263
oligarchs' impact, 253
oligarchs' rise, 107–08, 107*n*, 111–12
presidential or parliamentary rule issue, 240
privatization and, 79–81, 163, 249
Putin's Ukrainian policy, 9, 168–71, 263–64
referendum on Soviet Union (1991), 22
regions of Ukraine, 19*b*
rent seeking and early Ukrainian policy, 55–56
Russia-Belarus currency union project, 62

Soviet economic reforms and crisis, 18, 23–27
Soviet Union dissolution, 33*n*
Soviet Union formation, 17
taxation survey, 142
Tymoshenko governments, 207, 223
Ukrainian economic policy and, 3, 44, 72
Ukrainian parliamentary elections of 2002, 183
Ukrainian parliamentary elections of 2006, 214, 216
Ukrainian presidential election of 1994, 66–67
Ukrainian presidential election of 1999, 118–19, 183
Ukrainian presidential election of 2004, 9, 176, 181–84, 187, 190–91, 193–94, 198–99
underground economy size, 48
underreform trap, 121, 122–23
union of soviet states talks, 31
war in Georgia, 228
WTO accession and, 224–25
Yanukovych government, 217–18
Yushchenko's call for new elections, 232
Yushchenko's foreign policy, 204
Yushchenko's ouster as prime minister, 146
Yushchenko's reforms, 135, 138, 140
Russian Civil War, 12
Russian Club, 181, 183
Russian constitution, 85–86
Russian Duma. *See* Russian State Duma
Russian economic reforms. *See also* economic reforms
economic reform delays and consequences, 3
national independence as goal, 2
Russian Federal Security Service (FSB), 120*n*
Russian Federation Council, 102. *See also* Russian parliament
Russian financial crises
Ukraine's liberation from Russia, 37
Ukrainian crisis comparison, 229, 247
underreform trap and, 123
Yushchenko's reforms, 5, 128–31, 147
Russian language
changes in Kyiv, 1
constitution and, 85
Declaration of National Unity and, 216
history of Crimea, 57
international assistance and, 88
Kravchuk characteristics as president, 34
Kuchma's characteristics as president, 91
miners' strikes, 18
national independence and, 31–32
nation-building as goal, 2–3
new political forces and, 41–43
opposition conference coverage, 178
regions of Ukraine, 19*b*
transcription approach of book, 10
Ukrainian presidential election of 1994, 66–67
Ukrainian presidential election of 2004, 187, 189
Russian Ministry of Defense, 146
Russian nationalists. *See also specific individuals and entities*
Black Sea Fleet as issue, 101
Crimea secession threat, 57
NATO controversies, 228
Russian Orthodox Church, 14, 184
Russian parliament. *See also* Russian Federation Council; Russian State Duma
constitution and, 84
semiproportional system of, 116–17
shoot-out in, 65
Ukraine's liberation from Russia, 36–37
Russian State Duma, 21, 191, 193. *See also* Russian parliament
Russian-Ukrainian Treaty of 1997. *See* Treaty on Friendship, Cooperation and Partnership
Russification, 15, 19*b*, 56
Rybachuk, Oleh, 182, 203, 204, 209, 217

Saakashvili, Mikheil, 202, 228
Saddam Hussein, 145
Safire, William, 29*n*
salaries. *See* wages and salaries
sales taxes. *See* taxes and taxation
Savchenko, Oleksandr, 30, 30*n*
savings
economic growth program, 99
privatization vouchers and, 83
renewed financial crisis, 229
Tymoshenko government, 223
Yanukovych's reforms, 161
Yushchenko's reforms, 131
Scandinavian countries, as parliamentary stalwarts, 241. *See also specific entities*
Scheffer, Jaap de Hoop, 226
scientific exchanges and EU, 204
scrap iron, export tariffs, 225
security guards, prevalence of, 113, 115
security police, 14, 39, 95. *See also* law enforcement
Security Service of Ukraine (SBU)

crime and law enforcement, 113
Gongadze murder and, 145
orange coalition formation, 203
presidential election of 2004, 182, 185, 194–96, 198
Yanukovych government, 219
Yushchenko's poisoning and, 185
Semeniuk, Valentyna, 203, 216, 223
sensitive products, WTO accession and, 224
separatism
awakening under Gorbachev, 22
Crimea secession threat, 57, 63, 91
democracy's survival as concern, 258
nation-building as goal, 2
Serbia
NATO bombing of Yugoslavia and, 104, 226, 263
student organization in, 179
Sevastopol naval base, 9, 36–37, 57, 101–02, 227–28
Sevorodonetsk, presidential election of 2004, 195
shadow economy, economic statistics and, 167. *See also* underground economy
Shcherban, Yevhen, 95, 113
Shcherbytskiy, Volodymyr, 15, 18, 20*b*
Shelest, Petro, 14–15, 23
shestidesyatniki. See Children of the 20th Party Congress
Shevardnadze, Eduard, 31, 197
Shevchenko, Taras, 12
"shock therapy" (economic policy), 44
shortages of goods. *See also* food and food supplies
author's 1991 Ukraine trip, 29
awakening under Gorbachev, 18, 22
Soviet economic reforms and crisis, 24–25
Shpek, Roman, 45, 60, 69–70, 70*n*, 74
Shushkevich, Stanislav, 32–33
Siberia
amnesty for prisoners, 16
miners' strikes, 18
Sintoza, 109
Slovakia
author's trip through western Ukraine, 59
EU membership, 172
Russian gas embargo, 211
taxation survey, 142
Yushchenko's privatization reforms, 141
Slovenia, EU membership, 172
small enterprises. *See also* privatization
central-regional relations, 244
Kuchma's reforms, 45, 70, 79–81
presidential election of 2004, 179
underreform trap, 121
Yushchenko's reforms, 128, 135, 141–43, 149
Smeshko, Ihor, 185, 195
soap, miners' demands for, 18
social costs of economic crisis
capitalist transformation and, 246–47
Kravchuk as Father of Nation, 58
Kuchma's reforms as president, 72
rent seeking and early economic policy, 56
social costs of reform delays
lessons from Ukraine's transformation, 237
Yushchenko's reforms, 126
social costs of transition, national independence as goal, 2
Social Democratic Party (United)
parliamentary elections of 1998, 118
parliamentary elections of 2002, 155–56
presidential election of 2004, 159
Yekhanurov government, 210
Yushchenko's ouster as prime minister, 145
social democrats. *See also specific individuals and entities*
new political forces, 42
Orange Revolution aftermath, 201
presidential election of 2004, 195
socialism and socialists. *See also specific individuals and entities*
awakening under Gorbachev, 21
constitutional reform legislation, 177
history of Ukraine, 14
Kuchma's reforms as president, 85, 88
national independence and, 32
NATO controversies background, 226
opposition organization, 155
orange coalition formation, 203
Orange Revolution aftermath, 201
parliamentary elections of 1994, 64
parliamentary elections of 1998, 117
parliamentary elections of 2002, 155–56, 159
parliamentary elections of 2006, 213–16
parliamentary elections of 2007, 220
presidential election of 1994, 67
presidential election of 1999, 119
presidential election of 2004, 188–90
Soviet economic reforms and crisis, 23
underreform trap and, 121
Yanukovych government, 217, 218
Yekhanurov government, 210

socialist economy, market economy versus, 5, 126. *See also* Soviet economic system
Socialist International, 220
Socialist Party
  Gongadze murder and, 144
  new political forces, 41–42
  orange coalition formation, 203
  parliamentary elections of 1998, 118
  parliamentary elections of 2002, 156
Socialist Party of Ukraine, 64, 67
social sector. *See also specific aspects*
  economic growth program, 99–100
  Kuchma's reforms as president, 75, 86, 89
  social reform achievements, 232–36
  Yushchenko's government reforms, 136
social security, Kuchma's reforms as president, 75
social transfers
  oligarchs' impact, 251
  parliamentary elections of 2007, 220
  Tymoshenko's reforms, 207
Sokil (Hawk), 144
Solana, Javier, 194
Solidarity movement (Poland), 18, 193–94
songs of celebration, 196–97
Soros Foundation, 42, 250
Soros, George
  author's 1991 Ukraine trip, 29
  Kuchma's economic reforms, 60, 62, 68, 89, 89*n*
  Kuchma's policy stagnation, 100*n*
Soros International Economic Advisory Group, 62, 100*n*
South Ossetia, Russia's war in Georgia, 228
sovereignty issues. *See also* national independence
  awakening under Gorbachev, 21–22
  challenges ahead, 264
  constitution and, 84
  denuclearization concerns and, 40
  Kravchuk as Father of Nation, 58
  Kuchma's foreign policy, 102, 104
  lessons from Ukraine's transformation, 237
  NATO controversies, 227–28
  Putin and, 9
  Soviet economic reforms and crisis, 26
  Ukraine's liberation from Russia, 36
Soviet central planning system, revival attempt, 47
Soviet economic reforms and crisis. *See also* economic reforms
  awakening under Gorbachev, 18
  impact of reforms and crisis, 23–27
Soviet economic system
  hyperinflation and economic crisis, 54
  Kuchma's reforms as president, 75
  nation-building as goal, 3
  Ukrainian economic crisis, 23
  Ukrainian nationalist economic policy, 44
Soviet enterprise privatization. *See* privatization
Soviet flag, replacement of, 33
Soviet nationality policy, 15
Soviet parliament. *See* USSR Congress of People's Deputies
Soviet Savings Bank, 223
Soviet State Price Committee, 99
Soviet Ukrainian Constitution of 1978, 35, 58, 64, 83–84. *See also* constitution, Ukrainian
Soviet Union. *See also specific issues and entities*
  author's 1991 Ukraine trip, 29–31
  central-regional relations and, 243
  European economic convergence, 260
  formation of, 17
  Gorbachev reforms and Ukraine, 15–18, 21–22
  history of Ukraine, 11–15
  judicial reform needs and, 245
  Kravchuk as Father of Nation, 58
  male life expectancy, 24
  media of, 115
  oligarchs' rise and, 111–12
  referendum on (1991), 22
  regions of Ukraine, 19*b*
  trade comparison, 103
  Ukraine policy environment comparison, 60–61
  Ukraine's liberation from Russia, 36–39
  Ukrainian independence and, 31–33
  US Trade Act and, 225
Soviet Union dissolution
  Crimea secession threat, 57
  democracy's survival as concern, 254, 256, 258
  enterprise productivity after, 78
  Kravchuk characteristics as president, 34–35
  national independence and, 2, 31–33
  new political forces and, 42
  peace as priority, 3
special forces. *See also* armed forces
  dissolution of parliament, 219
  Orange Revolution demonstrations and, 192

Springtime of Nations, 179
Stalin, Joseph, 13–14, 56
starvation, imposed, 13
Stasiuk, Volodymyr, 185–86
state agencies. *See also specific entities*
challenges ahead, 265
crime and law enforcement, 115
economic growth program, 99
European economic convergence, 259
government reforms of Yushchenko, 134
oligarchs' impact, 253
reduction in number of, 143
state assets decline and privatization, 223
state bankruptcy concerns. *See also* foreign debt
presidential election of 1994, 66
rent seeking and early Ukrainian policy, 56
state-building. *See also* institution-building; *specific entities*
Kuchma's characteristics as president, 91
national independence and, 32
State Committee for Regulatory Policy and Entrepreneurship, 142
State Committee for the State of Emergency (GKChP), 31
state credits. *See also* banking sector; *specific entities*
rent seeking and early economic policy, 55–56
rise of US oligarchs, 110
Soviet economic reforms and crisis, 25
state debt, as percent of GDP, 129, 130*f*, 131, 147. *See also* arrears; foreign debt
state enterprise managers
awakening under Gorbachev, 21
economic growth program and, 97
hyperinflation and economic crisis, 54
Kinakh and, 152
Kuchma's reforms as president, 78–83
Kuchma's reforms as prime minister, 45–46
Lazarenko and, 95
nation-building as goal, 2–3
new political forces and, 42–43
oligarchs' rise, 108
presidential election of 1994, 66–67
rent seeking and early economic policy, 55
Soviet economic reforms and crisis, 24–25
Yushchenko's privatization reforms, 140
Zviahilskiy and rent seeking, 47
State Planning Committee, 97, 246
State Program for the Privatization of State Enterprises, 79
State Property Fund of Ukraine, 78–80, 203, 216, 249
State Savings Bank of Ukraine, 79
state subsidies. *See also* state credits
capitalist transformation and, 246, 249
competitive oligarchy and growth, 6
hyperinflation and economic crisis, 49, 52
Kuchma's reforms as president, 5
nationalist economic policy, 44
rent seeking and early economic policy, 56
underreform trap and, 121
WTO accession, 225
Yanukovych governments, 218
Yushchenko's reforms, 6, 136, 138
Zviahilskiy and rent seeking, 47
State Tax Administration
crime and law enforcement, 113, 115
establishment of, 54
media as repressed by, 159
opposition conference, 178
parliamentary elections of 1998, 117
presidential election of 2004, 180
Yanukovych's reforms, 161–62
Yushchenko's ouster as prime minister, 146
Yushchenko's reforms, 142
state-trading countries, market economy definition, 5–6
steel trade. *See also* metal trade
CES launching, 171
competitive oligarchy and growth, 6
economic boom of 2004, 164
economic reform delays and consequences, 4
Kuchma's foreign policy, 103
Kuchma's reforms as president, 74
new political forces and, 42
oligarchs' impact, 252–53
oligarchs' rise, 107–10, 109*n*
privatization and, 152, 163–64
renewed financial crisis, 230–31
Ukraine's turning to West, 9
WTO accession, 224–25
Yekhanurov government, 210–11
Yushchenko's reforms, 140, 148
Stelmakh, Volodymyr, 160–61
stock exchange, parliament as, 65, 118
stock market collapse, US, 229
stock ownership and privatization, 81, 111, 249. *See also* joint stock companies
stock sales via initial public offerings, 253
Strategic Arms Reduction (START) Treaty, 39–40, 264

United Nations, 35, 40, 145
United Russia Party, 220
United States
campaign financing in, 242
denuclearization concerns, 39–41, 58, 228, 261
homicide rate comparison, 113
Kuchma's foreign policy, 102–03, 104, 172, 226
Kuchma's radar sales to Iraq, 145
Kuchma's reforms as president, 60, 88–89, 91
Larenko's excesses, 96–97
market economy definition, 5
oligarchy and, 107, 110–11, 158
opposition conference, 178
technical assistance from, 62
Ukraine acknowledged as market economy, 225
Ukraine's liberation from Russia, 36
Ukraine's turning to West, 9
Ukrainian diaspora, 13
Ukrainian financial crisis renewal, 229
Ukrainian presidential election of 2004, 176, 181, 185, 193–94
Ukrainian security concerns and, 228, 264
Yushchenko's foreign policy, 204
urban-rural class divide, 221
US Agency for International Development (USAID), 62, 80, 88–89, 251
US Central Intelligence Agency (CIA), 56
US Civil War, 110
US Congress, Yushchenko address to, 204
US Customs Code, market economy definition, 5
US Department of Commerce, market economy definition, 5
US dollar
currency reform and, 76
exchange rate and, 129, 229
Soviet economic reforms and crisis, 25–26
Ukrainian exports and imports in terms of, 165*f*
Ukrainian GDP in terms of, 54, 259, 260*f*
Ukrainian trade and current account balances in terms of, 166*f*
US House of Representatives, campaign financing, 242
US robber barons, oligarchs' rise, 110
US-Russian-Ukrainian declaration of January 14, 1994, 228, 264
US Senate, as club of millionaires, 158
USSR Congress of People's Deputies, 17–18, 26
USSR Law on Cooperatives, 24, 110
USSR Law on Individual Labor Activity, 24
USSR Law on State Enterprises, 25
USSR Ministry of Foreign Trade, 24
US stock market collapse, 230
US Trade Act, Jackson-Vanik amendment to, 225
US Treasury, Ukraine's liberation from Russia, 38
UT-1 channel, 116, 180
Uzbekistan
Andijan massacre, 104, 199
Russian gas embargo, 212
Soviet Union dissolution, 33*n*
Uzhhorod, author's trip through western Ukraine, 59

value-added tax. *See* taxes and taxation
Vasyunyk, Ivan, 222
Vekselberg, Viktor, 141
Venice Commission, 103
vertically integrated companies. *See also specific entities*
oligarchs' impact, 253
oligarchs' rise, 109, 111
veterans, awakening under Gorbachev, 17
vetoes by parliament
agricultural land privatization, 139
constitution and, 85
Kuchma's criticisms of parliament, 131
vetoes by president
constitution and, 85, 217
presidential or parliamentary rule issue, 8, 239
Tymoshenko government, 222–23
visas. *See* travel regulations
Vitrenko, Natalia, 42, 119–20, 120*n*, 184, 189–90
vodka
factory inspections, 97
imports, 38
Voice of America, demise of media, 116
Volkov, Oleksandr
Gongadze murder and, 143
oligarchs' rise, 107, 112
Orange Revolution aftermath, 201
parliamentary elections of 1998, 118
presidential election of 1999, 119
Yushchenko's ouster as prime minister, 145–46
Yushchenko's reforms, 134, 138–39, 148–49
Voloshin, Aleksandr, 182–83
Volsky, Arkady, 66

Voltaire, 12
volume of money as ratio of GDP, 259, 261*f*
Volyn, regions of Ukraine, 19*b*
Voronin, Ihor, 170, 218
voucher privatization. *See* privatization vouchers
Vseukrainskie vedomosti, demise of media, 116
Vyakhirev, Rem, 106, 169

wages and salaries. *See also* income
  author's 1991 Ukraine trip, 29
  hyperinflation and economic crisis, 54
  Kuchma's reforms as president, 72, 75, 83
  oligarchs' impact, 251
  real wages, recovery of, 164, 169*f*
  Soviet economic reforms and crisis, 25
  Tymoshenko's reforms, 207
  Yushchenko's reforms of 2000, 125, 136, 147
Western Military Command, 194
West, Ukraine's turning to. *See also specific countries and organizations*
  Kuchma's reforms as president, 70–71, 88–89
  lessons from Ukraine's transformation, 238, 261–64
  oligarchs' impact, 253–54
wheat, Soviet economic reforms and crisis, 23
wineries, Soviet economic reforms and crisis, 23
World Bank
  Business Environment and Enterprise Performance Survey, 256
  Doing Business Index, 246, 247*f*, 248*f*
  economic growth program and, 97
  on inspections management, 142
  Kuchma's reforms as president, 61, 80, 88–90, 131
  lessons from Ukraine's transformation, 251
  nationalist economic policy and, 44
  pension guidelines, 161
  presidential or parliamentary rule issue, 239
  Yushchenko's reforms of 2000, 125, 149
World Economic Forum, 35
world market prices. *See* prices
World Trade Organization (WTO)
  CES launching and, 170–71
  Declaration of National Unity and, 216
  European economic convergence, 259
  Kuchma's foreign policy, 102
  lessons from Ukraine's transformation, 238
  Tymoshenko governments, 204–05, 209, 223
  Ukraine becomes member, 9, 202, 224–25, 263
  Yanukovych governments, 162, 218
  Yushchenko's foreign policy, 204
World War I, 12
World War II, 3, 13
Writers' Union, 16

Yakovlev, Aleksandr, 31
Yanukovych, Viktor
  CES launching and, 171
  dissolution of parliament, 219
  first government of, 151, 159–63, 202
  as globally renowned, 175
  NATO controversies, 226
  opposition conference, 178, 178*n*
  Orange Revolution aftermath, 201–02, 216
  parliamentary elections of 2006, 214–15
  parliamentary elections of 2007, 219, 221
  presidential election of 2004, 153, 159–60, 175–76, 180–85, 187–95, 197–98, 201
  presidential election of 2010, 231, 232
  regions of Ukraine, 20*b*
  Russia's war in Georgia, 228
  second government of, 202, 204, 216–19
  Tuzla incident and, 171
  Tymoshenko's reforms and, 222–23
Yatseniuk, Arseniy, 210, 222, 226
Yekhanurov, Yuriy
  capitalist transformation and, 249
  government of, 202, 209–12, 214, 217–18
  Kuchma's reforms as president, 69, 80–83, 89
  opposition organization, 153
  orange coalition end, 209
  parliamentary elections of 2006, 213–15
  Tymoshenko government, 222
  underreform trap and, 122
  Yushchenko's ouster as prime minister, 153
  Yushchenko's reforms, 132, 133, 142
Yeltsin, Boris
  awakening under Gorbachev, 21–22
  Crimea secession threat, 57, 58
  democracy's survival as concern, 254, 256, 258
  denuclearization concerns, 40, 228
  Kuchma's foreign policy, 8, 9, 101
  Kuchma's reelection and, 94, 118

Kuchma's reforms as president, 71, 91
legislative powers and, 35
presidential or parliamentary rule issue, 240
privatization and, 81, 163
Putin anointed president by, 168
reform speech by, 71
Soviet Union dissolution, 3, 32–33
Ukraine's liberation from Russia, 35–38
Yekhanurov government, 210
Yemelianov, Oleksandr, 30, 43–44
youth, higher education pursuit by, 235–36, 236*f*, 260
Yugoslavia
hyperinflation and economic crisis, 49
Kuchma's foreign policy, 104, 172
NATO bombing of, 104, 226, 263
Yushchenko, Viktor
capitalist transformation and, 249
dissolution of parliament, 219, 231
economic growth program and, 97
European Square speech, 186–87
German Advisory Group on Economic Reforms, 62
as globally renowned, 175
Kuchma's reforms as president, 69, 73, 75
Kuchma's reforms as prime minister, 45–46
Mukachevo mayoral elections, 184
NATO controversies, 226–28
opposition conference, 178*n*
opposition organization, 151, 153–55
orange coalition beginning, 202
orange coalition end, 208–09
Orange Revolution aftermath, 201, 231–32
ouster as prime minister, 5, 145–46, 151, 153, 153*n*
parliamentary elections of 2002, 155, 158
parliamentary elections of 2006, 213–16
parliamentary elections of 2007, 219, 221
poisoning of, 39, 185–86, 188, 203
as political personality, 132, 148, 154
presidential election of 1999, 119
presidential election of 2004, 7, 158–59, 175–98, 201
presidential election of 2010, 231, 232
presidential or parliamentary rule issue, 239
Putin's Ukrainian policy, 263
reforms of 2000, 5–6, 125–50, 151–53, 250
renewed financial crisis and, 232
Russia's war in Georgia, 227–28
Tyhypko and, 160
Tymoshenko's reforms, 205–09, 222–23
Ukraine's turning to Europe, 203–04
underreform trap and, 122
WTO accession and, 224
Yanukovych government, 217–18
Yekhanurov government, 209–11

Zaporizhe, regions of Ukraine, 20*b*
Zaporizhstal, 109*n*, 118
Zelenyi Svit. See Green World
Zerkalo nedeli, on revolutionary populism, 208
Zhevago, Konstantin, 109*n*, 221
Zhvania, David, 154, 178–79, 185, 203
Zienchuk, Michael, 60*n*
Zinchenko, Oleksandr, 179, 192, 203, 208–09
Ziuganov, Genady, 118–19
Zubr, 179
Zvarych, Roman, 61
Zviahilskiy, Yukhym
Kuchma administration and, 87
new political forces and, 42–43
oligarchs' rise, 107
regions of Ukraine, 20*b*
rent seeking and, 47–48, 55

Other Publications from the
Peterson Institute for International Economics

WORKING PAPERS

94-1 **APEC and Regional Trading Arrangements in the Pacific** Jeffrey A. Frankel with Shang-Jin Wei and Ernesto Stein
94-2 **Towards an Asia Pacific Investment Code** Edward M. Graham
94-3 **Merchandise Trade in the APEC Region: Is There Scope for Liberalization on an MFN Basis?** Paul Wonnacott
94-4 **The Automotive Industry in Southeast Asia: Can Protection Be Made Less Costly?** Paul Wonnacott
94-5 **Implications of Asian Economic Growth** Marcus Noland
95-1 **APEC: The Bogor Declaration and the Path Ahead** C. Fred Bergsten
95-2 **From Bogor to Miami . . . and Beyond: Regionalism in the Asia Pacific and the Western Hemisphere** Jeffrey J. Schott
95-3 **Has Asian Export Performance Been Unique?** Marcus Noland
95-4 **Association of Southeast Asian Nations (ASEAN) and ASEAN Free Trade Area (AFTA): Chronology and Statistics** Gautam Jaggi
95-5 **The North Korean Economy** Marcus Noland
95-6 **China and the International Economic System** Marcus Noland
96-1 **APEC after Osaka: Toward Free Trade by 2010/2020** C. Fred Bergsten
96-2 **Public Policy, Private Preferences, and the Japanese Trade Pattern** Marcus Noland
96-3 **German Lessons for Korea: The Economics of Unification** Marcus Noland
96-4 **Research and Development Activities and Trade Specialization in Japan** Marcus Noland
96-5 **China's Economic Reforms: Chronology and Statistics** Gautam Jaggi, Mary Rundle, Daniel Rosen, and Yuichi Takahashi
96-6 **US-China Economic Relations** Marcus Noland
96-7 **The Market Structure Benefits of Trade and Investment Liberalization** Raymond Atje and Gary Hufbauer
96-8 **The Future of US-Korea Economic Relations** Marcus Noland
96-9 **Competition Policies in the Dynamic Industrializing Economies: The Case of China, Korea, and Chinese Taipei** Edward M. Graham
96-10 **Modeling Economic Reform in North Korea** Marcus Noland, Sherman Robinson, and Monica Scatasta
96-11 **Trade, Investment, and Economic Conflict Between the United States and Asia** Marcus Noland
96-12 **APEC in 1996 and Beyond: The Subic Summit** C. Fred Bergsten
96-13 **Some Unpleasant Arithmetic Concerning Unification** Marcus Noland
96-14 **Restructuring Korea's Financial Sector for Greater Competitiveness** Marcus Noland
96-15 **Competitive Liberalization and Global Free Trade: A Vision for the 21st Century** C. Fred Bergsten
97-1 **Chasing Phantoms: The Political Economy of USTR** Marcus Noland
97-2 **US-Japan Civil Aviation: Prospects for Progress** Jacqueline McFadyen
97-3 **Open Regionalism** C. Fred Bergsten
97-4 **Lessons from the Bundesbank on the Occasion of Its 40th (and Second to Last?) Birthday** Adam S. Posen
97-5 **The Economics of Korean Unification** Marcus Noland, Sherman Robinson, and Li-Gang Liu
98-1 **The Costs and Benefits of Korean Unification** Marcus Noland, Sherman Robinson, and Li-Gang Liu
98-2 **Asian Competitive Devaluations** Li-Gang Liu, Marcus Noland, Sherman Robinson, and Zhi Wang
98-3 **Fifty Years of the GATT/WTO: Lessons from the Past for Strategies or the Future** C. Fred Bergsten
98-4 **NAFTA Supplemental Agreements: Four Year Review** Jacqueline McFadyen
98-5 **Local Government Spending: Solving the Mystery of Japanese Fiscal Packages** Hiroko Ishii and Erika Wada
98-6 **The Global Economic Effects of the Japanese Crisis** Marcus Noland, Sherman Robinson, and Zhi Wang
99-1 **Rigorous Speculation: The Collapse and Revival of the North Korean Economy** Marcus Noland, Sherman Robinson, and Tao Wang
99-2 **Famine in North Korea: Causes and Cures** Marcus Noland, Sherman Robinson, and Tao Wang
99-3 **Competition Policy and FDI: A Solution in Search of a Problem?** Marcus Noland

- 99-4 **The Continuing Asian Financial Crisis: Global Adjustment and Trade** Marcus Noland, Sherman Robinson, and Zhi Wang
- 99-5 **Why EMU Is Irrelevant for the German Economy** Adam S. Posen
- 99-6 **The Global Trading System and the Developing Countries in 2000** C. Fred Bergsten
- 99-7 **Modeling Korean Unification** Marcus Noland, Sherman Robinson, and Tao Wang
- 99-8 **Sovereign Liquidity Crisis: The Strategic Case for a Payments Standstill** Marcus Miller and Lei Zhang
- 99-9 **The Case for Joint Management of Exchange Rate Flexibility** C. Fred Bergsten, Olivier Davanne, and Pierre Jacquet
- 99-10 **Does Talk Matter After All? Inflation Targeting and Central Bank Behavior** Kenneth N. Kuttner and Adam S. Posen
- 99-11 **Hazards and Precautions: Tales of International Finance** Gary Clyde Hufbauer and Erika Wada
- 99-12 **The Globalization of Services: What Has Happened? What Are the Implications?** Gary C. Hufbauer and Tony Warren
- 00-1 **Regulatory Standards in the WTO: Comparing Intellectual Property Rights with Competition Policy, Environmental Protection, and Core Labor Standards** Keith Maskus
- 00-2 **International Economic Agreements and the Constitution** Richard M. Goodman and John M. Frost
- 00-3 **Electronic Commerce in Developing Countries: Issues for Domestic Policy and WTO Negotiations** Catherine L. Mann
- 00-4 **The New Asian Challenge** C. Fred Bergsten
- 00-5 **How the Sick Man Avoided Pneumonia: The Philippines in the Asian Financial Crisis** Marcus Noland
- 00-6 **Inflation, Monetary Transparency, and G-3 Exchange Rate Volatility** Kenneth N. Kuttner and Adam S. Posen
- 00-7 **Transatlantic Issues in Electronic Commerce** Catherine L. Mann
- 00-8 **Strengthening the International Financial Architecture: Where Do We Stand?** Morris Goldstein
- 00-9 **On Currency Crises and Contagion** Marcel Fratzscher
- 01-1 **Price Level Convergence and Inflation in Europe** John H. Rogers, Gary Clyde Hufbauer, and Erika Wada
- 01-2 **Subsidies, Market Closure, Cross-Border Investment, and Effects on Competition: The Case of FDI on the Telecommunications Sector** Edward M. Graham
- 01-3 **Foreign Direct Investment in China: Effects on Growth and Economic Performance** Edward M. Graham and Erika Wada
- 01-4 **IMF Structural Conditionality: How Much Is Too Much?** Morris Goldstein
- 01-5 **Unchanging Innovation and Changing Economic Performance in Japan** Adam S. Posen
- 01-6 **Rating Banks in Emerging Markets: What Credit Rating Agencies Should Learn from Financial Indicators** Liliana Rojas-Suarez
- 01-7 **Beyond Bipolar: A Three-Dimensional Assessment of Monetary Frameworks** Kenneth N. Kuttner and Adam S. Posen
- 01-8 **Finance and Changing US-Japan Relations: Convergence Without Leverage—Until Now** Adam S. Posen
- 01-9 **Macroeconomic Implications of the New Economy** Martin Neil Baily
- 01-10 **Can International Capital Standards Strengthen Banks in Emerging Markets?** Liliana Rojas-Suarez
- 02-1 **Moral Hazard and the US Stock Market: Analyzing the "Greenspan Put"?** Marcus Miller, Paul Weller, and Lei Zhang
- 02-2 **Passive Savers and Fiscal Policy Effectiveness in Japan** Kenneth N. Kuttner and Adam S. Posen
- 02-3 **Home Bias, Transaction Costs, and Prospects for the Euro: A More Detailed Analysis** Catherine L. Mann and Ellen E. Meade
- 02-4 **Toward a Sustainable FTAA: Does Latin America Meet the Necessary Financial Preconditions?** Liliana Rojas-Suarez
- 02-5 **Assessing Globalization's Critics: "Talkers Are No Good Doers???"** Kimberly Ann Elliott, Debayani Kar, and J. David Richardson
- 02-6 **Economic Issues Raised by Treatment of Takings under NAFTA Chapter 11** Edward M. Graham
- 03-1 **Debt Sustainability, Brazil, and the IMF** Morris Goldstein
- 03-2 **Is Germany Turning Japanese?** Adam S. Posen
- 03-3 **Survival of the Best Fit: Exposure to Low-Wage Countries and the (Uneven) Growth of US Manufacturing Plants** Andrew B. Bernard, J. Bradford Jensen, and Peter K. Schott

03-4 **Falling Trade Costs, Heterogeneous Firms, and Industry Dynamics** Andrew B. Bernard, J. Bradford Jensen, and Peter K. Schott

03-5 **Famine and Reform in North Korea** Marcus Noland

03-6 **Empirical Investigations in Inflation Targeting** Yifan Hu

03-7 **Labor Standards and the Free Trade Area of the Americas** Kimberly Ann Elliott

03-8 **Religion, Culture, and Economic Performance** Marcus Noland

03-9 **It Takes More than a Bubble to Become Japan** Adam S. Posen

03-10 **The Difficulty of Discerning What's Too Tight: Taylor Rules and Japanese Monetary Policy** Adam S. Posen/ Kenneth N. Kuttner

04-1 **Adjusting China's Exchange Rate Policies** Morris Goldstein

04-2 **Popular Attitudes, Globalization, and Risk** Marcus Noland

04-3 **Selective Intervention and Growth: The Case of Korea** Marcus Noland

05-1 **Outsourcing and Offshoring: Pushing the European Model Over the Hill, Rather Than Off the Cliff!** Jacob Funk Kirkegaard

05-2 **China's Role in the Revived Bretton Woods System: A Case of Mistaken Identity** Morris Goldstein and Nicholas Lardy

05-3 **Affinity and International Trade** Marcus Noland

05-4 **South Korea's Experience with International Capital Flows** Marcus Noland

05-5 **Explaining Middle Eastern Authoritarianism** Marcus Noland

05-6 **Postponing Global Adjustment: An Analysis of the Pending Adjustment of Global Imbalances** Edwin Truman

05-7 **What Might the Next Emerging Market Financial Crisis Look Like?** Morris Goldstein, assisted by Anna Wong

05-8 **Egypt after the Multi-Fiber Arrangement** Dan Magder

05-9 **Tradable Services: Understanding the Scope and Impact of Services Offshoring** J. Bradford Jensen and Lori G. Kletzer

05-10 **Importers, Exporters, and Multinationals: A Portrait of Firms in the US that Trade Goods** Andrew B. Bernard, J. Bradford Jensen, and Peter K. Schott

05-11 **The US Trade Deficit: A Disaggregated Perspective** Catherine L. Mann and Katharina Plück

05-12 **Prospects for Regional Free Trade in Asia** Gary C. Hufbauer/Yee Wong

05-13 **Predicting Trade Expansion under FTAs and Multilateral Agreements** Dean A. DeRosa and John P. Gilbert

05-14 **The East Asian Industrial Policy Experience: Implications for the Middle East** Marcus Noland and Howard Pack

05-15 **Outsourcing and Skill Imports: Foreign High-Skilled Workers on H-1B and L-1 Visas in the United States** Jacob Funk Kirkegaard

06-1 **Why Central Banks Should Not Burst Bubbles** Adam S. Posen

06-2 **The Case for an International Reserve Diversification Standard** Edwin M. Truman and Anna Wong

06-3 **Offshoring in Europe—Evidence of a Two-Way Street from Denmark** Peter Ørberg Jensen, Jacob F. Kirkegaard, Nicolai Søndergaard Laugesen

06-4 **The External Policy of the Euro Area: Organizing for Foreign Exchange Intervention** C. Randall Henning

06-5 **The Eurasian Growth Paradox** Anders Åslund and Nazgul Jenish

06-6 **Has EMU Had Any Impact on the Degree of Wage Restraint?** Adam S. Posen and Daniel Popov Gould

06-7 **Firm Structure, Multinationals, and Manufacturing Plant Deaths** Andrew B. Bernard and J. Bradford Jensen

07-1 **The Trade Effects of Preferential Arrangements: New Evidence from the Australia Productivity Commission** Dean A. DeRosa

07-2 **Offshoring, Outsourcing, and Production Relocation—Labor-Market Effects in the OECD Countries and Developing Asia** Jacob Funk Kirkegaard

07-3 **Do Markets Care Who Chairs the Central Bank?** Kenneth N. Kuttner/ Adam S. Posen

07-4 **From Industrial Policy to Innovative Policy: Japan's Pursuit of Competitive Advantage** Marcus Noland

07-5 **A (Lack of) Progress Report on China's Exchange Rate Policies** Morris Goldstein

07-6 **Measurement and Inference in International Reserve Diversification** Anna Wong

07-7 **North Korea's External Economic Relations** Stephan Haggard and Marcus Noland

07-8 **Congress, Treasury, and the Accountability of Exchange Rate Policy: How the 1988 Trade Act Should Be Reformed** C. Randall Henning

08-1 **Exit Polls: Refugee Assessments of North Korea's Transitions** Yoonok Chang, Stephan Haggard, Marcus Noland
08-2 **Currency Undervaluation and Sovereign Wealth Funds: A New Role for the WTO** Aaditya Mattoo and Arvind Subramanian
08-3 **Exchange Rate Economics** John Williamson
08-4 **Migration Experiences of North Korean Refugees: Survey Evidence from China** Yoonok Chang, Stephan Haggard, and Marcus Noland
08-5 **Korean Institutional Reform in Comparative Perspective** Marcus Noland and Erik Weeks
08-6 **Estimating Consistent Fundamental Equilibrium Exchange Rates** William R. Cline
08-7 **Policy Liberalization and FDI Growth, 1982 to 2006** Matthew Adler and Gary Clyde Hufbauer
08-8 **Multilateralism Beyond Doha** Aaditya Mattoo and Arvind Subramanian
08-9 **Famine in North Korea Redux?** Stephan Haggard and Marcus Noland
08-10 **Distance Isn't Quite Dead: Recent Trade Patterns and Modes of Supply in Computer and Information Services in the United States and NAFTA Partners** Jacob Funk Kirkegaard
08-11 **On What Terms Is the IMF Worth Funding?** Edwin M. Truman
08-12 **The (Non) Impact of UN Sanctions on North Korea** Marcus Noland
09-1 **The GCC Monetary Union: Choice of Exchange Rate Regime** Mohsin S. Khan
09-2 **Policy Liberalization and US Merchandise Trade Growth, 1980–2006** Gary Clyde Hufbauer and Matthew Adler
09-3 **American Multinationals and American Economic Interests: New Dimensions to an Old Debate** Theodore H. Moran
09-4 **Sanctioning North Korea: The Political Economy of Denuclearization and Proliferation** Stephan Haggard and Marcus Noland
09-5 **Structural and Cyclical Trends in Net Employment over US Business Cycles, 1949–2009: Implications for the Next Recovery and Beyond** Jacob Funk Kirkegaard
09-6 **What's on the Table? The Doha Round as of August 2009** Matthew Adler, Claire Brunel, Gary Clyde Hufbauer, and Jeffrey J. Schott
09-7 **Criss-Crossing Globalization: Uphill Flows of Skill-Intensive Goods and Foreign Direct Investment** Aaditya Mattoo and Arvind Subramanian

POLICY BRIEFS

98-1 **The Asian Financial Crisis** Morris Goldstein
98-2 **The New Agenda with China** C. Fred Bergsten
98-3 **Exchange Rates for the Dollar, Yen, and Euro** Simon Wren-Lewis
98-4 **Sanctions-Happy USA** Gary Clyde Hufbauer
98-5 **The Depressing News from Asia** Marcus Noland, Sherman Robinson, and Zhi Wang
98-6 **The Transatlantic Economic Partnership** Ellen L. Frost
98-7 **A New Strategy for the Global Crisis** C. Fred Bergsten
98-8 **Reviving the "Asian Monetary Fund"** C. Fred Bergsten
99-1 **Implementing Japanese Recovery** Adam S. Posen
99-2 **A Radical but Workable Restructuring Plan for South Korea** Edward M. Graham
99-3 **Crawling Bands or Monitoring Bands: How to Manage Exchange Rates in a World of Capital Mobility** John Williamson
99-4 **Market Mechanisms to Reduce the Need for IMF Bailouts** Catherine L. Mann
99-5 **Steel Quotas: A Rigged Lottery** Gary C. Hufbauer and Erika Wada
99-6 **China and the World Trade Organization: An Economic Balance Sheet** Daniel H. Rosen
99-7 **Trade and Income Distribution: The Debate and New Evidence** William R. Cline
99-8 **Preserve the Exchange Stabilization Fund** C. Randall Henning
99-9 **Nothing to Fear but Fear (of Inflation) Itself** Adam S. Posen
99-10 **World Trade after Seattle: Implications for the United States** Gary Clyde Hufbauer
00-1 **The Next Trade Policy Battle** C. Fred Bergsten
00-2 **Decision-making in the WTO** Jeffrey J. Schott and Jayashree Watal
00-3 **American Access to China's Market: The Congressional Vote on PNTR** Gary C. Hufbauer and Daniel Rosen
00-4 **Third Oil Shock: Real or Imaginary? Consequences and Policy Alternatives** Philip K. Verleger Jr.

- 00-5 **The Role of the IMF: A Guide to the Reports** John Williamson
- 00-6 **The ILO and Enforcement of Core Labor Standards** Kimberly Ann Elliott
- 00-7 **"No" to Foreign Telecoms Equals "No" to the New Economy!** Gary C. Hufbauer/Edward M. Graham
- 01-1 **Brunei: A Turning Point for APEC?** C. Fred Bergsten
- 01-2 **A Prescription to Relieve Worker Anxiety** Lori Kletzer/Robert E. Litan
- 01-3 **The US Export-Import Bank: Time for an Overhaul** Gary C. Hufbauer
- 01-4 **Japan 2001—Decisive Action or Financial Panic** Adam S. Posen
- 01-5 **Fin(d)ing Our Way on Trade and Labor Standards?** Kimberly A. Elliott
- 01-6 **Prospects for Transatlantic Competition Policy** Mario Monti
- 01-7 **The International Implications of Paying Down the Debt** Edwin Truman
- 01-8 **Dealing with Labor and Environment Issues in Trade Promotion Legislation** Kimberly Ann Elliott
- 01-9 **Steel: Big Problems, Better Solutions** Gary Clyde Hufbauer/Ben Goodrich
- 01-10 **Economic Policy Following the Terrorist Attacks** Martin Neil Baily
- 01-11 **Using Sanctions to Fight Terrorism** Gary Clyde Hufbauer, Jeffrey J. Schott, and Barbara Oegg
- 02-1 **Time for a Grand Bargain in Steel?** Gary C. Hufbauer and Ben Goodrich
- 02-2 **Prospects for the World Economy: From Global Recession to Global Recovery** Michael Mussa
- 02-3 **Sovereign Debt Restructuring: New Articles, New Contracts—or No Change?** Marcus Miller
- 02-4 **Support the Ex-Im Bank: It Has Work to Do!** Gary Clyde Hufbauer and Ben Goodrich
- 02-5 **The Looming Japanese Crisis** Adam S. Posen
- 02-6 **Capital-Market Access: New Frontier in the Sanctions Debate** Gary C. Hufbauer and Barbara Oegg
- 02-7 **Is Brazil Next?** John Williamson
- 02-8 **Further Financial Services Liberalization in the Doha Round?** Wendy Dobson
- 02-9 **Global Economic Prospects** Michael Mussa
- 02-10 **The Foreign Sales Corporation: Reaching the Last Act?** Gary Clyde Hufbauer
- 03-1 **Steel Policy: The Good, the Bad, and the Ugly** Gary Clyde Hufbauer and Ben Goodrich
- 03-2 **Global Economic Prospects: Through the Fog of Uncertainty** Michael Mussa
- 03-3 **Economic Leverage and the North Korean Nuclear Crisis** Kimberly Ann Elliott
- 03-4 **The Impact of Economic Sanctions on US Trade: Andrew Rose's Gravity Model** Gary Clyde Hufbauer and Barbara Oegg
- 03-5 **Reforming OPIC for the 21st Century** Theodore H. Moran/C. Fred Bergsten
- 03-6 **The Strategic Importance of US-Korea Economic Relations** Marcus Noland
- 03-7 **Rules Against Earnings Stripping: Wrong Answer to Corporate Inversions** Gary C. Hufbauer and Ariel Assa
- 03-8 **More Pain, More Gain: Politics and Economics of Eliminating Tariffs** Gary C. Hufbauer and Ben Goodrich
- 03-9 **EU Accession and the Euro: Close Together or Far Apart?** Peter B. Kenen and Ellen E. Meade
- 03-10 **Next Move in Steel: Revocation or Retaliation?** Gary Clyde Hufbauer and Ben Goodrich
- 03-11 **Globalization of IT Services and White Collar Jobs: The Next Wave of Productivity Growth** Catherine L. Mann
- 04-1 **This Far and No Farther? Nudging Agricultural Reform Forward** Tim Josling and Dale Hathaway
- 04-2 **Labor Standards, Development, and CAFTA** Kimberly Ann Elliott
- 04-3 **Senator Kerry on Corporate Tax Reform: Right Diagnosis, Wrong Prescription** Gary Clyde Hufbauer and Paul Grieco
- 04-4 **Islam, Globalization, and Economic Performance in the Middle East** Marcus Noland and Howard Pack
- 04-5 **China Bashing 2004** Gary Clyde Hufbauer and Yee Wong
- 04-6 **What Went Right in Japan** Adam S. Posen
- 04-7 **What Kind of Landing for the Chinese Economy?** Morris Goldstein and Nicholas R. Lardy
- 05-1 **A Currency Basket for East Asia, Not Just China** John Williamson
- 05-2 **After Argentina** Anna Gelpern
- 05-3 **Living with Global Imbalances: A Contrarian View** Richard N. Cooper
- 05-4 **The Case for a New Plaza Agreement** William R. Cline
- 06-1 **The United States Needs German Economic Leadership** Adam S. Posen
- 06-2 **The Doha Round after Hong Kong** Gary C. Hufbauer and Jeffrey J. Schott
- 06-3 **Russia's Challenges as Chair of the G-8** Anders Åslund
- 06-4 **Negotiating the Korea–United States Free Trade Agreement** Jeffrey J. Schott, Scott C. Bradford, and Thomas Moll
- 06-5 **Can Doha Still Deliver on the Development Agenda?** Kimberly Ann Elliott
- 06-6 **China: Toward a Consumption Driven Growth Path** Nicholas R. Lardy

06-7 **Completing the Doha Round** Jeffrey J. Schott
06-8 **Choosing Monetary Arrangements for the 21st Century: Problems of a Small Economy** John Williamson
06-9 **Can America Still Compete or Does It Need a New Trade Paradigm?** Martin N. Baily and Robert Z. Lawrence
07-1 **The IMF Quota Formula: Linchpin of Fund Reform** Richard N. Cooper and Edwin M. Truman
07-2 **Toward a Free Trade Area of the Asia Pacific** C. Fred Bergsten
07-3 **China and Economic Integration in East Asia: Implications for the United States** C. Fred Bergsten
07-4 **Global Imbalances: Time for Action** Alan Ahearne, William R. Cline, Kyung Tae Lee, Yung Chul Park, Jean Pisani-Ferry, and John Williamson
07-5 **American Trade Politics in 2007: Building Bipartisan Compromise** I. M. Destler
07-6 **Sovereign Wealth Funds: The Need for Greater Transparency and Accountability** Edwin M. Truman
07-7 **The Korea-US Free Trade Agreement: A Summary Assessment** Jeffrey J. Schott
07-8 **The Case for Exchange Rate Flexibility in Oil-Exporting Economies** Brad Setser
08-1 **"Fear" and Offshoring: The Scope and Potential Impact of Imports and Exports** J. Bradford Jensen and Lori G. Kletzer
08-2 **Strengthening Trade Adjustment Assistance** Howard F. Rosen
08-3 **A Blueprint for Sovereign Wealth Fund Best Practices** Edwin M. Truman
08-4 **A Security and Peace Mechanism for Northeast Asia: The Economic Dimension** Stephan Haggard/ Marcus Noland
08-5 **World Trade at Risk** C. Fred Bergsten
08-6 **North Korea on the Precipice of Famine** Stephan Haggard, Marcus Noland, and Erik Weeks
08-7 **New Estimates of Fundamental Equilibrium Exchange Rates** William R. Cline and John Williamson
08-8 **Financial Repression in China** Nicholas R. Lardy
09-1 **Did Reagan Rule In Vain? A Closer Look at True Expenditure Levels in the United States and Europe** Jacob Funk Kirkegaard
09-2 **Buy American: Bad for Jobs, Worse for Reputation** Gary Clyde Hufbauer and Jeffrey J. Schott
09-3 **A Green Global Recovery? Assessing US Economic Stimulus and the Prospects for International Coordination** Trevor Houser, Shashank Mohan, and Robert Heilmayr
09-4 **Money for the Auto Industry: Consistent with WTO Rules?** Claire Brunel and Gary Clyde Hufbauer
09-5 **The Future of the Chiang Mai Initiative: An Asian Monetary Fund?** C. Randall Henning
09-6 **Pressing the "Reset Button" on US-Russia Relations** Anders Åslund and Andrew Kuchins
09-7 **US Taxation of Multinational Corporations: What Makes Sense, What Doesn't** Gary Clyde Hufbauer and Jisun Kim
09-8 **Energy Efficiency in Buildings: A Global Economic Perspective** Trevor Houser
09-9 **The Alien Tort Statute of 1789: Time for a Fresh Look** Gary Clyde Hufbauer
09-10 **2009 Estimates of Fundamental Equilibrium Exchange Rates** William R. Cline and John Williamson
09-11 **Understanding Special Drawing Rights (SDRs)** John Williamson
09-12 **US Interests and the International Monetary Fund** C. Randall Henning
09-13 **A Solution for Europe's Banking Problem** Adam S. Posen and Nicolas Véron
09-14 **China's Changing Outbound Foreign Direct Investment Profile: Drivers and Policy Implications** Daniel H. Rosen and Thilo Hanemann
09-15 **India-Pakistan Trade: A Roadmap for Enhancing Economic Relations** Mohsin S. Khan
09-16 **Pacific Asia and the Asia Pacific: The Choices for APEC** C. Fred Bergsten
09-17 **The Economics of Energy Efficiency in Buildings** Trevor Houser
09-18 **Setting the NAFTA Agenda on Climate Change** Jeffrey J. Schott and Meera Fickling

* = out of print

POLICY ANALYSES IN INTERNATIONAL ECONOMICS Series

1 **The Lending Policies of the International Monetary Fund*** John Williamson
August 1982 ISBN 0-88132-000-5

2 **"Reciprocity": A New Approach to World Trade Policy?*** William R. Cline
September 1982 ISBN 0-88132-001-3

3 **Trade Policy in the 1980s***
C. Fred Bergsten and William R. Cline
November 1982 ISBN 0-88132-002-1

4 **International Debt and the Stability of the World Economy*** William R. Cline
September 1983 ISBN 0-88132-010-2

5 **The Exchange Rate System,* 2d ed.**
John Williamson
Sept. 1983, rev. June 1985 ISBN 0-88132-034-X

6 **Economic Sanctions in Support of Foreign Policy Goals***
Gary Clyde Hufbauer and Jeffrey J. Schott
October 1983 ISBN 0-88132-014-5

7 **A New SDR Allocation?*** John Williamson
March 1984 ISBN 0-88132-028-5

8 **An International Standard for Monetary Stabilization*** Ronald L. McKinnon
March 1984 ISBN 0-88132-018-8

9 **The Yen/Dollar Agreement: Liberalizing Japanese Capital Markets***
Jeffrey Frankel
December 1984 ISBN 0-88132-035-8

10 **Bank Lending to Developing Countries: The Policy Alternatives*** C. Fred Bergsten, William R. Cline, and John Williamson
April 1985 ISBN 0-88132-032-3

11 **Trading for Growth: The Next Round of Trade Negotiations*** Gary Clyde Hufbauer and Jeffrey J. Schott
September 1985 ISBN 0-88132-033-1

12 **Financial Intermediation Beyond the Debt Crisis*** Donald R. Lessard, John Williamson
September 1985 ISBN 0-88132-021-8

13 **The United States-Japan Economic Problem*** C. Fred Bergsten and William R. Cline
October 1985, 2d ed. January 1987
ISBN 0-88132-060-9

14 **Deficits and the Dollar: The World Economy at Risk*** Stephen Marris
December 1985, 2d ed. November 1987
ISBN 0-88132-067-6

15 **Trade Policy for Troubled Industries***
Gary Clyde Hufbauer and Howard R. Rosen
March 1986 ISBN 0-88132-020-X

16 **The United States and Canada: The Quest for Free Trade*** Paul Wonnacott, with an appendix by John Williamson
March 1987 ISBN 0-88132-056-0

17 **Adjusting to Success: Balance of Payments Policy in the East Asian NICs***
Bela Balassa and John Williamson
June 1987, rev. April 1990 ISBN 0-88132-101-X

18 **Mobilizing Bank Lending to Debtor Countries*** William R. Cline
June 1987 ISBN 0-88132-062-5

19 **Auction Quotas and United States Trade Policy*** C. Fred Bergsten, Kimberly Ann Elliott, Jeffrey J. Schott, and Wendy E. Takacs
September 1987 ISBN 0-88132-050-1

20 **Agriculture and the GATT: Rewriting the Rules*** Dale E. Hathaway
September 1987 ISBN 0-88132-052-8

21 **Anti-Protection: Changing Forces in United States Trade Politics*** I. M. Destler and John S. Odell
September 1987 ISBN 0-88132-043-9

22 **Targets and Indicators: A Blueprint for the International Coordination of Economic Policy** John Williamson/ Marcus H. Miller
September 1987 ISBN 0-88132-051-X

23 **Capital Flight: The Problem and Policy Responses*** Donald R. Lessard and John Williamson
December 1987 ISBN 0-88132-059-5

24 **United States-Canada Free Trade: An Evaluation of the Agreement***
Jeffrey J. Schott
April 1988 ISBN 0-88132-072-2

25 **Voluntary Approaches to Debt Relief***
John Williamson
Sept.1988, rev. May 1 ISBN 0-88132-098-6

26 **American Trade Adjustment: The Global Impact*** William R. Cline
March 1989 ISBN 0-88132-095-1

27 **More Free Trade Areas?*** Jeffrey J. Schott
May 1989 ISBN 0-88132-085-4

28 **The Progress of Policy Reform in Latin America*** John Williamson
January 1990 ISBN 0-88132-100-1

29 **The Global Trade Negotiations: What Can Be Achieved?*** Jeffrey J. Schott
September 1990 ISBN 0-88132-137-0

30 **Economic Policy Coordination: Requiem for Prologue?*** Wendy Dobson
April 1991 ISBN 0-88132-102-8

31 **The Economic Opening of Eastern Europe***
John Williamson
May 1991 ISBN 0-88132-186-9

32 **Eastern Europe and the Soviet Union in the World Economy*** Susan Collins/ Dani Rodrik
May 1991 ISBN 0-88132-157-5

33 **African Economic Reform: The External Dimension*** Carol Lancaster
June 1991 ISBN 0-88132-096-X

34 **Has the Adjustment Process Worked?***
Paul R. Krugman
October 1991 ISBN 0-88132-116-8

35 **From Soviet DisUnion to Eastern Economic Community?***
Oleh Havrylyshyn and John Williamson
October 1991 ISBN 0-88132-192-3

36 **Global Warming: The Economic Stakes***
William R. Cline
May 1992 ISBN 0-88132-172-9

37 Trade and Payments after Soviet Disintegration* John Williamson
June 1992 ISBN 0-88132-173-7

38 Trade and Migration: NAFTA and Agriculture* Philip L. Martin
October 1993 ISBN 0-88132-201-6

39 The Exchange Rate System and the IMF: A Modest Agenda Morris Goldstein
June 1995 ISBN 0-88132-219-9

40 What Role for Currency Boards?
John Williamson
September 1995 ISBN 0-88132-222-9

41 Predicting External Imbalances for the United States and Japan* William R. Cline
September 1995 ISBN 0-88132-220-2

42 Standards and APEC: An Action Agenda*
John S. Wilson
October 1995 ISBN 0-88132-223-7

43 Fundamental Tax Reform and Border Tax Adjustments* Gary Clyde Hufbauer
January 1996 ISBN 0-88132-225-3

44 Global Telecom Talks: A Trillion Dollar Deal* Ben A. Petrazzini
June 1996 ISBN 0-88132-230-X

45 WTO 2000: Setting the Course for World Trade Jeffrey J. Schott
September 1996 ISBN 0-88132-234-2

46 The National Economic Council: A Work in Progress* I. M. Destler
November 1996 ISBN 0-88132-239-3

47 The Case for an International Banking Standard Morris Goldstein
April 1997 ISBN 0-88132-244-X

48 Transatlantic Trade: A Strategic Agenda*
Ellen L. Frost
May 1997 ISBN 0-88132-228-8

49 Cooperating with Europe's Monetary Union
C. Randall Henning
May 1997 ISBN 0-88132-245-8

50 Renewing Fast Track Legislation*
I. M. Destler
September 1997 ISBN 0-88132-252-0

51 Competition Policies for the Global Economy Edward M. Graham and J. David Richardson
November 1997 ISBN 0-88132-249-0

52 Improving Trade Policy Reviews in the World Trade Organization
Donald Keesing
April 1998 ISBN 0-88132-251-2

53 Agricultural Trade Policy: Completing the Reform Timothy Josling
April 1998 ISBN 0-88132-256-3

54 Real Exchange Rates for the Year 2000
Simon Wren Lewis and Rebecca Driver
April 1998 ISBN 0-88132-253-9

55 The Asian Financial Crisis: Causes, Cures, and Systemic Implications
Morris Goldstein
June 1998 ISBN 0-88132-261-X

56 Global Economic Effects of the Asian Currency Devaluations
Marcus Noland, LiGang Liu, Sherman Robinson, and Zhi Wang
July 1998 ISBN 0-88132-260-1

57 The Exchange Stabilization Fund: Slush Money or War Chest? C. Randall Henning
May 1999 ISBN 0-88132-271-7

58 The New Politics of American Trade: Trade, Labor, and the Environment
I. M. Destler and Peter J. Balint
October 1999 ISBN 0-88132-269-5

59 Congressional Trade Votes: From NAFTA Approval to Fast Track Defeat
Robert E. Baldwin/Christopher S. Magee
February 2000 ISBN 0-88132-267-9

60 Exchange Rate Regimes for Emerging Markets: Reviving the Intermediate Option
John Williamson
September 2000 ISBN 0-88132-293-8

61 NAFTA and the Environment: Seven Years Later Gary Clyde Hufbauer, Daniel Esty, Diana Orejas, Luis Rubio & Jeffrey J. Schott
October 2000 ISBN 0-88132-299-7

62 Free Trade between Korea and the United States? Inbom Choi and Jeffrey J. Schott
April 2001 ISBN 0-88132-311-X

63 New Regional Trading Arrangements in the Asia Pacific? Robert Scollay and John P. Gilbert
May 2001 ISBN 0-88132-302-0

64 Parental Supervision: The New Paradigm for Foreign Direct Investment and Development Theodore H. Moran
August 2001 ISBN 0-88132-313-6

65 The Benefits of Price Convergence: Speculative Calculations
Gary C. Hufbauer, Erika Wada, and Tony Warren
December 2001 ISBN 0-88132-333-0

66 Managed Floating Plus Morris Goldstein
March 2002 ISBN 0-88132-336-5

67 Argentina and the Fund: From Triumph to Tragedy Michael Mussa
July 2002 ISBN 0-88132-339-X

68 East Asian Financial Cooperation
C. Randall Henning
September 2002 ISBN 0-88132-338-1

69 Reforming OPIC for the 21st Century
Theodore H. Moran
May 2003 ISBN 0-88132-342-X

70 Awakening Monster: The Alien Tort Statute of 1789 Gary C. Hufbauer/ Nicholas Mitrokostas
July 2003 ISBN 0-88132-366-7

71 Korea after Kim Jong-il
Marcus Noland
January 2004 ISBN 0-88132-373-X

72 **Roots of Competitiveness: China's Evolving Agriculture Interests**
Daniel H. Rosen, Scott Rozelle, and Jikun Huang
July 2004 ISBN 0-88132-376-4

73 **Prospects for a US-Taiwan FTA**
Nicholas R. Lardy and Daniel H. Rosen
December 2004 ISBN 0-88132-367-5

74 **Anchoring Reform with a US-Egypt Free Trade Agreement** Ahmed Galal and Robert Z. Lawrence
April 2005 ISBN 0-88132-368-3

75 **Curbing the Boom-Bust Cycle: Stabilizing Capital Flows to Emerging Markets**
John Williamson
July 2005 ISBN 0-88132-330-6

76 **The Shape of a Swiss-US Free Trade Agreement** Gary Clyde Hufbauer/ Richard E. Baldwin
February 2006 ISBN 978-0-88132-385-6

77 **A Strategy for IMF Reform**
Edwin M. Truman
February 2006 ISBN 978-0-88132-398-6

78 **US-China Trade Disputes: Rising Tide, Rising Stakes** Gary Clyde Hufbauer, Yee Wong, and Ketki Sheth
August 2006 ISBN 978-0-88132-394-8

79 **Trade Relations Between Colombia and the United States** Jeffrey J. Schott, ed.
August 2006 ISBN 978-0-88132-389-4

80 **Sustaining Reform with a US-Pakistan Free Trade Agreement** Gary C. Hufbauer and Shahid Javed Burki
November 2006 ISBN 978-0-88132-395-5

81 **A US–Middle East Trade Agreement: A Circle of Opportunity?** Robert Z. Lawrence
November 2006 ISBN 978-0-88132-396-2

82 **Reference Rates and the International Monetary System** John Williamson
January 2007 ISBN 978-0-88132-401-3

83 **Toward a US-Indonesia Free Trade Agreement** Gary Clyde Hufbauer and Sjamsu Rahardja
June 2007 ISBN 978-0-88132-402-0

84 **The Accelerating Decline in America's High-Skilled Workforce**
Jacob Funk Kirkegaard
December 2007 ISBN 978-0-88132-413-6

85 **Blue-Collar Blues: Is Trade to Blame for Rising US Income Inequality?**
Robert Z. Lawrence
January 2008 ISBN 978-0-88132-414-3

86 **Maghreb Regional and Global Integration: A Dream to Be Fulfilled**
Gary Clyde Hufbauer and Claire Brunel, eds.
October 2008 ISBN 978-0-88132-426-6

87 **The Future of China's Exchange Rate Policy**
Morris Goldstein and Nicholas R. Lardy
July 2009 ISBN 978-0-88132-416-7

88 **Capitalizing on the Morocco-US Free Trade Agreement: A Road Map for Success**
Gary Hufbauer and Claire Brunel, eds
September 2009 ISBN 978-0-88132-433-4

89 **Three Threats: An Analytical Framework for the CFIUS Process** Theodore H. Moran
August 2009 ISBN 978-0-88132-429-7

BOOKS

IMF Conditionality* John Williamson, editor
1983 ISBN 0-88132-006-4

Trade Policy in the 1980s* William R. Cline, ed.
1983 ISBN 0-88132-031-5

Subsidies in International Trade*
Gary Clyde Hufbauer and Joanna Shelton Erb
1984 ISBN 0-88132-004-8

International Debt: Systemic Risk and Policy Response* William R. Cline
1984 ISBN 0-88132-015-3

Trade Protection in the United States: 31 Case Studies* Gary Clyde Hufbauer, Diane E. Berliner, and Kimberly Ann Elliott
1986 ISBN 0-88132-040-4

Toward Renewed Economic Growth in Latin America* Bela Balassa, Gerardo M. Bueno, Pedro Pablo Kuczynski, and Mario Henrique Simonsen
1986 ISBN 0-88132-045-5

Capital Flight and Third World Debt*
Donald R. Lessard and John Williamson, editors
1987 ISBN 0-88132-053-6

The Canada-United States Free Trade Agreement: The Global Impact*
Jeffrey J. Schott and Murray G. Smith, editors
1988 ISBN 0-88132-073-0

World Agricultural Trade: Building a Consensus*
William M. Miner and Dale E. Hathaway, editors
1988 ISBN 0-88132-071-3

Japan in the World Economy*
Bela Balassa and Marcus Noland
1988 ISBN 0-88132-041-2

America in the World Economy: A Strategy for the 1990s* C. Fred Bergsten
1988 ISBN 0-88132-089-7

Managing the Dollar: From the Plaza to the Louvre* Yoichi Funabashi
1988, 2d. ed. 1989 ISBN 0-88132-097-8

United States External Adjustment and the World Economy* William R. Cline
May 1989 ISBN 0-88132-048-X

Free Trade Areas and U.S. Trade Policy*
Jeffrey J. Schott, editor
May *1989* ISBN 0-88132-094-3

Dollar Politics: Exchange Rate Policymaking in the United States*
I. M. Destler and C. Randall Henning
September 1989 ISBN 0-88132-079-X

Latin American Adjustment: How Much Has Happened?* John Williamson, editor
April 1990 ISBN 0-88132-125-7

The Future of World Trade in Textiles and Apparel* William R. Cline
1987, 2d ed. June *1999* ISBN 0-88132-110-9

Completing the Uruguay Round: A Results-Oriented Approach to the GATT Trade Negotiations* Jeffrey J. Schott, editor
September 1990 ISBN 0-88132-130-3

Economic Sanctions Reconsidered (2 volumes)
Economic Sanctions Reconsidered: Supplemental Case Histories
Gary Clyde Hufbauer, Jeffrey J. Schott, and Kimberly Ann Elliott
1985, 2d ed. Dec. 1990 ISBN cloth 0-88132-115-X
ISBN paper 0-88132-105-2

Economic Sanctions Reconsidered: History and Current Policy Gary Clyde Hufbauer, Jeffrey J. Schott, and Kimberly Ann Elliott
December 1990 ISBN cloth 0-88132-140-0
ISBN paper 0-88132-136-2

Pacific Basin Developing Countries: Prospects for Economic Sanctions Reconsidered: History and Current Policy Gary Clyde Hufbauer, Jeffrey J. Schott, and Kimberly Ann Elliott
December 1990 ISBN cloth 0-88132-140-0
ISBN paper 0-88132-136-2

Pacific Basin Developing Countries: Prospects for the Future* Marcus Noland
January 1991 ISBN cloth 0-88132-141-9
ISBN paper 0-88132-081-1

Currency Convertibility in Eastern Europe*
John Williamson, editor
October 1991 ISBN 0-88132-128-1

International Adjustment and Financing: The Lessons of 1985-1991* C. Fred Bergsten, editor
January 1992 ISBN 0-88132-112-5

North American Free Trade: Issues and Recommendations*
Gary Clyde Hufbauer and Jeffrey J. Schott
April 1992 ISBN 0-88132-120-6

Narrowing the U.S. Current Account Deficit*
Alan J. Lenz/*June 1992* ISBN 0-88132-103-6

The Economics of Global Warming
William R. Cline/*June 1992* ISBN 0-88132-132-X

US Taxation of International Income: Blueprint for Reform Gary Clyde Hufbauer, assisted by Joanna M. van Rooij
October 1992 ISBN 0-88132-134-6

Who's Bashing Whom? Trade Conflict in High-Technology Industries
Laura D'Andrea Tyson
November 1992 ISBN 0-88132-106-0

Korea in the World Economy* Il SaKong
January 1993 ISBN 0-88132-183-4

Pacific Dynamism and the International Economic System*
C. Fred Bergsten and Marcus Noland, editors
May 1993 ISBN 0-88132-196-6

Economic Consequences of Soviet Disintegration* John Williamson, editor
May 1993 ISBN 0-88132-190-7

Reconcilable Differences? United States-Japan Economic Conflict*
C. Fred Bergsten and Marcus Noland
June 1993 ISBN 0-88132-129-X

Does Foreign Exchange Intervention Work?
Kathryn M. Dominguez and Jeffrey A. Frankel
September 1993 ISBN 0-88132-104-4

Sizing Up U.S. Export Disincentives*
J. David Richardson
September 1993 ISBN 0-88132-107-9

NAFTA: An Assessment Gary Clyde Hufbauer and Jeffrey J. Schott/*rev. ed.*
October 1993 ISBN 0-88132-199-0

Adjusting to Volatile Energy Prices
Philip K. Verleger, Jr.
November 1993 ISBN 0-88132-069-2

The Political Economy of Policy Reform
John Williamson, editor
January 1994 ISBN 0-88132-195-8

Measuring the Costs of Protection in the United States Gary Clyde Hufbauer and Kimberly Ann Elliott
January 1994 ISBN 0-88132-108-7

The Dynamics of Korean Economic Development* Cho Soon
March 1994 ISBN 0-88132-162-1

Reviving the European Union*
C. Randall Henning, Eduard Hochreiter, and Gary Clyde Hufbauer, editors
April 1994 ISBN 0-88132-208-3

China in the World Economy
Nicholas R. Lardy
April 1994 ISBN 0-88132-200-8

Greening the GATT: Trade, Environment, and the Future Daniel C. Esty
July 1994 ISBN 0-88132-205-9

Western Hemisphere Economic Integration*
Gary Clyde Hufbauer and Jeffrey J. Schott
July 1994 ISBN 0-88132-159-1

Currencies and Politics in the United States, Germany, and Japan C. Randall Henning
September 1994 ISBN 0-88132-127-3

Estimating Equilibrium Exchange Rates
John Williamson, editor
September 1994 ISBN 0-88132-076-5

Managing the World Economy: Fifty Years after Bretton Woods Peter B. Kenen, editor
September 1994 ISBN 0-88132-212-1

Reciprocity and Retaliation in U.S. Trade Policy Thomas O. Bayard and Kimberly Ann Elliott
September 1994 ISBN 0-88132-084-6

The Uruguay Round: An Assessment*
Jeffrey J. Schott, assisted by Johanna Buurman
November 1994 ISBN 0-88132-206-7

Measuring the Costs of Protection in Japan*
Yoko Sazanami, Shujiro Urata, and Hiroki Kawai
January 1995 ISBN 0-88132-211-3

Foreign Direct Investment in the United States, 3d ed., Edward M. Graham and Paul R. Krugman
January 1995 ISBN 0-88132-204-0

The Political Economy of Korea-United States Cooperation* C. Fred Bergsten and Il SaKong, editors
February 1995 ISBN 0-88132-213-X

International Debt Reexamined*
William R. Cline
February 1995 ISBN 0-88132-083-8
American Trade Politics, 3d ed. I. M. Destler
April 1995 ISBN 0-88132-215-6
Managing Official Export Credits: The Quest for a Global Regime* John E. Ray
July 1995 ISBN 0-88132-207-5
Asia Pacific Fusion: Japan's Role in APEC*
Yoichi Funabashi
October 1995 ISBN 0-88132-224-5
Korea-United States Cooperation in the New World Order* C. Fred Bergsten/Il SaKong, eds.
February 1996 ISBN 0-88132-226-1
Why Exports Really Matter!* ISBN 0-88132-221-0
Why Exports Matter More!* ISBN 0-88132-229-6
J. David Richardson and Karin Rindal
July 1995; February 1996
Global Corporations and National Governments Edward M. Graham
May 1996 ISBN 0-88132-111-7
Global Economic Leadership and the Group of Seven C. Fred Bergsten and C. Randall Henning
May 1996 ISBN 0-88132-218-0
The Trading System after the Uruguay Round*
John Whalley and Colleen Hamilton
July 1996 ISBN 0-88132-131-1
Private Capital Flows to Emerging Markets after the Mexican Crisis* Guillermo A. Calvo, Morris Goldstein, and Eduard Hochreiter
September 1996 ISBN 0-88132-232-6
The Crawling Band as an Exchange Rate Regime: Lessons from Chile, Colombia, and Israel John Williamson
September 1996 ISBN 0-88132-231-8
Flying High: Liberalizing Civil Aviation in the Asia Pacific* Gary Clyde Hufbauer and Christopher Findlay
November 1996 ISBN 0-88132-227-X
Measuring the Costs of Visible Protection in Korea* Namdoo Kim
November 1996 ISBN 0-88132-236-9
The World Trading System: Challenges Ahead
Jeffrey J. Schott
December 1996 ISBN 0-88132-235-0
Has Globalization Gone Too Far? Dani Rodrik
March 1997 ISBN paper 0-88132-241-5
Korea-United States Economic Relationship*
C. Fred Bergsten and Il SaKong, editors
March 1997 ISBN 0-88132-240-7
Summitry in the Americas: A Progress Report
Richard E. Feinberg
April 1997 ISBN 0-88132-242-3
Corruption and the Global Economy
Kimberly Ann Elliott
June 1997 ISBN 0-88132-233-4
Regional Trading Blocs in the World Economic System Jeffrey A. Frankel
October 1997 ISBN 0-88132-202-4
Sustaining the Asia Pacific Miracle: Environmental Protection and Economic Integration Andre Dua and Daniel C. Esty
October 1997 ISBN 0-88132-250-4
Trade and Income Distribution
William R. Cline
November 1997 ISBN 0-88132-216-4
Global Competition Policy
Edward M. Graham and J. David Richardson
December 1997 ISBN 0-88132-166-4
Unfinished Business: Telecommunications after the Uruguay Round
Gary Clyde Hufbauer and Erika Wada
December 1997 ISBN 0-88132-257-1
Financial Services Liberalization in the WTO
Wendy Dobson and Pierre Jacquet
June 1998 ISBN 0-88132-254-7
Restoring Japan's Economic Growth
Adam S. Posen
September 1998 ISBN 0-88132-262-8
Measuring the Costs of Protection in China
Zhang Shuguang, Zhang Yansheng, and Wan Zhongxin
November 1998 ISBN 0-88132-247-4
Foreign Direct Investment and Development: The New Policy Agenda for Developing Countries and Economies in Transition
Theodore H. Moran
December 1998 ISBN 0-88132-258-X
Behind the Open Door: Foreign Enterprises in the Chinese Marketplace Daniel H. Rosen
January 1999 ISBN 0-88132-263-6
Toward A New International Financial Architecture: A Practical Post-Asia Agenda
Barry Eichengreen
February 1999 ISBN 0-88132-270-9
Is the U.S. Trade Deficit Sustainable?
Catherine L. Mann
September 1999 ISBN 0-88132-265-2
Safeguarding Prosperity in a Global Financial System: The Future International Financial Architecture, Independent Task Force Report
Sponsored by the Council on Foreign Relations
Morris Goldstein, Project Director
October 1999 ISBN 0-88132-287-3
Avoiding the Apocalypse: The Future of the Two Koreas Marcus Noland
June 2000 ISBN 0-88132-278-4
Assessing Financial Vulnerability: An Early Warning System for Emerging Markets Morris Goldstein, Graciela Kaminsky, and Carmen Reinhart
June 2000 ISBN 0-88132-237-7
Global Electronic Commerce: A Policy Primer
Catherine L. Mann, Sue E. Eckert, and Sarah Cleeland Knight
July 2000 ISBN 0-88132-274-1
The WTO after Seattle Jeffrey J. Schott, ed.
July 2000 ISBN 0-88132-290-3
Intellectual Property Rights in the Global Economy Keith E. Maskus
August 2000 ISBN 0-88132-282-2

The Political Economy of the Asian Financial Crisis Stephan Haggard
August 2000 ISBN 0-88132-283-0

Transforming Foreign Aid: United States Assistance in the 21st Century Carol Lancaster
August 2000 ISBN 0-88132-291-1

Fighting the Wrong Enemy: Antiglobal Activists and Multinational Enterprises
Edward M. Graham
September 2000 ISBN 0-88132-272-5

Globalization and the Perceptions of American Workers Kenneth Scheve/Matthew J. Slaughter
March 2001 ISBN 0-88132-295-4

World Capital Markets: Challenge to the G-10
Wendy Dobson and Gary Clyde Hufbauer, assisted by Hyun Koo Cho
May 2001 ISBN 0-88132-301-2

Prospects for Free Trade in the Americas
Jeffrey J. Schott
August 2001 ISBN 0-88132-275-X

Toward a North American Community: Lessons from the Old World for the New
Robert A. Pastor
August 2001 ISBN 0-88132-328-4

Measuring the Costs of Protection in Europe: European Commercial Policy in the 2000s
Patrick A. Messerlin
September 2001 ISBN 0-88132-273-3

Job Loss from Imports: Measuring the Costs
Lori G. Kletzer
September 2001 ISBN 0-88132-296-2

No More Bashing: Building a New Japan–United States Economic Relationship
C. Fred Bergsten, Takatoshi Ito, and Marcus Noland
October 2001 ISBN 0-88132-286-5

Why Global Commitment Really Matters!
Howard Lewis III and J. David Richardson
October 2001 ISBN 0-88132-298-9

Leadership Selection in the Major Multilaterals
Miles Kahler
November 2001 ISBN 0-88132-335-7

The International Financial Architecture: What's New? What's Missing? Peter Kenen
November 2001 ISBN 0-88132-297-0

Delivering on Debt Relief: From IMF Gold to a New Aid Architecture
John Williamson and Nancy Birdsall, with Brian Deese
April 2002 ISBN 0-88132-331-4

Imagine There's No Country: Poverty, Inequality, and Growth in the Era of Globalization Surjit S. Bhalla
September 2002 ISBN 0-88132-348-9

Reforming Korea's Industrial Conglomerates
Edward M. Graham
January 2003 ISBN 0-88132-337-3

Industrial Policy in an Era of Globalization: Lessons from Asia Marcus Noland and Howard Pack
March 2003 ISBN 0-88132-350-0

Reintegrating India with the World Economy
T. N. Srinivasan and Suresh D. Tendulkar
March 2003 ISBN 0-88132-280-6

After the Washington Consensus: Restarting Growth and Reform in Latin America Pedro-Pablo Kuczynski and John Williamson, editors
March 2003 ISBN 0-88132-347-0

The Decline of US Labor Unions and the Role of Trade Robert E. Baldwin
June 2003 ISBN 0-88132-341-1

Can Labor Standards Improve under Globalization? Kimberly A. Elliott and Richard B. Freeman
June 2003 ISBN 0-88132-332-2

Crimes and Punishments? Retaliation under the WTO Robert Z. Lawrence
October 2003 ISBN 0-88132-359-4

Inflation Targeting in the World Economy
Edwin M. Truman
October 2003 ISBN 0-88132-345-4

Foreign Direct Investment and Tax Competition John H. Mutti
November 2003 ISBN 0-88132-352-7

Has Globalization Gone Far Enough? The Costs of Fragmented Markets
Scott Bradford and Robert Z. Lawrence
February 2004 ISBN 0-88132-349-7

Food Regulation and Trade: Toward a Safe and Open Global System
Tim Josling, Donna Roberts, and David Orden
March 2004 ISBN 0-88132-346-2

Controlling Currency Mismatches in Emerging Markets
Morris Goldstein and Philip Turner
April 2004 ISBN 0-88132-360-8

Free Trade Agreements: US Strategies and Priorities Jeffrey J. Schott, editor
April 2004 ISBN 0-88132-361-6

Trade Policy and Global Poverty
William R. Cline
June 2004 ISBN 0-88132-365-9

Bailouts or Bail-ins? Responding to Financial Crises in Emerging Economies
Nouriel Roubini and Brad Setser
August 2004 ISBN 0-88132-371-3

Transforming the European Economy
Martin Neil Baily and Jacob Kirkegaard
September 2004 ISBN 0-88132-343-8

Chasing Dirty Money: The Fight Against Money Laundering
Peter Reuter and Edwin M. Truman
November 2004 ISBN 0-88132-370-5

The United States and the World Economy: Foreign Economic Policy for the Next Decade
C. Fred Bergsten
January 2005 ISBN 0-88132-380-2

Does Foreign Direct Investment Promote Development? Theodore Moran, Edward M. Graham, and Magnus Blomström, editors
April 2005 ISBN 0-88132-381-0

American Trade Politics, 4th ed. I. M. Destler
June 2005 ISBN 0-88132-382-9

Why Does Immigration Divide America? Public Finance and Political Opposition to Open Borders Gordon Hanson
August 2005 ISBN 0-88132-400-0

Reforming the US Corporate Tax
Gary Clyde Hufbauer and Paul L. E. Grieco
September 2005 ISBN 0-88132-384-5

The United States as a Debtor Nation
William R. Cline
September 2005 ISBN 0-88132-399-3

NAFTA Revisited: Achievements and Challenges Gary Clyde Hufbauer and Jeffrey J. Schott, assisted by Paul L. E. Grieco and Yee Wong
October 2005 ISBN 0-88132-334-9

US National Security and Foreign Direct Investment
Edward M. Graham and David M. Marchick
May 2006 ISBN 978-0-88132-391-7

Accelerating the Globalization of America: The Role for Information Technology
Catherine L. Mann, assisted by Jacob Kirkegaard
June 2006 ISBN 978-0-88132-390-0

Delivering on Doha: Farm Trade and the Poor
Kimberly Ann Elliott
July 2006 ISBN 978-0-88132-392-4

Case Studies in US Trade Negotiation, Vol. 1: Making the Rules Charan Devereaux, Robert Z. Lawrence, and Michael Watkins
September 2006 ISBN 978-0-88132-362-7

Case Studies in US Trade Negotiation, Vol. 2: Resolving Disputes Charan Devereaux, Robert Z. Lawrence, and Michael Watkins
September 2006 ISBN 978-0-88132-363-2

C. Fred Bergsten and the World Economy
Michael Mussa, editor
December 2006 ISBN 978-0-88132-397-9

Working Papers, Volume I Peterson Institute
December 2006 ISBN 978-0-88132-388-7

The Arab Economies in a Changing World
Marcus Noland and Howard Pack
April 2007 ISBN 978-0-88132-393-1

Working Papers, Volume II Peterson Institute
April 2007 ISBN 978-0-88132-404-4

Global Warming and Agriculture: Impact Estimates by Country William R. Cline
July 2007 ISBN 978-0-88132-403-7

US Taxation of Foreign Income
Gary Clyde Hufbauer and Ariel Assa
October 2007 ISBN 978-0-88132-405-1

Russia's Capitalist Revolution: Why Market Reform Succeeded and Democracy Failed
Anders Åslund
October 2007 ISBN 978-0-88132-409-9

Economic Sanctions Reconsidered, 3d. ed.
Gary C. Hufbauer, Jeffrey J. Schott, Kimberly Ann Elliott, and Barbara Oegg
November 2007
ISBN hardcover 978-0-88132-407-5
ISBN hardcover/CD-ROM 978-0-88132-408-2

Debating China's Exchange Rate Policy
Morris Goldstein and Nicholas R. Lardy, eds.
April 2008 ISBN 978-0-88132-415-0

Leveling the Carbon Playing Field: International Competition and US Climate Policy Design Trevor Houser, Rob Bradley, Britt Childs, Jacob Werksman, and Robert Heilmayr
May 2008 ISBN 978-0-88132-420-4

Accountability and Oversight of US Exchange Rate Policy C. Randall Henning
June 2008 ISBN 978-0-88132-419-8

Challenges of Globalization: Imbalances and Growth
Anders Åslund and Marek Dabrowski, eds.
July 2008 ISBN 978-0-88132-418-1

China's Rise: Challenges and Opportunities
C. Fred Bergsten, Charles Freeman, Nicholas R. Lardy, and Derek J. Mitchell
September 2008 ISBN 978-0-88132-417-4

Banking on Basel: The Future of International Financial Regulation
Daniel K. Tarullo
September 2008 ISBN 978-0-88132-423-5

US Pension Reform: Lessons from Other Countries Martin N. Baily/Jacob Kirkegaard
February 2009 ISBN 978-0-88132-425-9

How Ukraine Became a Market Economy and Democracy Anders Åslund
March 2009 ISBN 978-0-88132-427-3

Global Warming and the World Trading System Gary Clyde Hufbauer, Steve Charnovitz, and Jisun Kim
March 2009 ISBN 978-0-88132-428-0

The Russia Balance Sheet
Anders Åslund and Andrew Kuchins
March 2009 ISBN 978-0-88132-424-2

The Euro at Ten: The Next Global Currency?
Jean Pisani-Ferry and Adam S. Posen, eds.
July 2009 ISBN 978-0-88132-430-3

SPECIAL REPORTS

1 **Promoting World Recovery: A Statement on Global Economic Strategy***
by 26 Economists from Fourteen Countries
December 1982 ISBN 0-88132-013-7

2 **Prospects for Adjustment in Argentina, Brazil, and Mexico: Responding to the Debt Crisis*** John Williamson, editor
June 1983 ISBN 0-88132-016-1

3 **Inflation and Indexation: Argentina, Brazil, and Israel*** John Williamson, editor
March 1985 ISBN 0-88132-037-4

4 **Global Economic Imbalances***
C. Fred Bergsten, editor
March 1986 ISBN 0-88132-042-0

5 **African Debt and Financing***
Carol Lancaster and John Williamson, eds.
May 1986 ISBN 0-88132-044-7

6 **Resolving the Global Economic Crisis: After Wall Street*** by Thirty-three Economists from Thirteen Countries
December 1987 ISBN 0-88132-070-6

7 **World Economic Problems***
Kimberly Ann Elliott/John Williamson, eds.
April 1988 ISBN 0-88132-055-2
Reforming World Agricultural Trade*
by Twenty-nine Professionals from Seventeen Countries
1988 ISBN 0-88132-088-9

8 **Economic Relations Between the United States and Korea: Conflict or Cooperation?***
Thomas O. Bayard and Soogil Young, eds.
January 1989 ISBN 0-88132-068-4

9 **Whither APEC? The Progress to Date and Agenda for the Future***
C. Fred Bergsten, editor
October 1997 ISBN 0-88132-248-2

10 **Economic Integration of the Korean Peninsula** Marcus Noland, editor
January 1998 ISBN 0-88132-255-5

11 **Restarting Fast Track*** Jeffrey J. Schott, ed.
April 1998 ISBN 0-88132-259-8

12 **Launching New Global Trade Talks: An Action Agenda** Jeffrey J. Schott, ed.
September 1998 ISBN 0-88132-266-0

13 **Japan's Financial Crisis and Its Parallels to US Experience**
Ryoichi Mikitani and Adam S. Posen, eds.
September 2000 ISBN 0-88132-289-X

14 **The Ex-Im Bank in the 21st Century: A New Approach** Gary Clyde Hufbauer and Rita M. Rodriguez, editors
January 2001 ISBN 0-88132-300-4

15 **The Korean Diaspora in the World Economy** C. Fred Bergsten and Inbom Choi, eds.
January 2003 ISBN 0-88132-358-6

16 **Dollar Overvaluation and the World Economy** C. Fred Bergsten and John Williamson, eds.
February 2003 ISBN 0-88132-351-9

17 **Dollar Adjustment: How Far? Against What?** C. Fred Bergsten and John Williamson, eds.
November 2004 ISBN 0-88132-378-0

18 **The Euro at Five: Ready for a Global Role?** Adam S. Posen, editor
April 2005 ISBN 0-88132-380-2

19 **Reforming the IMF for the 21st Century**
Edwin M. Truman, editor
April 2006 ISBN 978-0-88132-387-0

20 **The Long-Term International Economic Position of the United States**
C. Fred Bergsten, ed.
May 2009 ISBN 978-0-88132-432-7

WORKS IN PROGRESS

Reassessing US Trade Policy: Priorities and Policy Recommendations for the Next Decade
Jeffrey J. Schott

China's Energy Evolution: The Consequences of Powering Growth at Home and Abroad
Daniel H. Rosen and Trevor Houser

Global Identity Theft: Economic and Policy Implications
Catherine L. Mann

Growth and Diversification of International Reserves
Edwin M. Truman

Financial Regulation after the Subprime and Credit Crisis
Morris Goldstein

Globalized Venture Capital: Implications for US Entrepreneurship and Innovation
Catherine L. Mann

Forging a Grand Bargain: Expanding Trade and Raising Worker Prosperity
Lori Kletzer, J. David Richardson, and Howard Rosen

East Asian Regionalism and the World Economy
C. Fred Bergsten

The Strategic Implications of China-Taiwan Economic Relations
Nicholas R. Lardy

Reform in a Rich Country: Germany
Adam S. Posen

Second Among Equals: The Middle-Class Kingdoms of India and China
Surjit Bhalla

Global Forces, American Faces: US Economic Globalization at the Grass Roots
J. David Richardson

Financial Crises and the Future of Emerging Markets
William R. Cline

Global Services Outsourcing: The Impact on American Firms and Workers
J. Bradford Jensen, Lori G. Kletzer, and Catherine L. Mann

Policy Reform in Rich Countries
John Williamson, editor

The Impact of Financial Globalization
William R. Cline

Banking System Fragility in Emerging Economies
Morris Goldstein and Philip Turner

Reengaging Egypt: Options for US-Egypt Economic Relations
Barbara Kotschwar and Jeffrey J. Schott

DISTRIBUTORS OUTSIDE THE UNITED STATES

Australia, New Zealand, and Papua New Guinea
D. A. Information Services
648 Whitehorse Road
Mitcham, Victoria 3132, Australia
Tel: 61-3-9210-7777
Fax: 61-3-9210-7788
Email: service@dadirect.com.au
www.dadirect.com.au

India, Bangladesh, Nepal, and Sri Lanka
Viva Books Private Limited
Mr. Vinod Vasishtha
4737/23 Ansari Road
Daryaganj, New Delhi 110002
India
Tel: 91-11-4224-2200
Fax: 91-11-4224-2240
Email: viva@vivagroupindia.net
www.vivagroupindia.com

Mexico, Central America, South America, and Puerto Rico
US PubRep, Inc.
311 Dean Drive
Rockville, MD 20851
Tel: 301-838-9276
Fax: 301-838-9278
Email: c.falk@ieee.org

Asia *(Brunei, Burma, Cambodia, China, Hong Kong, Indonesia, Korea, Laos, Malaysia, Philippines, Singapore, Taiwan, Thailand, and Vietnam)*
East-West Export Books (EWEB)
University of Hawaii Press
2840 Kolowalu Street
Honolulu, Hawaii 96822-1888
Tel: 808-956-8830
Fax: 808-988-6052
Email: eweb@hawaii.edu

Canada
Renouf Bookstore
5369 Canotek Road, Unit 1
Ottawa, Ontario KIJ 9J3, Canada
Tel: 613-745-2665
Fax: 613-745-7660
www.renoufbooks.com

Japan
United Publishers Services Ltd.
1-32-5, Higashi-shinagawa
Shinagawa-ku, Tokyo 140-0002
Japan
Tel: 81-3-5479-7251
Fax: 81-3-5479-7307
Email: purchasing@ups.co.jp
For trade accounts only. Individuals will find Institute books in leading Tokyo bookstores.

Middle East
MERIC
2 Bahgat Ali Street, El Masry Towers
Tower D, Apt. 24
Zamalek, Cairo
Egypt
Tel. 20-2-7633824
Fax: 20-2-7369355
Email: mahmoud_fouda@mericonline.com
www.mericonline.com

United Kingdom, Europe *(including Russia and Turkey)*, Africa, and Israel
The Eurospan Group
c/o Turpin Distribution
Pegasus Drive
Stratton Business Park
Biggleswade, Bedfordshire
SG18 8TQ
United Kingdom
Tel: 44 (0) 1767-604972
Fax: 44 (0) 1767-601640
Email: eurospan@turpin-distribution.com
www.eurospangroup.com/bookstore

Visit our website at:
www.piie.com
E-mail orders to:
petersonmail@presswarehouse.com